GENERAL WALTER BEDELL SMITH
AS DIRECTOR OF CENTRAL INTELLIGENCE

General Walter Bedell Smith

GENERAL WALTER BEDELL SMITH AS DIRECTOR OF CENTRAL INTELLIGENCE

OCTOBER 1950–FEBRUARY 1953

Ludwell Lee Montague

With an Introduction by
Bruce D. Berkowitz and Allan E. Goodman

THE PENNSYLVANIA STATE UNIVERSITY PRESS
University Park, Pennsylvania

Library of Congress Cataloging-in-Publication Data

Montague, Ludwell Lee, 1907–
    General Walter Bedell Smith as director of Central Intelligence,
October 1950–February 1953 / Ludwell Lee Montague ; with an
introduction by Bruce D. Berkowitz and Allan E. Goodman.
        p.   cm.
    Includes bibliographical references and index.
    ISBN 0-271-00750-8 (alk. paper).—ISBN 0-271-00751-6 (pbk. :
alk. paper)
    1. United States. Central Intelligence Agency—History.
2. Intelligence service—United States—History.   3. Smith, Walter
Bedell, 1895–1961.   I. Title.
JK468.I6M65   1992
327.1273′0092—dc20   90-21196
                                                                                          CIP

It is the policy of The Pennsylvania State University Press to use acid-free paper
for the first printing of all clothbound books. Publications on uncoated stock
satisfy the minimum requirements of American National Standard for Information Sciences—Permanence of Paper for Printed Library Materials, ANSI Z39.48–
1984.

Contents

Introduction

This book is the second in a series of studies released by the Central Intelligence Agency describing the establishment and development of the modern U.S. intelligence community. It focuses on the term of the fourth Director of Central Intelligence (DCI), Lieutenant General Walter Bedell Smith, a period extending from late 1950 to early 1953. Originally published internally by the CIA in 1971 and declassified in February 1990, this study was written by Ludwell Lee Montague, a long-time intelligence official who participated in many of the events that are chronicled here.

Smith's term as DCI is significant and deserves study for at least three reasons. First, Smith was the first "successful" DCI and established the role and responsibilities of the office for the next twenty years. Up until his term in office, Directors of Central Intelligence had been unable to perform their role as the leading U.S. intelligence official because the existing intelligence services in the military services and the State Department refused to recognize the DCI's authority (despite Executive Orders and statute). Smith, through determination, personal prestige, and an understanding of the national security bureaucracy, succeeded where his three predecessors had not. After Smith the DCI was recognized as the President's top intelligence adviser, as the coordinator and publisher of U.S. intelligence estimates, and as the U.S. official with primary responsibility for covert operations.

Second, it was under Smith that many of the enduring institutions of the U.S. national intelligence community were established. One of the most important of these was the National Intelligence Estimate (NIE), the intelligence community's primary vehicle for expressing its coordinated, comprehensive view on a particular subject of concern to U.S. policymakers. Smith instituted the NIE, as well as the organizations responsible for producing it, namely, the Office of National Estimates and the Board of National Estimates.

Third, Smith was responsible for putting life into the CIA itself. Although the CIA had been established by the National Security Act of 1947 and had grown significantly during the late 1940s, in 1950 the CIA was, as an organization, moribund. It did publish a daily intelligence summary for the President, but it had failed to carve out a significant mission of its own in the area of intelligence analysis. It was simply a compiler of information, and dependent on the other intelligence services for expertise and raw information. Under Smith the CIA provided the organizational base for coordinating national intelligence estimates. It also became the lead agency with responsibility for new areas of concern, such as scientific and economic intelligence.

Also, under Smith, the CIA was recognized as the U.S. agency with primary responsibility for covert action. Smith effectively consolidated the offices responsible for U.S. covert operations into the CIA's Directorate for Plans (today known as the Directorate for Operations). After Smith the CIA became known as the U.S. covert action agency, often at the expense of its analytical role.

According to Montague, the history of the CIA and the office of the DCI can be divided into two distinct periods: pre-Smith and post-Smith. This may be an overstatement today, as there have been events and Directors of Central Intelligence that have probably had at least as much influence as Smith. The investigations of the mid-1970s, which are closely tied to William Colby, and the assertion of the role of DCI under William Casey in the early 1980s come to mind. However, Montague does have a point. Prior to Smith the DCI and the CIA were latent capabilities that had yet to be realized, and after Smith much of this potential capability had been made real.

The "DCI Historical Series" of declassified, official studies on the origins of the CIA and of the leadership and problems faced by the early Directors of Central Intelligence makes available to scholars an unparalleled—and, in terms of the literature available on the national intelligence service of any country, a unique—public resource about a subject usually shrouded in secrecy. The present manuscript, combined with the first document to be released (*The Central Intelligence Agency: An Instrument of Government, to 1950*),[a] provides more than two thousand pages of previously classified analysis and documentation of the U.S. intelligence community's formative years. The official histories thus far released cover the period from the earliest debates during World War Two over the need for a peacetime national foreign intelligence service up to February 1953 when Walter "Beetle" Smith left the post of DCI to become Under Secretary of State.

---

[a]Written in 1950 by the CIA's first official historian, Arthur Darling, declassified in November 1989, and also published by The Pennsylvania State University Press.

Both studies document how difficult the development of a national, centralized intelligence community proved to be. They shed considerable light, moreover, not only on intelligence matters but also on how the U.S. government organized its national security apparatus as a whole after World War Two, what the motives of some of the key personalities involved were, and how the executive branch prepared for the policy of containment of Communism on a global scale.

Each study is distinctive because of the author's experience and outlook. Arthur Darling was brought in from outside government to do an official history, much as he had done in his academic career. He had no previous exposure to intelligence work. Ludwell Montague, on the other hand, was trained as a historian but had spent more than thirty years as an intelligence community insider by the time he wrote this study. Moreover, as his Preface to the present study makes clear, Montague believed that this experience and his personal familiarity with Smith made him especially qualified to write about this period.

Both authors appear to have had full access to the records and other files of the Office of Strategic Services (OSS), the CIA, and the National Security Council (NSC) for the period they studied. They also had the benefit of interviews with many key officials to get behind the reasons for decisions taken. Montague was able to have his entire draft read and commented upon by Sidney Souers, who was both a former DCI himself and Executive Secretary of the NSC, and William Jackson, who was a member of a key study group on the reorganization of the CIA and later the Deputy Director of Central Intelligence under Smith.

By the time Montague wrote this study, portions of the Darling manuscript had been published in the CIA's internal professional journal, *Studies in Intelligence*. Montague makes clear that he was conscious of Darling's study as he developed his own, but he also makes clear that he believed the earlier work was flawed in several respects.

Montague is generous to Darling, but in a backhanded fashion. He acknowledges that Darling performed a demanding task by collecting a documentary record of the early years of the intelligence community and provided a valuable service in doing so. But, according to Montague, Darling arrived as CIA Historian with no background in intelligence and no experience in the organizational disputes that had plagued the agency's creation and, as a result, arrived at flawed conclusions. Montague believed that Darling considered the first Directors of Central Intelligence heroes, thwarted by the military services and State Department in carrying out the mission assigned to the DCI. As a result, claims Montague, the Darling study is flawed, as it unfairly casts all the officials who opposed the DCI as opponents of a centralized intelligence system and fails to pay due credit to the arguments of the agencies that tried to limit the authority of the DCI. Montague also believed that Darling was led astray because he did not fully understand the motives of the personalities who took part in the events.

Consequently, the manuscript Montague wrote first focuses on "setting the record straight" and does so by explaining the personal relationships and antipathies that accompanied the struggle to establish the CIA (and, incidentally, also by attempting to establish his own personal claim as the originator of the modern intelligence community's structure). Because of the emphasis on personalities—and the clashes between them that shaped the early post–World War Two intelligence community—it is not surprising that Montague begins his study by recounting how the principal characters came to be involved in the craft of intelligence in the first place. Whether or not Montague's criticisms of Darling are entirely valid, he does provide valuable insights into the outlook of the men who led it.

Central to the narrative of both this study and the earlier one by Darling are two concepts. The first is that, in order to be effective in framing and conducting American foreign policy, the President needed to have an agency that could provide "national intelligence." This term refers to information of all sorts about other countries that was collected and assessed by recognized experts independently of the viewpoints and biases of particular departments and the policies they represented.

While reasonable in theory, the idea of a national intelligence community was very difficult to realize in practice because the authority and resources it required inevitably would come at the expense of established organizational interests in the U.S. national security community. In the years immediately following the war (as always) there was a struggle over who was to be in charge of American foreign policy. Responsibility for intelligence was one part of this struggle, and the proponents of a national intelligence community were weak players in this competition. The established departments maintained that they were already in the business of providing intelligence information and that they could do so as well as—if not better than—a new agency. The State Department argued that covert action was a tool of foreign policy and rightly belonged within its jurisdiction.

The second concept that emerges throughout the manuscripts (and that explains the difficulty encountered in creating a central intelligence function in the U.S. government) is that a national intelligence community should be headed by a person who would be the President's chief adviser on intelligence matters. The title chosen by President Harry S

Truman was that of Director of Central Intelligence (DCI) rather than Director of the CIA because the objective was to have someone in charge of all the intelligence operations and functions of the government and not just those of a particular agency. But as most individuals who have been DCI have discovered, the position is an anomalous one in the U.S. national security power structure. In the period about which Darling wrote (1945–50) and with which Montague begins his study, this was especially problematic because, although all the early DCIs were general officers, they had other ambitions and a host of senior officers above them. As such they were outranked by the Chiefs of Staff of the Armed Services, were technically under the control of the Secretary of Defense, and, when it came to clear foreign policy matters, should also be under the control of the Secretary of State. And in the case of the DCI on whom most of Darling's study concentrates, Rear Admiral Roscoe Hillenkoetter, the problems faced were acute because the Admiral was outranked by nearly everyone over whom he was bound to try to exert his authority.

The DCI was also supposed to have independent access to the President and had the obligation to provide information and viewpoints about issues on which the Secretaries of State and Defense were frequently at odds. None of the early DCIs relished being put in this position, and few had such access to the President. Some, in fact, held the post hoping for other assignments that would bring them back into active command. But each tried to act with the independence and authority of DCI. Why they failed but Smith did not is the subject of the present study.

Montague regards Smith as the real founder of the postwar intelligence community because Smith fought the bureaucratic battles that established the role of intelligence in the U.S. foreign policy decisionmaking process and appeared to understand better than his predecessors how to function effectively as DCI. In this account "Beetle" Smith assumes nearly legendary proportions and appears to have come from central casting. He was both a manager and a thinker; lacking a college education (because he had to take care of a severely disabled parent), he was probably better read in world history than most of the leaders and foreign policy experts of his day. He was a soldier, coming up through the ranks, and then an outstanding officer during World War Two. And he probably deserves as much credit for his behind-the-scenes contribution to the allied victory as the American generals whose names became household words. He was close personally to at least one President and greatly respected by another. He also served for three years as Ambassador to the Soviet Union, so he would have known at first hand the nature of the primary target of early U.S. intelligence activities. According to his memoirs, this time in Moscow gave Smith an early picture of the type of threat the Soviet Union would represent to the United States.

Smith took the job of DCI claiming "I know nothing about this business" (see Part Two, page 56). But as Montague makes clear, this was not altogether true. During the war Smith exhibited a deep and enduring interest in intelligence matters, read widely about the creation of the OSS, and exposed himself to the thinking of Donovan a number of times on the subject of how best to centralize intelligence for national security in peacetime situations. Smith also had the advantage of having an experienced team with which to work in the persons of William Jackson and Allen Dulles as, respectively, Deputy Director of Central Intelligence (DDCI) and Deputy Director (of the CIA) for Plans (DDP, the acronym by which the head of the CIA's clandestine operations was known). None of Smith's predecessors had the benefit of such a knowledgeable team. And he benefited from the growing realization and acceptance in Washington that in dealing with the rapidly increasing military and subversive threat posed by the Soviet Union the intelligence community had just as vital a role to play as did the OSS in the European theater during World War Two.

Montague organized his study into five "volumes," here designated "parts." Each was designed to tell a particular story up to a specific point in time. Part One contains what Montague regarded as essential background to understanding the nature of the challenges and problems that confronted Smith when he was appointed DCI. In fact, this part reads much like the introductory chapters of a dissertation (Montague had a Ph.D. in history), in which an author traces the evolution of the problem with which the study will deal. But Montague also uses this platform to correct what he thought were the shortcomings of the official history prepared by Arthur Darling and to establish the importance of the findings of the study of the CIA conducted by Dulles, Jackson, and Matthias Correa (formerly an aide to Secretary of Defense Forrestal and then in private law practice). It was on the basis of this report that the NSC mandated a reorganization of the CIA, and how Smith carried it out is the subject of Part Three.

Part One analyzes the evolution of the concept of centralized intelligence as well as the baronial politics among the chiefs of the military intelligence services, which the CIA was intended to supplant. The discussion of the impact of leaks to the press of national security plans and documents, as well as the disputes (which probably led to these leaks) among the various cabinet secretaries and national security aides about who was in charge and whether the United State could develop a coherent foreign policy, has a very familiar ring. It is important to understand today that these types of problems have plagued national security decisionmaking for some time and have limited our ability to gather intelligence and make the best use of it. It is also important to realize that these difficulties reflect the essential untidiness that our democratic process invites when it comes to foreign affairs.

Montague also hints at a much more proactive role in the creation of the CIA by President Truman. Although the evidence behind Montague's account of Truman's desire to have a peacetime intelligence agency—and to have access himself to information that was independent of the viewpoints of the Departments of State and Defense—is slim (amounting to only two footnoted sources), the narrative suggests that this President as much as his more knowledgeable advisers wanted foreign policy decisions to be based on some form of intelligence. Further indication of Truman's avid interest in intelligence matters and the use of intelligence information (especially when conveyed personally by the DCI) is given in Part Five.

Part Two, "Bedell Smith Takes Command," deals with the appointment of Smith as DCI and the condition in which he found the CIA. From the outset it was clear that Smith had done considerable thinking and much homework on how the CIA ought to function and what it would take for the authority of the DCI to be accepted within the military services and the national security community generally. The heart of Part Two deals with the specific steps Smith took to establish command and control of the CIA and the other components of the intelligence community, especially that section responsible for planning and conducting covert action operations, the Office of Policy Coordination (OPC). These were also exciting times for the intelligence community owing to the onset of the Korean War and the need to produce estimates of what would happen next. It is striking that Montague says Smith was less concerned about whether these estimates said anything new or about why some proved to be wrong than he was about making sure the process that produced them did not make the job of establishing the authority of the CIA more difficult.

Smith's vision of how a central intelligence community should function involved establishing a system for effective command and control as well as clarifying the role of the DCI and his authority to direct all aspects of intelligence activities. One of the first steps he took to do this was to regain control of covert action operations, which at the time were lodged in and directed by officers of the Department of State. Even today many people still do not realize that in the early years of the Cold War the most enthusiastic proponents of the use of covert action were members of the foreign service, not CIA officers. But because the former did not fully understand how difficult such operations were to mount, Smith probably wanted to make sure that as their use increased—as seemed very likely—the DCI would personally be able to monitor their effectiveness and impact on other facets of intelligence work.

More than any of his predecessors, Smith worked to put the administration and day-to-day management of the CIA on a sound and business-like footing. As this part of the study outlines, during his tenure as DCI, Smith created the essential structure under which the Agency has operated for most of its existence. Smith was especially concerned with enabling the DCI to manage the entire agency closely and with paying adequate attention to details. He did much to instill in the field units the clear recognition that their work and reports were to be done in response to DCI directives and addressed to the DCI, rather than for fiefdoms within the operations directorate.

Smith also introduced measures for providing agency-wide administrative and logistical services, so that scarce resources could be managed and monitored effectively, and for making sure that DCI directives and national policy were followed. All these steps helped ensure that the DCI would not be blindsided by the traditional secrecy of operations officers should an operation fail or cause major embarrassment to the U.S. government.

Smith's vision extended into the future. He wanted to ensure that the CIA would be thought of as a career service, and he took steps to come up with a training and rotation system so that he could create a corps of managers raised within the CIA and familiar with the full range of the Agency's operations. From the viewpoint of this study, it is notable that Smith established the Historical Staff as part of the Office of the DCI so that an institutional memory would be available.

Part Three, entitled "Reorganization Pursuant to NSC 50," highlights how Smith applied his vision to effect the reorganization of the CIA. Of particular interest here are the discussion of how the institutions for producing National Intelligence Estimates were created and Smith's views of how national intelligence analyses should be developed, coordinated, and provided to users. "National estimate" refers to a brief report prepared for the President and the others members of the NSC on a current situation posing a direct threat to U.S. national security and how it might develop over some specified period of time. It is "national" in the sense that the report should be the product of the collaborative efforts of the intelligence community. It is an "estimate" because it contains some forecast of what was to develop about a problem or in a situation with which policymakers were already and deeply concerned. Smith had a very clear sense both of what policymakers at the time needed and of the kinds of personnel and organization that could produce it. His three qualities of a good estimator were experience, imagination, and intellect, which are the same qualities required today, and qualities that Smith thought essential if estimates were to make sense of rapidly changing situations on which information is usually incomplete. Here Montague's work also foreshadows the bureaucratic problems that would plague the estimating process after Smith moved on and that eventually led to the demise of the Office of National Estimates in 1973.

Part Four is entitled "The War Emergency and the Clandestine Services." While not an overstatement of its contents, this title makes it sound more exciting than it is, for what Montague does here is tell the story of how Smith reorganized the operations side of the CIA in light of mounting Soviet subversion and the onset of the Korean War, which he and others thought might be a prelude to the outbreak of World War Three. The material is consequently interesting, but not because it reveals long-held CIA secrets about exciting covert action operations. Even the deleted portions of the text do not appear to contain such details, and Gregory Treverton's *Covert Action* remains about the best source there is for information on the nature of these operations.

Montague's account is significant because it details the tensions between Smith and Allen Dulles (who was to be Smith's successor) over the scope and freedom that the clandestine part of the CIA should have in general and Smith's concern that the Agency's involvement in covert action operations—and the growing number of such operations that seemed to be demanded by policymakers in the State and Defense Departments—would detract from the effectiveness of the CIA at collecting and analyzing intelligence. This is a concern subsequent DCIs expressed as well, and it is a problem still very much debated in intelligence and foreign policy circles today.

Part Five is entitled "External Relations." It deals with Smith's and the CIA's interactions with the foreign affairs and national security agencies as well as with Congress. Unfortunately, the entire second section of this part—some forty pages—has been excised, and we can only speculate that the material covers the Agency's developing relations with foreign intelligence services. Much of what is described in Part Five, however, has a very contemporary ring. Montague records what Smith learned about the difficult role the DCI must play as a senior policy adviser to the President but without the responsibilities for advocating or implementing policy of either the Secretaries of State or Defense or the Joint Chiefs of Staff. Much of this part concentrates on struggles that Smith did not win because of this anomaly and that have remained problems for his successors even to this day. Finally, there is a brief account of how the intelligence community began to survey systematically the shortcomings of the way communications intelligence was being directed and handled. From this review effort the National Security Agency was to emerge as a new member of the intelligence community—and one nominally under the command and control of the DCI.

Ludwell Lee Montague's career was to a large degree a personification of the establishment, development, and maturing of the Central Intelligence Agency. As his autobiographical statement in the Preface indicates, Montague was trained as a historian and was an academician until the outbreak of World War Two. After that point Montague spent the remainder of his life using his skills in the world of intelligence, serving as an intelligence staff officer in the Army. In the latter stages of the war Montague developed draft policy positions on intelligence issues for the Joint Chiefs.

One of these drafts was the response of the Joint Chiefs to William Donovan's proposal for a postwar intelligence community. Under the Donovan plan, most organizations responsible for collecting and analyzing intelligence would have been placed under the direct control of the Director of Central Intelligence. This reallocation of authority would have come at the expense of the military services and State Department, which naturally opposed the plan. The Joint Chiefs, in response, proposed an alternative. Under their plan, a Director of Central Intelligence would be established and would have authority to coordinate national intelligence estimates, but most of the organizations responsible for producing intelligence would be left in the military services and the State Department.

This proposal, JIC 239/5 (dated 1 January 1945), was revised and incorporated in other policy documents, including President Truman's order of January 1946 establishing the Central Intelligence Group and the Director of Central Intelligence. The general approach advocated by JIC 239/5, in which authority and responsibility are "split" between the DCI and the operating departments, persists to this day. The only organizations that are "owned" by the DCI are the CIA and the relatively small Intelligence Community Staff. All other intelligence community components—the military intelligence offices, the State Department's Bureau for Intelligence and Research, the National Security Agency, and other special collection offices—are located in some other department of the Government. The DCI has authority over tasking these components and approves their budgets, but he shares authority in the sense that some other official is responsible for the day-to-day operations of these agencies.

Montague was responsible for drafting JIC 239/5, so he has a legitimate claim as the originator for the basic organizing principle of the modern U.S. intelligence community. Some would view this as a dubious honor, because the division of authority has often proved a major stumbling block to the effectiveness of the U.S. intelligence community. Locating intelligence organizations within the Departments of Defense, State, Treasury, and Energy allows them to draw on the resources and expertise of these agencies. It also locates these intelligence organizations close to some of their most important clients. It is useful, for example, to have the office of the Director of the Defense Intelligence Agency around the corner from the Chairman of the Joint Chiefs of Staff. The DCI, however, is the only intelligence official in a position to represent *national* intelligence priorities. Without his guidance, intelligence agencies are apt to respond mainly to the requirements of their parent organizations or, even worse, their own organizational interests. Because officials in an agency such as NSA know that their careers are affected at least as much by the JCS as by the DCI, they often act accordingly.

As a result, the intelligence community contained an institutional bias toward decentralization that has acted against the efforts of the DCI to set priorities in intelligence planning and to coordinate the national intelligence product. Directors of Central Intelligence have varied considerably in the degree to which they have succeeded in overcoming this institutional bias. Some, such as Hillenkoetter, have proven relatively weak and were unable to exercise effective leadership over agencies determined to act independently. Others, such as Hoyt Vandenberg and Stansfield Turner, have tried to provide firm direction but were probably too direct or too blunt, met stout resistance by the departmental intelligence organizations, and ultimately were also thwarted by the bureaucracy.

Some Directors of Central Intelligence have been successful managers and were able to overcome this separation of authority and exercise direction. A few were especially successful, and Smith was one of them. Smith was able to use his own personal dynamism and keen understanding of how organizations operate to win the bureaucratic contest. Others who were successful included William Casey, who used the support he knew he enjoyed from the President (as well as considerable assistance from his Deputy Director, Bobby Inman). These Directors not only provided a clear set of priorities and plans for the intelligence community; they also left the office of DCI stronger than it was when they assumed it. The important point, however, is that although Montague may claim authorship for this principle of "separation of powers" within the intelligence community, the principle itself has been a mixed blessing.

Montague was among the first officers to report for work at the new Central Intelligence Group (CIG), and he spent the next twenty-five years in leading positions in the intelligence community. As Assistant Director of the CIG, he headed its Central Reports Staff and its successor organization, the Intelligence Staff. He remained in this post after the CIG was reorganized as the Central Intelligence Agency. When Smith was appointed DCI, he selected Montague as a member of the Board of National Estimates, the group of senior analysts responsible for drafting and supporting the coordination of NIEs for the DCI. Montague remained in this position until his retirement in July 1970. It was during his retirement years that Montague completed this study. Ludwell Montague died on 29 February 1972.

The manuscript was completed in December 1971 and classified at the "Secret" level. It was declassified and released under the Historical Review Program on 16 February 1990 and presented to the National Archives by the Chief Historian of the CIA, Dr. J. Kenneth McDonald. Dr. McDonald told us of the existence of this manuscript during the course of our research in preparing the introductions to the study by Professor Arthur Darling mentioned above, and he has been extremely helpful to us in many ways on both projects. We obtained a reprint of copy number three of the Montague manuscript from the National Archives in the form of a microfiche; the Penn State Press made a photocopy from the fiche and used it for typesetting. Neither we nor the editors at the Press have made changes to the text (including notes) of any sort besides minor copyediting for correctness and consistency of spelling, punctuation, and other grammatical matters.

By making the Darling and Montague manuscripts available to the National Archives, the government has put the historical study of U.S. intelligence on much more solid ground. Unfortunately, however, even these studies do not tell the entire story of CIA operations and other intelligence activities in the early 1950s. As the reader will note, there are a large number of excisions in the text (with approximate length indicated in brackets) in passages that relate to the sizes of various units and offices within the CIA, identities of some CIA officials, covert action operations, and liaison relationships with foreign intelligence services. The Montague manuscript contains a much larger number of deletions than the Darling study.

One might disagree with the standards that dictated that certain passages be deleted or with the strictness with which they were applied.

We strongly believe that intelligence sources and methods need to be protected; nevertheless, we seriously question whether the size of the staff of the Office of National Estimates in November 1950 (an example of one piece of data that was excised) is truly sensitive information. Not only is this a fairly arcane statistic that is more than forty years old, but that office no longer even exists in any recognizable form in the intelligence community. We would also note that many of the references to specific covert operations that fell victim to the sanitization process have been written about in exquisite detail not only by scholars and the media but also in memoirs by CIA personnel who have had their writings cleared by the Agency.

In fairness to the CIA and the Historical Review Program, though, we would like to point out that our research has not uncovered any effort by the intelligence community to slant these histories for political reasons in either their original drafting or in the process through which they were declassified. Neither does any effort appear to have been made to hide the fact that the founders of the early intelligence community disagreed with each other—and also about the need for a central intelligence agency in the first place—or that there were shortcomings and outright failures in management, operations, and analysis.

Finally, we would note that the CIA was not the only organization that was responsible for determining which information was to be deleted in the review of the manuscript; other departments and agencies, such as the Department of State, also had their say. It is entirely possible that those other agencies are responsible for many of the deletions in the text, in which case they, rather than the CIA, must take responsibility for them.

Practically speaking, the material missing from the present text does not, in our view, diminish the value of what has been released. For we believe there has been considerable misunderstanding about why the CIA was established and, equally important, insufficient comprehension of how difficult it was to organize the nation's national security agencies and policies after the end of World War Two. And those topics are really the subject of this manuscript.

In preparing this manuscript for publication, we want to thank our Research Assistant, Sandy Bogart, for her work in obtaining information concerning Montague's career from the archivists and alumni offices at Duke University and Virginia Military Institute. Finally, we want to commend The Pennsylvania State University Press and its director, Sanford G. Thatcher, for the idea to publish this and the Darling manuscript and to do so in timely fashion. We think the publication of these studies is useful to remind us that, even at a time when the nation is celebrating the end of the Cold War, the government established a national intelligence community for the long haul. The office of the DCI, the Central Intelligence Agency, and the idea of a national intelligence community were intended not just as an immediate response to the perceived threat from the Soviet Union, but as recognition of the basic fact that the United States requires the ability to assess the widest possible range and nature of threats to American security. And the period ahead—as was the case with the period about which Montague wrote— seems no less fraught with such risks and in need of strategic intelligence.

Foreword

This is the second volume in the DCI Historical Series that the Central Intelligence Agency has declassified and transferred to the National Archives for release to the public under the CIA Historical Review Program. This program resulted from the passage by Congress of the CIA Information Act of 1984, which relieved the Agency from the burden of searching certain designated operational files in response to Freedom of Information Act requests. At the request of Congress, and with our earlier declassification of the Office of Strategic Services records as precedent, the Agency agreed to undertake new efforts to declassify and transfer historically significant CIA records to the National Archives. This declassified version of *General Walter Bedell Smith as Director of Central Intelligence, October 1950–February 1953*, by Ludwell L. Montague, is a result of these efforts.

Like the first CIA history released under this program, Arthur B. Darling's *The Central Intelligence Agency: An Instrument of Government, to 1950*, this history has a distinct point of view. Indeed, Montague's opening chapters take issue with the Darling history's generally favorable view of the first three Directors of Central Intelligence who preceded General Smith. Whereas Darling found the State Department, the FBI, and heads of the military intelligence services principally responsible for the hardships that the CIA and its predecessor, the Central Intelligence Group, endured from 1946 to 1950, Montague holds the first Directors of Central Intelligence answerable for these problems and for the interdepartmental dissension that produced them. Montague contends that it was Walter Bedell Smith who finally established the CIA in the role that the President and Congress had originally intended. According to Montague, the history of U.S. intelligence is "clearly divisible into two distinct eras, before Smith and after Smith."

The interpretive differences between Darling and Montague involve more than their assessments of the contributions of General Smith's three predecessors. Also at stake was the reputation of his successor, Allen Dulles, whose 1949 report—known informally as the Dulles-Jackson-Correa Report—had heavily criticized Rear Admiral Roscoe Hillenkoetter, Director of Central Intelligence from May 1947 to October 1950, for a major ongoing failure in intelligence coordination. Darling defended Hillenkoetter's record against these charges, and Montague tells us that Dulles disapproved of Darling's history and as Director restricted access to it. (Darling's work was nevertheless published in the CIA's classified internal journal, *Studies in Intelligence*, in the late 1960s, and declassified and released to the public in November 1989.)

Ludwell Montague completed this five-part history, which was originally classified "Secret," in December 1971 for the History Staff in the Office of the Director of Central Intelligence. As part of its accountability to the American people, the Central Intelligence Agency is pleased to open this important study to the public under the Historical Review Program. We hope that its account of General Smith as Director of Central Intelligence will make possible a more accurate record and fuller understanding of his and the CIA's role in this period of our nation's history.

19 January 1990   J. Kenneth McDonald
                                                              Chief Historian

Preface

I am grateful to have been given the opportunity to write about General Walter Bedell Smith as Director of Central Intelligence from 1950 to 1953. As this history will demonstrate, it was General Smith who finally established the Central Intelligence Agency in the role that had been intended for it by the President in 1946 and the Congress in 1947. That conception, which was worked out in JIC 239/5 dated 1 January 1945, had been lost from sight in the conflict with the departmental intelligence agencies precipitated by General Vandenberg and inherited by Admiral Hillenkoetter. It took a man of Smith's prestige, character, and ability to restore order and to create, for the first time, a really effective United States intelligence community. Thus, the history of U.S. intelligence is clearly divisible into two distinct eras, before Smith and after Smith.

Let me set forth my qualifications to undertake this history and, incidentally, my point of view.

I have a Ph.D. in history (Duke, 1935) and was Assistant Professor of History at the Virginia Military Institute until October 1940, when, as a reserve captain, I was called to active duty in the Military Intelligence Division of the War Department General Staff.

During 1942, as a lieutenant colonel and Secretary of the Joint Intelligence Committee, I was closely associated with Brigadier General Walter Bedell Smith, then Secretary of the Joint Chiefs of Staff. Our relationship at that time is indicated by the fact that in 1943, when Smith was Chief of Staff at Allied Force Headquarters in Algiers, he asked for me by name to be the Chief Historian at that headquarters. (I was not allowed to go, on the ground that my services were indispensable to the JIC.)

In December 1944, as a colonel and the senior Army member of the Joint Intelligence Staff, I participated in the fierce debate in the JIC over General Donovan's proposal for a "central intelligence service" and personally drafted JIC 239/5, the compromise that eventually served as the basis for the President's letter of 22 January 1946, establishing the Central Intelligence Group, and for the provisions of the National Security Act of 1947, establishing the Central Intelligence Agency. The conception of the CIA that Bedell Smith finally established was derived from JIC 239/5, not from the Donovan plan.[a]

In January 1946 I was one of the eight men who reported for duty with the Central Intelligence Group on the first day of its existence and personally drafted NIA Directives Nos. 1 and 2. Thereafter I was Acting Assistant Director, CIG, under both Admiral Souers and General Vandenberg as DCI. Later I was Chief of the Intelligence Staff, ORE (1946–47), under General Vandenberg, and CIA member of the NSC Staff (1947–51), under both Admiral Hillenkoetter and General Smith as DCI.

On 10 October 1950 (three days after he had taken office as DCI), General Smith put me in personal charge of the urgent production of national intelligence estimates pending the creation of an Office of National Estimates. In November he made me a charter member of the Board of National Estimates.

I am not the first to have worked in this field of history. In 1951 William Jackson, Smith's Deputy, engaged Arthur Darling, a professional historian, to prepare a "historical audit" of the "evolution of the concept of a national intelligence system" for the information of the President, the National Security Council, and the Intelligence Advisory Committee, as well as the DCI, so that all might learn from the CIA's past successes and failures. Darling's history extends from William Donovan's conception of a presidential "coordinator of information" (1941) through Bedell Smith's initial reorganization of the CIA (1950).[b]

Arthur Darling accomplished a monumental work in assembling from many scattered sources documents of historical value relating to the "evolution of the concept of a national intelligence system" and in recording interviews with the leading participants in that evolution who were available to him from 1951 to 1952. All concerned with the subject are indebted to him for that service. Darling's history, however, does not provide an entirely adequate basis for understanding Bedell Smith's problems and actions as DCI. For one thing, Darling had little experience in government, and he sometimes failed to comprehend the full significance of the material that he had collected.[c] For another, Darling, working for the DCI, took as his heroes the predecessor DCIs, Vandenberg and Hillenkoetter, and condemned, at least by implication, all those who had hindered and persecuted them—including William Jackson and

---

[a]General Donovan understood the difference. He bitterly opposed JIC 239/5.

[b]Arthur Darling, *The Central Intelligence Agency: An Instrument of Government, to 1950*, 12 vols., CIA Historical Staff, HS-1.

[c]Darling honestly recorded that William Donovan laughed when he read Darling's introductory essay on the nature of intelligence.

Allen Dulles![a] That was not only impolitic; it was also a distortion of the history of the pre-Smith period.[b]

For this reason I have felt obliged to review the pertinent aspects of the pre-Smith period in summary fashion in order to establish an adequate basis for an understanding of the proceedings of Bedell Smith and his deputies, William Jackson and Allen Dulles.

There is also an "organizational history" of the Bedell Smith period prepared by George Jackson and Martin Claussen as a sequel to Darling's history.[c] It is a well-researched and straightforward account of the structural changes within the Agency during the Smith regime, except as regards the clandestine services, which are not covered, and is an excellent source of factual information in greater detail than I have thought it necessary to present. In general, however, it does not go beneath the surface of events in order to explain them in terms of internal and external relationships and personal motivations, as I have endeavored to do.

[fourteen lines deleted]

I am especially indebted to Sidney Souers and William Jackson for their interest and assistance. Souers was the first Director of Central Intelligence (1946), the first Executive Secretary of the National Security Council (1947–51), and Special Consultant to the President (1951–53). Jackson was a member of the NSC Survey Group (1948), Deputy Director of Central Intelligence (1950–51), and Senior Consultant to the DCI (1951–53). Both men granted me day-long interviews and subsequently read and commented on the draft text.[d]

I am likewise especially indebted to Walter Pforzheimer, who was the CIA's Legislative Counsel (1946–55), and is now (1971) the Curator of its Historical Intelligence Collection. He has given me the benefit of his personal recollections and has read and commented on the entire draft text—as have Howard Ehrmann, Chief of the Historical Staff, and Bernard Drell, his deputy.

---

[a]Darling may have intended to assert his intellectual integrity and professional independence in the face of Jackson's evident purpose to condemn Vandenberg and Hillenkoetter in order to exalt Smith.

[b]Infuriated, Allen Dulles decreed that no one should ever see Darling's history without his express permission. He was not concerned with security, but with what he regarded as historical misrepresentation. Dulles's own understanding of the history of the period was diametrically opposite Darling's but itself less than perfect.

[c]George Jackson and Martin Claussen, *Organizational History of the Central Intelligence Agency, 1950–1953*, 10 vols., Historical Staff, HS-2.

[d]Souers has read and commented on the entire draft. Jackson had read only through Chapter VI when illness prevented him from assisting me further.

Others who have given me valuable oral testimony are, in the order of their first appearance in my source references, Averell Harriman, Lawrence Houston, Meredith Davidson, Robert Amory, John Earman, [name deleted], Lawrence White, Wayne Jackson, Frank Reynolds, Gordon Butler, James Reber, John Bross, Sherman Kent, Abbot Smith, James Graham, Willard Matthias, Otto Guthe, Virginia Long, [name deleted], Arthur Lundahl, Phyllis Beach, Thomas Lawler, Karl Weber, Louise Davison, Richard Helms, Gordon Stewart, James Lay, Burney Bennett, and Ray Cline. Most of those listed have also read and commented on the parts of the draft text with reference to which they had special competence. Mr. Helms was pleased to say that Chapter X, in which he appears, succeeded in giving the essence of the subject, and even the flavor of the time, without getting lost in the minutiae—which is, of course, what I endeavored to do.

I am grateful to all of these informants for their generous contributions of information and judgment. Needless to say, however, I am solely responsible for the judgments that I have expressed and the passing comments that I have made.

[eleven lines deleted]

December 1971   Ludwell Lee Montague

PART ONE

THE
ESSENTIAL
BACKGROUND

I

A BIOGRAPHICAL
INTRODUCTION

*As Director of Central Intelligence, he made an outstanding contribu-
tion to the national security of the United States. Through his firmness
and tact, perceptiveness and judgment, and withal, through his brilliant
leadership in a position of highest responsibility, he assured the realization of that ideal of a coordinated intelligence effort which was set
forth by the Congress in 1947, and brought to a new height of effectiveness the intelligence machinery of the United States Government.
Through his well-grounded and clearly defined concept of intelligence,
reinforced by his recognized integrity and high personal prestige, he
won acceptance of the principle that policy decisions must be based
upon sound intelligence.*

*—Dwight D. Eisenhower
21 February 1953*[a]

As President Eisenhower justly recognized, it was General Walter Bedell
Smith who first brought into effective existence the Central Intelligence
Agency and the U.S. intelligence community that had been contemplated
in the President's letter of 22 January 1946 and in the National Security
Act of 1947 and who first established intelligence in its proper role in the
policymaking processes of the Government. In this sense, Bedell Smith
deserves to be remembered as the real founder of the CIA.

He had precursors, of course. William Donovan first conceived of a
central intelligence agency in the service of the President, but his

---

[a]On presenting to General Walter Bedell Smith the first National Security Medal ever
awarded.

authoritarian attitude—his zealous inability to consider any other point of view than his own—prevented him from accomplishing his purpose. Sidney Souers, the first Director of Central Intelligence (DCI), served for five months. He never undertook to do more than get that office established and capable of development by a "permanent" successor. His successor, Hoyt Vandenberg, stayed for only eleven months. Vandenberg had a grand conception of a totally self-sufficient, authoritarian central agency that went even beyond Donovan. He sowed the wind and left his successor, Roscoe Hillenkoetter, to reap the whirlwind. Hillenkoetter never wanted to be DCI and probably never should have been. He was unable to cope with the situation in which he found himself and gladly relinquished it to go to sea, which he said was the proper place for a sailor in time of war.

Thus, it remained for Bedell Smith to accomplish what the President and the Congress had intended. That could have been done only by a man of his immense personal prestige and brilliantly perceptive judgment, firmness—and tact.

Bedell Smith did not achieve perfection in a little more than two years, nor did the CIA remain static under his successors, each of whom made his own constructive contribution. The Agency developed notably during the long tenure of Smith's immediate successor, Allen Welsh Dulles, who was DCI for nine years, far longer than any other man. Dulles certainly knew more of "the craft of intelligence" than Smith did. His understanding was not narrowly limited to covert operations, although his primary personal interest certainly was. His decisions as DCI were generally wise and constructive. It cannot be said, however, that the development of the Agency during his time was in accordance with any grand conception or preconceived plan. The Agency, like Topsy, "just growed," in accordance with its inherent nature—which had been established by Bedell Smith.

Thus, the history of the Central Intelligence Agency and of the U.S. intelligence community is clearly divisible into two distinct eras—before Smith, and after him.

Lieutenant General Walter Bedell Smith took office as Director of Central Intelligence on 7 October 1950.[a] On that same day William Harding Jackson took office as Smith's Deputy. Three months later, on 2 January 1951, Allen Welsh Dulles took office as Deputy Director for Plans (DDP)—that is, for covert activities. Jackson departed in August 1951, and Dulles then succeeded him as Deputy Director. Smith departed in February 1953, and Dulles then succeeded him as Director.

The character of Smith's administration as DCI was strongly affected by the personalities and past experiences of these three men. This history

---

[a]Smith was a four-star general effective 1 August 1951.

therefore opens with biographical sketches of each of them before taking up the problems they faced and the solutions that they devised for them.

WALTER BEDELL SMITH

Walter Bedell Smith was born in Indianapolis on 5 October 1895, the son of a local merchant. He attended St. Peter and Paul's School and entered Butler University, but in his freshman year he had to withdraw and go to work, because his father had become an invalid. He afterward sought to compensate for his lack of a college education by extensive professional and historical reading, with the result that he became a better read man than most college graduates.

In 1911, when he was sixteen, Smith enlisted in the Indiana National Guard. Two years later he was an eighteen-year-old first sergeant. In 1917 he was selected for officer training and was commissioned a reserve second lieutenant in November. He went to France with the 4th Division, was wounded at St. Mihiel (September 1918), and was then ordered to duty with the War Department's Bureau of Intelligence in Washington. That assignment was his only intelligence service prior to his appointment as Director of Central Intelligence in 1950.

After the war Smith obtained a commission in the Regular Army. In addition to the usual assignments of an infantry officer in time of peace, he had one very unusual one, to be assistant to the chief coordinator of the Bureau of the Budget (1925–29).

At the Infantry School in 1931, Captain Smith came to the favorable notice of Colonel George Catlett Marshall, the assistant commandant in charge of instruction. Upon Smith's graduation, Marshall had him appointed Secretary of the School. When Marshall became Chief of Staff of the Army in August 1939, he had Major Smith assigned as Assistant Secretary of the War Department General Staff. Smith consequently became Secretary of the General Staff in September 1941 and Secretary of the Joint Chiefs of Staff and the Combined Chiefs of Staff in February 1942.

Despite his outstanding qualities, Smith had had a hard struggle to win recognition in the Army, because he was not a West Pointer. Marshall, who was not a West Pointer either, was not affected by that consideration. Smith remained deeply grateful to Marshall for his recognition and patronage.[1]

When General Dwight David Eisenhower was assigned to command the U.S. forces in the European Theater of Operations, Marshall suggested that he take Smith to be his Chief of Staff.[2] As Assistant Chief of Staff for War Plans, Eisenhower had been impressed by Smith's managerial performance as Secretary; he was glad to accept Marshall's suggestion. Thus, Smith become Chief of Staff of the Allied Forces, first in North Africa and then in Europe.

Eisenhower later described Smith as "the general manager of the war" (of Eisenhower's part of it, that is) and as "a Godsend—a master of detail with clear comprehension of the main issues."[3] Some say that Smith actually commanded the Allied Expeditionary Forces while Eisenhower played bridge, or at least that Smith was Eisenhower's real deputy as Supreme Commander[a] rather than merely his Chief of Staff.[4] There can be no doubt of the importance of the role that Smith played at SHAEF,[b] but Smith himself gave Eisenhower full credit for his crucial command decisions.[5]

When Eisenhower returned to Washington, late in 1945, to succeed Marshall as Chief of Staff of the Army, he summoned Smith to be his Assistant Chief of Staff for Operations and Planning. Smith had hardly arrived in Washington, however, when he was asked to go to Moscow as Ambassador. President Truman and Secretary Byrnes considered that a general of Smith's reputation would be a more effective ambassador in Moscow than any civilian could be at that time.[6]

Bedell Smith went to Moscow supposing (as did Truman, Byrnes, Marshall, and Eisenhower) that, although Marshal Stalin was certainly a suspicious and difficult man, he could be reached by a bluff soldier-to-soldier approach, and that mutual confidence and cooperation between the United States and the Soviet Union could thereby be established.[7c] The prevailing thought at that time was that the future peace of the world depended on the establishment of such a relationship; the alternative was too terrible to contemplate.

Three years in Moscow disillusioned Smith. His conclusion from that experience was that

> . . . we are forced to a continuing struggle for a free way of life that may extend over a period of many years. We dare not allow ourselves any false sense of security. We must anticipate that the Soviet tactic will be to attempt to wear us down, to exasperate us,

---

[a]The nominal Deputy Supreme Commander was British Air Marshal Tedder.

[b]Supreme Headquarters, Allied Expeditionary Forces.

[c]General Marshall retained this illusion until he himself went to Moscow as Secretary of State in 1947.

to keep probing for weak spots, and we must cultivate firmness and patience to a degree that we have never before required.[8a]

Smith returned from Moscow in March 1949 to become the Commanding General of the First Army, with headquarters on Governor's Island in New York harbor. It was from that post that he was called to be Director of Central Intelligence.

President Eisenhower later said of Smith that, "strong in character and abrupt by instinct, he could achieve harmony without appeasement."[9] Smith did indeed "achieve harmony without appeasement" in his relations with the Intelligence Advisory Committee (IAC), which was composed of the heads of the departmental intelligence agencies under his chairmanship as DCI. His reputation as a strong and abrupt character was an important, but latent, factor in that success. The operative factor was his calculated effort to create an atmosphere of mutual consideration and goodwill.[b] General Smith could be a very engaging man when he set out to be. According to his deputy, his every action, "abrupt" or ingratiating, was calculated for effect.[10] He could be ingratiating without compromising his authority, without leading anyone to mistake that as a sign of weakness.[c] The force of his personality was such that, from the moment he entered a room, he commanded the respectful attention of all present there.[11]

Vivid recollections of General Smith's "abrupt" and forceful expressions of impatience have tended to obscure the memory of his basic kindness and consideration, and of his strong sense of humor.

It happens that the author twice served General Smith directly, in 1942 and again in 1950, without ever experiencing from him anything other than friendly good humor and kind consideration. One understood that the General was a forceful and demanding man, impatient when disappointed, but one could approach him with confidence, if confident that one was serving him well.[12]

Others who knew General Smith well testify also to his kindness and his good humor.[d] He was not only considerate, but even sentimental. He found his relaxation in tending a rose garden. He greeted with a kiss all the women of his familiar acquaintance, young or old, pretty or not. He

---

[a]This is an apt sermon for our own time (1971).

[b]See Part Two, Chapter V.

[c]As had happened when Admiral Hillenkoetter attempted the same approach in 1947. See Part One, Chapter II.

[d]For example, Meredith Davidson, John Earman, William Jackson, Walter Pforzheimer, Sidney Souers.

was a shareholder in a toy factory, and he delighted to shower toys on the fathers of young children.[13]

Bedell Smith never failed to recognize, and to remember, a subordinate's good performance, but he was indeed a terror to anyone who disappointed him. His general reputation was that of an "ogre" whom it would be unwise to provoke. The beginning of the explanation of the contradiction between his true character and his reputation is to be found in his own testimony. Noting that he had become first sergeant of an infantry company at the age of eighteen, he said, "It is possible that some of the less attractive characteristics of my personality were acquired at a very early age as an infantry first sergeant."[14]

One can imagine the performance that an eighteen-year-old first sergeant would have had to put on to dominate an infantry company, especially as such things were done in 1913. Sergeant Smith learned that it worked with buck privates. Lieutenant General Smith knew that it worked also with major generals. It is remembered of him that on one occasion, in October 1950, he "chewed out" a major general, a member of the Intelligence Advisory Committee, in the language of a drill sergeant addressing a lackadaisical recruit—but at the same time calling him familiarly by his Army nickname.[15]

Bedell Smith hazed the members of his personal staff unmercifully. It appears that in part he did so deliberately, as a technique for keeping them alert and hustling. They came to realize that it was also, sometimes, the expression of a teasing sense of humor.[16] But more often than not it was the expression of a genuine impatience. William Jackson, Smith's Deputy, understood that. Smith, he said, was an extremely brilliant man, very quick in his perceptions. He simply had no patience with men less brilliantly perceptive than he.[17]

No matter what the occasion for it, a broadside from Bedell Smith was always a shattering experience. Characteristically, Smith never apologized for his impatient outbursts, but he always found an early opportunity to demonstrate to his victims his continuing goodwill toward them. Members of his staff lived in a state of constant tension, but they remained personally devoted to the General.[18a]

His personal staff members were not the only ones to receive such expressions of his displeasure. Such dignitaries as William Jackson, Allen

---

[a]Smith's basic kindness is illustrated by the story of a member of his personal staff who became so terrified of him that his effectiveness was impaired. Smith was highly displeased to observe this reaction, but he neither kept the man near him, where he would inevitably be subjected to further hazing, nor did he summarily fire him. Instead, he quietly transferred him to a position of dignity in which he would be under less pressure.

Dulles, and Frank Wisner felt the same pressure.[a] Jackson, who was highly esteemed by Smith,[b] said that he could never feel at ease with Smith until they were being driven home together at the end of the working day.[19]

Indeed, Jackson, Dulles, and Wisner felt Smith's ire more severely than did lesser folk. General Smith considered that senior officers ought to be able to defend themselves, but was solicitously concerned regarding the well-being and the morale of the troops.[20]

In sum, Bedell Smith defensively concealed his essentially kind and generous nature and deliberately cultivated a reputation for irritable impatience as a managerial technique.[c] Eventually his "abrupt" manner became habitual—instinctive, as Eisenhower put it. But Bedell Smith could also be ingratiating and conciliatory when that suited his purpose, as this history will show.

Those who ventured to speak familiarly of Bedell Smith called him "Beetle." That nickname, obviously derived from his middle name, expressed his hyperactivity. It pleased him; he had a small black beetle embossed on his personal stationery. But Winston Churchill preferred to call him, admiringly, "the American Bulldog"[22]—presumably for his seamed countenance and his indomitable tenacity of purpose.

WILLIAM HARDING JACKSON

William Harding Jackson was born in 1901 at "Belle Meade," the estate of his grandfather, General William Harding Jackson, near Nashville. General Jackson had commanded a cavalry division in the Confederate Army of Tennessee. "Belle Meade" was famous for the breeding of thoroughbred horses.[d] During Jackson's childhood, however, his father and grandfather died and "Belle Meade" was sold.[e] His maternal grand-

---

[a]The radically different reactions of Dulles and Wisner are reported below, Part Two, page 92.

[b]Smith gave evidence of this esteem in several ways, notably by leaving a substantial and unexpected bequest to Jackson's son.

[c]One of Smith's favorite sayings was "I have a more even disposition than anyone here—always terrible." Another was "Every officer is entitled to make *one* mistake. *You* have just made yours."[21]

[d]Portraits of famous "Belle Meade" stallions adorn Jackson's living room in Tucson, Arizona.

[e]"Belle Meade" is now owned by the State of Tennessee and maintained by the Association for the Preservation of Tennessee Antiquities.

father, James B. Richardson of Nashville, decided that he should be sent to school in New England, where he attended Faye School and then St. Mark's.[23]

Jackson graduated from Princeton University in 1924 and from Harvard Law School in 1928. He began his career as a New York lawyer with Cadwalader, Wickersham & Taft, but went to work with Carter, Ledyard & Milburn in 1930 and became a partner in that firm in 1934. During these prewar years he was an active polo player and also an active pilot of light private aircraft.

On the morrow of Pearl Harbor, Tommy Hitchcock, the famous polo player, led Jackson into obtaining a commission as captain in the Army Air Corps, for service in air intelligence. After graduation from the Air Intelligence School in Harrisburg, Jackson was assigned to the headquarters of the Army Air Force Anti-Submarine Command, which operated under the control of the Navy's Eastern Sea Frontier. There, after a period of extreme boredom, Captain Jackson had the temerity to produce an analysis of the effectiveness of antisubmarine warfare as it was then being conducted off the U.S. East Coast. He showed that it was a dismal failure and urged that the Army units involved be sent to reinforce the RAF Coastal Command for a concerted attack on the German submarines at their source in the Bay of Biscay.

Captain Jackson's paper infuriated the U.S. Navy, from Admiral King on down, but it delighted the Army Air Force. Jackson was reassigned to be Assistant Military Air Attaché in London, in liaison with the Coastal Command. His recommendation was eventually carried out, although it took the personal intervention of the Secretary of War to overcome the bitter opposition of the Navy.[24]

Jackson went on from this success to become a colonel and Deputy G-2 on the staff of General Omar Nelson Bradley, who was in command of the 12th Army Group. In addition to his official duties, he became Bradley's personal counsellor, particularly with regard to his relations with SHAEF. Bradley strongly resented what he regarded as SHAEF's undue favor toward Field Marshal Montgomery at the expense of the 12th Army Group. Since he was psychologically unable to blame his disappointments on his West Point classmate and old friend, "Ike" Eisenhower, he blamed them on the malign influence of that military upstart, Bedell Smith, Eisenhower's Chief of Staff. Thus, there were elements of personal jealousy and military snobbery in Bradley's attitude toward Smith. Seeing all this only from Bradley's point of view, Jackson regarded Smith as "that ogre at SHAEF."[25]

At the same time, Jackson came into cooperative contact with Allen Welsh Dulles, the chief of the OSS mission in Switzerland. Jackson had known Dulles as a lawyer in New York. They met in France to confer on how Dulles's clandestine operations into Germany might be made to serve the intelligence needs of the 12th Army Group.[26]

At the end of the war Jackson proposed to take advantage of the intimacy of U.S.–U.K. military relations to make a thorough study of the British intelligence system, before the Foreign Office got around to regarding Americans once more as foreigners. It was arranged for him to do so under OSS auspices. Jackson spent two weeks in London conferring on the subject. His principal informant was Anthony Eden.[27] That was, of course, at too high a level for him to get a realistic, working-level view. He came away an enthusiastic admirer of the British Joint Intelligence Committee, which then did indeed enjoy the highest reputation in intelligence.[a]

Jackson submitted his report to General William J. Donovan, Director of Strategic Services. Donovan already knew all about the British JIC and could not have been less interested in any joint committee system. But Jackson later sent a summary to James Forrestal, Secretary of the Navy, with whom he was personally acquainted,[b] and that established in Forrestal's mind the idea that Jackson was an expert on the British intelligence system. This letter was significant in that it first articulated the "board of directors" concept strongly advocated by Admiral Inglis (1947–49).[c]

Jackson returned to his law practice in New York, but his reputation as an authority on the British intelligence organization was such that in July 1946 General Vandenberg, then DCI, sent him, with Kingman Douglass,[d] [three lines, with [e]note, deleted].[28] Jackson considered Douglass's participation superfluous.[29]

Jackson and Douglas were included in the "Advisory Committee" that Vandenberg created in August 1946. That group was composed entirely of investment bankers and associated lawyers, but all had some acquaintance with the problem of interdepartmental intelligence coordination.[30f]

In January 1948 James Forrestal, then Secretary of Defense, called on Jackson to participate with Allen Dulles and Matthias Correa in an investigation of the Central Intelligence Agency on behalf of the National

---

[a][note deleted]

[b]Jackson had done legal work for Forrestal in New York before the war. He considered Forrestal a good man for whom to work, although he did not like him personally.

[c]See pages 31–34.

[d]Douglass had been the senior U.S. intelligence liaison officer in the British Air Ministry during the war and Acting Deputy DCI under Souers.

[e][note deleted]

[f]The others were Allen Dulles, Robert Lovett, Paul Nitze, and Sidney Souers.

Security Council. This Survey Group rendered its devastating report in January 1949.[a]

Meanwhile, in 1947, Jackson had left his law firm to become the managing partner in the investment banking firm of J. H. Whitney & Company. He was intent on achieving financial independence in this role when, to his surprise and dismay, the "ogre of SHAEF" asked him to drop this plan and return to Washington to be the Deputy Director of Central Intelligence.[b]

ALLEN WELSH DULLES

Allen Welsh Dulles was born in Watertown, New York, in 1893. His father was a Presbyterian clergyman. His grandfather, John Foster, was an eminent lawyer who had been Secretary of State from 1892 to 1893. Robert Lansing, another lawyer who was Secretary of State from 1915 to 1920, was his uncle by marriage. His brother, John Foster Dulles, was five years older than he.

John Foster Dulles accompanied John Foster to the Hague Convention of 1907, which was held during his junior year at Princeton. In 1911 John Foster placed John Foster Dulles with the New York law firm of Sullivan & Cromwell, which specialized in international law. Through the Lansing connection, John Foster Dulles was a member of the U.S. Delegation to the Paris Peace Conference in 1919.

These connections and influences led Allen Dulles first into the diplomatic service and then into the law firm of Sullivan & Cromwell.

Allen Dulles graduated from Princeton University in 1914. He then taught English for one year at the Presbyterian missionary school in Allahabad, India, before returning to Princeton, where he received his M.A. degree in 1916.

In 1916 Dulles was commissioned in the diplomatic service and assigned to the American Legation in Vienna. He was transferred to Bern and served there during the war from 1917 to 1918. He was then (with his brother) a member of the U.S. Delegation to the Paris Peace Conference. After further diplomatic service in Berlin (1919) and Constantinople (1920–22), he was recalled to the State Department to be the chief of its Near East Division.

---

[a]See page 43.
[b]See Part Two, page 57.

While in Washington (1922–26), Dulles studied law at George Washington University. In October 1926 he resigned from the diplomatic service and joined the firm of Sullivan & Cromwell in New York. He kept up his connections in the State Department, however, and served as legal adviser to the U.S. delegations at the Geneva Conferences of 1927 and 1932. He was also active in the Council on Foreign Relations in New York.[a]

In 1942 William Donovan, who had known Dulles in legal circles in New York, recruited him for the Office of Strategic Services. From October 1942 until November 1945 Dulles was chief of the OSS clandestine operations based in Switzerland and of the OSS mission that entered Germany after the surrender. His achievements in that role are well known; he gave his own account of them in *Germany's Underground* (1947) and *The Secret Surrender* (1966).[31]

For these achievements Allen Dulles came to be regarded as the American master of the craft of intelligence. In November 1945, when Robert Lovett was asked who should be the director of the central intelligence agency, he replied that the only name he had heard mentioned was that of Allen Dulles.[32]

At the end of 1945 Dulles returned to his law practice in New York. In August 1946, however, General Vandenberg enlisted him in the DCI's "Advisory Committee."[b] In February 1947, when Vandenberg's intention to resign as DCI became known, the State Department considered commending Dulles to succeed him, only to discover that Admiral Hillenkoetter had already been selected.[33]

In April 1947, when Congress was considering the statutory establishment of a central intelligence agency, Dulles submitted a nine-page memorandum on the subject. That memorandum consisted in large part of reiteration of the point that the Director of Central Intelligence and his principal lieutenants should be civilians of a judicial temperament, men willing to dedicate the remainder of their active lives to the task, rather than transient military officers looking elsewhere for the ultimate fulfillment of their careers.[34c] That point was well taken and well argued—but one cannot escape the impression that Dulles was then thinking of himself as the judicious and dedicated civilian who ought to be Director of Central Intelligence.

---

[a]He became President of the Council in 1946.

[b]See page 11.

[c]Admiral Souers had been DCI for less than five months, General Vandenberg for less than eleven. Souers, a reserve officer, had been impatient to return to his private business. Vandenberg, a career officer, had consented to become DCI only as a step toward the realization of his ambition to become Chief of Staff of the prospectively independent Air Force.[35]

Allen Dulles had made his reputation as a clandestine operator—and later, as DCI, he certainly was CIA's "Great White Case Officer." It is notable, then, that in this 1947 memorandum he argued that 80 percent of the CIA's information would come from open sources and only 20 percent from secret sources, a term that he used to cover communications intelligence as well as espionage. He stressed that in time of peace the great bulk of the information required would be of a civil rather than a military character: scientific, economic, social, and political. It would be of greater importance to understand the mind of the Kremlin and to trace the Soviet development of advanced weapons than to count the number of Soviet divisions. The collection of a vast amount of information would be futile unless it was evaluated and interpreted by knowledgeable, experienced, and mature men.[a] For such men to be available, it would be necessary to establish intelligence as an attractive professional career.[36]

It has been said that Allen Dulles's interest was too narrowly confined to clandestine operations.[37] This memorandum written in 1947 shows that even then he had a good grasp of the entire subject, no matter how much his personal interest continued to be drawn primarily to clandestine operations.

In January 1948 Secretary Forrestal asked Dulles to head a three-man survey group appointed to investigate the functioning of the Central Intelligence Agency on behalf of the National Security Council. Thus, Dulles had another opportunity to express himself on the subject. In January 1949 the survey group rendered a devastating report.

At some time during the fall of 1950 Bedell Smith asked Allen Dulles to come to Washington to supervise the clandestine operations of the CIA. Dulles came in November, as a consultant. He was appointed Deputy Director for Plans on 2 January 1951.

---

[a]Dulles's specific suggestion on this point was that the Research and Analysis Branch of the OSS, which had been transferred to State, be retransferred to the CIA.

II

THE CRUCIAL PROBLEM

The director shall be advised by a board consisting of the heads of the principal military and civilian intelligence agencies having functions related to the national security.

—JIC 239/5
1 January 1945

When General Smith became Director of Central Intelligence in October 1950, the proper relationship between the DCI and the heads of the departmental intelligence agencies who collectively composed the Intelligence Advisory Committee had been the subject of bitter controversy for six years. General Smith's unique personal contribution as DCI was his astute resolution of that controversy. A full appreciation of that achievement requires a summary review of the various concepts of that relationship that had been advanced during those six years (1944–50). Such a review is presented in this chapter and the one on NSC 50 that follows.

THE JIS CONCEPT, 1944

The wartime Joint Intelligence Committee (JIC) was composed of six intelligence powers, each jealous of its own sovereignty and jurisdiction.[a]

---

[a]To wit: the Assistant Chief of Staff G-2, War Department General Staff; the Director of Naval Intelligence; the Assistant Chief of Air Staff A-2; and representatives of the Department of State, the Foreign Economic Administration, and the Office of Strategic Services.

There was no one in a position of leadership: the chairman (the senior military member by date of personal rank) was only first among equals, with merely procedural functions. No one represented the national interest as distinguished from conflicting departmental interests. The committee strove to achieve a consensus because the Joint Chiefs of Staff (JCS) were known to regard "split papers" with strong disfavor.[a] Disagreements could be resolved, however, only if someone backed down or if, as more often happened, someone could devise an ambiguous formulation that would cover both opposing points of view. Joint estimates prepared on this basis tended to become vague and meaningless precisely at those points that were of most significance.

The Joint Intelligence Staff (JIS), the full-time working group that prepared papers for JIC consideration and adoption, was a band of brothers who lived and worked together. Despite their different departmental origins, they had a common point of view. They could almost always achieve agreement among themselves without strain—but of course each was subject to instruction by a JIC principal who had considered the matter from only a departmental point of view.

The members of the JIS agreed among themselves that a headless joint committee like the JIC was the worst possible mechanism for producing intelligence estimates or for coordinating intelligence activities. On their own initiative, during the fall of 1944, they began to develop a plan for a better postwar interdepartmental intelligence organization. Inasmuch as every department concerned with national security or foreign relations would require a departmental intelligence agency to serve its peculiar operational needs, there would have to be an interdepartmental committee to bring together the heads of those departmental agencies to deal with matters beyond the exclusive competence of any one department. The members of the JIS felt strongly, however, that any such committee would have to have an independent chairman, appointed by the President, responsible solely to him, and free of the influence of departmental special interests. This chairman, having heard the argument on points in dispute among the departmental agencies, should have the power to decide what the text of the estimate or recommendation would say, on the basis of his own personal judgment. To prevent the suppression of responsible differing judgments, however, any member of the committee who objected to the chairman's decision on a substantial issue should have the right to express his position and the reasons for it in a dissenting

---

[a]The device of that time for presenting a disagreement was to present alternative texts in parallel columns—that is, "to split the text." The wartime JIC sent forward only one split paper. It related to the functions of the OSS, and the OSS split the text.

footnote. This device was intended to obviate the evasion or obfuscation of critical issues and to give the reader the benefit of a clear expression of both the chairman's considered judgment and the dissenter's opposing view.[a]

This concept, developed by the men who had had the most direct and practical experience of the functioning of a joint committee, is the touchstone for all that follows and the essential element in the role of the Director of Central Intelligence today.

THE STATE DEPARTMENT PLAN,
SEPTEMBER 1944

Meanwhile, the Department of State was developing a plan for a postwar "Office of Foreign Intelligence" within that Department. This plan was premised on the exclusive responsibility and authority of the Secretary of State for conducting the foreign relations of the United States, subject only to the direction of the President. It made no provision for the interdepartmental coordination of intelligence activities or of intelligence estimates. State simply assumed that it would dominate the field in time of peace, that the military intelligence services would be concerned only with such technical specialties as order of battle and weaponry.[b] State would maintain "close liaison" with them and would obtain through liaison whatever military inputs it needed for its own estimates. It had no idea of allowing the military a voice in those estimates, which would provide the intelligence foundation for national policy.[39]

THE DONOVAN PLAN, NOVEMBER 1944

In October 1944 a working draft of this State Department plan came into the possession of General William J. Donovan, the Director of Strategic

---

[a]The author, then senior Army member of the JIS, participated in the development of this concept.[38]

[b]The authors of this plan evidently had a strong sense of State's mission but no acquaintance with the world of intelligence. Army doctrine of that time held, for example, that political, social, and economic considerations were essential elements of *military* intelligence, which properly included anything that might affect Army operations.

Services. Donovan moved quickly to forestall State by submitting to the President a draft Executive Order releasing the Office of Strategic Services from its wartime subordination to the Joint Chiefs of Staff and transferring it to the Executive Office of the President.[40] His talking points, unexpressed in that curt document, were (1) that Presidential decisions on national policy and strategy should be based on intelligence free of the distorting influence of departmental policy and (2) that an organization capable of providing such intelligence already existed in the Office of Strategic Services.

It appears that Isadore Lubin dissuaded Donovan from presenting this draft Executive Order to the President and persuaded the President to request of Donovan a fully developed plan for a postwar intelligence service.[41] Donovan complied by submitting, on 18 November, a memorandum enclosing a draft order establishing a "central intelligence service" in the Executive Office of the President.[42]

Donovan distinguished between the "operational intelligence" required by the several departments in the performance of their respective departmental functions and the intelligence required by the President and his immediate advisers in order to plan and carry out national policy and strategy. He contemplated that departmental intelligence services would continue to exist to meet departmental needs, but he made the central service exclusively responsible for the production of strategic and national policy intelligence. The director of the central service would determine what information was required for that purpose and how it should be collected—whether by the central service directly or through the departmental services. He would coordinate (that is, direct) the activities of all the intelligence agencies of the Government so as to ensure an integrated national intelligence effort. He would have access to all intelligence information available to the Government and would accomplish the final evaluation, synthesis, and dissemination of the intelligence required for national policy planning purposes.

Donovan emphasized that the director of the central service should be responsible solely to the President. He made clear his strongly held opinion that the director should not be required to obtain the concurrence of the heads of the departmental services with regard to his national intelligence reports and estimates, or even with regard to his coordination of their activities. Indeed, he made no provision even to consult them.[a] As a grudging concession, he did include in his November proposals

---

[a]Donovan regarded the existing JIC with anger and contempt. He had suffered both insult and injury from it, and he considered that any joint committee system must necessarily be incompetent and ineffectual.

provision for occasional consultation with the Secretaries of State, War, and Navy jointly, but their role would be only advisory. The director would act with the authority of the President.

JIC 239/5, 1 JANUARY 1945

Donovan's proposals were referred to the Joint Chiefs of Staff, and by them to the Joint Intelligence Committee, for comment and recommendation. That threw the fat into the fire! The three service members of the JIC reacted violently to the idea of having "Wild Bill" Donovan authorized to direct and control their activities and to present to the President strategic intelligence estimates in which they had had no voice.[a]

The Army G-2 then had the ablest policy staff in the intelligence community (if it could be called a community at that time). The G-2 staff agreed that there were three functions that could be centralized to advantage: (1) the coordination of all intelligence activities; (2) the performance of services of common concern; and (3) the production of "strategic and national policy intelligence." It argued, however, that no one operating service (OSS, alias CIS) should be given the power to coordinate (that is, to direct) the operations of the others. Such authority would violate the principle of the chain of command: for example, it would make the operations of the Army G-2 subject to the control of an agency not responsible to the Chief of Staff or the Secretary of War. Moreover, such a coordinating agency would naturally favor its own operations, and that would eventually lead to a single intelligence service not necessarily responsive to departmental requirements. For these reasons, Army G-2 held that the coordinating function should not be assigned to the director of a central intelligence service, but rather to the Secretaries of State, War, and Navy, acting jointly, since they, individually, had the authority to direct the activities of their respective departmental intelligence agencies.[43]

That was sound doctrine, but the organization with which Army G-2

---

[a]The State Department was strangely passive about this matter, considering the impact of Donovan's proposals on the basic premise of the Department's own plan. The Foreign Economic Administration was indifferent, but its representative in the JIS became the most passionate advocate of the Donovan Plan—a reflection of his personal disgust with joint committees as a way of doing business.

proposed to implement it was a four-part contraption: (1) a *central intelligence authority* composed of the three Secretaries; (2) a *central intelligence planning agency*,[a] to plan for coordination and submit recommendations to the authority; (3) a separate *joint intelligence service*, to perform services of common concern; and (4) *the existing JIC* to produce "strategic and national policy intelligence."[44]

JIC 239/5, the eventual compromise reached after a month of contention, combined the doctrine of the Army G-2 with the unitary and independent central intelligence service proposed by General Donovan. It proposed that the coordinating function be assigned to a *National Intelligence Authority* composed of the three Secretaries and that the other three functions identified in the Army's scheme—to plan for coordination, to perform services of common concern, and to produce national intelligence—be assigned to a *Central Intelligence Agency*.[45] Be it noted that the director of this agency could only submit plans and recommendations to the Authority, which alone had the power to coordinate by decree.[b]

In JIC 239/5 the director of the central agency not only was made responsible to the three Secretaries but also was required to consult the heads of the departmental intelligence agencies. He was not made responsible to them, however. Their relationship to him was expressly described as only advisory.[46]

The original JIS concept[c] was not spelled out in JIC 239/5, but was understood by all concerned to apply to the relationship between the director and his advisory board. It was thought to be sufficiently implicit in the assignment of functions to the central agency and the explicit designation of the board as advisory to its director.

There would have been no Central Intelligence Agency without General Donovan's initiative, but it is historically erroneous to suppose, as is commonly done, that the CIA is based on the Donovan plan. Actually, the CIA is based on the much more sophisticated doctrine of the Army G-2 Policy Staff and on the agreement reached in JIC 239/5, which was significantly different from the Donovan plan, as General Donovan himself well understood.

---

[a]This "agency" was actually a joint committee different from the existing JIC. It would consist of a director appointed by the President and members appointed by the Secretary of State and the three Chiefs of Staff.

[b]In 1958 the NSC delegated to the DCI the task of coordinating intelligence activities, but the word was then used in a sense different from that understood by it in 1944—i.e., coordination through leadership, persuasion, and agreement rather than by command. It is still true that only the NSC has the power to coordinate by decree (1971).

[c]See page 16.

On 9 and 11 February 1945 the *Chicago Tribune* and the *Washington Times-Herald* published the secret texts of JCS 1181 (the Donovan plan) and JCS 1181/1 (JIC 239/5 as submitted to the JCS with insignificant amendments by the Joint Strategic Survey Committee). The publication of these secret documents was accompanied by an outcry that an American Gestapo was about to be created.[a] This outcry moved the JCS to shelve the entire subject indefinitely.[47]

On 5 April 1945 President Roosevelt asked General Donovan to see whether he could sell his 18 November plan to the Cabinet. Donovan got uncomprehending and negative responses from the Secretaries of State and Treasury, the Attorney General and the Postmaster General, and the Secretaries of the Interior, Agriculture, and Labor. The decisive response was from the Secretary of War. Mr. Stimson indicated that he strongly preferred the JCS plan (JIC 239/5) and said that State, War, Justice, and the Navy had agreed that the subject should be deferred until the conclusion of hostilities.[48]

At this point Donovan's Deputy, General John Magruder, pleaded with him to accept JIC 239/5 in lieu of his own plan.[b] He could thus disarm the opposition and get the Central Intelligence Agency established without delay, while the OSS was still in being to serve as its nucleus. With that foundation established, other desiderata could be obtained through normal development in practice.[49] That was wise counsel, but General Donovan refused to consider it. The result was the destruction of the OSS.

THE BUDGET BUREAU PLAN, SEPTEMBER–DECEMBER 1945

In April 1945 the Bureau of the Budget was already at work on a plan for a postwar intelligence system. The Bureau ignored both the Donovan

---

[a]This contention was absurd on the face of the documents quoted. J. Edgar Hoover, Director of the Federal Bureau of Investigation, is believed to have been responsible for this breach of security, his purpose being to prevent the creation of a central intelligence agency based on the OSS. Hoover then had a scheme for the development of the FBI into a "worldwide secret intelligence" agency. That agency would have been concerned only with clandestine collection. The functions of evaluation and analysis would have been assigned to the Department of State.

[b]As the OSS member of the JIC, Magruder had voted for JIC 239/5 as a reasonable compromise. Characteristically, General Donovan paid no attention to the considerations adduced in the JIC debate.

plan and JIC 239/5. Instead, it produced a less parochial version of the State Department plan of 1944.[a] The difference was provision for an elaborate structure of interdepartmental committees under State's control for the coordination of intelligence programs. The basic premise remained the same: the responsibility and authority of the Secretary of State for the conduct of all foreign affairs.

The Bureau went into action soon after the surrender of Japan. On 20 September 1945 it persuaded President Truman to sign two documents. One was an Executive Order dissolving the Office of Strategic Services, transferring its Research and Analysis Branch to State and its remaining elements to the War Department—all to take effect only ten days later, on 1 October.[50] The other was a memorandum directing the Secretary of State to take the lead in developing a comprehensive and coordinated foreign intelligence program through the creation of an interdepartmental group "heading up under the State Department."[51][b]

These two related developments were a shock to the Foreign Service officers who dominated the Department of State. They failed to perceive the advantages thus presented to State and vehemently resented the intrusion of strange men and ideas into their preserve.[52] The ensuing contention and confusion within the Department was such that eleven weeks passed before Alfred McCormack, the Secretary's new Special Assistant for Research and Intelligence,[c] was ready to present his proposals to the War and Navy Departments, even though what he then proposed was substantially what the Bureau of the Budget had prepared before 20 September.

The State Department (Bureau of the Budget) plan presented on 3 December provided for an Interdepartmental Intelligence Coordinating Authority, composed of the Secretaries of State, War, and Navy, which would determine the intelligence requirements of all the departments and agencies of the Government and the appropriate means to satisfy them. It would assign operating responsibilities, review the adequacy and efficiency of all intelligence programs, and establish centralized operating agencies as needed. Actually, this work would be done, subject to the Authority's approval, by an Executive Secretary, an officer of the Department of State. He would manage the Authority's agenda, submit his

---

[a]See page 17.

[b]War and Navy contended that this ambiguous expression meant that an interdepartmental group should be formed to devise a plan. State, proceeding unilaterally to devise a plan, held it to mean that the permanent structure should "head up" under State, which was evidently Budget's intention.

[c]Colonel McCormack was a New York lawyer who had been Chief of the Special Branch, G-2, during the war.

recommendations to it, and see to the proper execution of its decisions. He would be assisted by an Advisory Group composed of full-time representatives of the Assistant Chief of Staff G-2, the Director of Naval Intelligence, and the Assistant Chief of Air Staff A-2.[a] Analyses and proposed programs would be submitted to him by a proliferation of "Interdepartmental Coordinating Committees" on every conceivable topic. For a start, twelve such committees were proposed, each of which would be chaired by an Assistant Secretary.[53b]

Thus, unlike General Donovan, the Department of State was now willing to consult in every case with each interested party—but it was obvious that the whole elaborate committee structure was intended to be merely consultative and that effective control of the coordination process would be vested in the Executive Secretary and his Assistant Secretaries, officers of the Department of State.

The State Department and Budget Bureau exhausted themselves in devising this mechanism for coordination. With regard to services of common concern, they could only provide that the Authority might establish centralized agencies for such purposes if it perceived a need to do so. It was agreed in principle that there should be a central agency to conduct clandestine operations. Other central agencies might be established for other purposes, but each would be separate and limited to a particular task. It was stated as a principle that no central agency should be established if any departmental agency could perform the task as a service to the other departmental agencies.[54]

With regard to "strategic and national policy intelligence" the Department of State was adamant. Such intelligence would be produced by the Department, on the authority of the Secretary of State alone, as a necessary consequence of his unique responsibility for foreign affairs. The staff to be established within the Department for this purpose would accept the participation of officers seconded to it by the War and Navy Departments but would not be bound to obtain their concurrence or that of the service intelligence chiefs. There would be no advisory board like that contemplated in JIC 239/5.[55]

This plan had been prepared without consulting anyone in the War and Navy Departments. Their reaction remained to be reckoned with.

---

[a]Note that these officers themselves were nowhere in the picture, not even as an advisory board like that contemplated in JIC 239/5.

[b]This plan provided also for a separate Interdepartmental Security Coordinating Authority to be served by the same Executive Secretary with the aid of a second advisory group and a second proliferation of topical committees (eight to begin with).

JCS 1181/5 AND THE LOVETT REPORT

In August 1945, on the initiative of the Deputy Director of Naval Intelligence, Rear Admiral Sidney W. Souers, the Joint Chiefs of Staff were reminded of JIC 239/5.[56] On 19 September the Chiefs adopted JCS 1181/5, which was substantially identical to JIC 239/5,[a] and requested the Secretaries of War and Navy to forward their recommendation to the President.[57] They were, of course, too late. On 20 September, when President Truman signed the papers presented to him by the Bureau of the Budget,[b] he was unaware that the Joint Chiefs of Staff had an alternative plan.

While they waited for the Secretary of State to set up an interdepartmental committee to devise a plan or else to present his own plan, the Secretaries of War and Navy commissioned studies of their own on the subject. The report submitted to Secretary Forrestal by Ferdinand Eberstadt on 22 October contained a strong endorsement of JCS 1181/5 (JIC 239/5).[58c] So did the report submitted to Secretary Patterson by Robert Lovett on 3 November.[59]

The Lovett Report was, in general, a paraphrase of JCS 1181/5, but, significantly, Lovett took the trouble to spell out the JIS concept of the relationship between the Director, the CIA, and his advisory board,[d] as follows:

> The Director shall consult with and secure the opinion of the Board on all important questions that may arise. . . . In the event of a difference of opinion . . . the decision of the Director shall be controlling, subject, however, to the right of any member of the Board to have the question submitted for final decision to the National Intelligence Authority. The Director should also consult with the Board before delivering any estimates and appreciations to the President or any member of the Cabinet, and if there shall be any difference of opinion . . . the differing opinion should accompany the Director's report.

At the regular periodic meeting of the Secretaries of State, War, and Navy held on 14 November, Forrestal insisted that action be taken to

---

[a]The difference, which was essentially rhetorical, increased emphasis on the subordination of the director of the central agency to the National Intelligence Authority.

[b]See page 22.

[c]Souers wrote the intelligence chapter of the Eberstadt Report.

[d]See pages 16–17. Presumably Lovett was advised on this point by John Magruder, then Chief of the Strategic Services Unit in the War Department.

establish a central intelligence agency without further delay, and Patterson had Lovett present his summary report on the subject. Byrnes, unbriefed for this, agreed in principle to the Lovett concept and an ad hoc committee was formed to work out the details.[60a] In that committee, however, McCormack proved to be intransigent,[61] and on 3 December he presented his version of the Budget Bureau plan as though the 14 November meeting of the three Secretaries had never been held.

The War and Navy Departments refused to accept McCormack's plan, even after he had modified it superficially to meet some of their objections.[62] They thought absurd the idea of twenty different coordinating committees and several separate central intelligence agencies, but their main objection was that they would be denied any effective voice in the intelligence to be presented to the President as the basis for national policy and strategy. They were determined to have the Lovett plan, which was JCS 1181/5, which was JIC 239/5.

THE PRESIDENT'S LETTER, 22 JANUARY 1946

By the end of December, President Truman's patience had been exhausted. He called for copies of the State Department and JCS plans[63] in order to see for himself what the difference was. Having seen, he decided emphatically in favor of the JCS plan, overrode the demur of the Director of the Budget, and summoned Admiral Souers to the White House to help draft the necessary action paper.[64b]

The President's action took the form of a letter to the Secretaries of State, War, and Navy.[66] Its substance was adapted by Souers from the draft directive annexed to JIC 239/5.[67] It established a National Intelligence Authority and directed this Authority to establish a Central Intelligence Group, to be composed of personnel and facilities to be provided by the State, War, and Navy Departments[c] under a Director to be appointed by the President.

---

[a]The members of this committee were McCormack and Russell for State, Lovett and Brownell for War, and Souers and Correa for Navy.

[b]Souers was not a Truman "crony"; he first met the President when he went to the White House for this purpose. Truman already knew Souers's name, however, as that of a pillar of the Democratic Party in St. Louis and as that of an officer who had played an important role in the development of the JCS plan and was high in the confidence of Admiral Leahy and Secretary Forrestal.[65]

[c]This arrangement was deemed legally necessary pending the enactment of legislation to establish a Central Intelligence Agency. Such an independent Agency could not be created by Executive Order.

The title "Director of Central Intelligence" (instead of Director, Central Intelligence Agency) first appeared in the President's letter. Presumably the change was made because there was, in fact, no Agency. It was retained in the National Security Act of 1947 and afterward proved useful in disinguishing between the DCI as head of the intelligence community and as head of a particular agency, one constituent in that community.

The title "Intelligence Advisory Board" also first appeared in the President's letter. The text of that paragraph was taken verbatim from JIC 239/5, except for the use of proper titles for the director and the board. The language of JIC 239/5 and the President's letter was then understood by all in terms of Secretary Lovett's more explicit text on the same subject.

ADMIRAL SOUERS AND THE IAB, FEBRUARY–JUNE 1946

Rear Admiral Souers was appointed to be the first Director of Central Intelligence on 23 January 1946. He emphasized that the Central Intelligence Group was a "cooperative interdepartmental activity"[68]—as of course it had to be as long as the DCI remained dependent on the departments for personnel and facilities. Souers fully understood the JIS–Lovett concept regarding the relationship between the DCI and the IAB, but, having been through the battles over the Donovan and McCormack plans, he was primarily concerned with retaining the confidence and cooperation of the members of the IAB.

Souers met five times with the IAB during his less than five months as DCI. He cleared with the IAB his drafts for NIA Directives Nos. 1, 2, and 3 and discussed with it a variety of problems relating to the functions and internal organization of the Central Intelligence Group. None of these matters occasioned any difficulty, except his proposal to publish an interpretive *Weekly Summary* in addition to the CIG *Daily*, from which comment was excluded.[a] State was alarmed by the idea of the CIG's publishing uncoordinated comment on current intelligence but received no support and reluctantly acquiesced. Since no national intelligence

---

[a] A single, all-sufficient daily summary of current information was all that President Truman particularly desired to get from CIG. The Secretary of State jealously insisted that this *Daily* contain no comment on the reports summarized, reserving that function for State. (See Part Three, page 158.)

estimates were produced during Souers's brief tenure, no precedents were established with regard to their consideration and adoption. The intention was to proceed in accordance with the JIS-Lovett concept.[69]

GENERAL VANDENBERG AND THE IAB, JUNE 1946–MAY 1947

Admiral Souers, a reserve officer, was impatient to return to his private business in St. Louis. He had consented to serve as DCI only in order to get the Central Intelligence Group started without further delay and only until agreement could be reached on a "permanent" successor. On 10 June 1946 he was relieved as DCI by Lieutenant General Hoyt Vandenberg.[70]

An obvious reason for Vandenberg's selection to be DCI was that he was the ranking member of the Intelligence Advisory Board. As the highly decorated former commanding general of the Ninth Army Air Force,[a] he was also, personally, the Board's most distinguished member. Another consideration was that he was a nephew of Senator Vandenberg; there was at the time a special concern to prevent the legislation to establish a Central Intelligence Agency from becoming a party issue.[71] In relation to these impressive credentials, the General's relative lack of experience in intelligence must have seemed unimportant. Indeed, it was probably thought good that a man of Vandenberg's distinction had had any such experience at all.[b]

The fact was that General Vandenberg had no interest in pursuing a career in intelligence. His ambition was to become the Chief of Staff of the prospectively independent Air Force. He sought to avoid being named DCI, until it was pointed out to him that as DCI he could make himself personally known to the President, the three Secretaries, and the Chairman of the Joint Chiefs of Staff, and thus advance toward his true goal.[72]

Although Vandenberg had no long-term interest in the subject, he had very positive ideas about the proper role of the DCI and the CIA. He held

---

[a]The U.S. tactical air component of General Eisenhower's command in Europe.

[b]During the preceding eleven months Vandenberg had been Assistant Chief of Staff G-2. He had had no part in the battle over the Donovan plan, which might have been instructive to him, and had been only a remote observer of the battle over the McCormack plan.

a poor opinion of Souers's cautious, consultative approach to the IAB and was resolved not to follow it. As a youthful, vigorous, and self-confident man at forty-seven, his instinct was to take command and issue orders. In this he was a reincarnation of General Donovan. Indeed, he outdid Donovan, who had been more realistic. Vandenberg's simple conception was to build up the prospective CIA into an independent, entirely self-sufficient, national intelligence service. He would then discover wasteful duplication of intelligence effort and reduce the departmental intelligence services to mere staffs of briefers for presenting the CIA product in their respective departments.[73] Thus, Vandenberg's purpose was to create the single intelligence service that the wartime G-2 Policy Staff had warned against.[a] Moreover, it was entirely contrary to the intention of JIC 239/5, JCS 1181/5, the Lovett Report, and the President's letter.

Vandenberg brought with him from G-2 a group of Army colonels headed by Edwin K. Wright, who had been for a few months the G-2 Executive but who had had no other intelligence experience.[b] These men closeted themselves, consulted no one who had been through the debates of 1944–46, and, ten days after Vandenberg took office, produced a draft NIA directive that was designated to enable Vandenberg to carry out his intention.[74] It would have authorized the DCI to do three new things:

(1) To undertake any research and analysis that he deemed necessary in order to produce "strategic and national policy intelligence." It was pointed out that the DCI could not meet his personal responsibility for the accuracy, adequacy, and timeliness of such intelligence if he was required to rely solely on evaluated intelligence from the various departments.

(2) To centralize the production of any intelligence of interest to more than one department whenever, in his judgment, that work could be more efficiently done centrally, and, in such cases, to take over the departmental organizations engaged in such work, including their funds, personnel, and facilities.[c]

---

[a]See page 19.

[b]Wright enlisted in the Army in 1920, when he was twenty-one, and three years later was made a second lieutenant. He achieved distinction as an Armored Force instructor and staff officer and served on the staff of the 12th Army Group (1944–45). Apparently General Bradley recommended him to General Vandenberg when the latter became G-2. Wright was DDCI under both Vandenberg and Hillenkoetter.

[c]Two such "services of common concern" were specified: (1) all federal espionage and counterespionage for the collection of foreign information; (2) all federal monitoring of the foreign press and foreign propaganda broadcasts.

(3) To act as the executive agent of the NIA in coordinating and supervising all federal foreign intelligence activities related to the national security.

As should have been expected, this document produced an explosion in the IAB. Vandenberg's response was disarmingly disingenuous. He had meant only to engage in a little supplementary research to find and close gaps in coverage. He accepted verbal amendments that limited his research to that purpose, required him to obtain the agreement of the interested IAB members before centralizing any intelligence function, and specified that he should "act for" the NIA (instead of as its executive agent) in coordinating (but not supervising) federal foreign intelligence activities. Thus amended, the draft directive went to the NIA with the concurrence of the IAB and was adopted as NIA Directive No. 5, dated 8 July 1946.[75]

It may be doubted whether the members of the National Intelligence Authority would have grasped the differences implied by these textual changes, even if they had been made aware of them. They had no time to devote to the active coordination and supervision of intelligence activities. They were glad to have a vigorous young DCI act for them in such matters. As for General Vandenberg, he had gotten the substance of what he wanted, at some cost in verbal clarity. Given authority to engage in research, he could undertake any research he pleased, for it was a sure thing that departmental research could be found wanting in adequacy and timeliness. He moved at once to convert Souers's Central Reports Staff, designed to produce current intelligence and to coordinate "strategic and national policy intelligence," with an authorized strength of sixty, into an Office of Research and Evaluation (ORE)[a] recruiting toward a strength of two thousand![76] The members of the IAB soon began to realize that, even in the NIA directive's amended form, they had been outmaneuvered. Thus, Vandenberg got the authority he wanted, at the cost of thoroughly antagonizing the IAB.

Two weeks after the adoption of NIA Directive No. 5, the DCI produced the first national intelligence estimate, ORE 1, "Soviet Foreign and Military Policy." The President had called for it on Friday morning, for delivery to him at noon on Tuesday.[b] By dint of a crash effort, a draft text

---

[a]Established 22 July 1946; changed to Reports and Estimates 27 October, in deference to State's sensitivity about CIG research. Vandenberg was ever ready to give words to get substance.

[b]President Truman had little, if any, conception of any differences between current intelligence, basic intelligence, and estimative intelligence. To him, intelligence was simply the information that one had on hand.

coordinated with representatives of the departmental intelligence services was delivered to the DCI shortly after noon on Tuesday. Vandenberg sent it on to the President without consulting the IAB. His later excuses for that omission were: (1) the President had asked him for his personal estimate; (2) the President had called for a separate estimate on the same subject from the JIC, the membership of which was identical with that of the IAB, and had received a separate response from them, so that he was aware of their views[a]; (3) in any case, ORE 1 had in fact been coordinated with the departmental agencies, and there had been no time left for any further formalities.[77]

Rear Admiral Thomas B. Inglis, the Chief of Naval Intelligence, was not disposed to let this incident pass as an extraordinary scramble setting no precedent. He took occasion to make the point that the DCI's estimates must include a statement of the personal concurrence or dissent of each member of the IAB—a reasonable interpretation of the intent of the President's letter and NIA Directive No. 1.[b]

Admiral Inglis did not, however, want the IAB to meet to discuss the substance of estimates. All that he wanted was an opportunity to vote on them by the "voting slip" method that the JIC had devised to avoid the necessity of meeting.[78c]

There was a lengthy IAB meeting on this proposal. Vandenberg sought to substitute for it an idea that had been approved in NIA Directive No. 2 but had never been implemented, that of having full-time representatives of the IAB agencies participate in the preparation of CIG estimates. Vandenberg's counterproposal was adopted,[79] but, in the context of his steadily worsening relations with the IAB, it was never effectively implemented.[d]

In the course of this heated debate Inglis made a pronouncement that went far beyond the interdepartmental coordination of national intelligence estimates. He declared that the IAB had the authority and responsibility to direct and supervise all the operations of the CIG. Vandenberg rejected that idea, and no one then supported Inglis,[80] but Inglis would raise it again with IAB support to plague Vandenberg's successor. It therefore requires examination.

---

[a]The JIC response was a hasty hodge-podge, not comparable to ORE 1 in analytical quality, but there was no contradiction between the two estimates.

[b]This idea was explicit in the Lovett Report. NIA Directive No. 1 contained such a provision with regard to recommendations to the NIA, but inadvertently did not with regard to intelligence estimates.

[c]This system meant, of course, that the members of the JIC acted on joint estimates without joint consideration of the subject. If any member objected to some point in the draft, the JIS would have to find a way to paper over the difficulty.

[d]See Part Three, pages 121–22.

ADMIRAL INGLIS AND THE "BOARD OF DIRECTORS" CONCEPT

Admiral Inglis was not an enemy of the Central Intelligence Group, or of the prospective Central Intelligence Agency. He had strongly supported JIC 239/5, and it was he (prompted by Souers) who had brought that proposal again to the attention of the Joint Chiefs of Staff,[81] which led to JCS 1181/5 and the President's letter.[a] But Inglis was outraged by Vandenberg's departures from what Inglis knew to be the true intent of those documents. He saw emerging a Director as arbitrary in his relations with the departmental agencies as General Donovan would have been. But in his reaction Admiral Inglis went to the opposite extreme. His doctrine that the operations of the CIG were subject to the control of the IAB was as much a deviation from the intent of the President's letter as was Vandenberg's plan.

Inglis was not opposed, as was the Department of State, to the development of a large CIG Office of Research and Evaluation generally competent in the fields of political, economic, social, and geographic intelligence. In April 1946 he had united with Vandenberg in proposing to Souers that the former Research and Analysis Branch (R&A) of OSS be transferred from State to CIG.[82b] Inglis wanted CIG to do all of ONI's basic research work, as a "service of common concern" presumably useful to the other departments as well. Even while objecting to Vandenberg's publication of a national intelligence estimate without first obtaining his personal concurrence, he was demanding that ORE produce at once a great volume of descriptive ("basic") intelligence for the benefit of the departmental intelligence agencies.[85] Thus, Inglis wanted a productive ORE, but only as a servant of the departmental agencies—as the Research and Analysis Branch of OSS had been, with its program under the control of the IAB.

But where did Inglis get the idea that the IAB was a "board of directors" in control of the CIG, with the DCI no more than its executive officer?

---

[a]See pages 19–20 and pages 24–26.

[b]At that time R&A was being dismembered by its enemies within State.[83] Transfer to the CIG would have preserved its integrity and would have obviated any need to create a duplicate research office in the CIG. Souers, however, feared that it would draw down upon the CIG the departmental jealousy and hindrance that had frustrated the OSS—which indeed happened in the case of the ORE. In February 1947 Secretary of State Marshall reintegrated the former R&A as the Office of Research and Intelligence (ORI).[84] Inevitably, ORI regarded ORE's research and reporting as an intolerable duplication and a direct threat to ORI's still insecure existence, if not to the military intelligence services as well. (ORI was redesignated OIR—Office of Intelligence Research—in March 1947.)

Certainly he could not find that idea in JIC 239/5, the Lovett Report, or the President's letter. He got it from William H. Jackson's letter to James Forrestal, the Secretary of the Navy, dated 14 November 1945.[a] No doubt the Secretary forwarded this letter to his Chief of Naval Intelligence.

In this letter, by a line of reasoning akin to that which underlay JIC 239/5, Jackson proposed a similar system for the coordination of all intelligence activities, the performance of services of common concern, and the "coordination of intelligence opinion in general estimates of a broad strategic nature." The significant difference between his proposals and those of the contemporary Lovett Report[b] was in his prescription regarding the relationship between the director of the central agency and the heads of the departmental agencies, which is quoted below.[86]

> The active direction of the Central Intelligence Agency should be in a Directorate of Intelligence, consisting of the chief intelligence officers in the Army, Navy, and Air Forces, a representative of the Department of State and, perhaps, representatives of other departments. . . .
>
> Acting under the general supervision of the Directorate of Intelligence would be the Director of the Central Intelligence Agency. This Director, a man of the highest intelligence qualifications available in the United States, regardless of military or civilian background, should be appointed by the President upon the advice of the Department of Defense, or the [National Security] Council, or the various Secretaries described above [that is, the NIA as subsequently established.][c]
>
> The Central Intelligence Agency, which should be run by the Director, would have various departments comprising the intelligence facilities and services of common usefulness.[d]

Admiral Inglis made only one heated reference to the "board of directors" concept during Vandenberg's tenure as DCI. He developed the issue more fully during his conflict with Vandenberg's successor, Admiral Hillenkoetter.[e] It is convenient, however, to present here the principal points of argument in that debate.

---

[a]See page 11.

[b]See page 24.

[c]These were Jackson's contingent recommendations regarding the NIA function.

[d]Jackson suggested that political, economic, scientific, topographic, photographic, and communications intelligence be centralized in the CIA. Apparently he assumed that the former R&A Branch of OSS would be transferred from State to the CIA. For his position in the different circumstances of 1948 and 1950, see pages 42 and 112.

[e]See page 37.

Given a strong sense of need to curb Vandenberg and Jackson's articulation of the "board of directors" concept, Inglis could find some few debater's points in support of his thesis. JCS 1181/5 had referred to a "common intelligence agency"—that is, a conception of the central agency as the common property of the participating departments. NIA Directive No. 1 had described the CIG as a "cooperative interdepartmental activity." As a matter of practical fact, the DCI had been dependent on the three departments for personnel and facilities.[a] In consulting the IAB, Admiral Souers had made no distinction between interdepartmental coordination and the internal affairs of the CIG.

In pursuing this line of argument, Admiral Inglis had to ignore the antecedents of the President's letter. In particular, Lovett had considered and rejected the "board of directors" concept, and the three Secretaries had based their recommendation to the President on Lovett's report. The interest and authority of the three departments were represented by the NIA, not by the IAB. The President's letter expressly described the IAB as advisory to the DCI. Its very name declared its function to be only advisory.[b]

When the National Security Act of 1947 was under consideration by Congress, Admiral Inglis gave strong testimony in favor of the establishment of a Central Intelligence Agency with ample powers and functions. He stressed the importance of subordinating the DCI to the NIA, alias the NSC, a reprise of his position in the JIC debate in 1944. Given that, he thought that the DCI should be the executive agent of the NSC, with power to give direction to the departmental intelligence agencies in the name of the NSC. He never mentioned the idea of the IAB as a "board of directors" empowered to give direction to the DCI. The duty of the IAB members, he said, was to ensure the effective collaboration of the departmental agencies with the central agency. To that extent they would share with the DCI responsibility for the success of the Central Intelligence Agency.[88]

Thus, it would appear, the "board of directors" concept was not, for Admiral Inglis, a fundamental principle that should be incorporated in the statute, but rather a tactical weapon to be employed, within the IAB, against any DCI whom he deemed to be too arbitrary.

---

[a]Vandenberg escaped from this dependency. He was able to show that the departmental agencies had failed to supply properly qualified personnel to the CIG and therefore that he needed authority for direct recruitment. The fact was that few well-qualified intelligence officers were available in the military services. Most men with modern intelligence experience were reserve officers eager to return to their homes now that the war was over.[87]

[b]Inglis later sought to evade this obvious point by contending that the IAB (IAC) was advisory to the NIA (NSC). That was sheer sophistry.

With regard to Admiral Inglis, a nagging question obtrudes, whether his clash with General Vandenberg and his bitter conflict with Admiral Hillenkoetter were motivated in any degree by disappointment that he had not been chosen to be DCI in their stead. Inglis himself denied that he had any such ambition, but one may still wonder about that.

Hillenkoetter and his aides came to regard Inglis as the implacable enemy of the CIA. In fact, however, he was opposed only to the trend of the CIA's development under Vandenberg and Hillenkoetter. Admiral Inglis should be remembered as one of the founders of the CIA (as Vandenberg and Hillenkoetter were not) and as a staunch advocate of a strong and broadly competent Agency. If he had ever been made DCI, he would have been a good one.

THE NATIONAL SECURITY ACT OF 1947

From the beginning it had been understood that the CIG was only a temporary expedient, and that a central intelligence agency should be established by Act of Congress as soon as practicable. General Vandenberg's staff prepared the draft of a bill for that purpose. It was overtaken by the development of the National Security Act of 1947, which was designed to reorganize the entire national security apparatus of the Government. Among other things, it provided for the establishment of the National Security Council and, subject to that Council's direction and control, the Central Intelligence Agency.[a]

As regards the CIA, the intention of the Act was to give legislative sanction to the provisions of the President's letter of 22 January 1946, with the substitution of "NSC" for "NIA." In an early version of the bill, the provisions of the President's letter had been incorporated by reference. There was objection to that as bad legislative practice. Therefore, the four functions assigned to the DCI in the President's letter were copied into the final text of the Act, with some editorial revision,[b] and

---

[a]Other relevant provisions were for the establishment of a Secretary of Defense (but as yet no Department of Defense), for the division of the War Department into the Departments of the Army and the Air Force, and for the statutory establishment of the Joint Chiefs of Staff. Until 1947 the JCS organization derived its existence solely from President Roosevelt's agreement to implement Prime Minister Churchill's plan for a Combined Chiefs of Staff organization.

[b]The only change of substantive significance was the requirement that the CIA make "appropriate" (rather than "full") use of the departmental agencies. It was evidently intended to make the CIA less dependent on the departmental agencies, more free to exercise independent judgment.

one more function was added: to "advise" the NSC regarding the activities of the departmental agencies—as distinguished from making recommendations for their coordination. The idea seems to have been that recommendations for coordination would have to carry the concurrence or dissent of the IAB members, and that the DCI needed additional authority to advise the NSC regarding their activities without obtaining their concurrence or even, necessarily, consulting them. Thus, the purpose was to free the DCI from the trammels of the IAB, at least to that extent.[89]

Ironically, one incidental consequence of dropping the intended reference to the President's letter was that the National Security Act of 1947, as finally adopted, contained no reference, direct or indirect, to the Intelligence Advisory Board. When the Act went into effect, on 17 September 1947, the IAB was left without any warrant for its continued existence!

ADMIRAL HILLENKOETTER AND THE IAB/IAC, MAY 1947–JANUARY 1949

Early in 1947, when the War Department requested the return of General Vandenberg to duty in the Air Force, the only question considered with regard to his successor was which *admiral* he should be. On 17 February 1947 the NIA agreed upon the selection of Rear Admiral Roscoe H. Hillenkoetter.[a] He demurred—he had just settled himself in an assignment that he preferred, as Naval Attaché in Paris—but his preference was overruled, and he was ordered to be DCI. Moreover, in evident sensitivity to criticism of the brevity of the tenure of Souers and Vandenberg, Hillenkoetter was committed to devote the remainder of his active service (eleven years) to that assignment.

At the age of fifty-one, Admiral Hillenkoetter already had behind him a distinguished career in intelligence. His service as Naval Attaché at Vichy had strongly impressed Admiral Leahy, then Ambassador there, now the President's personal representative in the NIA. During the war he had

---

[a]The Special Assistant to the Secretary of State remained ignorant of this fact for two more weeks and then learned of it by accident from a member of his office seconded to the CIG. The Special Assistant was then preparing to nominate Allen Dulles to be DCI. Obviously the Secretary had not consulted him with regard to Hillenkoetter's appointment, and indeed had not even informed him of it.[90]

organized the Joint Intelligence Center at Pearl Harbor, and for that had won high commendation from Admiral Nimitz. In late 1945, when Souers had declined consideration to be DCI, Secretary Forrestal had thought next of Captain Hillenkoetter, but had been dissuaded, on the grounds that Hillenkoetter was too junior to the members of the prospective IAB and that he was not familiar with the background of JCS 1181/5.[91] Souers had then been drafted, but now, little more than a year later, Admiral Leahy proposed Hillenkoetter's name, and the three Secretaries agreed[a] that it was a fine choice.

Despite this distinguished patronage, Rear Admiral Hillenkoetter took office as DCI on 1 May 1947 under two severe handicaps. One was the embattled attitude of the IAB toward the DCI, which had been provoked by Vandenberg. The other was the fact that, in point of personal rank, Hillenkoetter was junior to every military member of the IAB.[b]

Hillenkoetter, by nature an amiable man, realized that he must pacify the IAB if he was to accomplish his task as DCI. On 26 June he told the NIA that he did not need the authority granted to Vandenberg to "operate within his jurisdiction as an agent of the Secretaries of State, War, and Navy" whose "decisions, orders, and directives" should have the same force and effect within those departments as though they had been issued by the Secretary himself.[c] Hillenkoetter recommended that this interpretation be revoked, in order to quiet the apprehensions of the IAB members and restore a spirit of mutual confidence and goodwill. Secretaries Marshall and Patterson and Admiral Leahy were doubtful of this act of abnegation—Vandenberg had persuaded them that the DCI really needed such authority—but Secretary Forrestal considered that the interpretation had caused unnecessary friction and it was revoked.[93]

Moreover, when it was observed that the National Security Act of 1947 contained no warrant for the continued existence of the IAB, Hillenkoetter proposed to reconstitute that board as the Intelligence Advisory Committee (IAC).[d] He wished to do that on his own authority as DCI

---

[a]In the author's observation, Admiral Hillenkoetter was a first-rate naval aide and current intelligence briefing officer, with little depth of perception in anything else. Admiral Souers considered him no more than an "amiable Dutchman."

[b]The military members of the IAB at this time were Major General Stephen Chamberlin (Army), Rear Admiral Thomas Inglis (Navy), and Major General George McDonald (Air Force).

[c]In February 1947 Vandenberg had obtained from the NIA this interpretation of the meaning of "act for" in NIA Directive No. 5. It overrode the contention of the IAB that the DCI could "act for" the NIA only with the agreement of the IAB. Vandenberg had been able to show that it had taken him up to eight months to obtain watered-down agreement from the IAB.[92]

[d]Under the 1947 Law the NIA, the CIG, and presumably the IAB were all to expire when

(which would show who was boss), but was persuaded that it should be done by an NSC directive.

Instead of responding to Admiral Hillenkoetter's conciliatory approach, the embittered military members of the former IAB interpreted that as a sign of weakness and set out to impose on him the "board of directors" concept. Their plan was to interpose the contemplated IAC between the NSC and the DCI, making it advisory to the NSC, and making the DCI the executive agent of the proposed IAC rather than the agent of the NSC.[a] Coached by the staff that he had inherited from Vandenberg,[b] Hillenkoetter resisted that attempt, with some support from the State Department member of the former IAB.[c] A bitter wrangle over this issue went on from July until December. In its latter stages it was over the terms of NSC Intelligence Directive No. 1. Hillenkoetter was finally compelled to invoke the authority of the Secretary of Defense. Forrestal thereupon laid down the law to the Secretaries of the Army, Navy, and Air Force, and to their intelligence chiefs, that Hillenkoetter's version of NSCID No. 1 was to be accepted.[94]

Even with this authoritative support, Hillenkoetter was conciliatory when, on 8 December, he met with the former members of the IAB as, in effect, a drafting committee to perfect the DCI's draft for NSCID No. 1. He recognized that there were two opposing and strongly held points

---

the DCI took office. On 26 September, the day that Hillenkoetter was sworn in under the new legislation, the NSC, meeting for the first time, extended the life of all directives of the former NIA applicable to the late CIG until they were superseded by NSC directives. In the same measure the NSC instructed the DCI to submit appropriate draft directives within sixty days. Understandably, in developing these proposals, the DCI chose to regard the IAB as corporately defunct, although he convened its former members on 20 November and 8 December, in their capacities as departmental intelligence chiefs, to consult on his recommendations to the NSC, including his plan to create a new kind of IAC.

[a]During this same period the JIC (the military members of the IAB) succeeded in imposing the "board of directors" concept on the Deputy Director of the Joint Staff for Intelligence. The JCS directive establishing the Joint Staff had emphasized its independence of the Departments of the Army, the Navy, and the Air Force, but the recommendations and estimates of the Deputy Director for Intelligence could reach the JCS only through the JIC and with its approval. That provision effectively reduced the Deputy Director of the Joint Staff to the status of a servant of the JIC. The military members of the IAB (the JIC) were seeking to reduce the DCI to the same status in relation to the IAC.

[b]His Deputy, Brigadier General Edwin K. Wright, and his General Counsel, Lawrence R. Houston. In the ensuing debate Hillenkoetter himself frequently expressed personal indifference regarding the issue, but insisted that the CIA position should be presented to the NSC with any IAB dissents, so as to obtain a command decision from the NSC.

[c]The State representatives (William Eddy and his successor, Park Armstrong) were determined to destroy Vandenberg's ORE, but otherwise upheld the authority of the DCI, which they wished to invoke to make weight against the enemies of the OIR within the State Department.

of view. He would not presume to judge between them. Without rancor among themselves, they should pass any substantial issue to the NSC for a command decision, by means of a draft text with appropriate dissents. He would accept whatever the NSC decided, and so, he presumed, would they.[95]

When they got down to consideration of the text, Admiral Inglis and General Chamberlin abandoned their more extreme contentions, but Admiral Hillenkoetter accepted a number of verbal amendments that, in cumulative effect, substantially eroded the authority that Vandenberg had claimed for the DCI and that Congress had presumably intended him to exercise. Hillenkoetter later explained that he accepted these compromises in order to get agreement and end the controversy, hoping to be able to develop the CIA-IAC relationship along more positive lines after mutual confidence and goodwill had thereby been established.[96]

Hillenkoetter had opened the meeting of 8 December by reading aloud a passage from a letter from Dr. Vannevar Bush to Secretary Forrestal. Bush had referred to the controversy between the DCI and IAB, and had urged that "someone at the highest level" should break the deadlock and decide the issue without further delay. That was Hillenkoetter's theme at the beginning of the meeting—that they should stop wrangling and refer the issue to the NSC for an authoritative decision.

In his letter Dr. Bush referred incidentally to "the imminence of a vigorous inquiry." Hillenkoetter did not know what that meant. Neither, apparently, did any member of the former IAB. What was meant is the subject of the next chapter.

III

THE "DULLES REPORT" AND NSC 50

General Smith stated that NSC 50, giving effect in substance to the recommendations of the so-called Dulles Committee Report, had not yet been carried out by the Central Intelligence Agency, but that it was his intention promptly to carry out this directive.

—IAC Minutes
20 October 1950

THE IDEA OF AN INDEPENDENT SURVEY

Sidney W. Souers was called back to Washington to be the Executive Secretary of the National Security Council to be established pursuant to the National Security Act of 1947. Souers asked Secretary Forrestal how he expected the NSC to exercise its statutory responsibility to supervise the operations of the Central Intelligence Agency.[a] Forrestal responded that the Council would have no time for that; Souers should do it, as Executive Secretary. Souers replied that, if he had wished to supervise the CIA, he would still be DCI, which he was not. Neither he nor Forrestal was at that time aware of any particular problem with regard to the CIA. They were talking about routine supervision. Both men realized

---

[a]Forrestal conceived that, as Secretary of Defense, he would be in charge of the NSC, because the Act described the Secretary of Defense as the President's principal assistant "in all matters relating to the national security." (Actually, that language was intended only to give the Secretary precedence over the Joint Chiefs of Staff.) At the first meeting of the NSC, however, President Truman decided that the Secretary of State (Marshall) should preside in the absence of the President.[97]

that, while the NSC could act on the recommendations of the DCI, it had no way to keep check on the general performance of the CIA.[98]

Hillenkoetter suggested to Forrestal that it might be well to have some independent and impartial consultants review the organization and procedures of the CIA and define more clearly how the Agency should function under the Act of Congress.[99] His motives for making this suggestion may be inferred. Hillenkoetter had had no part in developing the idea of a central intelligence agency. He had no preconceptions as to the role and mission of the CIA, but he did know that Vandenberg and the IAB had had a furious quarrel about this matter, and that the members of the IAB were still angry and sensitive about it. It would be helpful to him, in his relations with them, if some body not involved in the dispute were to lay down a clear doctrine on the subject. Hillenkoetter did not care personally what the doctrine might be, so long as it was clearly established by authority of the NSC. He and his colleagues would then know how to carry out their assigned functions in a disciplined military manner.

Hillenkoetter did not press his suggestion on Forrestal, and Forrestal was preoccupied by other problems. Hillenkoetter was left to struggle with the IAB over issues that meant nothing to him but a great deal to his advisers in the CIA—until, finally, he appealed to Forrestal for a command decision.[a]

In October 1947—when Hillenkoetter's struggle with the IAB over the NSC intelligence directives was at its height—Hanson Baldwin published an article the theme of which was that the greatest weakness of the United States was in intelligence, its real first line of defense. Baldwin was not attacking the CIA, but rather was advocating a stronger CIA, more centralization of intelligence rather than less. He dwelt upon the general decline of the quality of intelligence personnel since the postwar demobilization, and also on the general incompetence of the military mind to grasp the intelligence problems of the day, which were political, economic, and psychological rather than military. He deplored the domination of all of the intelligence agencies by military men[b] and the subordination of the national interest in the coordination of intelligence activities to a struggle for power among them. The Director of Central Intelligence should be a civilian with authority to control the departmental agencies and to impose coordination upon them.[100]

This Baldwin article impressed Robert Blum, who had just become

---

[a]See pages 36–38.

[b]Colonel Park Armstrong, the Special Assistant to the Secretary of State, was a lawyer rather than a soldier, but he had served in Army G-2 during the war.

Secretary Forrestal's staff assistant for NSC and CIA affairs. Blum was concerned about the competence of the three military intelligence agencies, as well as about the competence of the CIA and the interdepartmental coordination of intelligence activities. Blum proposed that a group of qualified consultants be formed to survey the situation.[101] It appears that it was this proposal that led to the creation of the NSC Survey Group.[a]

THE NSC SURVEY GROUP

On 13 January 1948 the NSC recommended to the President that a group of individuals from outside of the Government service be appointed to make a "comprehensive, impartial, and objective survey of the organization, activities, and personnel of the Central Intelligence Agency" and to report to the NSC on (1) the adequacy and effectiveness of the present organizational structure of the CIA, (2) the value and efficiency of existing CIA activities, (3) the relationship of those activities to those of the other departments and agencies, and (4) the utilization and qualifications of CIA personnel.[102]

It is notable that these terms of reference confined the investigation to the CIA. They did not encompass Blum's concern regarding the competence of the departmental intelligence agencies and their cooperation with the central agency. The reason was that some question had been raised regarding the authority of the NSC to investigate the departmental agencies. Supplemental terms of reference authorized the Survey Group to examine the departmental agencies in relation to the problem of interdepartmental coordination, but the emphasis remained on the presumed shortcomings of the CIA.[103] In any event, the competence of the departmental agencies to supply the CIA with timely and reliable finished intelligence was never thoroughly examined, although the question was germane to the CIA's requirement for integral research capabilities. Thus, the investigation had from its inception a perhaps unintended anti-CIA bias.

Secretary Forrestal selected all three of the members of the Survey

---

[a]In commenting on this passage, Admiral Souers insisted that it was he who proposed the independent survey, on the occasion mentioned above, page 39. That was six months before the Survey Group was established. The more immediate impulse seems to have come from Hanson Baldwin and Robert Blum, through Forrestal, but Souers could reasonably believe that he had inspired Forrestal's proposal to the NSC.

Group, subject to President Truman's approval, of course. They were Allen W. Dulles (Chairman), William H. Jackson, and Matthias F. Correa.[a] These particular men were chosen simply because Forrestal knew them personally and deemed them specially knowledgeable in relation to the subject. They were chosen without regard to the doctrinal controversy between the CIA and the IAC over the "board of directors" concept.[104]

This was indeed a highly qualified group, but it was hardly impartial. Dulles was predisposed to be critical of a military director and deputy director, and the generally military administration of the CIA.[b] He was also predisposed to listen with special sympathy to the complaints of the former OSS men in the OIR (State) and the OSO (the CIA's office of clandestine collection). Both groups were highly critical of Hillenkoetter.[c] Jackson was naturally sympathetic to the point of view of the IAC members who had been advocating his own "board of directors" concept in opposition to Hillenkoetter.[d] Correa was still doubtful of the wisdom of entrusting interdepartmental coordination to an agency that was itself engaged in intelligence operations.[e]

It appeared to Jackson that Dulles had no plan to conduct a systematic survey, that he was interested only in writing out his personal prescription for the proper organization of clandestine operations. Jackson therefore went to Forrestal and obtained the assignment of Robert Blum to head an investigative staff for the Survey Group [most of three lines, with note, deleted].[f] Since he had instigated the appointment of the Survey Group, he was no doubt glad to have an active part in the investigation.

Jackson and Blum quickly identified the DCI-IAC relationship as the crucial problem and wished to concentrate on that, but Dulles was interested only in specific operational problems.[g] This difference led to

---

[a]Regarding Dulles and Jackson, see above, pages 9–14. Correa was a New York lawyer with considerable civil and military experience in criminal investigation and security. In 1945, as a Marine major and Secretary Forrestal's favorite aide, he had been associated with Souers in defeating the McCormack plan and promoting the JCS plan. (See pages 24–25.)

[b]See page 13.

[c]The OIR's attitude toward the ORE has been mentioned above, at pages 31 and 37. The OSS veterans in the OSO complained that they had no access to Hillenkoetter and that tyros in the administrative staff surrounding him were interfering with their operations. In their view, the proper remedy would be to break up the CIA's "Kremlin" and to make Dulles the DCI.[105]

[d]See pages 32–33 and 37.

[e]See pages 19–20 and 29. The distinction between the NIA and the DCI in relation to coordination had been lost in NIA Directive No. 5.

[f][note deleted]

[g]On 30 June 1948 Dulles told the Eberstadt Committee that there was nothing the matter with the CIA that the recruitment of more competent personnel would not correct.[107] (Cf. his testimony in 1947, pages 13–14.)

an early division of labor within the Survey Group. Jackson took interdepartmental coordination as his province, with regard to planning, estimates, and research services of common interest. Dulles concentrated on the CIA's intelligence collection services, overt as well as covert. Correa got what was left: general administration and relations with the FBI.[108]

In the end, Robert Blum drafted the body of the Survey Group's report, and William Jackson drafted the summary.[a] The report, dated 1 January 1949, was delivered to the NSC Secretariat on 18 January.

THE DULLES REPORT

The report of the NSC Survey Group was devastating. It found that the CIA had failed in its responsibilities with regard to both the coordination of intelligence activities and the production of national intelligence estimates, and it attributed those failures primarily to a lack of understanding and leadership on the part of the Director of Central Intelligence.[109][b]

That indictment was true in all particulars, but it did not tell the whole story. The situation that the Survey Group rightly deplored was also attributable in large part to the recalcitrance and incompetence of the departmental intelligence agencies.[c] The Survey Group apparently assumed that they would cooperate, competently and without reservation, if given a stronger sense of participation in an IAC more effectively led by a more enterprising DCI. The report correctly held that, in the last

---

[a]The reference to "the so-called Dulles Committee Report" in the IAC minutes for 20 October 1950 may reflect Jackson's sense that *he* was the true author of the "Dulles Report." Jackson wrote the minutes of that meeting.

[b]The report contained fifty-seven specific conclusions and recommendations. They will be taken up in subsequent chapters, as they applied to the Smith-Jackson reorganization of the CIA.

[c]This aspect of the matter was recognized in the contemporary Eberstadt Report. It held that a vigorous effort was required to improve the internal structure of the CIA and the quality of its product, but that an equal improvement of the departmental intelligence agencies was also essential. It also called for positive efforts to foster relations of mutual confidence between the CIA and the departmental agencies, noting that the CIA deserved and must have a greater degree of acceptance and support from the old-line intelligence services than it had hitherto had.[110] (For further reference to the Eberstadt Report, see Part Two, page 59, and Part Three, page 124.)

analysis, the DCI was personally responsible for making the system work. If he could not obtain the cooperation of the IAC, he had recourse to the NSC.

The report held that the IAC was "soundly conceived"—as a committee *advisory* to the DCI, in accordance with NSCID No. 1—but that it should participate more actively with the DCI in the continuing coordination of intelligence activities.[a] It observed that coordination could best be accomplished by mutual agreement in the IAC. That was obvious, but agreement had been impossible to obtain without compromise, obfuscation, and delay. The Survey Group was confident that effective coordination by agreement could be accomplished with the right measure of leadership by the DCI.[112]

Nowhere did the report mention the "board of directors" concept, but its ghost walked in the passages relating to the production of national intelligence estimates. There it was held that such estimates should derive their authority from the "collective responsibility" of all of the members of the IAC.[113][b] Finally, the report strongly urged that the Director of Central Intelligence should be a civilian.[114] Its text on that point was derived from the text of Dulles's testimony given in 1947.[c]

RESPONSES TO THE DULLES REPORT

Souers referred the Dulles Report to the IAC for comment, and the IAC met on 18 February 1949 to consider a CIA draft for that purpose. General Wright, the Deputy Director, was in the chair. Admiral Hillenkoetter had found it necessary to pay a visit to the [words deleted].[115]

At this meeting Park Armstrong (State) proved to be a remarkably well-informed interpreter of the intent and meaning of the Dulles Report. He was the only person present who had a good word to say for it. The other members of the IAC condemned it roundly, though for different reasons.

---

[a]Since personally revising the DCI's draft NSCIDs, in December 1947 (page 37, above), the IAC had met only once, on 16 June 1948. It had been functioning, however, by the voting-slip method preferred by Admiral Inglis. The June 1948 meeting had been held at Souers's suggestion, after Forrestal had vetoed, at the NSC level, a DCID on which the IAC had agreed.[111]

[b]The subtle difference between the report's discussion of the IAC as a consultative body with regard to the coordination of intelligence activities and as a joint committee for the production of estimates seems to reflect a personal difference between Dulles, who favored a strong DCI, and Jackson, who was still impressed by the British JIC.

[c]See page 13.

General Wright scorned it as a mass of platitudinous observations leading to impractical recommendations. Admiral Inglis was even more vehement. Agreeing with Wright's general remarks (which was remarkable in itself), he denounced the report for calling upon the IAC to "assume" collective responsibility without according to it a corresponding collective authority. In the end, the IAC agreed that it could never agree on a single set of comments, and that each member should comment separately.[116]

Admiral Hillenkoetter's lengthy comments in the Agency's response to the Dulles Report were generally conciliatory. He praised the Survey Group for an admirable and constructive effort to direct the CIA to fundamentals. He agreed that its observations were generally accurate and its objectives sound, but held that its conclusions were faulty in many respects and its recommendations unfeasible. He concurred in thirty-seven of the report's fifty-seven specific conclusions and recommendations, sometimes observing that what had been recommended was already in effect. Where he disagreed, he patiently explained why, generally with good reason.[117]

Admiral Hillenkoetter was evidently confident that he had made a reasoned and reasonable defense, and that the NSC would accept it as such. He permitted himself to remark that, if intelligence coordination were as yet less than might be desired, the members of the NSC would understand the difficulties that had been encountered, particularly anyone (Forrestal) who had been concerned with the unification of the Armed Services. Only one note of personal resentment appeared in his fifty-three pages of comment: his reference to rumors in the fall of 1948 that one member of the Survey Group (Dulles) would be named DCI when Mr. Dewey took office as President.[118]

The comments of General Irwin, the Director of Intelligence, Army General Staff, were notable only for his flat rejection of the Survey Group's finding that the DCI had failed in his responsibility for the coordination of intelligence activities. The DCI, forsooth, had no such responsibility. That was a function of the IAC![119a]

The comments of Admiral Inglis showed his better understanding of the case. He knew that Irwin was dead wrong under the terms of NSCID No. 1, and that was the substance of his complaint. He denied that the IAC was "soundly conceived" and proposed a revision of NSCID No. 1 to establish an "Intelligence Coordinating Committee" (ICC) that would be directly subordinate to the NSC and would be charged by it with authority and responsibility for the coordination of intelligence activities and the

---

[a]Theoretically, coordination was a function of the NSC. The DCI could only submit recommendations to it, after consulting the IAC.

production of national intelligence estimates. Inglis realized, of course, that under the statutes these were functions of the DCI. Consequently he had to allow to the DCI a right of independent communication with the NSC without ICC concurrence. His plan was thus theoretically monstrous: two parallel authorities charged with the same functions.[120] His purpose, of course, was to force the DCI to pay attention to the IAC, and to give the IAC direct access to the NSC if he did not. Admiral Inglis also argued at length against the idea that the DCI should be a civilian, emphasizing the advantages of having a professional military officer in that position.[121]

The position of the Department of State was, of course, a general endorsement of the Dulles Report.

NSC 50

The NSC readily agreed that it could not act on the basis of almost three hundred pages of controversial literature. It asked the Secretaries of State and Defense[a] to review the papers in the case and to recommend what action the NSC should take. NSC 50, the report of the two Secretaries to the Council, was actually prepared by General Joseph McNarney, with the nominal participation of Carlisle Humelsine and the active assistance of Robert Blum. Blum was amused to find himself drafting the NSC action on the recommendations that he had drafted for the Survey Group.[122b]

On 7 July 1949 the NSC adopted the conclusions and recommendations of NSC 50. By so doing, it agreed that the Survey Group's condemnation of Hillenkoetter and the administration of the CIA had been "too sweeping," but generally approved the Survey Group's recommendations for the reorganization and reform of the CIA, with one notable exception. The NSC emphatically rejected the doctrine of "collective responsibility" for national intelligence estimates on the ground that the inevitable consequence would be estimates watered down to obtain agreement. It

---

[a]That is, Dean Acheson and Louis Johnson. Acheson succeeded Marshall as Secretary of State in January 1949. Johnson succeeded Forrestal as Secretary of Defense in March.

[b]McNarney was chairman of the Management Committee in the Office of the Secretary of Defense. Humelsine was Director of the State Department's Executive Secretariat. Impartial judgment at the managerial level seems to have been intended, excluding the contentious DCI and IAC, but Blum was now an interested party and Armstrong had some voice in the matter vice Humelsine.

reaffirmed that the IAC was advisory to the DCI, but enjoined the DCI to enlist the more active participation of the IAC in the coordination of intelligence activities and the production of national estimates. The CIA should, "as far as possible," refrain from duplicating departmental intelligence research and production.[123]

The DCI was directed to reorganize the CIA generally along the lines recommended by the Survey Group and to report progress within ninety days. The DCI and IAC were directed to address themselves to eight particular problems of coordination identified by the Survey Group and to report progress within six months.[124]

HILLENKOETTER'S REACTION TO NSC 50

Whereas Admiral Hillenkoetter had responded to the Dulles Report with confidence, his spirit was crushed by the NSC's approval of NSC 50—even though the NSC had discounted the Survey Group's personal criticism of him as "too sweeping" and had reaffirmed the DCI's leading role in the coordination of intelligence activities and in the production of national intelligence estimates. Instead of being stimulated to exert the "forthright leadership" called for by the Dulles Report and NSC 50, he became psychologically withdrawn—still amiably approachable, but more than ever unwilling to exercise initiative and leadership.[125] Since his Deputy, General Wright, had departed on 9 March and had not been replaced, this withdrawal on the part of the DCI in effect left no one in charge at the CIA.[a]

In these circumstances, the component offices of the CIA were left to determine for themselves how they would comply with the direction of the NSC in NSC 50. With one conspicuous exception, the reorganization plans submitted by Hillenkoetter were in dutiful compliance. That they were not implemented was not the fault of the CIA. Rather, it was attributable to the unwillingness of the Department of State to accept the implications of the recommendation that it had endorsed.[b]

---

[a] To illustrate the point: when the author, who then represented the CIA in the NSC Staff, as one familiar with the substance of intelligence, sought instruction from the DCI on a matter of CIA policy, he was told "I will support whatever position you take." If the author had thought himself qualified to take a position for the CIA in that matter, he would not have sought instruction. The DCI's response was an abdication, not a proper delegation of authority. It was typical, however, of his attitude at that time. The occasion was that mentioned below, Part Four, page 196.

[b] See Part Three, page 111, and Part Four, page 218.

The conspicuous exception was the reorganization plan proposed by the ORE and passively adopted by Hillenkoetter. It was, palpably, an attempt to perpetuate the status quo under a pretense of compliance.[a]

In the IAC Hillenkoetter's attitude was passive, his tone sarcastic. He declared that, since coordination by mutual agreement was now the order of the day, he would vote with the majority—but would the members please hurry up and agree among themselves, so that he could have a majority to vote with. That was, of course, an abdication of his responsibilities as DCI. In these circumstances, the IAC proceeded to prove its incapacity to function as a collective authority without strong leadership. Its Standing Committee[b] was unable to deal promptly and effectively with the particular problems identified by the Survey Group.[126]

THE "WEBB STAFF STUDY"

Admiral Inglis having retired, Park Armstrong, the Special Assistant to the Secretary of State, assumed such leadership as there was in the IAC. On 2 August he submitted to the IAC four proposals that, he said, were designed to carry out the provisions of NSC 50 with regard to the coordination of intelligence activities, the production of national intelligence estimates, the definition of the research to be performed by the CIA as a service of common interest, and the allocation of responsibility for the production of "political summaries."[127]

These proposals were referred to the Standing Committee of the IAC, where the service members refused to consider those that related to the internal organization of the CIA, a remarkable reversal of Admiral Inglis's doctrine, but a position consistent with NSC 50. All agreed that the problem should be passed to the DCI's own coordinating staff for further study. On 21 December that staff submitted a report that, on the whole, rejected Armstrong's proposals as contrary to the National Security Act of 1947 and having a tendency to revive the "board of directors" concept rejected by the NSC in approving NSC 50. This response was in substantial agreement with the views of the service members of the Standing Committee. Thus, State was isolated within the IAC.[128c]

---

[a]See Part Three, pages 125–26.

[b]A representative working group to prepare papers for IAC consideration.

[c]One may surmise that the service intelligence chiefs were beginning to see Hillenkoetter as a military man being persecuted by civilians—perhaps also as a weak DCI who offered no real threat to them.

State's failure at the IAC level coincided with Hillenkoetter's submission of his proposed "reorganization" of the ORE to the NSC. That flagrant evasion of the plain intent of NSC 50 provoked General John Magruder, in the Office of the Secretary of Defense, to prepare a staff study on the "Production of National Intelligence."[a] This study concluded with a draft NSC Intelligence Directive to be proposed by the Secretaries of State and Defense, acting jointly. That draft directive prescribed in some detail how the DCI should reorganize the ORE in accordance with NSC 50.[b] It also gave to the IAC effective control over all finished intelligence produced by the CIA. It would have established the principle of "collective responsibility" that the NSC had expressly rejected in approving NSC 50.[130]

It is remarkable that John Magruder, the former Deputy Director of the OSS and a champion of JIC 239/5,[c] should have been the author of such a plan. His own explanation was that Hillenkoetter's contumacy in perpetuating the ORE forced State and Defense to go to that extreme in order to obtain any effective voices in the production of national intelligence estimates.[131] It should be noted that Magruder emphasized the obligation of the departmental agencies to participate constructively in the production of such estimates, which they had never yet done. His proposed organization for the purpose within the CIA was substantially identical with that which Souers had adopted in 1946—that is, with the accepted concept before the advent of Vandenberg—except that he vested control in the IAC as a committee, rather than in the DCI.

On 7 July 1950 James E. Webb, the Under Secretary of State, forwarded Magruder's staff study, dated 1 May, to the DCI for comment, as a joint proposal of the Departments of State and Defense.[132] That is, of course, how it came to be known as the "Webb Staff Study."

The response of the CIA, prepared by Lawrence Houston, the General Counsel, boldly rejected the "Webb Staff Study" as flagrantly contrary to the National Security Act of 1947 and to NSC 50 as well. It effectively demonstrated that the study was also contrary to the known views of the Secretary of Defense.[133][d] The CIA's counterproposal was a draft revision of NSCID No. 1 that clarified and elaborated all that had been obfuscated in Hillenkoetter's compromise with the IAC in December 1947.[e] This

---

[a]Although this document became known as "the Webb Staff Study," Magruder was the initiator as well as the author.[129]

[b]For the particulars, see Part Three, pages 126–27.

[c]See page 21.

[d]Fortuitously, Secretary Johnson had rejected an agreed plan for coordination by committee on the ground that it tended to obscure and obstruct the personal responsibility and authority of the DCI.

[e]See page 37.

draft reaffirmed the primary personal responsibility of the DCI for the coordination of intelligence activities and the production of national intelligence and commanded the loyal cooperation of the departmental intelligence agencies in the national interest. Moreover, it restored to the DCI the authority that Vandenberg had obtained and Hillenkoetter had dissipated—to function as the executive agent of the NSC, whose decisions, orders, and directives concerning the coordination of intelligence activities should have the same force and effect within the several departments as if they had been issued by the Secretary concerned, subject to that Secretary's right of appeal to the NSC.[134a]

This CIA response, sent to Under Secretary Webb on 26 July, had an electric effect. Webb hastened to say that the intent of his Staff Study had been "misconstrued." On 14 August he sent over a "corrected" copy.[135] Hillenkoetter and Houston met with Magruder to discuss the new version on 21 August, but that meeting was a standoff—no progress whatever was made toward a reconciliation of the opposing State–Defense and CIA positions.[b] The CIA remained resolved to press for NSC consideration of its proposed revision of NSCID No. 1.[136]

At that point the Executive Secretary of the NSC advised that further action should be suspended pending the arrival of a new Director of Central Intelligence.

---

[a]See page 36.
[b]Author's conversation with Lawrence Houston, May 1970.

PART TWO

BEDELL SMITH TAKES COMMAND

IV

THE SELECTION OF SMITH AND JACKSON

It is a pity that a qualified civilian could not have been found for this key post. But, barring a civilian, Gen. Bedell Smith is, by common consent, a good choice.

—*Washington Post*
21 August 1950

President Truman could not have made a better choice.

—*New York Times*
22 August 1950

THE SEARCH FOR A NEW DCI

From the time of the submission of the Dulles Report to the National Security Council in January 1949, it was understood in that circle that Admiral Hillenkoetter had to be replaced as DCI.[1] Souers, however, insisted that Hillenkoetter could not be relieved until his successor had been chosen and was immediately available to take over. The reason was that there was no Deputy Director at the CIA who could serve as Acting Director.[a] It took twenty-one months to satisfy Souers's requirement.

Hillenkoetter himself was quite willing to be relieved, especially after the adoption of NSC 50 (July 1949). He had never wanted to be DCI. It had been a painfully frustrating and thankless experience. He was convinced that the Survey Group, General McNarney, and the National

---

[a]The Survey Group had condemned Wright even more severely than it had Hillenkoetter. Wright departed for another assignment on 10 March 1949 and was not replaced.

Security Council had never understood the problem, that they had all been misled by a clever clerk, Robert Blum. At about the time that he emphatically rejected Armstrong's four proposals (December 1949), he suggested that the proper place for a sailor was at sea.[2] His transition from shocked passivity to aggressive reaction, as with regard to the "Webb Staff Study," probably reflected a realization that he was a short-timer with nothing to gain and nothing to lose.

One reason for the long delay in finding a successor to Hillenkoetter was President Truman's antagonism toward his Secretary of Defense, Louis Johnson.[3] The Secretary proposed the appointment of General Joseph McNarney, which was a good idea. The author of NSC 50 would certainly have known what action it required. He had a forceful character that would have been able to exercise "forthright leadership" in the IAC. As the ruthless four-star "Manager" of the Department of Defense, he was already regarded with awe by the military members of the IAC. But Truman would not consider McNarney, because he had been proposed by Johnson. The Secretary suggested other names, but none of them was ever seriously considered.[4]

Secretary of State Acheson, on the other hand, was unwilling to suggest anyone to succeed Hillenkoetter unless the President expressly asked him to do so, which he never did.[5] There can be no doubt that Armstrong would have proposed Allen Dulles[a]— perhaps he did, within the Department—but Acheson knew that Truman would never appoint Dulles, who was closely identified with Dewey. Thus, despite his great reputation in the field, his at least nominal authorship of the Dulles Report, and his evident ambition to be DCI, Allen Dulles was never even considered as a possible successor to Hillenkoetter.[6]

Gordon Gray, the Secretary of the Army, nominated himself to be the DCI and was a very active candidate, but was never seriously considered.[7]

When it became more widely known that a successor to Hillenkoetter was being sought, there arose some public demand that a civilian be appointed (as had been recommended in the Dulles Report), but apparently there was no demand for the appointment of Dulles. William Donovan, William Foster, J. Edgar Hoover, and Dean Rusk were mentioned,[b] but none of them was seriously considered by the President. Apparently the President did sound out Robert Lovett and David Bruce,[c] but both declined the appointment.[8]

---

[a]See Part One, pages 35 and 44.

[b]Donovan was practicing law in New York. Foster was Acting Administrator, Economic Cooperation Administration. Hoover was even then the long-time Director of the Federal Bureau of Investigation. Rusk was Deputy Under Secretary of State.

[c]Lovett had recently resigned as Under Secretary of State to return to Brown Brothers, Harriman & Company. Bruce, who had been the director of OSS operations in Europe during the war, was Ambassador to France.

THE SELECTION OF BEDELL SMITH

One morning in May 1950 Sidney Souers again reminded the President of the need to find a successor to Admiral Hillenkoetter. The President's response was, "How would Bedell Smith do?"[9]

That Smith would be a good choice was probably Truman's own idea. He had held Smith in high regard as his Ambassador to Moscow and believed that Smith really understood the Russians. He would have considered, moreover, that a general who had been an ambassador should be agreeable to both State and Defense. It is unlikely that the President's consideration went much deeper than that,[10] but he may have taken into account Smith's reputation as an able and forceful organizer and manager. He may also have considered that Smith's personal prestige and three-star rank would ensure his ascendancy over the military members of the IAC.

Souers thought that Smith would do very well indeed. The trouble was that Smith had long suffered severely from a stomach ulcer and was even then in Walter Reed General Hospital for treatment.[11] This time the medics did not let him go until they had operated to remove most of his stomach.[a]

Bedell Smith did not want to be Director of Central Intelligence. Several times he begged off, with reference to the state of his health.[13] His intention at the time was to retire from the Army and to seek a remunerative position in industry or the presidency of a university.[14] But it is unlikely that President Truman considered anyone else after he had thought of Smith. In addition to Truman's own predilection, Averell Harriman, who joined the White House staff late in June, was strongly urging Smith's appointment.[15] Even the President of the United States, however, had to wait to see how well Smith would recover from his operation.

On the 25th of June North Korean forces invaded South Korea. On the 27th the President decided to commit U.S. air and naval forces in support of the South Koreans; on the 30th he committed U.S. ground forces as well.[16] At some time during those last days of June, Admiral Hillenkoetter asked directly to be reassigned to duty at sea.[17] To request such an

---

[a]This operation solved the ulcer problem, but Smith never recovered his former robust appearance. Lacking a stomach, he was simply undernourished. That condition may have aggravated his irritable impatience (see Part One, page 8), but was not the prime cause of it.[12]

assignment in time of war was, for him, an honorable way out of an impossible situation.[a]

In late July or early August, when it became evident that Bedell Smith would make a good recovery from his operation, the President ordered him to accept appointment as Director of Central Intelligence.[18] It was an order that General Smith could not refuse in a time of national peril. His view of the gravity of the changed situation is indicated by the fact that, as DCI, he persuaded several reluctant men to come to the CIA by convincing them that World War III was imminent.[19]

Smith's nomination was announced to the press on 18 August and sent to the Senate on the 21st. He appeared before the Senate Armed Services Committee on the 24th. No member of that committee was in any doubt regarding his qualifications, but Senator Saltonstall inquired, for the record, regarding his health. Smith declared that, as a result of his operation, his health was now better than it had ever been during the war.[20] The Senate confirmed his appointment unanimously on 28 August.

The confirmation of Smith's appointment to be DCI had been treated as a matter of the utmost urgency, yet his entry on duty was postponed, first until late September, ultimately until 7 October. That delay must have been found necessary in order to give him more time in which to recover his strength and to prepare for the heavy task that he was to assume.

THE SELECTION OF WILLIAM JACKSON

Having told the President that he would accept appointment to be the Director of Central Intelligence, Bedell Smith spoke privately to Sidney Souers. "I know nothing about this business," he said. "I shall need a Deputy who does."[21]

Souers suggested William H. Jackson, whom he considered to be the preferable member of the late NSC Survey Group. In particular, Jackson had represented the "cooperative" approach to the coordination of intelligence activities, which had been Souers's own approach. Souers considered that Dulles's interest and experience were too narrowly confined to clandestine operations, a minor and incidental part of the DCI's respon-

---

[a]He was eventually assigned to command the cruisers of the Seventh Fleet, in the Far East.

sibilities, and that Dulles represented the "dictatorial" (OSS) concept of coordination.[22a]

When Smith returned to Governor's Island, he called Jackson in New York and invited him to lunch at the 21 Club. Jackson was surprised by this invitation from "the Ogre of SHAEF" and was disposed to evade it, but Smith was urgent and Jackson finally accepted. Jackson did not know that Smith was to be DCI, and consequently had no idea what Smith's purpose was.[23]

At this luncheon Smith turned on his charm, and Jackson was surprised to discover that "the Ogre of SHAEF" had a great sense of humor. But when Smith presented his proposition, Jackson recoiled in dismay. He was then intent on making a fortune at Whitney & Company. If he left there to go to Washington, he would have everything to lose and nothing to gain. Moreover, he did not intend to expose himself to being bawled out by a "tyrannical soldier." At that, Smith laughed and said that his bark was worse than his bite.

Smith appealed to Jackson's patriotism. The war in Korea might be the opening move of World War III. Smith knew nothing about intelligence and needed Jackson's help. Smith would take care of external relations (the President, the NSC, the IAC) and would rely on Jackson to accomplish the internal reorganization of the CIA in accordance with NSC 50. In the end, Jackson agreed to come for six months on three conditions: (1) a free hand in reorganizing the CIA; (2) [two lines, with [b] note, deleted]; and (3) no bawlings out.[24] When Smith's appointment was publicly announced, on 18 August, Smith immediately announced that William H. Jackson would be his Deputy.[25]

SMITH'S PREPARATION FOR THE TASK

Bedell Smith was not as ignorant of intelligence as he made out to Souers and Jackson. As Secretary of the War Department General Staff and of the Joint Chiefs of Staff, 1939–42, he had become well aware of the inadequacies of the departmental intelligence agencies and the joint intelligence committee system. For that reason, no doubt, he worked with William Donovan to create the Office of Strategic Services directly

---

[a]Whatever may be thought of Donovan, Dulles certainly was not "dictatorial" as DCI (1953–61).

[b][note deleted]

subordinate to the Joint Chiefs of Staff.[a] Both men probably expected that the OSS, in that relationship, would make a more direct contribution to strategic planning than it was in fact able to do, trammeled as it was by the departmental intelligence agencies and the Joint Intelligence Committee.[27]

Even after his departure to become Eisenhower's Chief of Staff, Smith remained interested in the idea of a centralized and professional intelligence service. On 9 September 1943, as the U.S. Fifth Army was storming ashore at Salerno, Smith took time out from the cares of that day to request of Donovan a written exposition of his views on that subject. Donovan's response was a document almost as formidable as its title: "The Need in the United States on a Permanent Basis as an Integral Part of Our Military Establishment of a Long-Range Strategic Intelligence Organization with Attendant 'Subversion' and 'Deception of the Enemy' Functions."[28b]

As Chief of Staff in Algiers, Smith demonstrated his personal disdain for joint committees. When a newly arrived G-2, British Brigadier Kenneth Strong, suggested that Smith might wish to obtain the views of the local JIC established by his predecessor, Smith replied, with his customary vigor: "We've hired you for your knowledge and advice. If you are wrong too often, we'll fire you and hire someone else to take your place."[30]

Thus made personally responsible, Strong forgot his British upbringing and assumed personal authority. He convened his JIC on occasion, for consultation and coordination of activities, but there was no doubt about who was in charge. The intelligence estimates that Strong submitted to Eisenhower and Smith were Strong's own personal estimates—made with the aid of an able staff, of course.

Smith was impressed by Strong's success in getting good intelligence from a staff composed of many disparate elements: British, American, and French; Army, Navy, and Air Force. It was a fully integrated staff under the direction of a single strong and able mind, not a collection of representatives. Smith must have contrasted its smooth efficiency with the contentions that had wracked the U.S. JIC in Washington.

---

[a]Smith considered that he had saved Donovan and the COI organization from extinction at that time. Donovan acknowledged that Smith had been helpful in the creation of the OSS.[26]

[b]Be it noted that in 1943 Donovan conceived of this "strategic intelligence organization" as an integral part of the military establishment—indeed, as a fourth service, coequal with the Army, Navy, and Air Force—which shows that he was thinking primarily of paramilitary operations.[29] In 1944 he returned to the idea of a coordinator of information reporting directly to the President and responsible only to him, which had been his conception in 1941.

The high value that Smith put upon Strong's services as G-2 is indicated by the furious quarrel that he had with General Sir Alan Brooke, Chief of the Imperial General Staff, over the latter's refusal to transfer Strong from AFHO to SHAEF. Smith thought this to be a matter of sufficient importance to warrant the use of his ultimate weapon, an appeal by Eisenhower over Brooke's head to Churchill.[31]

The surprise achieved by the German offensive in the Ardennes in December 1944 was potentially embarrassing for the G-2, SHAEF. There was talk of an intelligence failure. But on all occasions Smith loyally declared that Strong had given ample warning of the possibility, which had been disregarded by Smith himself and others. Smith learned an important lesson from this experience, one that he remembered as DCI: that the most prescient intelligence is unavailing unless delivered in such a way as to make an impact on the minds of opinionated decisionmakers.[32]

When Bedell Smith came himself to be Director of Central Intelligence, he had in mind the model of an effective director of intelligence. That model was Kenneth Strong, who had been able to get British, American, and French soldiers, sailors, and airmen to work effectively together by exerting a vigorous and decisive leadership.

Bedell Smith was not in Washington when the Donovan plan, JIC 239/5, the McCormack plan, JCS 1181/5, the Lovett Report, the President's letter, and the Dulles Report were under consideration,[a] and there is no indication that he ever studied any of those papers. Jackson was quite sure that he had never read the Dulles Report. Neither did he discuss CIA problems with Jackson before they took office. Jackson was not surprised by that. Smith had delegated to him the internal reorganization of the CIA. He would expect Jackson to submit plans for his approval. Until then, he was not concerned. Conversely, he did not seek Jackson's advice on how to handle the IAC. That was his business in the agreed division of labor.[33]

At the Armed Services Committee hearing on his nomination (24 August), General Smith declared that, deliberately, he had studied only two documents. One was the National Security Act of 1947. The other was the Hoover Task Force report on the Agency—that is, the Eberstadt Report.[34] Both of those documents were available to the members of the committee. (The Hoover Commission had reported to the Congress as well as to the President.) Smith was tactful in not referring to any classified Executive document to which the senators would not have had access. It is of interest that he had read the Eberstadt Report, for it was a

---

[a]See Part One, Chapters II and III.

good deal more sympathetic toward the CIA than the Dulles Report had been.[a]

On 23 August (the day before Smith's appearance before the Senate committee in Washington), Lawrence Houston, the CIA General Counsel, took to Smith at Governor's Island an organization chart of the CIA on which the names of the incumbent officers had been entered, at Smith's request. Smith took advantage of the opportunity to question Houston at length regarding the problems confronting the CIA and requested Houston to produce a memorandum on the subject.[35]

Houston's memorandum was dated 29 August 1950. With regard to the coordination of intelligence activities, he pointed out that, as a result of the requirement to obtain IAC agreement, the recommendations submitted to the NSC had not been those of the DCI, as Congress had intended, but instead had been watered-down compromises, replete with loopholes and therefore ineffectual. The compromised language of the NSCIDs had, indeed, enabled the IAC to pretend to be advisory to the NSC and a board of directors supervisory to the DCI.[36]

With regard to the production of estimates, Houston pointed out that the departmental intelligence agencies tended to disregard the CIA's overt collection requests, that they withheld intelligence information from the CIA on various pretexts, that they imposed intolerable delays in the process of coordination, that their action on draft estimates was generally governed by policy and budgetary considerations, and that their dissents were often insubstantial and quibbling.[37]

Houston noted also a number of specific problems—for example, [words deleted] with the JCS regarding the status of the CIA in time of war. His general conclusion was that the solution to all these problems required the grant of adequate authority to the DCI to achieve coordination by direction without relying any longer on a spirit of cooperation and goodwill.[38b]

To support this memorandum, Houston attached to it seven documents. They were:

(1) The CIA's draft revision of NSCID 1, as sent to Under Secretary Webb on 26 July.[c]

(2) A draft covering memorandum to the NSC designed to explain and justify this proposed revision of NSCID 1.

---

[a]See Part One, page 43.

[b]The tone of this conclusion reflects the desperation felt in the CIA after four years of futile effort to achieve effective coordination by IAC agreement.

[c]See Part One, pages 49–50.

(3) The current NSCID 1, dated 19 January 1950—that is, as revised pursuant to NSC 50.

(4) A memorandum by the General Counsel, dated 27 September 1949, interpreting the intent of the National Security Act of 1947.

(5) The "Webb Staff Study," dated 1 May 1950, and the "corrected" version sent to the CIA on 14 August.[a]

(6) JIC 445/1, "The Wartime Status and Responsibilities of the Central Intelligence Agency and Its Field Agencies," 25 July 1950.

(7) The CIA's response to JIC 445/1, a memorandum from Hillenkoetter for Magruder dated 16 August 1950.

General Smith evidently studied those documents carefully, for he later showed himself to be familiar with them. He did not, however, adopt the conclusion that Houston derived from them.[b]

Finally, General Smith must have studied NSC 50. He may also have discussed it with Souers and McNarney.

During September, in addition to studying these documents, Bedell Smith discussed the subject with William Donovan and Allen Dulles in New York and with Admiral Hillenkoetter in Washington.[c] The result of his discussion with Donovan was six written communications from the latter transmitting old OSS documents, giving current advice on organization, and recommending former OSS personnel.[40] Smith accepted as much of Donovan's advice as he liked[d] and disregarded the rest.[e] He persuaded Allen Dulles to come to the CIA for six weeks as a consultant.[42]

On 21 September 1950 Donovan warned Smith not to "let them ruin CIA before you get there."[43] Smith was receiving the same advice covertly from Lyle T. Shannon, Hillenkoetter's Acting Executive, whom Smith had known at SHAEF.[44] Both men were apprehensive lest lame-duck Hillenkoetter sell out the CIA in his current negotiations with Webb and Magruder over the "Webb Staff Study." Souers's instruction to Hillenkoetter to suspend action on that matter pending Smith's arrival was probably given at the request of Smith.[f]

---

[a]See Part One, pages 48–50.

[b]See Chapter V.

[c]In contrast to William Jackson's animosity toward Hillenkoetter, Smith's attitude toward him was sympathetic.[39]

[d]See Part Three, pages 128–29.

[e]Lawrence Houston recalls that at this time Donovan and Smith were rather patronizing in their attitudes toward each other.[41]

[f]See Part One, pages 48–50. Actually, Hillenkoetter was adamant in his attitude toward Webb and Magruder.

Smith suggested to Hillenkoetter that William Jackson be appointed immediately to the vacant office of Deputy Director, but Hillenkoetter refused.[45] He could not forgive Jackson for his personal strictures in the "Dulles Report." He did consent to make Jackson a consultant to the DCI. In that capacity Jackson occupied the Deputy Director's vacant office on 2 October 1950 and immediately began directing the preparation of papers for General Smith's consideration on his arrival, as though Hillenkoetter were not still DCI.[a]

On Saturday, 7 October, General Smith finally relieved Admiral Hillenkoetter as DCI. At the same time William Jackson took office as DDCI.

Before meeting formally with the IAC, General Smith saw the Secretaries of State and Defense and obtained their agreement to drop the subject of the "Webb Staff Study," on his assurance that NSC 50 was a sufficient directive for him. He met with the National Security Council on 12 October and told them that he would carry out NSC 50, with one exception: he would not carry out the merger of OSO and OPC[b] that NSC 50 had prescribed. The NSC approved this modification of its directive by the DCI.[46]

There was no substantive discussion between the National Security Council and the new Director of Central Intelligence. The Council did not even inquire why Smith made an exception regarding the prescribed merger of OSO and OPC. As Forrestal had said in 1947, the National Security Council really had no time and attention to give to understanding the problems of the CIA and to supervising its management.[c] What the NSC wanted was for somebody in whom it had confidence to take charge and run the show, without all this bickering and contention.[47] It was sure that it had the right man in Lieutenant General Walter Bedell Smith. Indeed it had.

---

[a]See pages 78–79.
[b]The CIA Offices of Special Operations and Policy Coordination.
[c]See Part One, page 39.

V

BEDELL SMITH AND THE INTELLIGENCE ADVISORY COMMITTEE

General Smith . . . stated that the Intelligence Advisory Committee must be geared for rapid cooperative work.

—*IAC Minutes*
20 October 1950

THE STRENGTH OF SMITH'S POSITION

The members of the Intelligence Advisory Committee knew in advance that in Bedell Smith they would face a more formidable Director of Central Intelligence than they had ever faced before. One may surmise that they approached the confrontation with no little apprehension.

Smith's personal rank as the senior lieutenant general of the Army was the least factor in that connection, though an appreciable one. Vandenberg had been a lieutenant general, and that had not deterred the IAB from opposing him. They had not been able to cope with him before the National Intelligence Authority, but they had sabotaged him in subtle ways with impunity.[a]

Smith, however, was a far more formidable character than Vandenberg. He enjoyed immense personal prestige as the organizer of victory in Europe and as a man who had dealt with Stalin face to face. He could count on the personal esteem and strong support of the President, the

---

[a]One cannot know what would have happened if Vandenberg had had time to exercise the powers granted to him by the NIA in February 1947. (See Part One, page 36.) When Vandenberg then obtained authority to give direction to the departmental agencies, he already knew that he was leaving the CIA.

Secretary of State, and the Secretary of Defense.[a] And he was well known to be a forceful and impatient man, one likely to react explosively if crossed.

SMITH'S APPROACH TO THE IAC

Bedell Smith's instinct was to take command. He understood that as DCI he was responsible not only for the administration of the CIA but also for leadership of the entire intelligence community. He understood that personal responsibility implied commensurate authority. He knew that he could obtain from the President and the NSC, or from the Congress if need be, whatever authority he told them he required in order to accomplish his mission.

Thus, Bedell Smith had the option of demanding the authority that Hoyt Vandenberg had obtained and of imposing his will on the IAC. Lawrence Houston had advised him that he would need to have and to exercise such authority.[b] Yet Bedell Smith, a naturally imperious man, deliberately decided not to exercise that option. It is unlikely that he knew much, if anything, of Vandenberg's experience. He knew intuitively that that was not the way to get the best results.

As Smith pondered the problem, he must have thought of SHAEF, of Eisenhower and Kenneth Strong, of their success in leading disparate and discordant elements to work effectively together in the common cause. He evidently came to a deliberate conclusion that he could obtain better results by adopting that approach to the IAC—by exerting strong leadership in an atmosphere of mutual consideration and respect, of common effort and responsibility.

THE 10TH OF OCTOBER

As it happened, General Smith's first meeting with the IAC was entirely unplanned, but it served to set the tone of the new regime.

---

[a]George Marshall replaced Louis Johnson as Secretary of Defense on 21 September 1950.

[b]See page 60.

After close of business on Tuesday, 10 October (Smith's second work-ing day in office), Smith was informed that the President desired six estimates to take with him to his meeting with General MacArthur at Wake Island. The six subjects were: (1) the threat of full-scale Chinese Communist intervention in Korea, (2) the threat of direct Soviet interven-tion in Korea, (3) the threat of a Chinese Communist invasion of Formosa, (4) the threat of a Chinese Communist invasion of Indochina, (5) Communist capabilities and threat in the Philippines, and (6) general Soviet and Chinese Communist intentions and capabilities in the Far East. The President would be leaving for Wake Island within twenty hours.[a]

During the war scare of March 1948, a joint ad hoc committee had been set up to estimate, over the weekend, whether the USSR intended deliberately to initiate general war.[48] The Dulles Report had cited that improvisation as a model of how national intelligence estimates should be made.[49][b] Consulted by telephone at his home, Jackson recommended that the 1948 procedure be followed in this emergency. Smith himself telephoned each member of the IAC, summoning them to a meeting in his office at 7:00 P.M. At least one member of the IAC objected to being called away from his dinner table. Smith straightened him out in the language of a drill sergeant addressing a lackadaisical recruit.[50]

There is no record of this meeting of the IAC in General Smith's office, because there was no secretary present, only Smith himself and five members of the IAC.[c] Smith explained the situation, and the IAC agreed to set up six joint ad hoc committees (one for each subject) to meet in the Pentagon and produce the desired estimates overnight. When one member objected that he could not possibly obtain the required clear-ances within his Department before 8:00 A.M., Smith declared that to be the objector's problem. Smith would expect to receive the required estimates at that hour.[51]

The members of the IAC departed in haste to call up their men for this task. Smith then summoned to his office Dr. Ludwell Montague, Chief of the Global Survey Group in ORE, and sent him to the Pentagon to take charge of the joint committees already assembling there. The CIA was otherwise unrepresented in this operation.[d]

---

[a]President Truman never made any distinction between current and estimative intelli-gence. (See Part One, pages 29–30.)

[b]Actually, a worse model could not have been found. However, the point that the Dulles Report sought to make was that there should be departmental participation in the prepara-tion of national intelligence estimates and shared responsibility for them.

[c]Representing State, Army, Navy, Air Force, and the Joint Staff.

[d]Jackson (who was not at the IAC meeting) must have suggested Montague for this role

Montague reported to Smith in the morning with six fully coordinated estimates in finished form. Meanwhile, the President had called for a seventh estimate, on the likelihood of a deliberate Soviet decision to precipitate global war. Fortunately, that requirement could be met by quotation from an estimate that had been fully coordinated only a few days before.[a] The IAC did not meet to ratify these estimates; the concurrences of its members were obtained through their senior representatives in the ad hoc working group. As General Vandenberg had remarked on a previous occasion, there was no time for "further formalities."[54b]

These seven estimates were subsequently published under one cover as ORE 58–50—although ORE had nothing whatever to do with them except to reproduce them. They were joint estimates reflecting the conventional wisdom of the day, without any exercise of superior judgment. The conclusions were negative in every case. The estimate of greatest historical interest held that, although the Chinese could intervene in Korea with massive ground forces, they would be unlikely to do so for fear of U.S. retaliation against China.[55]

ORE 58–50 provided an exciting opening for a new era in DCI-IAC relations. If some members of the IAC were sluggish in their initial response to the DCI's call, the obvious importance and urgency of the President's requirements produced urgent action thereafter, with no time for quibbling. And, if General Smith's demands upon them were peremptory, what he was demanding was their active participation in the preparation of a national intelligence estimate—as distinguished from merely registering concurrence or dissent with regard to a CIA draft, as had hitherto been the practice.[c]

THE 20TH OF OCTOBER

General Smith's first formal meeting with the IAC was held on the 20th of October. His performance that afternoon was masterful.

---

when consulted by telephone. Smith had known Montague in the JCS Secretariat in 1942, but could not have known that he was present in the CIA. Jackson had discussed the ORE problem with Montague in 1948, and on 7 October 1950 had requested of him a plan for an Office of National Estimates, which Montague had delivered earlier on the 10th.[52] Jackson later explained that Montague had been chosen for this task because Smith and Jackson had no confidence in ORE, but knew Montague to be experienced in joint intelligence estimating and sympathetic toward the idea of departmental participation in national intelligence estimates.[53]

[a][note deleted.]

[b]See Part One, pages 29–30.

[c]See Part Three, pages 121–23.

The General opened the meeting by announcing that both the "Webb Staff Study" and the CIA's counterproposal for the revision of NSCID 1 had been dropped from further consideration.[56] To his audience that must have said that he would entertain no further scheming to make of the IAC a "board of directors" and that, reciprocally, he would subject them to no further lectures on the statutory authority of the DCI.

NSC 50 provided a sufficient directive for the present, the General continued. (NSC 50 declared that the IAC was soundly conceived as an advisory body and specifically rejected the idea of "collective responsibility," but held that the IAC should participate more actively in the coordination of intelligence activities and the discussion and approval of intelligence estimates, under the forthright initiative and leadership of the DCI.)[57]

General Smith declared that he would promptly carry out NSC 50 (which prescribed the reorganization of ORE desired by members of the IAC), except as regards the OSO-OPC merger (which was not of concern to them). The NSC had approved this exception. (It would have been noted that he could get the NSC to change its directives at his request, without the concurrence of the IAC.)

General Smith then declared that the IAC must be geared for "rapid cooperative work." All present would have been reminded of the 10th of October.

General Smith next read a six-paragraph memorandum on "The Responsibility of the Central Intelligence Agency for National Intelligence Estimates." This paper was said to have been dictated by William H. Jackson in August as background information for Walter Lippman.[58] Actually, it was a verbatim quotation from Chapter V of the Dulles Report, omitting some unnecessary paragraphs and sentences. But in reading Jackson's text Smith made one significant verbal amendment. Where Jackson had said that the ultimate approval of national intelligence estimates should rest on the "collective responsibility" of the IAC, Smith read "collective judgment."[59]

The background of that change is interesting. In September, Jackson had submitted his text to Lawrence Houston, the General Counsel, for comment, and Houston had strongly objected to the idea of "collective responsibility" as contrary to the National Security Act of 1947 and to NSC 50. In passing the paper to Smith, on 16 October, Jackson had covered it with a note warning Smith that the term "collective responsibility" should not be used.[60] Since Jackson offered no substitute, he evidently intended the paper for Smith's background information only and did not anticipate that Smith would read it in full to the IAC. Smith did not discuss the paper with Jackson. He decided on his own to read it with the change indicated, which was his own verbal choice.[61]

The IAC readily agreed with Jackson's doctrine that, although the Act of 1947 apparently gave the CIA the independent and exclusive right to produce national intelligence, as a practical matter such estimates could be produced only with the cooperation of the departmental intelligence agencies. Jackson went on to say that such estimates should be "compiled and assembled" centrally (which implied a merely editorial function) by an agency whose "objectivity and disinterestedness" were not open to question (which implied an exercise of judgment regarding the validity of departmental contributions). Even as Smith read it, however, final approval would rest on the "collective judgment" of the IAC. Smith added that future national intelligence estimates would be published under a cover showing plainly that they were the product of a "collective effort."[62]

In this connection, Smith announced that he would establish as soon as possible an Office of National Estimates (ONE) to be concerned solely with the production of national intelligence estimates and an Office of Research and Reports (ORR) to engage in such intelligence research as the IAC agreed could best be done centrally, specifically excluding the political intelligence research to which State had objected.[63a]

There was further agreement upon a procedure for the production of national intelligence estimates. The IAC would consider and adopt an estimates program in order of priority and the terms of reference for particular estimates. Departmental contributions would be forwarded to ONE in accordance with an agreed schedule. On the basis of these contributions ONE would produce a first draft and send it to the departmental agencies for review. After working-level discussion of this draft and the departmental comments on it, ONE would submit to the IAC a revised draft for final discussion, resolution of differences, and approval, subject to the notation of dissents on any substantial differences remaining unresolved at the IAC level.[b] The business of the next meeting would be the adoption of an estimates program and of terms of reference for an estimate on Indochina.[64]

As the members of the IAC left this meeting, they must have been jubilant. Instead of being overwhelmed by the "Ogre of SHAEF," they had been taken into partnership! In the circumstances, there would be

---

[a]This reorganization of ORE had been proposed by the Dulles Report and enjoined by NSC 50.

[b]This is, of course, the procedure still in effect twenty years later, except that the IAC soon ceased to consider terms of reference on which agreement had been reached at the ONE level.

no point whatever in a contentious attempt to define more precisely the relative authority of the DCI and the IAC. In their enthusiasm the members of the IAC may not have noticed that General Smith had done almost all of the talking.

"RAPID COOPERATIVE WORK"

The IAC met again on 26 October and adopted a program of eleven estimates in the following order of priority: the Philippines, Indochina, Soviet Capabilities and Intentions, Germany, Chinese Communist Capabilities and Intentions, Yugoslavia, Iran, Greece, Turkey, India, and Austria. This list reflected general apprehension that the Russians and the Chinese might take advantage of the U.S. involvement in Korea to commit local armed aggression elsewhere around their periphery. There was particular concern regarding Berlin.[65]

General Smith announced that Dr. Montague would be in charge of the production of these estimates pending the establishment of an Office of National Estimates.[a] The General wanted them to be produced as rapidly as possible. The military members of the IAC doubted that their respective staffs could act on more than three or four estimates simultaneously. State (Armstrong) and the CIA (Montague) thought that they could maintain a faster pace than that. Smith declared that Montague would set the pace. If the military could not keep up, that would be just too bad; Montague would proceed without them. The military members of the IAC would at least get a voice in the matter when it came before the IAC.[66]

Thus instructed, Montague submitted six coordinated estimates to the IAC during the next four weeks. Three of them (the Philippines, Soviet Capabilities and Intentions, Yugoslavia)[b] were from the program. Three others were crash estimates related to the Chinese Communist intervention in Korea.[c] In addition, Montague turned over to the Board of National Estimates four draft estimates ready for interdepartmental coordination. Two of them (Indochina, Germany)[d] were from the initial program. Two

---

[a]ONE was formally established on 13 November 1950, but Montague remained in charge of the production of national estimates through the IAC meeting held on 21 November.

[b]NIE-1, NIE-3, and NIE-7.

[c]NIE-2, NIE-2/1, and NIE-2/2.

[d]NIE-4 and NIE-5.

others had been undertaken by the IAC in response to urgent requests. They were "Future Military Capabilities of the Western European Countries in the Light of Present NATO Programs" and "Importance of Iranian and Middle East Oil to Western Europe."[67a]

This remarkable achievement was possible only because General Smith had transformed the relationship between the CIA and the departmental intelligence agencies. Gone was the departmental indifference, not to say hostility, that had hindered ORE's production and coordination of estimates. The IAC members had evidently instructed their subordinates to do their utmost to meet Montague's requirements. No one wanted General Smith to hear that he or his agency was hindering the production of estimates. Beyond that, however, there was also a new and positive sense of comradely collaboration in a common effort.[68]

It may be said that the Chinese Communists helped, too, by creating a real sense of national emergency like that which had prevailed in the days following Pearl Harbor.

THE 11TH OF NOVEMBER

During this period General Smith concluded every meeting of the IAC with a speech in praise of its members for the remarkably fine collaborative effort that was being made in the production of national intelligence estimates. At the close of the meeting held on Saturday, 11 November, he laid it on thicker than ever. It was wrong, he said, to call the Intelligence Advisory Committee merely *advisory*.[b] Together they were really the United States Joint Intelligence Board![69]

Montague heard these words with dismay. It appeared that General Smith was abdicating the statutory responsibilities (and authority) of the DCI and accepting the doctrine of a "collective responsibility" vested in the IAC, with all of the attendant evils of a joint intelligence system.

A member of the IAC, Brigadier General Vernon E. Megee, USMC, Deputy Director for Intelligence of the Joint Staff, understood it that way also. General Megee had come late to the meeting, explaining genially that he had been celebrating the anniversary of the Marine Corps. That fact was evident. It had contributed to the congeniality of the occasion.

---

[a]NIE-13 and NIE-14.

[b]Stress upon that word had been Hillenkoetter's defense against the "board of directors" concept.

Now General Megee was moved to interrupt the DCI by exclaiming, "Yes, we are the Board of Directors!"

An awful silence ensued. Everyone present, including Megee, knew that Megee had said a bad word. Everyone held his breath, waiting for the explosion. But when General Smith resumed speaking, it was in a quiet and somber tone, in marked contrast to his previous ebullience. He was speaking of the lonely personal responsibilities of the DCI, responsibilities that he could not share with his colleagues in the IAC, no matter how kindly they might wish to share that burden with him.[70] General Smith never had to make that speech but once. He was understood.

It is significant that General Smith recognized instantly the connotations of the expression "board of directors"—and that, despite all his persiflage about a collective effort and achievement (which confused a good many people in the CIA), he understood clearly his unique personal responsibility as Director of Central Intelligence. The members of the IAC understood that, too (though General Megee was slow to catch on). They were glad enough to collaborate with him in partnership on his generous terms. Nothing was ever heard again of the "board of directors" concept.

OVER THE LONGER TERM

General Smith continued to meet regularly with the IAC and to talk up the cooperative participation of the departmental intelligence chiefs in the coordination of intelligence activities and in national intelligence estimates. At the same time, he sought to avoid conflict with them by bringing nothing seriously controversial before the IAC. For example, in April 1951 he inquired of his staff why an NSCID on Economic Intelligence was being prepared.[a] The terms of a legalistic formulation on the subject might provoke controversy in the IAC. He preferred to achieve a mutually accepted working relationship with the departmental agencies through the gradual accretion of practice and precedent, without writing a formal directive.[71] Actually, substantial agreement with the IAC agencies had already been achieved. It was duly recorded in NSCID 15, dated 13 June 1951.[b]

---

[a]The purpose was to register NSC approval of the functions of the newly created Office of Research and Reports, as a "service of common concern." That was required by literal application of the terms of the National Security Act of 1947, Section 102(d)(4).

[b]See Part Three, pages 153–54.

Smith's attitude is further illustrated by his response to a complaint that the conclusions of national intelligence estimates were rather commonplace. He accepted that criticism, observing that the estimates were being watered down in order to obtain agreement and avoid dissenting footnotes. Personally, he said, he would be willing to publish an estimate to which every member of the IAC dissented, and someday it might be necessary to do that in order to present a good estimate, but to do so now would set back the development of the CIA for several years.[72] In other words, Smith recognized his unique personal responsibility for the substance of national intelligence estimates and was prepared to assert his prerogative in that respect if the occasion were of sufficient importance to require it, but he would not sacrifice his good relations with the IAC in order to assert his personal view with regard to an inconsequential difference.

Inevitably, a time did come when General Smith was hindered and frustrated by his inability to obtain agreement in the IAC. He was then heard to remark, "I don't see how Hillenkoetter ever accomplished as much as he did."[73] But these difficulties were primarily with the Joint Chiefs of Staff, and only secondarily with the service members of the IAC.[74] Moreover, such obstruction as Smith encountered in the IAC never involved such a challenge to his authority as Hillenkoetter had faced. In these cases of disagreement, the IAC members were operating within the system that Smith himself had established between 10 October and 11 November 1950, a system based on mutual respect and consideration such as had never existed before.

In September 1951 Smith received a demonstration that the members of the IAC thoroughly appreciated his policy of collaboration with them in that spirit.

A fourth report to the NSC was then required, on progress in the implementation of NSC 68, which called for an intensification of intelligence activities to meet the growing Soviet threat to U.S. security.[a] The previous report in this series had contained a reference to substantial progress in interdepartmental cooperation and coordination through the active participation of the IAC.[75] It had been prepared by Dr. Montague, as the Intelligence member of an NSC drafting committee, and had been cleared directly with the IAC. The September 1951 draft was prepared by James Reber, Assistant Director, Intelligence Coordination, in coordination with the IAC representatives with whom he normally dealt regarding

---

[a]The general subject of NSC 68 and its implementation is discussed in Part Four, Chapter XVI.

the coordination of intelligence activities. Unlike their colleagues who had participated in the preparation of national intelligence estimates, these men had no appreciation of the new spirit that Smith had created in the IAC. They were still imbued with the previously existing attitude of suspicion and antagonism toward the CIA, and they were particularly incensed by the current difficulties in coordination mentioned above. From their point of view, Smith was contumaciously frustrating in the IAC the sacred will of the Joint Chiefs of Staff. When the September 1951 draft came before the IAC, it bore a notation that the representatives of the service intelligence agencies recommended the deletion of the paragraph in praise of the IAC as an effective instrument for coordination.[76]

When the IAC met to consider this draft, on 10 September 1951, General Smith coldly observed that this disagreement indicated a feeling at the working level that the IAC was not as effective as hitherto he had supposed it to be. That being the case, he would ask the NSC to appoint an impartial board (like the Dulles Survey Group) to investigate the matter and propose a remedy. In response to this threat,[a] the service members of the IAC fell over one another in their haste to repudiate their representatives as parochial fellows ignorant of the IAC and its good works. They declared that General Smith's "reactivation" of the IAC had been an outstanding development that had made possible great forward strides in intelligence coordination. Inwardly, Smith must have been highly amused by this scene, but he kept a stern countenance and seemed only reluctantly dissuaded from demanding a thorough investigation of the IAC.[77]

Thus, the IAC, which had bullied and badgered Admiral Hillenkoetter, found itself supplicating the gracious favor of his successor!

Initially, Smith's primary problem had been how to obtain the cooperation of the members of the IAC, but during his tenure as DCI the IAC became progressively less important to him. He was spending more and more of his time and attention at a higher level, with the President, the Secretaries of State, Defense, and the three services, and their principal deputies and assistants. He was in high favor in all these quarters and had trouble only with the Joint Chiefs of Staff. The members of the IAC were far down on his totem pole.

Nevertheless, good relations with the heads of the departmental intel-

---

[a]By this time it could be anticipated that any such board would recommend less consideration for the departmental intelligence agencies, rather than more.

ligence agencies are a matter of considerable importance to a Director of Central Intelligence. General Smith bequeathed to his successors a DCI-IAC relationship that gave real meaning to the idea of an intelligence community.[a]

---

[a]This term first appeared, as "the Federal intelligence community," in IAC-D-29/8, 9 April 1952, para. 1.

VI

COMMAND AND CONTROL OF THE CENTRAL INTELLIGENCE AGENCY

The Director said that he wished to have it clearly understood what he meant by staff work. He stated that he considered the Assistant Directors to be his staff and used the analogy of a Special Staff in any large military headquarters. . . . He stated that his staff headed by Mr. Kirkpatrick could be compared to the Secretary of the General Staff in a military headquarters.

—SC-M-4
8 January 1951

PREVIOUS PRACTICES

Naturally, each of General Smith's predecessors as DCI brought his own personal style to the exercise of command and control over the CIG/CIA. Although the Dulles Report complained of military predominance in the administration of the CIA, it was the former Chief of Staff at SHAEF who first organized the top management of the CIA by analogy to a major military headquarters.

NIA Directive No. 2 had authorized Admiral Souers to select one assistant director from each of the four personnel contingents contributed to the Central Intelligence Group by State, Army, Navy, and the Army Air Forces, and to make one of them his deputy.[78] Each of them was expected to represent the interest of his Department in the Group, but it was also understood that each should serve primarily as a lieutenant of the DCI. In that role each was expected to advocate the interest of the CIG before the member of the IAB who had seconded him.

Admiral Souers regarded his three Assistant Directors as indeed Assistant DCIs. He and his Deputy consulted them frequently, as a council, on the problems of the CIG as a whole. Only secondarily were they also the chiefs of the three component units of Souers's simple organizational structure.[a]

With the advent of General Vandenberg as DCI, these consultations ceased. If Vandenberg had a privy council, it was the cabal of colonels that he brought with him from G-2.[b] Later he depended entirely on his Deputy, Colonel Edwin Wright, in matters of internal organization and administration, and on Donald Edgar, the Chief of his Interdepartmental Coordinating and Planning Staff (ICAPS), with regard to external relations.[c] Within the CIG, Vandenberg was not particularly secretive about his purposes and plans, but, jealously insulated by Wright, he simply had no system for consulting, or even informing, his Assistant Directors. For example, one of them learned only by accident that it had already been decided to alter radically the functions of his office and to increase its recruiting goal from 60 to 2,000![79]

This situation obtained even when all that there was of the CIG was housed in a few rooms in the older part of the building now known as New State. It was not improved when the working components of the CIG were located in the former OSS complex at 2430 E Street, while the CIG headquarters was in the North Interior Building a half mile away.

Admiral Hillenkoetter inherited General Vandenberg's physical and procedural isolation from his Assistant Directors. Even when Hillenkoetter moved into the Administration Building at 2430 E Street, he still remained effectively isolated from them by his headquarters staff. Personally, Vandenberg and Hillenkoetter were both approachable men. Their isolation resulted from the procedural patterns established by Wright and Edgar[d] and from their own lack of interest in maintaining direct contact

---

[a]Souers's Deputy was Colonel Kingman Douglass, seconded by the Army Air Forces as a civilian. The three Assistant Directors were Captain William Goggins, Navy, in charge of the Central Planning Staff; Colonel Ludwell Montague, seconded by State as a civilian, in charge of the Central Reports Staff; and Colonel Louis Fortier, Army, in charge of "Central Intelligence Services," then an empty box on the organization chart. None of these four survived the advent of Colonel Edwin Wright as General Vandenberg's *éminence grise*. Only Montague remained with the Group.

[b]The most notable of them were Colonel Edwin Wright, who became DDCI, and Colonel Donald Galloway, who became ADSO.

[c]Vandenberg (Wright) dissolved Souers's Central Planning Staff and then created a replica of it as ICAPS. Edgar was seconded from State, but became a strong advocate of the prerogative of the DCI.

[d]Edgar was succeeded by Prescott Childs, from State, in 1947. Wright remained DDCI until 1949, when he departed and his office was left vacant.

with their operating units. The CIA became a sort of Holy Roman Empire in which the feudal barons pursued their respective interests subject to no effective direction and control by the titular emperor.[80a]

So commanding a character as Bedell Smith could not be expected to tolerate such a lack of system and order. One of his first concerns on taking office was to establish his effective command and control over all components of the Central Intelligence Agency. In doing that, he naturally thought and acted in terms of his military experience.

CONTROL OF THE OFFICE OF POLICY COORDINATION

General Smith's first move, on assuming command of the CIA, was to establish his control over the Office of Policy Coordination (OPC). That office had been created in 1948 to conduct covert "activities" other than the clandestine collection of intelligence, which was the function of the Office of Special Operations (OSO).[b] Although nominally a component of the CIA, OPC was effectively under the direction of the Departments of State and Defense, rather than that of the Director of Central Intelligence.

The idea of such an office had originated with a State Department proposal [word or number deleted] to establish within that Department a "Director of Special Studies" to coordinate plans for covert operations to be carried out by various agencies.[c] That proposal moved Allen Dulles[d] to advise the NSC that State's scheme would not work. The proposed Director must not only coordinate plans but direct and control the operations envisaged, in close conjunction with clandestine intelligence operations. Indeed, the two sorts of secret operations should have one director, as had been the case in the OSS, and as the British had now decided to do.[81e]

---

[a]It may be noted that the Assistant Director, Reports and Estimates, exercised no more control over the components of ORE than did the DCI over the CIA as a whole.

[b]The warrant for assigning the OPC function to the CIA was in the National Security Act of 1947, Section 102(d)(5): "to perform such other functions and duties *related to* intelligence affecting the national security" as the NSC might direct" (emphasis supplied).

[c]In this phase the idea was limited to covert political, or psychological, operations.

[d]As Chairman of the NSC Survey Group.

[e]At this time (May 1948) Dulles begged the question whether the combined secret service should be in the CIA or in an independent agency directly responsible to the NSC. The Dulles Report (January 1949) recommended that OPC and OSO be combined in one "Operations Division" within the CIA.

Hillenkoetter then proposed the creation of an Office of Special Services (OSS) within the CIA and of an Operations Advisory Board analogous to the IAC to provide authoritative policy guidance to the DCI.[82] The NSC finally decided (NSC 10/2) to locate the office in the CIA under a less revealing name[a] and subject to less formal policy guidance by the Departments of State and Defense. However, in a meeting held in the office of the Executive Secretary, NSC, on 6 August 1948, George Kennan, representing the Department of State, laid down the law that "political warfare" was essentially an instrument of foreign policy and that OPC, located in the CIA for expedient reasons, must be regarded as a direct instrumentality of State, not subject to the DCI's interference. The Executive Secretary, Sidney Souers, seconded Kennan, saying that the intention of the NSC was that State should control OPC's operations in time of peace and that Defense should do so in time of war. Hillenkoetter acquiesced, so long as State accepted political responsibility, as Kennan did.[83] Thus, Hillenkoetter surrendered operational control of OPC to State—and to Defense with regard to covert operations in time of war and to preparations for war. Hillenkoetter retained administrative control of OPC, a subordination that proved very irksome to the ADPC, but there is no indication that he ever used this power to impose his views on OPC, other than with regard to administrative accountability.[b]

State, with the concurrence of Defense, had chosen Frank Wisner to be Assistant Director, Policy Coordination. Born in Laurel, Mississippi, in 1909, he was a graduate of the University of Virginia (1931) and its Law School (1934). He had been a partner in Carter, Ledyard & Milburn (as had William H. Jackson). During the war he had served as a naval officer in ONI (1941–43) and OSS (1943–46)[c]; his OSS service was in North Africa, the Middle East, Rumania, France, and Germany. Afterward he was deputy to the Assistant Secretary of State for Occupied Areas from 1946 to 1948. He had been ADPC for two years when General Smith relieved Admiral Hillenkoetter.

Even before General Smith took office, his Deputy-designate, William H. Jackson, summoned Frank Wisner (his former law partner) and Lawrence Houston, the CIA General Counsel, and directed them to prepare a revision of NSC 10/2 that would clarify and confirm the DCI's

---

[a]Initially, the Office of Special Projects (OSP), soon changed to the Office of Policy Coordination (OPC).

[b]Lyle T. Shannon, Hillenkoetter's Deputy Executive, and Lawrence Houston, his General Counsel, did use this leverage, with some success, in a constant effort to exert some CIA control over OPC's operations.[84]

[c]When the OSS was dissolved on 1 October 1945, its clandestine services continued to operate as the Strategic Services Unit (SSU) of the War Department.

authority over covert operations.[a] Despite the "understanding" established in 1948, Wisner was willing to accept the authority of Bedell Smith. On 5 October he and Houston submitted to Jackson their proposals regarding the amendment of NSC 10/2.[85]

When Bedell Smith saw this paper, he cast it aside. He already had the requisite authority, he said. There was no need to amend NSC 10/2.[86b] Wisner demurred, saying that he was hindered by the ambiguities of 10/2 and embarrassed by the "understanding" of 1948. Smith told him to forget it. That "understanding" had been reached in circumstances that no longer pertained; it was no longer of any validity.[87] Smith desired to continue to receive advice and policy guidance through the existing arrangements, but it must be understood that this advice was given to the CIA, not to OPC as a separate entity, without any implication that State, Defense, or the JCS had any authority to give direction to OPC.[88]

It was left to Wisner to explain Smith's position to the representatives of State, Defense, and the JCS from whom he regularly received policy guidance.[c] He did so on 12 October. Smith's interpretation of NSC 10/2 and his repudiation of the "understanding" of 1948 were well received by those representatives, who gave their personal agreement and undertook to inform their principals.[89]

The differences between the circumstances of 1948 and those of 1950, to which General Smith referred, were three: (1) Kennan, who was determined to control covert political warfare, and Hillenkoetter, who was deemed inadequate for that role, were both gone; (2) Smith had reached his own understanding with the Secretaries of State and Defense; (3) all concerned were happy to accept General Smith's forthright assumption of command of covert action operations.[d]

THE OFFICE OF THE DIRECTOR

Having established his control over OPC, Smith turned his attention to the more effective organization of his own office as an instrument of

---

[a]See page 62.

[b]Smith was always opposed to writing a formal directive if he could establish his point in practice, lest the formulation of the directive provoke controversy. (See pages 71–72.)

[c]They were Robert Joyce (State), General John Magruder (OSD), and Admiral Leslie Stevens (JCS), called collectively the NSC 10/2 Committee, or the Senior Consultants.

[d]Smith soon became embroiled with the JCS over the control of covert operations in time of war. Then Smith himself desired to amend NSC 10/2 in order to resolve that issue.

command and control. The key to that was the selection of an officer who would serve the Director and Deputy Director as Smith himself had served General Marshall when he was Secretary of the War Department General Staff. That officer was given the title of Executive Assistant in order to distinguish him from the several personal assistants in the Office of the Director.[a]

Admiral Hillenkoetter's office had consisted only of himself and his Deputy, Brigadier General Edwin Wright. Immediately below them in the chain of command was the Executive, an office created by Wright in 1946. It was the focal point in the CIA. The Executive was directly supported by four staff units: Budget, Management, Personnel, and Procurement. Beneath him, but less immediately under his personal direction, were seven other staff units and the six line offices of the CIA.[b] In principle, and normally in practice, no Assistant Director could reach the DCI except through the Executive.

Wright had established this pattern in July 1946 for the purpose of preventing access to Vandenberg except through him. Even after he was named Deputy Director, Wright continued to function as the Executive until May 1947, when Hillenkoetter appointed a Navy captain to the vacant office. That too made no difference. Wright continued to function as, in effect, the director of the CIA, while Hillenkoetter took care of external representation and the Executive attended to internal administration as directed.

The NSC Survey Group criticized this setup on the ground that it permitted administrative officials to exercise policy control over the line offices of the CIA, with the result that CIA policy was determined by administrative rather than intelligence considerations. The Dulles Report urged that the DCI should regain direct contact with his Assistant Directors and consult them as staff advisers in the determination of CIA policy.[90]

This advice was disregarded, since the persons criticized were in actual control of the CIA. When Wright departed in March 1949, Hillenkoetter allowed the administration of the CIA to devolve to his own man, Captain Walter Ford, USN, the Executive.[c] When Ford's successor, Captain Clarence Winecoff, USN, also departed, in April 1950, Hillenkoetter

---

[a]They were Lieutenant Colonel Henry Mueller, the General's personal military aide; John Earman, held over from the Hillenkoetter regime; and Joseph Larocque, Jackson's man. Larocque had been Jackson's classmate at St. Mark's and a staff assistant to the NSC Survey Group.

[b]See Organization Chart, 1 October 1950, Part Three, page 113.

[c]Hillenkoetter offered the Deputy Directorship to George Carey, who declined it. (See Part Three, page 187.) Thereafter he made no effort to fill the vacancy.

already knew that his own days as DCI were numbered. The management of the CIA then devolved to Lyle T. ("Ted") Shannon, as Acting Executive.[a]

Shannon conceived his task to be to preserve the status quo pending the arrival of a new DCI. He feared that Hillenkoetter would sell the CIA down the river in his current negotiations with State and Defense regarding the "Webb Staff Study."[b] When General Smith's appointment was announced, in August, Shannon entered into out-of-channels communication with him.[92c]

Of course General Smith had no idea of leaving the management of the CIA to his Deputy, much less to a subordinate administrative officer. He conceived Jackson's function as Deputy to be analogous to that of a Chief of Staff; Jackson functioned in that way. At the same time, Smith realized that he could not deal directly with the chiefs of eleven staff units and six line offices. That would be too broad a span of control. Smith established a weekly Staff Conference with his Assistant Directors and a very few staff officers, as a means of dealing with problems of internal coordination and of laying down a general policy line.[d] From the beginning, however, he intended to reduce that span of control by appointing three specialized deputies, in addition to the DDCI.[e] Meanwhile, he needed a "secretary of the general staff," an executive assistant.

Jackson found the man for the job.[93] He was Lyman Kirkpatrick, then Deputy Assistant Director for Operations.

Kirkpatrick, thirty-five in 1951, was a native of Rochester, New York, and a graduate of Princeton University (1938). After four years as a journalist in Washington, he was recruited by the OSS. He became a major commanding the OSS intelligence unit at Headquarters, 12th Army Group, where he became well and favorably known to Brigadier General Edwin Sibert, the G-2, and Colonel William Jackson, the Deputy G-2. Eventually he became General Bradley's briefing officer. He returned to Washington in 1945 to be an editor of *World Report,* but in January 1947 General Sibert recruited him to be a member of his staff as ADO.[f]

---

[a]Shannon was born at Farmer City, Illinois, in 1909, enlisted as a private soldier in 1924, and rose from the ranks to the status of a colonel, GSC, at SHAEF in 1944. He came to the CIG as an administrative officer in August 1946 and retired from the Army in 1947.[91]

[b]Actually, Hillenkoetter, coached by Houston, stood firm for the authority of the DCI during these negotiations. (See Part One, pages 48–50.)

[c]Smith had known Shannon at SHAEF. He had personal reason to appreciate the ability indicated by Shannon's rise from private to colonel.

[d]See pages 84–85.

[e]See pages 85–96.

[f]See Part Three, page 186.

Kirkpatrick was in charge of [words deleted] from February 1948 until October 1950, when he was made DADO.[94]

Kirkpatrick was made Executive Assistant on 13 December 1950. His position differed from that of Hillenkoetter's Executive in that he was a staff officer, not in the chain of command. He was, however, the nexus between the Director and Deputy Director on the one hand and the specialized Deputies and Assistant Directors on the other. It was his function to see to it that every matter deserving the Director's attention was brought to his attention, and in proper form, thoroughly staffed out and coordinated. It was also his function to convey the Director's inquiries and decisions to the officers responsible to act on them, and to see to it that appropriate action was in fact taken.

When General Smith had explained these duties to Kirkpatrick, he remarked, "That year I spent working as secretary of the general staff for General Marshall was one of the most rewarding of my entire career and the unhappiest year of my life."[95]

In order to keep himself informed of the proceedings of the CIA, General Smith required Kirkpatrick to prepare a daily log listing all important incoming and outgoing communications, meetings, and conversations. The Assistant and Deputy Directors were required to propose to Kirkpatrick items for inclusion in this log. Smith reviewed it first thing in the morning, together with the *Daily Intelligence Summary*. Then Jackson and Kirkpatrick came in, explained to him more fully the items that interested him, and briefed him on matters requiring his personal attention.[96] Reference to items in the log often served as the basis for discussion at the Director's morning meetings with his Deputies.[a] Kirkpatrick kept the minutes of these meetings.

For his own convenience in keeping track of the flow of paper, Kirkpatrick established the Executive Registry.[97]

Kirkpatrick was Executive Assistant for six months and was then assigned to be Deputy Assistant Director, Special Operations. He was succeeded by Joseph Larocque, who held the office for five months and was then assigned to be Deputy Assistant Director, Operations. Larocque was succeeded by Loftus Becker,[b] who held the office for one month and

---

[a]See page 95.

[b]Becker, forty in 1951, was a native of Buffalo, New York, and a graduate of Harvard (1932) and Harvard Law School (1936). He practiced law in Honolulu from 1936 to 1938, and New York from 1938 to 1942, and then served in the Army from 1942 to 1945, rising in rank from private to major. In particular, he was an intelligence officer with the Ninth Army and later attended the Nuremberg trials as an expert on German military organizations. He returned to his law firm in New York in 1946, but in April 1951 was brought into the Director's Office by Jackson as an "intermittent" consultant. In fact, he served full-time but without a long-term commitment.

then was made Deputy Director, Intelligence.[a] Becker was succeeded by John Earman, who held the office for ten years, five months (until May 1962). The office was then superseded by the appointment of an Executive Director (Lyman Kirkpatrick), and Earman was made Inspector General.

THE DAILY STAFF MEETING

During his first two months in office, General Smith had all the officers in immediate attendance on him come into his office at nine in the morning, when he reviewed with them the problems of the day and gave them their instructions.[98] However, by the time that Kirkpatrick began to record minutes of these morning meetings, they were being held elsewhere, Smith was not present, Jackson was in the chair, and they were called the "Deputy Director's Staff Meeting."[99] At the conclusion of this daily staff meeting, Jackson and Kirkpatrick went in to brief the Director.

This procedure was similar to the former practice at SHAEF. There Bedell Smith, as Chief of Staff, had conducted an eight o'clock staff meeting to review the situation, after which he and a very few others went in to brief Eisenhower.[100]

The minutes of these meetings do not list the persons present; the attendance can only be inferred from indirect quotations in the text.[b] Jackson normally presided, and Kirkpatrick normally kept the minutes. The other regular attenders were Murray McConnel, Lyle Shannon, James Reber, Joseph Larocque, and John Earman. Allen Dulles and John O'Gara joined the group in January 1951.[c]

In mid-March 1951 the three Deputy Directors, Jackson, McConnel, and Dulles, ceased to attend this daily staff meeting. (They were attending another daily meeting with the Director.[d]) Nevertheless, the daily staff meeting continued to be held by the Executive Assistant. It was

---

[a]See page 92.

[b]The one indirect quotation of Smith (22 December 1950) was probably a report on what he had said elsewhere, rather than evidence of his presence in that meeting.

[c]McConnel was the Executive from 16 October until 1 December 1950, when he became Deputy Director, Administration. Shannon was Deputy Executive, then Assistant DDA. Reber bore the title of Assistant Director, Intelligence Coordination, but was actually the chief of a small staff section at Headquarters. Dulles was Deputy Director, Plans. O'Gara was Assistant DDA for Administration (Special).

[d]See page 95.

evidently Kirkpatrick's device for preparing himself to meet with the Director and his Deputies. Larocque and Becker continued the practice.[101]

The "daily" staff meeting was held very irregularly during January and February of 1952. On 25 February Earman announced that it would be held only weekly thereafter. Actually, only one more meeting was held, on 19 March.[102] The reason was that the Director's Office was by then functioning so efficiently that it was no longer necessary to hold a staff meeting in order to find out what was going on.

THE WEEKLY STAFF CONFERENCE

The weekly staff conference with the Assistant Directors was a more formal occasion than the daily staff meeting. The Director himself normally presided, and Kirkpatrick kept formal, numbered minutes—for example, SC-M-1, 18 December 1950.

At the first meeting General Smith explained that the functions of the staff conference were to consider the internal policy of the Agency[a] and to eliminate the present lack of cross-coordination within the Agency.[103] At the fourth meeting he assured the Assistant Directors that he would be directly accessible to them at any time, although it would be more difficult to reach him on Thursdays and Fridays.[b] He likened the Assistant Directors to the Special Staff at a military headquarters.[c] He took that occasion to lecture on the doctrine of "completed staff work."[104][d] Later he decreed that papers presented for his consideration must be in the established general staff format: statement of the problem, facts bearing on the problem, discussion, conclusions, and recommendations.[105]

---

[a]Cf. the recommendation of the Dulles Report to this effect, mentioned above, page 80.

[b]He met with the NSC and the IAC on Thursdays and briefed the President on Fridays.

[c]As distinguished from the members of the General Staff, who advise the commander and supervise (in his name) the execution of his orders but themselves have no command authority, the members of the Special Staff are the commanders of subordinate service units (Quartermaster, Engineer, Ordnance, etc.) who also serve as advisers to the commander with regard to their technical specialties.

[d]A paper presenting a problem and recommending that something be done about it is of no use to a commander. He requires a paper recommending a specific action, with that recommendation supported by reasoning and coordinated with all concerned, and with the action paper drawn up in such a way that he can sign it (if he approves), or reject it, or remand it for revision in accordance with his specific instructions.

The weekly staff conference was useful to Smith as a means of establishing contact with his Assistant Directors, making himself known to them and taking their measure, and laying down his general policy line. When he had accomplished those purposes, he began to urge them to settle their interoffice problems directly among themselves, instead of bringing them to the staff conference. He urged them to accomplish that by direct personal contact or by telephone, saying that written memoranda should be used only as a last resort.[106] When meetings of the weekly conference were canceled because no one had anything to propose for the agenda, he expressed his satisfaction, saying that it showed that direct lateral coordination was working.[107]

The last meeting of the staff conference was held on 17 December 1951. Thereafter the supervision of interoffice coordination was left to the three specialized Deputies, each in his own area,[a] and interarea coordination was accomplished at the Director's daily meeting with them. Like the daily staff meeting, the weekly staff conference had accomplished its purpose and was no longer required.

THE DEPUTY DIRECTOR FOR ADMINISTRATION (DDA)

Bedell Smith appreciated the ability of "Ted" Shannon, the Acting Executive, but Shannon was a controversial figure, implicated in the NSC Survey Group's indictment of the administration of the CIA[b] and embroiled in a continuing conflict with OPC and OSO over the control of administrative support for the clandestine services.[c] William Jackson, who had been a member of the Survey Group and was now Smith's Deputy, urged that Shannon be summarily fired.[108] Smith refused to do that, but he perceived that he had better bring in an outsider, a man not involved in these ancient quarrels, to head up his administrative organization.

Moreover, Smith himself considered that traditional military administrative methods were old-fashioned and inefficient. His thought was that a successful businessman could teach modern business techniques to his predominantly military (or ex-military) administrative personnel. The

---

[a]As DDI, Becker held biweekly meetings of the "IAD's" (Intelligence Assistant Directors).

[b]See page 81.

[c]See pages 87–88.

man he chose for that task was Murray McConnel, fifty-five, President of the Manufacturers Capital Corporation of New York City.[a]

McConnel entered on duty as the CIA Executive on 16 October 1950, only nine days after Smith himself took office. Shannon then reverted to his normal position as Deputy Executive. On 1 December McConnel was redesignated Deputy Director for Administration (DDA), and Shannon became the Assistant DDA for Administration.[b] On 4 January 1951 John O'Gara was made Assistant DDA for Administration (Special), in charge of administrative support for the clandestine services.[c] Shannon then became Assistant DDA for Administration (General).

These changes in the organizational structure were accompanied by heavy emphasis on the theme that the function of Administration was to serve, not to control. Jackson said later (13 June 1951) that he and Smith had found Administration (read Shannon) "running the show," that the purpose of the reorganization had been to "subordinate" Administration. McConnel himself emphasized that the DDA had a service function, not a command position.[110]

McConnel handled the myriad administrative consequences of Smith's radical reorganization of the CIA[d] with efficiency and dispatch—though it remains a question how much that was his doing, how much Shannon's. In any case, it appears that McConnel had committed himself to come to the CIA for only six months. His successor, Walter Reid Wolf, entered the DCI's office as a special consultant in February 1951 and was soon made Deputy Director for Administration effective 1 April.[e]

Wolf, fifty-seven, was the senior vice president of the City Bank Farmers Trust Company and a vice president of the National City Bank of New York, on indefinite leave of absence from both institutions. An investment

---

[a]There was a warm personal relationship between Smith and McConnel, but the basis for it is not apparent on the record. McConnel had pursued a long career in investment banking. Smith had become acquainted with him while at Governor's Island, from 1949 to 1950.[109]

[b]There were two other Assistants to the DDA, for Inspection and Security and for Communications.

[c]O'Gara, fifty-five, was probably the nominee of Allen Dulles. After an administrative career in R. H. Macy & Co., New York from 1922 to 1943, he served as a colonel in the Army Service Forces from 1943 to 1944 and as Deputy Director, Personnel, OSS from 1944 to 1945. He returned to Macy's from 1945 to 1949 but was in the State Department from October 1949 until called to the CIA. He remained Assistant DDA (Special) until that office was abolished on 28 July 1952 and continued to serve as a CIA administrative officer until his retirement in 1961.

[d]See Part Three.

[e]McConnel then took Wolf's place as special consultant, a position that he held until 30 June 1953.

banker, as was McConnel, he had had no experience in the management of an operating enterprise.[a] He had few, if any, ideas of his own to contribute to the better administration of the CIA. Indeed, he was overwhelmed by the responsibilities of his position and incapable of positive action, except insofar as he was instructed by Smith himself—or by Shannon.[111]

General Smith was not known for his tolerance of incompetence or passivity. It is, then, pertinent to ask why he kept Wolf as DDA for the remainder of his tenure as DCI. There was a well-concealed streak of kindness in General Smith's character; he did harbor in the CIA some few men, distinguished in their time, whose better days were behind them.[b] A reason for keeping Walter Wolf was a sense of personal obligation to him. Wolf had handled Smith's personal investments with great success indeed.[112]

When Smith did keep in a position of responsibility an officer who was not functioning effectively, he simply short-circuited that officer by appointing a deputy on whom he could depend.[113] Thus, Smith depended on Shannon to carry on as his working deputy for administration, with Wolf as a front. But there was one problem that Shannon could not resolve, partly because of the bitter enmity of the clandestine services toward him personally. That was the issue over the control of administrative support for the clandestine services. Shannon had been working on that for five years, on behalf of two successive DCIs, without being able to get the clandestine services to accept the DCI's position on the subject.

The clandestine services had always had a separate administrative apparatus of their own. When the OSS was dissolved (1 October 1945) and its clandestine services were transferred to the War Department as the Strategic Services Unit (SSU), they took with them the administrative apparatus of the OSS.[c] The CIG, in its earliest days, was dependent on this continuing OSS/SSU administrative organization for support. When OSO was created out of SSU (11 July 1946), it included an administrative organization corresponding to that of SSU. When OPC was created (1 September 1948), it looked to OSO, rather than to the CIA, for covert administrative support.

The central administration of the CIG/CIA was, essentially, the creation of Vandenberg and Wright. When it attempted to absorb the admin-

---

[a]McConnel was also President of the Cuno Engineering Corporation of Meriden, Connecticut.

[b]Two examples are Brigadier General Trubee Davison and Lieutenant General H. H. Morris, successive Assistant Directors for Personnel.

[c]No one actually moved, of course. As the remnant of the OSS, SSU simply continued to function in the OSS complex at 2430 E Street.

istrative elements of OSO, it was rebuffed. The clandestine services contended, with reason, that administrative support for covert operations must be itself a covert operation; identification with the overt administration of the CIA would result in exposure. There was also some merit in their contention that the administrative personnel of the CIA were not professionally qualified to understand the peculiar requirements of clandestine operations. The other side of the argument was, of course, the personal responsibility of the DCI for the use made of unvouchered funds.

Hillenkoetter ordered the centralization of administrative support for covert operations, but the clandestine services appealed to the NSC Survey Group, which found in their favor, as did the NSC in NSC 50. Thus, the issue became entangled in the stalemate regarding the implementation of NSC 50.[a]

General Smith characteristically decreed that his Deputy Director for Administration should have charge of all CIA administrative activities, but the DDCI (Jackson), the DDP (Dulles), the ADPC (Wisner), and the ADSO (Schow, later Wyman) were all personally committed to the concept that the clandestine services should control their own administrative support and there was no real change in the previously existing situation. The issue was papered over by various devices. John O'Gara was named Assistant DDA (Special) and at the same time Assistant DDP (Administration). The administrative services that had been in OSO were gradually brought under the direct control of the DDP. They were not in any effective sense under the control of the DDA.

On 10 December 1951 an exasperated DCI laid down the law in no uncertain terms. Those assembled to receive instruction were William Jackson (now the Senior Consultant), Allen Dulles (the DDCI), Frank Wisner (the DDP), Colonel Kilbourne Johnston (ADPC), General W. G. Wyman (ADSO), Walter Wolf (the DDA), and Colonel Lawrence White, who had been selected to replace Shannon as Assistant DDA. Characteristically, General Smith explained himself by an Army analogy, referring to the relationship of a unit quartermaster to the Quartermaster General of the Army on the one hand and to the unit commander on the other.

Smith reiterated that the DDA was directly responsible to the DCI for all administrative support within the Agency. He ordered the DDP not to establish any duplicate administrative organization in his own office, or in OSO or OPC. He authorized the DDP to install in his own office a senior administrative officer who would belong to the DDA (the Quarter-

---

[a]The complex situation summarized above will be reviewed in detail in the appropriate Directorate and Office histories.

master General), but would work for the DDP (the unit commander) to ensure adequate support services for his operations. There would be similar administrative officers in OPC and OSO; they would be the "quartermasters" of those offices, analogous to the quartermasters of Army divisions.

General Smith made it clear that the operating offices would exercise control over the employment of the men and material allocated to them, reserving to the DDA the function of inspection and audit over all programs to ensure that they were implemented properly and in accordance with approved directives.

At the conclusion of this performance Jackson polled all those present and made each agree that the system prescribed by the Director was a major change from that which had hitherto prevailed and that each would accept the minutes of the meeting as a memorandum of understanding on the subject.[a]

Concurrently with this personal intervention, Smith relieved Shannon as Assistant DDA[b] and designated Colonel Lawrence ("Red") White to replace him. Smith considered that White had the force of character that would be required to enforce Smith's will. White was embarrassed during the 10 December meeting as Smith kept saying what White (rather than Wolf) would do in that regard.[115]

"Red" White, thirty-nine, was a native of Union City, Tennessee, and a graduate of the U.S. Military Academy (1933). He had commanded an infantry regiment in combat in the Southwest Pacific. He was wounded in action in Luzon in April 1945, spent the next two years in military hospitals, and was retired for combat disability on 31 March 1947. Meanwhile, General Sibert had recruited him to be the Deputy Chief, later the Chief, of the Foreign Broadcast Information Branch.[c] In that role his particular task was to purge the FBIB of unclearable linguists and mediocre engineers. It was a task that required a certain ruthlessness for the good of the service. On 13 December 1950 he was made Deputy Assistant Director, Operations, replacing Kirkpatrick, who had been reassigned as Executive Assistant. He went to work as the Assistant DDA (in practical effect, the working DDA) on 11 December 1951.[116d]

General Smith's prescribed system was put into effect on 1 August 1952. John O'Gara was then relieved of his dual Assistantship and "Ted"

---

[a]White's minutes of the meeting were dated 12 December. Two days later Becker, the Executive Assistant, put out an insignificantly revised version.[114]

[b]For the time being Shannon was carried as Special Assistant to the DDA.

[c]White reported for duty as Deputy Chief, FBIB, on 9 January 1947. He became Chief effective 29 September.

[d]White was not formally appointed to that position until 1 January 1952.

Shannon was appointed to be the new Chief of Administration, DDP.[a] This change coincided with the general reorganization of the clandestine services under the direct command of the DDP.[b]

"Red" White had covered his minutes of the 10 December meeting with a personal memorandum that said:[117]

> No matter what is written on this or any other paper, it is not worth the paper it is written on unless those responsible for implementation cooperate in a sincere effort to make it work. . . . I know that we can do it if people would only forget their jurisdictional disputes and give us a chance!

So it was done, under the forceful leadership of "Red" White in carrying out Bedell Smith's forceful command—although the DDP continued to grumble about the hindrances he suffered from his loss of control over his own men and resources.[c]

THE DEPUTY DIRECTOR FOR PLANS (DDP)

The same general order that established the office of Deputy Director for Administration provided also for a Deputy Director for Operations, but showed that office to be vacant.[119] It was being held open for Allen Dulles.

The function of the Deputy Director for Operations (later redesignated Deputy Director for Plans) was to exercise general supervision of the Offices of Operations, Special Operations, and Policy Coordination.[120] The Dulles Report had recommended that those three offices be "integrated" into a new self-sufficient and semi-autonomous "Operations Division."[121] For his own reasons, however, Bedell Smith desired to avoid merging OSO and OPC.[d] To appoint a single Deputy Director in general charge of the three offices was a way of providing for the necessary coordination of

---

[a]The clandestine services came to appreciate Shannon's talents when he went to work for them. He had a long and successful career in DDP [one-and-a-half lines deleted].

[b]See Part Four, Chapter XVII.

[c]Wolf resigned as DDA after Smith's departure. White became Acting DDA on 1 July 1953 and DDA on 21 May 1954. According to Colonel White, the more than ten months' delay between those two dates was attributable to the new DCI's desire to obtain a more prestigious figure to be DDA.[118] Finally he realized that it would be better to retain White in that office.

[d]See Part Four, Chapters XVI and XVII.

their activities without actually integrating them. Bedell Smith must have had this arrangement already in mind on 12 October 1950, when he told the NSC that he would not at this time integrate OSO, OPC, and [words deleted] OO, as directed by NSC 50.[a]

Before leaving New York, Smith had discussed the subject with Allen Dulles and had persuaded him to come to the CIA for six weeks as a consultant.[122] Dulles came in that capacity on 16 November 1950. The Office of Deputy Director for Operations was created on 1 December. On or about 18 December Dulles agreed to accept appointment to it under a different title, Deputy Director for Plans.[123] That was thought to be a less revealing designation.

On 22 December Allen Dulles drew up a contract memorandum defining his position in the CIA. He would enter on duty full time as DDP on 2 January 1951, on a "without compensation" basis (except for per diem and travel expenses while away from New York) pending reconsideration of that matter before 1 July 1951.[124] Evidently Dulles was not yet willing to commit himself beyond that date.[b]

Dulles's initial avoidance of a long-term commitment probably reflected his awareness that there was a sharp policy difference between Bedell Smith and himself. Dulles was still convinced that the integration of OSO and OPC was indispensable to efficient and secure clandestine operations. When he accepted appointment as DDP, he must have known that Smith was diametrically opposed to that. As DDP, Dulles took care to avoid a flagrant violation of Smith's orders, but nevertheless worked steadily toward the eventual accomplishment of his own purpose in disregard of Smith's known policy.[c] So doing, he knew that he risked provoking a violent reaction by Smith that would make his own position in the CIA untenable.

Smith, for his part, did not engage Allen Dulles to carry out the recommendations of the Dulles Report, as is commonly (and logically) supposed. The evidence is clear that that was contrary to Smith's intention in 1950. Rather, Smith engaged Dulles despite his known views on that subject, because he valued Dulles's experience and skill as a clandestine operator and thought to make use of those qualities, while retaining policy control in his own hands.

Smith never felt the same confidence in Allen Dulles and Frank Wisner that he did in William Jackson. During 1951 he had Jackson "survey"

---

bDulles remained in this noncommittal status until 23 August 1951, when he took office as DDCI. He then had to commit himself, since that was a statutory office.

cSee Part Five, Chapter XXI.

(investigate) the offices under Dulles's supervision.[a] With reason, he came to suspect that Dulles and Wisner were actually pursuing a policy contrary to his own. In exasperation, he visited upon them more violent manifestations of his wrath than he did upon anyone else.[125]

The reactions of Dulles and Wisner to this treatment were markedly different. Allen Dulles was sufficiently self-assured to be able to laugh about it—out of Smith's presence, of course. In the security of his own office, Dulles would exclaim: "The General was in fine form this morning, wasn't he? Ha, ha, ha!"[126] But Frank Wisner was always shaken. He likened an hour with General Smith to an hour on the squash court[127]— and he did not mean by that to suggest that he enjoyed it.

William Jackson had engaged to remain as DDCI for only six months. Actually, he stayed for more than ten. When his departure was being contemplated, Allen Dulles was not his choice to be his successor—nor Smith's either, apparently.[128] Jackson persuaded Smith to offer the position to Gordon Gray, who declined it.[129b] Jackson's impatience to get back to Whitney & Company did not allow him to search further for a successor.

Jackson ceased to be DDCI on 3 August 1951.[c] After some hesitation, Allen Dulles was appointed to succeed him, on 23 August. Frank Wisner then succeeded Dulles as DDP.

THE DEPUTY DIRECTOR FOR INTELLIGENCE (DDI)

During October and November 1950 it was contemplated that there would be a third specialized deputy director, a Deputy Director for National Estimates.[130] That title was a misnomer in that this deputy would have supervised all of the components of the CIA not covered by the DDA and DDP, not just the Office of National Estimates. He would have been equivalent to the Deputy Director, Intelligence, as that office

---

[a]See page 105.

[b]Jackson had known Gray as a lawyer in New York. In 1949 Gray had been a candidate for appointment to be DCI (see page 54). Appointment as DDCI would have been a step toward the realization of that ambition. But in 1951 Gray was President of the University of North Carolina, only temporarily in Washington as Director of the staff of the Psychological Strategy Board (see Part Four, page 205). Evidently he was no longer interested in becoming DCI.

[c]He remained active in CIA affairs as the Director's "Special Assistant and Senior Consultant."

was eventually set up. It should be remembered, however, that in late 1950 it was not contemplated that the CIA would engage in much intelligence research, even as a "service of common concern," and what there was to be of that was thought of as primarily contributory to national estimates.

However, the general order issued on 1 December did not provide for a Deputy Director, National Estimates (DDNE), as it did for a Deputy Director, Operations, even though that office remained vacant at the time. The probable reason for that omission was that no suitable appointee had yet been found, as Dulles had been found for Operations. General Smith desired to make Admiral Leslie Stevens his deputy for National Estimates[a]—he had known Stevens as Naval Attaché in Moscow—but Stevens, the Deputy Director of the Joint Staff for Subsidiary Plans (covert operations), could not be persuaded to leave that position.

In these circumstances, the DDCI, William Jackson, exercised particular supervision over the offices that would have been allotted to a DDNE. Jackson did not confine his attention to those offices, but they were the ones that had particularly interested him as a member of the NSC Survey Group.[b]

When Allen Dulles became DDCI, he continued to function as a super-DDP and paid little attention to the offices that Jackson had supervised in particular. Thus, a need for a third specialized deputy came again to be felt. Loftus Becker, the Executive Assistant, proposed the appointment of Kingman Douglass to that position.[c] Douglass, however, had already committed himself to return to Dillon, Read & Company at an early date. He declined the appointment and returned the compliment by nominating Becker, who was appointed.[132] Becker took office as Deputy Director for Intelligence (DDI) on 1 January 1952.

The reorganization of the CIA pursuant to NSC 50 had already been accomplished before Becker was made DDI.[d] The six offices placed under his supervision initially were Collection and Dissemination (OCD), Current Intelligence (OCI), Intelligence Coordination (OIC), National Estimates (ONE), Research and Reports (ORR), and Scientific Intelligence (OSI). On 1 March 1952 the Office of Operations (OO) was transferred from the jurisdiction of the DDP to that of the DDI.

---

[a]Smith's statement to this effect is recorded in the notes that Colonel Howze prepared for General Bolling on Smith's first meeting with the IAC on 20 October 1950,[131] though not in IAC-M-1. In context it is implicit that Howze understood that Stevens would have had jurisdiction over both ONE and ORR.

[b]See Part One, page 43.

[c]Douglass had been Souers's DDCI and was then Smith's Assistant Director, Current Intelligence. (See Part Three, page 159.)

[d]See Part Three.

Becker understood the functions of the DDI to be threefold: (1) to gather the "fatherless" Assistant Directors together into one family and to resolve jurisdictional disputes among them,[a] thus reducing the DCI's span of control; (2) to deal on more even terms with the DDP in coordinating the relationship of those offices with the clandestine services; and (3) to serve as the DCI's principal adviser and representative with regard to the coordination of intelligence activities and in other external relationships.[133] When these functions were finally defined in regulations in March 1953, the last was made first: the DDI was to assist the DCI in the coordination of intelligence activities, and also to direct and coordinate the seven offices named above.[134] Becker briefed the DCI on the IAC and NSC agendas, presided at the IAC in his absence, and represented the CIA on the NSC Senior Staff.

The "fatherless" Assistant Directors found it hard to regard Becker, forty, as a father figure. That was particularly true of Sherman Kent, forty-eight, the newly appointed ADNE, and Raymond Sontag, fifty-four, Kent's deputy. Both of them regarded Loftus Becker with personal disdain. Kent dutifully attended Becker's meetings with the Assistant Directors under his supervision and recognized Becker's authority in administrative matters, but refused to submit to Becker's supervision in any matter of intelligence judgment. To Kent it was important to maintain the principle that the Board of National Estimates was directly in the service of the Director of Central Intelligence.[135]

Within a month after they both took office, the tension between Becker and Kent was such that Becker demanded of Smith that he have Stuart Hedden, the Inspector General,[b] investigate ONE. Smith took the occasion to teach Becker a lesson in command relationships. Hedden was Smith's Inspector General, not Becker's. Becker had supervisory authority over ONE. If he was not satisfied with ONE's performance, it was his responsibility to correct the situation himself. He should not call on Hedden or Smith to do that for him.[136]

That was all very well, but no help to Becker, especially when Smith went on to justify ONE against Becker's particular complaint.[c] It may have pleased Smith's sardonic humor to see whether Becker could indeed impose his authority on Kent.

If Bedell Smith had been dissatisfied with the existing situation, it

---

[a]The principal jurisdictional dispute requiring resolution was between OCI and ONE. (See Part Three, pages 164–70.)

[b]See page 107.

[c]See page 72 and Part Three, pages 145–46.

would have been changed in short order, but in fact Smith was satisfied with the situation as it stood. Becker had general supervision of the CIA's production of substantive intelligence to meet NSC requirements. In that capacity it was proper for him to make the Board of National Estimates pay attention to NSC requirements and schedules.[a] But Smith shared Kent's view of the direct relationship between the DCI and the Board of National Estimates with regard to the substance of estimates,[b] and he encouraged Kent to continue to come directly to him in such matters.

It worked out in practice in accordance with Smith's conception. ONE was subject to the administrative control of the DDI. Kent had to submit to Becker's direction with regard to the programming and production of estimates, but Kent continued to deal directly with the DCI with regard to the substance of estimates.

There was less strain in Becker's relations with the other IADs,[c] but the practice was similar. Becker exercised a general supervision of the production schedules of OCI, ORR, and OSI as well as ONE. He did not attempt to subject the substance of their intelligence production to his personal judgment prior to publication, but he did review their published works for relevance and cogency.[137]

THE DIRECTOR'S DAILY MEETING WITH HIS DEPUTIES

Beginning on 23 March 1951, General Smith met daily with his three (later four) Deputies, his Executive Assistant, and one or two others on occasion. These meetings were recorded as the "Director's Meeting" until 6 June 1952, when they came to be called the "Deputies' Meeting."[138] It was in these meetings that Smith exercised, primarily, his command and control of the CIA.

It has been said of Allen Dulles that, as DCI, he was too greatly preoccupied with covert operations, to the exclusion of his other responsibilities. It is pertinent to observe that Bedell Smith, who had never before been a covert operator, spent almost all of his time with his Deputies discussing covert operations: their proper organization within the CIA, interdepartmental relations with regard to them, and matters

---

[a]See Part Three, pages 147–48.
[b]See Part Three, pages 129 and 131.
[c]Intelligence Assistant Directors (those under the supervision of the DDI).

relating to particular operations in the field. Those were the besetting problems of the time, with a local war in progress in Korea and with general war deemed possibly imminent. The production of finished intelligence and the coordination of interdepartmental intelligence activities could be left to the DDI.[a] The general administration of the Agency could be left to an able Assistant DDA. But covert operations commanded the personal attention of the DCI.

One consequence of this situation was that, whereas the Assistant Director, National Estimates, was pretty much his own boss (subject to the concurrence of the IAC), the Assistant Directors for Policy Coordination and Special Operations had to function under the close scrutiny of a three-tiered hierarchy: the DDP, the DDCI, and the DCI himself.

The normal procedure in this daily morning meeting was that Bedell Smith opened the discussion by inquiring about items in the daily log that had particularly interested him. Then the others in turn brought up the matters that they particularly wished to bring to the attention of the Director. The discussion sometimes became general, but was more often a dialogue between the deponent and the DCI. On the basis of the discussion, Smith sometimes rendered his decision, sometimes called for a further study of the subject and report to him.[139]

The meeting began to resemble a squash court[b] when Bedell Smith began to cross-examine Allen Dulles and Frank Wisner. He suspected them both of being not entirely candid with him. He thought that Wisner in particular was unduly slow and vague in his responses. He was determined to make them both respond to him as he thought they should.[140]

THE CAREER SERVICE AND THE OFFICE OF TRAINING

One of General Smith's first concerns, on taking command of the CIA, was to establish service in the Agency as a professional career. Smith was certainly well aware of the deficiencies of the military intelligence services, which were primarily attributable to a lack of professional

---

[a]In practice the ADNE assumed responsibility for the production of national intelligence estimates and tended to ignore the DDI.

[b]See page 92.

training and continuity of experience in intelligence work.[a] He must also have heard the common criticism of OSS operations as amateurish—which was inevitable at that time. He had probably heard Allen Dulles's opinion that the chief thing the matter with the CIA was the generally low quality of its personnel, haphazardly recruited during Vandenberg's rapid expansion of the CIG.[b] His own view was that "continuity of high caliber personnel, possessing specialized training and experience, is essential for the conduct of the Agency's activities."[142]

In his initial approach to this problem, Smith was probably thinking primarily of operational personnel of the clandestine services. Academic training and experience might suffice for the DDI offices, but Smith wanted his young operators to be instilled with military discipline and devotion to duty.[143] He was also thinking in terms of a statutory establishment like those of the Foreign Service and the FBI, which would permit reassignment by order (rather than by negotiated personal agreement).[c] He realized that a career service under such discipline would have to be made attractive in other respects in order to obtain volunteers. In particular, he wanted authority to award decorations for valorous or meritorious service.[144][d]

On the recommendation of the DDCI, William Jackson, Smith recruited Colonel Matthew Baird to develop a career service program.[e] Smith, a graduate of the Infantry School, the Command and General Staff School, and the Army War College, if not of West Point, considered such formal mid-career training to be an essential element of career

---

[a]In the prewar Army, the "Manchu Law" prevented anyone from making a career of general staff service. Intelligence theory and practice were not taught in the service schools or in field exercises. The intelligence required in presenting operational problems was given: it did not have to be obtained. Intelligence staffs were merely token units, except on the Mexican border and in overseas commands. To be assigned to intelligence duties was to be sidetracked from the main line of professional advancement. The only men who could be considered professional intelligence officers were those with sufficient private means (and lack of military ambition) to be military attachés.[141]

[b]See Part One, pages 14 and 42.

[c]He was afterward persuaded that no statute was necessary.

[d]The first fruit of this idea was the National Security Medal authorized by Executive Order in January 1953. It was first awarded to Walter Bedell Smith himself, on his retirement as DCI, and has rarely been awarded since then. The Distinguished Intelligence Medal and Intelligence Medal for Merit came later.

[e]Baird, forty-nine, had been Jackson's roommate at Princeton.[145] A native of Ardmore, Pennsylvania, he held a Princeton M.A. (1925) and Oxford B. Litt. (1928) and had been Assistant Headmaster of Haverford School, Headmaster of Arizona Desert School, and owner-operator of the Ruby Star Ranch near Tucson. During the war he served in the South Pacific, finally as CO, 13th Air Force Service Command. He was recalled to active duty in December 1950 and assigned to the CIA.

development. Baird was therefore given the title of Director of Training, as a subordinate of the DDA.

Baird's appointment occasioned considerable bureaucratic anguish. The CIA already had two training programs. One, conducted by the Office of Personnel for overt employees, was taken over by Baird without too much trouble. The other was conducted by OSO for the instruction of covert employees in the techniques of clandestine operations. The clandestine services felt strongly that they must control that program, for professional as well as security reasons. They had frustrated previous attempts by the Office of Personnel to take it over. Thus, Baird found himself involved in the long-standing conflict between Administration and the clandestine services over the control of administrative support for clandestine operations.

On 22 March 1951 General Smith intervened to say that Baird was *his* director of training, and that he intended Baird to "plan, direct, and supervise the basic training for operational personnel."[146] Then, suiting the action to the word, on 18 April 1951 Smith removed Baird's Office of Training from the jurisdiction of the DDA and subordinated it to himself directly.[a] He then declared that the Director of Training was to "*supervise all* Agency training programs and *conduct* such *general* training programs as may be, required" (emphasis supplied).[147]

These terms left open the question as to who would conduct specialized operational training. In July, however, the entire clandestine training apparatus was subordinated to the Director of Training, although it continued to be shown as subordinate to DDP on the DDP organization chart.[148] The Director of Training did not get full control of it until the reorganization of the clandestine services in August 1952.[b] Meanwhile, on 3 July 1951, Baird produced a staff study proposing the establishment of a "small elite corps" within the Agency to be recruited from among recent college graduates and middle-grade employees. The provisions of this plan for career management and development were generally accepted, but the idea of an "elite corps" was universally condemned. On 17 September Smith vetoed the idea, saying that he wanted the career service to include all the professional employees of the CIA.[149] Implicit was the thought that any professional employee who could not be regarded as "elite," or who would not commit himself to career service, should be gotten rid of without delay.

---

[a]Smith's point having been made, on 3 February 1955, the Office of Training was subordinated to the new Deputy Director for Support (DDS).

[b]See Part Four, Chapter XIX. With regard to the training programs developed by Baird, see the history of the Office of Training.

Smith then referred the problem of developing a plan for a career service to a committee headed by the DDA, Walter Wolf. The plan produced by that committee was adopted in June 1952.[150] Its implementation was supervised, not by the Director of Training, but by a permanent Career Service Board composed of the DDA (Chairman), DDI, DDP, Director of Training, and Director of Personnel, supported by a career service committee or board in each office or area division.[151]

With regard to the career service, Smith had two superficially contradictory objectives: he wished to purge the CIA of incompetent or only marginally competent personnel, but at the same time he wished to establish continuity of service as the norm. This duality of purpose sometimes led him to zig-zag in his pronouncements. At the Director's meeting on 7 December 1951 he declared that the turnover rate was too high; he wanted recruiting to be more selective, with some assurance of at least three years of service.[152] A few days later Wolf reported that the turnover rate was actually very low. It had been 12.2 percent in April and 8.8 percent in August,[a] but was now only 1.4 percent per month, compared with 3.6 percent for the Government as a whole.[153] At the next staff conference Smith declared that the recent expansion of the Agency had been too rapid; recruitment should be slower and more selective. When General Trubee Davison, the Director of Personnel, demurred that the turnover rate was actually low, Smith responded emphatically that he wished it were higher, if that meant that the Agency was being purged of the unfit. He then declared that there was no need to slow down recruitment so long as recruiting standards were raised.[154]

General Smith repeatedly urged the recruitment of more young women into the professional ranks of the career service. In August 1951 he remarked that the CIA needed also some "good young Bunches," especially in the clandestine services.[155b]

In personnel policy General Smith sought also to bridge the chasm between the DDI and DDP areas. A good career service officer ought to be able to serve effectively on either side of the house. In December 1952 he was gratified to observe that a number of station chiefs were returning to headquarters and being replaced by personnel from headquarters. The replacements should be mature career service personnel from both sides

---

[a]These high rates reflected the impact of life under General Smith on the personnel inherited from Vandenberg and Hillenkoetter. Smith should have been gratified thereby.

[b]The reference was, of course, to Ralph Bunche, a former section chief in the R&A Branch of the OSS. In 1951 Bunche was Professor of Government at Harvard University and Director of the Trusteeship Department of the United Nations staff. He had come to public notice in 1949, when he succeeded in establishing an armistice between the Arabs and Israelis.

of the Agency, men who would be capable of functioning well overseas after a course of instruction. The returning chiefs should not be assigned to the same area at headquarters, but rather to a different service, in order to broaden their experience.[156a]

General Smith anticipated that eventually the most senior positions in the CIA would be filled by selection from the career service. Until career service officers had been qualified by training and experience, one of the Agency's greatest problems, he said, would be the difficulty of finding men adequately qualified for such positions.[157b]

THE OFFICE OF COMMUNICATIONS AND THE CABLE SECRETARIAT

For reasons similar to those that moved him to attach the Office of Training to his own office, General Smith a year later took the Office of Communications away from the DDP and subordinated it directly to himself.

The communications organization of the OSS survived in SSU and passed intact into the CIG Office of Special Operations. In October 1950, when General Smith became DCI, this unit was known as the Communications Division of OSO. In July 1951 it became the Office of Communications, directly subordinate to the DDP.[158]

During 1951 there was a sharp increase in the CIA's overseas operations, in response to the sense of war emergency then prevailing,[c] and a correspondingly sharp increase in the CIA's overseas communications.[159] In order to strengthen his communications system, General Smith enlisted the services of Major General Harold M. McClelland, USAF (Ret.).[160]

McClelland, fifty-eight in 1951, was a native of Tiffin, Iowa, and a graduate of Kansas State University (1916). He entered the Army in 1917 and became a pilot in the Army Air Service. As his career progressed, he became a specialist in meteorology and communications and the inventor

---

[a]This was an old Army assignment policy. Smith's intention was most conspicuously fulfilled in the case of Ray Cline. [five lines deleted]. In the end, however, Cline left the CIA to become Director of the Bureau of Intelligence and Research in the Department of State.

[b]The first career service officer to become DCI was, of course, Richard Helms, appointed in 1966.

[c]See Part Four, Chapters XVI and XVII.

of various electronic devices. At the onset of war in 1941 he was in charge of all aspects of Army Air Corps communications; he developed for the Army Air forces the largest communications system the world had yet seen. His last service before retirement was as the first Director of Communications and Electronics in the Department of Defense and Chairman of the Joint Communications and Electronics Committee.

General McClelland took office as Assistant Director, Communications, on 10 September 1951. In that office his primary concern was with the technical development and organization of a worldwide, secure communications system. He was only incidentally concerned with the control and distribution of messages received.

General Donovan, as Director, OSS, and General Magruder, as Director, SSU, had controlled the distribution of OSS and SSU cables through an Executive Secretariat in their own offices. No DCI, however, had ever exercised such control over the distribution of CIG/CIA cables. The communications system belonged to the ADSO, later to the DDP. The DCI saw only such cables as the ADSO, ADPC, and DDP chose to bring to his attention. Normally, the cables went directly to action officers in OSO and OPC and then took several days, or longer, to filter up through the hierarchy to the DCI—if he ever saw them at all.[161]

When General Smith realized how this system worked, he was intensely dissatisfied. He lacked confidence that the DDP was keeping him adequately informed. He feared that some blunder overseas might become public knowledge before he knew anything about the situation that had produced it. As he put it to Earman, a general who does not know what his field forces are doing is not in command.[162]

General Smith determined that all CIA cables should be addressed to the Director and that their distribution should be controlled by a Cable Secretariat located in his own office—the same device that Donovan and Magruder had employed. The chief of this secretariat, a man loyal to the Director exclusively, would select from the entire traffic those cables that he thought should be brought immediately to the Director's attention.[a]

General Smith had such a man in mind. He was Major Gordon Butler, USA, who had served Smith in the JCS Secretariat and in the general staff secretariats at AFHQ and at SHAEF. Smith arranged for Butler's prompt assignment to duty with the CIA. When Butler reported to him on 22 July 1952, his instructions were brief: "You know what I want. Any questions? See Jack Earman for anything that you need."[164]

General McClelland was in accord with General Smith's purpose, but

---

[a]Evidently at Smith's direction, McClelland submitted to Smith, on 9 July 1952, a plan for such a Cable Secretariat.[163]

the clandestine services strongly resented having their messages read by any outsider. In particular, they resisted revealing the identities concealed by the pseudonyms they used, without which their messages were usually unintelligible. This problem was eventually overcome, but only after General Smith had made some explosive remarks on the subject.[165]

When the clandestine services were organized, on 1 August 1952, under the direct control of the DDP, the Office of Communications was removed from DDP control and attached directly to the Office of the Director. The Cable Secretariat remained a separate entity within the office of the Director, under the supervision of the Executive Assistant rather than the Director of Communications.[166a]

THE HISTORICAL STAFF

In December 1950 William Jackson told his morning staff meeting that he wanted a history of the Agency prepared on a current basis, for the information of future Directors regarding the evolution of the organization.[167] A month later Jackson had developed this idea further. A Historical Branch would be formed in OIC. It not only would prepare and keep current a history of the CIA but also would prepare the Agency's annual reports and any speeches to be delivered by senior officials and would handle any necessary relations with the press.[168] Thus, Jackson conceived the CIA's interest in its own history to be closely related to public relations.[b]

Jackson's idea was put into effect in May 1951, when Lieutenant Colonel Chester Hansen, USAF, was appointed Assistant to the Director and Chief of the Historical Staff.[170] Thus, that Staff was located in the office of the Director rather than in OIC.

Hansen was a public relations man who had entered the Army in 1941 and had served for nine years as an aide to General Omar Bradley, in the 28th Division, II Corps, First Army, 13th Army Group, Veterans Administration, and Joint Chiefs of Staff. He was the ghostwriter of General

---

[a]Smith's point having been made, on 3 February 1955 the Office of Communications was subordinated to the new DDS. The Cable Secretariat remains (1971) within the office of the Director.

[b]Jackson's initial choice of a man for this work was Shane MacCarthy,[169] forty-two, a native of County Cork who must have kissed the Blarney Stone before leaving Ireland. MacCarthy had no qualifications as a historian but was a master of showmanship. He became Orientations Officer in the Office of Training.

Bradley's book, *A Soldier's Story*. That book went to press in March 1951[171]—which made Hansen available to Jackson in May.[a]

Hansen did not himself attempt to write the desired history of the CIA. He engaged the services of Arthur Darling, fifty-nine, head of the history department of the Phillips Academy at Andover, as a professional consultant to help to set up the project.[b] Darling came to the CIA in October 1951 on leave of absence from Andover until June 1952. He hoped, however, to remain permanently as the CIA Historian.[172]

After months of consultation between Hansen and Darling, it was Jackson who defined what the character of the history should be. It should be a "historical audit" of the "evolution of the concept of a national intelligence system," for the information of the President, the NSC, and the IAC as well as the DCI, so that all might learn from the Agency's successes and failures. The history should "pay close attention in historical perspective to any weaknesses in the organization and defects of administration that might emerge."[173] Darling understood that to mean that the history should set forth the horrors of the pre-Smith period in order to justify and applaud the reforms of the Smith era.[174] In short, the desired history was to be evaluative and instructive, not to say hortatory.

General Smith's comment on that idea was to say that what *he* wanted was a "dispassionate chronological history" (by which he presumably meant a strictly objective narrative). If Darling was not the man to do that, someone of the stature of S.L.A. Marshall should be engaged to do it.[175c] However, Darling's leave of absence from Andover was extended until June 1953, and he went to work on the history as instructed by Jackson.[d]

Hansen was not much interested in the Historical Staff. As Assistant to the DCI, he handled such public relations problems as the CIA then had. He was not much employed and, in July 1952, asked for a more interesting CIA assignment overseas.[176] Instead, he was released to the Air Force in October, and Colonel Stanley Grogan, USA (Ret.), was appointed to the position thus made vacant.[177] General Smith had known

---

[a]Jackson had known Hansen at 12th Army Group, of course, and also in Washington since October 1950. Jackson was in intimate contact with General Bradley's office; he married the General's secretary.

[b]Darling had been Associate Professor of History at Yale.

[c]Brigadier General Samuel Lyman Atwood Marshall was an outstanding military historian. A journalist until 1942 but a veteran of World War I, he had become an Army combat historian. Smith had known him in 1944–45 as the Army's Chief Historian in Europe. By 1952 he had published eight military historical works and had been chief Army historian in Korea.

[d]Jackson may have doubted that a historian of Marshall's stature would serve his purpose.

Grogan as a classmate at the Infantry School in 1931 and as the War Department's first public relations officer, in 1941.[a] Like Hansen, Grogan concerned himself with public relations almost exclusively and paid little attention to the Historical Staff.

Darling accomplished a monumental work in assembling from many scattered sources documents of historical value relating to the pre-Smith period of the CIA's history and in recording interviews with men who had played leading parts during that period. These papers became the basis of the Historical Staff's Historical Collection.[b] Darling's history, however, was not the "dispassionate" narrative that General Smith had wanted. Neither was it the elaboration of the Dulles Report that William Jackson had expected. Darling took as his heroes the embattled DCIs, Vandenberg and Hillenkoetter, and condemned at least by implication all those who had criticized and opposed them, including the NSC Survey Group.[178] When Allen Dulles became aware of that, he was very displeased.[179]

In January 1953 General Smith decided that Darling's services should not be retained beyond expiration of his leave from Andover in June and that Forrest Pogue should be invited to become the CIA Historian.[180] Smith had known Pogue as one of S.L.A. Marshall's military historians in Europe and as the author of the official U.S. history of SHAEF.[c]

That is where Bedell Smith left this matter. To finish the tale, one may add that Pogue indicated a willingness to come to the CIA early in 1954, when he would have completed his contract with the Operations Research Office of the Johns Hopkins University in Heidelberg.[d] Darling was therefore retained until December 1953 to complete his history,[e] but Allen Dulles, the new DCI, decreed that it must be kept under lock and key, to be seen by no one without the Director's express permission.[f]

---

[a]Grogan, age sixty-one in 1952, was a native of Archbald (near Scranton), Pennsylvania. After graduation from high school in 1909, he went to work as a newspaperman, but he obtained a Regular Army commission in 1917. Most of his Army career was spent in press relations work. He had been retired for about a year when General Smith found him to replace Hansen.

[b]Not to be confused with the Historical Intelligence Collection assembled by Walter Pforzheimer.

[c]*The Supreme Command* (Washington, 1954).

[d]Instead of coming to the CIA as had been expected, Dr. Pogue excused himself in March 1954 and accepted an appointment to be Professor of History at Murray State College, Murray, Kentucky. He was a graduate of that college and had been professor of history there before the war.

[e]After retiring from the Agency, Darling lived in Washington for a number of years. He died in Paris in November 1971.

[f]The Darling history is now available through the Historical Staff. Indeed, most of it has

THE INSPECTOR GENERAL

One of General Smith's first acts, on assuming command of the CIA, was to call for a series of briefings on the component offices of the Agency. He followed up these briefings with visits to each office in turn. The General held that a commander should get out of his headquarters and go to see the troops—and be seen by them. He urged his principal lieutenants to follow his example in that respect. In particular, he wanted the DDP, ADPC, and ADSO to make more frequent visits to overseas stations. But Smith did not suppose that such visits would constitute a thorough inspection. For that purpose, he said, the CIA should have one or two full-time inspectors.[181]

Meanwhile, Smith kept his Deputy, William Jackson, busy making surveys[a] of particular offices, notably of OPC, OSO, and OO, the three offices supervised by the DDP. Even after he ceased to be DDCI, Jackson continued this work, as the Director's "Special Assistant and Senior Consultant."[182] Apparently Smith considered Allen Dulles to be too intimately related to the clandestine services to be able to give him an independent and impartial check on them. Thus, William Jackson may be regarded as the CIA's first Inspector General, although he never bore that title.

In June 1951 the employment of Stuart Hedden was under consideration in the CIA.[183b] Jackson thought that he might do to head a certain covert project.[184] Late on a day in September Hedden paid a personal call on General Smith. He was expected to stay about fifteen minutes, but remained closeted with Smith for nearly two hours, well past the close of business. When he finally emerged, he told Earman that he might have upset the General; he had talked back to him.[185] On the contrary, Smith was delighted—few of his associates dared to do that—but Hedden could hardly have gotten away with it if Smith had not been strongly impressed by Hedden's quick intelligence and force of character. Smith told Hedden that a man of his ability ought to be working for the United States Government.[186] He told Earman that Hedden was just the man to be his Inspector.[187]

---

been published in *Studies in Intelligence*. It should be read, however, with cognizance that Allen Dulles considered it a misinterpretation of the history of the pre-Smith period—as does the present author.

[a]This term seems to have been carried over from the title of the NSC Survey Group (1948).

[b]Hedden, fifty-two in 1951, was a native of Newark, New Jersey, and a graduate of Wesleyan University (1919) and Harvard Law School (1921). After practicing law in New York, he had become an investment banker.

On 11 September Smith asked Jackson how Hedden would do as Inspector. Jackson's response was negative; Hedden would need considerable training before he could undertake that role. Smith replied with some umbrage that of course he had assumed that Hedden would have at least six months of training and experience before undertaking such duties.[188] Smith repeated the question on 16 October, and again Jackson's response was negative, although he conceded that he had no doubt of Hedden's character and ability.[189]

Stuart Hedden entered on duty as a Special Assistant to the Director on 30 October 1951 and was immediately associated with Jackson in the "survey" of OO. Their joint report was dated 13 November. Hedden also studied the feasibility of a separate administration for the clandestine services,[a] reporting to Jackson on 26 November, and undertook a Jackson-type "survey" of OCI, reporting on 7 December. Having had this training and experience, he was appointed Inspector General, effective 1 January 1952.[190]

The draft of the order appointing Hedden had designated him as "Inspector, with the rank of Assistant Director." That was a formula that the DCI had used in designating General Harold M. McClelland to be Director of Communications.[191] Smith, however, personally directed that the phrase designating the Inspector an Assistant Director be deleted.[192] He may have considered "Assistant Director" to be a title of command, inappropriate for a staff officer. He certainly considered his Inspector, who regularly attended his meetings with his Deputies, to be of higher personal rank than an Assistant Director.

The status and duties of the Inspector General were never formally defined during Hedden's tenure. General Smith probably assumed that everybody would know what that title meant. He made it clear that Hedden's requests for information were to be treated as requests from the DCI himself, and that Hedden was privileged to short-circuit the chain of command in seeking information. He did not make it clear to Hedden that the responsible officers in the chain of command were entitled to know and respond to whatever Hedden was reporting to Smith on the basis of information thus obtained.

The clandestine services never welcomed prying by any outsider into their affairs. There was notable animosity in the personal relationship between Hedden and Wisner, the DDP. In April 1952 Hedden made the mistake of submitting to Smith two operational recommendations without consulting the responsible officials. Wisner seized the opportunity to raise the general issue with Smith, who responded by enunciating the

---

[a]See pages 88–89.

standard Army doctrine on the subject: the Inspector had no command authority; Smith would not consider any recommendation from him unaccompanied by the comments and recommendations of the responsible officers in the chain of command.[193]

Wisner wanted a confrontation with Hedden in the presence of the DCI. Smith said no, they must first attempt to settle the matter between themselves. (After Wisner had left, he no doubt instructed Hedden privately.) On 13 May 1952 Wisner, Johnston, [name deleted], McClelland, and Hedden met and signed a formal memorandum of understanding regarding correct procedure.[a] In a postscript Hedden expressed disgruntlement that it should have been thought necessary to record in writing anything so obvious.[194]

An adequate definition of Stuart Hedden's functions as Inspector General would be that he was General Smith's personal handyman. He made a formal "survey" of OSI[b] and tours of inspection [one line deleted], but he served also as General Smith's personal agent in several covert matters having nothing to do with inspection.[195]

Stuart Hedden was no respecter of persons. His sharp criticisms antagonized many vested interests in the CIA, especially in the clandestine services.[c] But he retained the confidence of Bedell Smith, who admired his forthright honesty, toughness, and judgment[197]—and he conceived that he was working only for Bedell Smith. His advice to his successor, Lyman Kirkpatrick, was "insist that Allen [Dulles] agree that you are responsible only to him."[198]

Stuart Hedden resigned as soon as it became known that Bedell Smith was leaving the Agency. His letter of resignation stressed that it had always been his intention to leave when Smith did and that no want of confidence in Allen Dulles was to be inferred from his action.[199] He evidently expected that inference to be made. The fact was that he did not think Allen Dulles a good choice for DCI. He would have preferred William Donovan.[200]

---

[a]Frank Wisner was the DDP, of course. Kilbourne Johnston was the ADPC and [name deleted] was his Deputy. [name deleted] was the Acting ADSO, and Harold McClelland the AD, Communications.

[b]See Part Three, page 177.

[c]He held a generally poor opinion of the management of clandestine operations.[196] Smith, who thought that Dulles and Wisner were not being candid with him, must have valued Hedden's independent check on them.

PART THREE

REORGANIZATION
PURSUANT TO NSC 50

VII

THE REORGANIZATION

The Survey Group Report proposes a number of major changes in the internal organization of CIA. . . . We concur in them and in the concept of CIA upon which they are based. However, we recognize that there may be other methods of organization which will accomplish the same objectives.

—NSC 50
1 July 1949

In dutiful compliance with NSC 50, Admiral Hillenkoetter submitted, in August 1949, a plan for the integration of the Office of Policy Coordination (OPC), the Office of Special Operations (OSO), and the [words deleted] Office of Operations (OO), as recommended by the report of the NSC Survey Group.[1] The Department of State never acted on that proposal, which involved the amendment of NSC 10/2 in a way that would have reduced State's control over OPC. Consequently, it was never implemented.

On the other hand, Hillenkoetter's plan for the reorganization of the Office of Reports and Estimates (ORE), reported to the NSC on 27 December 1949,[2] was a transparent attempt to perpetuate the status quo under a specious pretense of compliance.[a] It was implemented, but was without any real effect.

Thus, the organization of the CIA in October 1950, when General Smith relieved Admiral Hillenkoetter, was substantially what it had been

---

[a]See pages 125–26 and Part One, page 47.

in July 1949, when the NSC had directed a radical reorganization, although there had been some few inconsequential changes in nomenclature. That organization is shown in the organizational chart (Figure 1).

General Smith assured the NSC and the IAC that he would proceed forthwith to reorganize the CIA in accordance with NSC 50, except that he would not merge OPC and OSO.[a] Smith looked to his Deputy, William Jackson, to prepare for his approval the specific plans required to carry out this commitment.[b] The new organizational structure that Jackson and Smith devised is shown in Figure 2.[c]

---

[a]See Part Two, pages 57 and 62.

[b]See Part Two, page 57.

[c]This chart, dated 19 January 1951, is of curious interest in that it shows the DDCI in the position later occupied by the DDI—that is, with no jurisdiction over the DDP and the DDA but in direct command of the six "DDI Offices." William Jackson did function as DDI while he was DDCI, but was not confined to that role. Allen Dulles did not function as DDI when he became DDCI in August 1951. Thus, the chart is not a true reflection of the facts in particular.

Fig. 1. Central Intelligence Agency (Organization as of 1 October 1950)

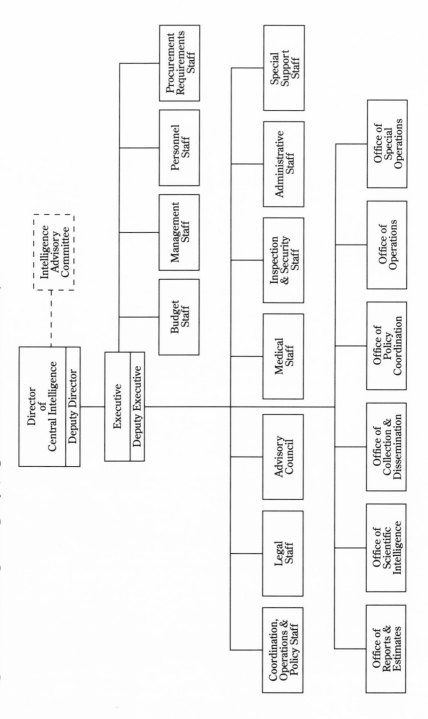

Fig. 2. Central Intelligence Agency

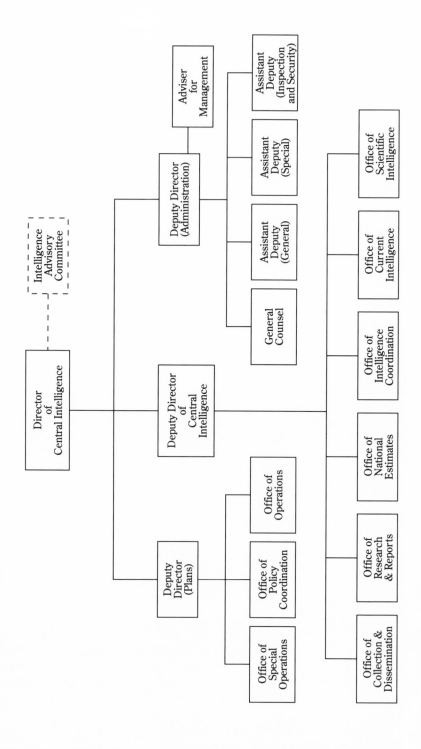

VIII

THE OFFICE OF INTELLIGENCE COORDINATION

To devise plans for the interdepartmental coordination of intelligence activities had been from the first an explicit function of the Director of Central Intelligence.[3] Admiral Souers created for that purpose a Central Planning Staff composed of officers seconded from the several departments,[4] not as instructed representatives but as men familiar with departmental interests and capabilities, working for the DCI. Vandenberg (Wright) abolished that staff by reassigning its members and then created another based on the same principle. It was grandiloquently styled the Interdepartmental Coordinating and Planning Staff (ICAPS).[5]

ICAPS was never able to accomplish much in the way of effective interdepartmental coordination. There were two reasons for its failure. One was that its members had had little or no practical experience as intelligence officers; they did not really understand the business. The other was the determined resistance of the IAC and its representative Standing Committee to the constant effort by ICAPS to assert the superior authority and prerogative of the DCI. The energies of ICAPS were spent in haggling with the Standing Committee over the verbal terms of draft directives that in the end were compromised into ambiguity or meaninglessness. Thus, frustrated in its true function, ICAPS turned instead toward giving direction to the line offices of the CIA in the name of the DCI, and supposedly in the interest of interdepartmental coordination.[6]

The NSC Survey Group noted, in 1948, that the responsibility of the ICAPS members (whether to the DCI or to the departments) was ambiguous, that they were not well qualified for their task, and that they tended to interfere with the operations of the line offices. It recommended that ICAPS be "reconstituted" as a staff responsible solely to the DCI and devoted solely to interdepartmental coordination.[7] That recommendation excited derision in the CIA, and even in the IAC, because that was what ICAPS was already supposed to be. Its only effect was to cause Hillenkoetter to delete "Interdepartmental" from the name of ICAPS, making it COAPS (the DCI's personal staff for "Coordination, Operations, and Policy"). That change enabled the same incompetent group to interfere even more readily in the affairs of the line offices of CIA—but the sands were already running out.[a]

Smith and Jackson had no use whatever for ICAPS, alias COAPS. They even refused to receive the respects of James Reber, the newly appointed Chief of COAPS.[b] For a time Jackson himself performed the functions of COAPS, personally planning the reorganization of the CIA and discussing its terms and implications with the members of the IAC, especially the State Department member. Jackson even functioned personally as the Secretary of the IAC, an incidental duty of the Chief of COAPS.

In early November (after about a month in office) Jackson summoned Reber and told him that General Smith wished to appoint an ambassador or a general to his position. If Reber were to be retained, however, how would he propose to proceed? Reber replied that, first, he would resign from the Department of State; the chief of the DCI's coordinating staff should be the DCI's own men. Second, he would request the immediate relief of all other members of COAPS, except any whom he might choose to retain and who might be willing to transfer to the CIA; the entire staff should be the DCI's men. Reber managed also to suggest that in the Committee Secretariat he had had more practical experience in interdepartmental coordination than any ambassador or general would be likely to have had.[8]

Jackson was impressed by Reber's good sense, right attitude, and address. He abolished COAPS on 1 December 1950 and on 13 December announced that Reber would serve as Acting Assistant Director for Intelligence Coordination and Secretary of the IAC. In May 1951 General Smith struck the "Acting" from Reber's title.

The Office of Intelligence Coordination consisted only of Reber and two assistants[9]; it was really a small staff section rather than a line office. Reber took the position that working liaison and coordination with the

---

[a]ICAPS became COAPS on 1 July 1950, only three months before General Smith took office as DCI.

[b]Reber, age thirty-nine in 1950, was a native of Elizabethtown, Pennsylvania, and held a Ph.D. in International Relations from the University of Chicago (1939). He entered the Department of State in 1943 and in 1950 was Chief of the Committee Secretariat in the office of the Secretary. State sent him to relieve Prescott Childs as Chief of COAPS on 1 October 1950, only six days before Smith and Jackson took office.

departmental agencies was properly a function of the line offices directly concerned, rather than of OIC.[10] With regard to problems of coordination requiring IAC action, he convened interdepartmental ad hoc committees with himself in the chair; the Standing Committee of the IAC was abolished.[11] On these occasions Reber followed the example of General Smith's approach to the IAC,[a] recognizing that departmental interests were entitled to consideration and respect. He bore in mind also Jackson's dictum that the CIA was not required to do all the coordinating that was done, so long as the DCI was in a position to assure himself that it was being done well.[12b]

In October 1951 Reber set forth more fully the six principles that governed his approach to interdepartmental coordination. He held that (short of an appeal to the NSC) the CIA must achieve such coordination by leadership, stimulation, and persuasion and that the primary role and expert knowledge of the substantively responsible agency must be recognized. Actual coordination on specific problems should be decentralized as far as possible to the offices and agencies having functional responsibility, but the DCI must retain a general supervisory role, with the ADIC as his assistant for that purpose. In the end, the effectiveness of interdepartmental coordination would depend on the personal relations of the intelligence chiefs themselves, especially in the IAC. In general, a flexible, practical attitude would be far more effective than a legalistic, doctrinaire approach.[13]

That was sound doctrine. It was also the reverse of what the ICAPS approach had been. In general, it worked well—given the entirely new DCI-IAC relationship that General Smith had created.[c]

On 1 January 1952 the OIC was subordinated to the DDI. Loftus Becker then superseded James Reber as the DCI's principal assistant for interdepartmental intelligence coordination.[d] Becker considered absorbing the small OIC into his personal staff but refrained from doing so, probably in order not to diminish Reber's standing as an Assistant Director, which was of value in his work as an external representative and negotiator.[e]

---

[a]See Part Two, Chapter V.

[b]For an example of the application of this principle in practice, General Smith deferred to the sensitivities of the Pentagon by appointing an Army G-2 officer to be the first Chairman of the Watch Committee (see page 171). ICAPS would have attempted to insist that the chair belonged to the CIA.

[c]An exceptional case is noted in Part Two, pages 72–73.

[d]See Part Two, pages 93–94.

[e]On 1 February 1954 Richard Bissell was appointed Special Assistant to the DCI for Planning and Coordination, and on 1 July 1954 he absorbed the DDI's responsibilities for interdepartmental coordination. OIC was then abolished, and its personnel were transferred from the DDI to the Special Assistant.

IX

THE OFFICE OF NATIONAL ESTIMATES

The other explicit function of the Director of Central Intelligence was to

> accomplish the correlation and evaluation of intelligence relating to the national security, and the appropriate dissemination within the Government of the resulting strategic and national policy intelligence.[14]

That formulation, in the President's letter of 22 January 1946, made it clear that the intelligence to be disseminated was the product of the DCI's correlation and evaluation.[a] The passage was commonly understood to refer only to the production of national intelligence estimates. Any other production of finished intelligence by the CIG/CIA was thought to come under another provision of the President's letter, to perform "services of common concern."[16] This distinction, clear in the minds of Admiral Souers and his colleagues, was lost in General Vandenberg's omnibus Office of Research and Evaluation, alias Reports and Estimates.[b]

THE CENTRAL REPORTS STAFF

To perform this estimating function, Admiral Souers created a Central Reports Staff (CRS) in February 1946, based on Ludwell Montague's plan

---

[a]In the National Security Act of 1947 this language was changed to read "to correlate and evaluate intelligence relating to the national security, and provide for the appropriate dissemination of such intelligence."[15] The revised language was less clear on the point in question, but there was no intent to change the meaning. (See Part One, pages 34–35.)
[b]See Part One, page 28.

for a "National Estimates Staff,ᵃ [words deleted].¹⁷ The immediate task of the CRS was to produce an all-sufficient daily summary of current intelligence, which was what President Truman particularly wanted from his Central Intelligence Group, but it was anticipated that eventually its principal function would be the drafting of national intelligence estimates for DCI-IAB consideration in accordance with the Lovett Report's doctrine—that is, in coordination with departmental representatives, but with a power of decision vested in the Chief, CRS, at his level, and in the DCI at his, subject to the notation of any dissents.ᵇ

The actual strength of the CRS never exceeded [number deleted], and it never got beyond the production of current intelligence. It was never able to obtain from the departments the assignment of men of sufficient experience and judgment to produce thoughtful estimates.ᶜ Consequently, it produced none and thus never set a precedent for the interdepartmental coordination of national intelligence estimates.

THE FAILURE OF ORE

For Souers's concept of a small, select estimates staff dependent on departmental research support, General Vandenberg substituted the concept of an entirely self-sufficient Office of Research and Evaluation with a strength of [number deleted]. Vandenberg's departure, however, arrested the growth of ORE at about [number deleted]. Thus, ORE conformed neither to Souers's concept nor to Vandenberg's. It continued to pretend to the self-sufficiency that Vandenberg had intended it to have, but lacked the manpower and the intellectual resources required to make good that pretension.

There were four reasons for the failure of ORE. One was its lack of a clearly defined and generally understood mission.¹⁸ Another was its lack

---

ᵃThe change in name was probably made to conform to the name of the Central Planning Staff and to allow for the Staff's current intelligence function. It was unfortunate in that it deemphasized its primary estimating function.

ᵇSee Part One, pages 15–17, 19–20, and 24–25. Montague, who had drafted JIC 239/5 and NIA Directives No. 1 and No. 2, was Chief of the Central Reports Staff.

ᶜActually, very few such men were available in the departments. During the war the military intelligence agencies had been manned for the most part by reserve officers who in 1946 were impatient to return to their homes. Similarly, the professorial types in State (in the former R&A Branch of the OSS) were generally impatient to return to their universities. The few qualified men who remained were not being given away to the CIG.

of a pertinently experienced and forceful Assistant Director.[a] A third was the generally poor quality of ORE personnel.[b] When ORE was recruiting toward [number deleted], anybody able to reach the door was admitted, but ORE had little more success than CRS in recruiting men for discernment and mature judgment. The fourth reason for ORE's failure was the hostility and obstructionism of the departmental intelligence agencies, antagonized by Vandenberg and ICAPS.

As Chief of the Intelligence Staff, ORE,[c] Montague strove to carry out the original conception of how national intelligence estimates should be produced, but he was frustrated by Admiral Inglis. Inglis demanded that Vandenberg make Montague stop calling for departmental contributions. He wanted ORE to work for ONI by producing basic intelligence as a "service of common concern." He did not want ONI to have to work for ORE. Vandenberg was delighted to comply with Inglis's demand, for Inglis was providing the CIG's need for independent research capabilities.[20]

When Montague called for the assignment of full-time IAB representatives to the Intelligence Staff, in accordance with NIA Directive No. 2, Admiral Inglis insisted that they could be only part-time "messenger boys."[22][d] These designated representatives not only refused to occupy offices in ORE but even refused to meet occasionally with the Intelligence Staff to discuss terms of reference and draft estimates. At their insistence ORE drafts were sent to them by courier, and after intolerable delays they sent back the generally scornful and captious written comments of the departmental analysts. Thus, they functioned only as post offices between ORE and those analysts.[e] Until July 1948 there was never

---

[a]In order to gain favor in the Department of State, Vandenberg solicited the assignment of a Foreign Service Officer to supersede Montague as ADRE. The senior FSO thus obtained knew nothing of intelligence research or estimates production and had no interest in taking charge of ORE. Within nine months he contrived an escape and was replaced by a State appointee who dared not assert his authority over his branch chiefs. They were seconded by the several departments and in no way beholden to him. Montague remained in ORE as Chief of the Intelligence Staff, 1946–47, and then as Chief, Global Survey Group.[19]

[b]Of course there were individual exceptions to this generalization. In 1950 ONE was well staffed with men selected from ORE, and other ORE men made their mark in other offices.

[c]The Intelligence Staff had charge of all ORE intelligence production until July 1947.

[d]Montague's idea was that, if the IAB representatives participated regularly in the work of the Intelligence Staff, they could and would serve also as advocates of the semi-coordinated ORE draft estimates in their respective agencies, as had the members of the Senior Team of the JIS with respect to JIC estimates.[21]

[e]These representatives were "policy" men without substantive competence to discuss and judge the issues raised by the analysts, even if they had been willing to meet.

any joint discussion of draft estimates such as would have made it possible to achieve mutual understanding and perhaps agreement.[a] ORE accepted as much, or as little, as it pleased of these working-level comments and then sent its unilaterally revised draft to the members of the IAC separately for concurrence, dissent, or comment.[b] Even the acceptance of all working-level proposals did not guarantee the concurrence of an IAC member, who might raise issues never before mentioned. Normally the IAC did not meet to discuss the substance of an estimate.[c] ORE either adjusted its text to satisfy each IAC member individually or elected to accept a dissent. The ADRE rarely saw the text of an estimate until it was disseminated in print. The DCI never did.[25]

The NSC Survey Group condemned ORE for failing to enlist the effective participation of the IAC agencies in the production of national intelligence estimates.[26] It was Admiral Inglis and his colleagues in the IAC who refused such participation when ORE sought it. The resulting procedures for the "coordination" of estimates could hardly have been more rigid, indirect, ineffective, and frustrating to ORE. They provided neither true independence of action and judgment for ORE, as a national agency free of departmental bias, nor a true collective effort in the national interest.

Despite these hindrances, ORE did produce, in response to NSC requirements, some few estimates as well considered and well coordinated as any later produced by ORE.[d] Such estimates, however, were certainly not typical of ORE intelligence production.

After the Intelligence Staff was dissolved in July 1947, no one exercised effective central direction and control over the intelligence production of ORE.[e] Each branch chief suited himself in that regard. The result was a diversion of effort away from production addressed to the level of the

---

[a]The two exceptions to this statement were a meeting with IAB representatives on ORE-1 (see Part One, page 29)[23] and the joint ad hoc committee convoked in March 1948 (see Part Two, page 65).[24] After the adoption of DCID-3/1, 8 July 1948, such working-level meetings were held regularly, but by that time the attitude of mutual disregard described in this paragraph had become firmly established.

[b]This procedure had been prescribed by Admiral Inglis (see Part One, page 30).

[c]It did meet for this purpose on two occasions. In both cases the circumstances were extraordinary.

[d]These estimates were produced under Montague's direction and control as the CIA member of the NSC Staff and therefore the attorney for the NSC Staff within ORE.[27] William Jackson seems not to have been aware of them. In the report of the NSC Survey Group he cited the work of the joint ad hoc committee of March 1948 as the only example of a properly prepared national intelligence estimate.[28]

[e]The Assistant Director assumed the functions of the Chief, Intelligence Staff, but did not exercise them.[29]

President and the NSC, a standard that the Intelligence Staff had endeavored to maintain, and into current and descriptive reporting at a level more commensurate with the limited capabilities of ORE's inexperienced analysts. Some of this trend was responsive to new requirements for intelligence support for OPC and the NSRB,[a] but most of ORE's intelligence production was self-initiated. It included a proliferation of duplicatory current intelligence publications intended only for internal or, at most, for working-level distribution. These publications were said to be needed in order to provide training for junior analysts. They also helped morale by giving every analyst the satisfaction of seeing his work published, regardless of whether it was worthy of high-level consideration. The greater part of ORE's work came to be done for no better reason than its own satisfaction. Moreover, even its more serious undertakings tended increasingly to be published as uncoordinated intelligence memoranda, in order to avoid the vexations and delays of interdepartmental coordination. These "memoranda" were generally descriptive rather than analytical in content; some of them ran to as many as one hundred pages. Finally, most of those papers that ORE did coordinate as national estimates were actually a mélange of current and descriptive reporting with little, if any, analytical or estimative content.[30]

The comment of the NSC Survey Group on this situation was that ORE had conspicuously failed to produce national intelligence estimates and instead had busied itself with producing "miscellaneous reports and summaries which by no stretch of the imagination could be considered national estimates.[31b]

FIVE PROPOSALS FOR REMEDIAL ACTION

The situation described above still existed when Bedell Smith and William Jackson took office in October 1950. They were then cognizant of five separate proposals for remedial action, made by John Bross, William Jackson, John Magruder, Ludwell Montague, and William Donovan (in chronological order). These proposals were similar in most respects, although there were significant differences among them. All recom-

---

[a]The National Security Resources Board, the Chairman of which was a statutory member of the NSC, depended on ORE for the satisfaction of its extensive requirements for intelligence support.

[b]ORE held that anything that it chose to produce was, ipso facto, national intelligence.

mended the creation of a well-qualified body to be concerned solely with the production of national intelligence estimates. Each contributed in some respect to the solution devised by Smith and Jackson—the creation of the Office of National Estimates.

During the summer of 1948 John Bross[a] investigated the CIA for the Eberstadt Committee[b] and came to the following conclusion:

> The greatest need in the CIA is [for] the establishment at a high level of a small group of highly capable people, freed from administrative detail, to concentrate upon intelligence evaluation. The Director and his Assistants have had to devote so large a portion of their time to administration that they have been unable to give sufficient time to analysis and evaluation. A small group of mature men of the highest talents, having full access to all information, might well be released completely from routine and set to thinking about intelligence only. Many of the greatest failures in intelligence have not been failures in collection, but failures in analyzing and evaluating correctly the information available.[32c]

Bross's concept was reflected in the recommendation of the Eberstadt Committee that there be established in the CIA "at the top echelon, an evaluation board or section composed of competent and experienced personnel who would have no administrative responsibilities and whose duties would be confined solely to intelligence evaluation."[34]

Bedell Smith had certainly read this recommendation by the Eberstadt Committee. It is likely that he had read also Bross's more extended treatment of the subject.[d]

The remedy proposed by William Jackson in the report of the NSC Survey Group was similar, though less explicit. It was premised upon a return to the distinction understood in early 1946, between the production of national intelligence estimates and the performance of "services

---

[a]Bross, a New York lawyer, had been in the OSS. [sentence deleted] From 9 September 1963 until his retirement in January 1971 he was Deputy to the DCI for National Intelligence Programs Evaluation (NIPE).

[b]The Commission on Organization of the Executive Branch of the Government ("the Hoover Commission") established a Committee on National Security Organization headed by Ferdinand Eberstadt. That Committee's principal recommendation was for the creation of the Department of Defense.

[c]Bross had consulted Montague. His conception of a small group of mature men released from administrative responsibilities and set to thinking about the substance of intelligence was derived from Montague's conception of the role of the Global Survey Group within ORE.[33]

[d]See pages 59 and 130.

of common concern."[a] Out of ORE there should be created two bodies: "a small, high-level Estimates Division," concerned solely with the production and coordination of national estimates, and a "Research and Reports Division" to perform such research services as it might be agreed could best be performed centrally. The remainder of ORE's activities—and personnel—should be discarded.[35]

The text of the Survey Group's report shows that, when Jackson proposed this "small, high-level Estimates Division," he had in mind the "small organization of highly qualified individuals" that Admiral Souers had intended the Central Reports Staff to be.[36] Montague had spent an afternoon with Jackson explaining his "National Estimates Staff" (CRS) concept and how it had been lost in ORE.[37]

Montague was pleased, of course, when the NSC Survey Group adopted his proposal, first made in 1946,[b] but he feared that the Group's emphasis on the "collective responsibility" of the IAC would nullify the Lovett doctrine[c] and reduce national estimates to the level of joint estimates.[39] In approving NSC 50, however, the NSC rejected the idea of "collective responsibility" while endorsing the idea of "a small, high-level Estimates Division" and a separate "Research and Reports Division."[40]

The direction given by the NSC could have been met by making the Global Survey Group of ORE the nucleus of a "National Estimates Staff" directly subordinate to the DCI—which is, in simple terms, what finally was done in November 1950.[d] Within ORE it was generally supposed that that was what the NSC Survey Group had intended. Admiral Hillenkoetter, however, left it to ORE to decide how to comply with the NSC's direction[e]—and ORE had no interest in reforming itself.[41]

The "organizational realignment" that the ADRE proposed, and that ICAPS and Hillenkoetter accepted without question, was designed to preserve ORE's existing structure and practices while pretending to comply with NSC 50. Within the [number deleted] regional divisions of ORE,[f] the editors, whose function it was to render into acceptable English the scribblings of the analysts, were solemnly declared to be divisional "estimates staffs" producing "high-level estimates" (as well as all the other miscellaneous publications of their divisions). The Assistant Director's routine administrative meeting with his division chiefs was

---

[a]See page 119.

[b]See page 119. Since then Montague had proposed the same plan three times—in October 1946, April 1947, and August 1947—without effect.[38]

[c]See Part One, page 24.

[d]See page 136.

[e]See Part One, page 47.

[f]These divisions had previously been called branches, as on page 122.

declared to be the "Estimates Production Board" (although it never considered the substance of any estimate). Three odd elements of ORE were declared to be the "Central Research Group" (although these disparate elements never had a common chief and never functioned as a group).[42a] Thus, the prescribed words were used, but nothing whatever was changed.[b]

The CIA's obvious refusal to comply with the intent of NSC 50 as regards ORE, while pretending to have done so, provoked John Magruder's proposals, alias "the Webb staff study."[c] Magruder's draft NSC directive provided for the establishment in the CIA (not in ORE) of a "National Intelligence Group" to be composed of a "National Estimates Staff" and a "Current Intelligence Staff." The strength of the group was not to exceed [number deleted] of whom no more than [number deleted] might be from the departmental intelligence agencies; the rest would be CIA employees. The chief of the group, representing the DCI, would be advised and assisted by full-time representatives of the members of the IAC. These IAC representatives would play an active part in framing terms of reference, obtaining responsive and timely departmental contributions, and reviewing draft estimates. The members of the IAC would themselves participate actively in advising the DCI on the initiation and adoption of estimates.[44]

Magruder's plan would certainly have satisfied the requirement of NSC 50 for a small estimates office distinctly separated from any CIA research activity. Incidentally, it was in effect a revival of Admiral Souers's projected Central Reports Staff, which would have had both current intelligence and estimates branches under a chief advised by full-time IAB representatives.[45] Thus, Magruder's plan may have been derived from NIA Directive No. 2 and CIG Administrative Order No. 3, although Magruder was certainly capable of devising an identical plan for himself. Montague's plan of 1946 and Magruder's plan of 1950 were both derived from a common source, the known intent of JIC 239/5, JCS 1181/5, and the President's letter of 22 January 1946.

John Magruder had been a strong advocate of JIC 239/5. He was probably responsible for Robert Lovett's exposition of the doctrine that the DCI should have the deciding voice in the IAC.[d] He was not an enemy of the DCI's prerogative—rather the contrary—but he was outraged by the contumacy of the CIA as represented by ORE, ICAPS, and

---

[a][three-line note deleted]
[b]Montague dissociated himself in writing from any responsibility for this palpable fraud.[43]
[c]See Part One, pages 48–49.
[d]See Part One, pages 21 and 24.

Hillenkoetter. That outrage no doubt affected the tone and style of his original staff study. The "corrected copy" (from which the preceding paragraph is derived) was probably truer to his essential thought. He was making an earnest effort to obtain for the departmental agencies an effective voice in national intelligence estimates, but also to ensure that they made an effective contribution to such estimates—which they had not been doing. Because he sought an active role for the departmental agencies, he was denounced by the CIA as an advocate of the "board of directors" concept[46]—which he certainly was not. Such was the state of mutual sensitivity and incomprehension that existed between the CIA and the departmental agencies when General Smith took office.

In late August 1950 Lawrence Houston presented both versions of Magruder's staff study to General Smith as evidence of a current effort on the part of State and Defense to impose their will on the DCI by curbing his independence of judgment.[47] On 3 October Jackson recommended Magruder's "corrected" version to Smith as "sound."[48] Smith adopted the essential substance of Magruder's proposal, though with important variations.

One of William Jackson's first acts as DDCI was to call on DeForest Van Slyck for a plan for an office of estimates. Van Slyck was a personal friend of Jackson. He was also Montague's deputy as Chief of the Global Survey Group, ORE. He invited the participation of Theodore Babbitt, ADRE, as a matter of courtesy, and of Montague, because he knew that Montague already had a plan in mind.

What Jackson got on 10 October 1950 was the sixth edition of Montague's plan of 1946 for a "National Estimates Staff." As such, this plan was essentially identical with Magruder's, but it went into greater organizational and procedural detail. In particular, Montague elaborated every procedural step in the production of a national intelligence estimate, from the perception of an NSC Staff requirement through final adoption by the DCI with the advice and concurrence (or dissent) of the members of the IAC. And Montague set forth explicitly the Lovett doctrine,[a] as Magruder had not.[49]

Furthermore, Montague warned Jackson that in the circumstances of 1950 this plan could not be made effective unless and until positive action was taken to ensure the satisfaction of four prior conditions, to wit:

(1) Action to make sure of the availability of research support from the departmental agencies adequate as to both timeliness and content. "This condition cannot be met at present."

---

[a]See Part One, page 24.

(2) The establishment of a research office in the CIA capable of providing like support in fields of "common concern" (scientific, economic, geographical).

(3) The recruitment of requisite senior personnel. "The contemplated Office cannot be adequately manned with personnel now in CIA."

(4) Thorough indoctrination of the IAC agencies in the new cooperative concept and a new start in relations with them. "This plan will not work except on a basis of mutual confidence and cooperation in the national interest."[50]

Montague's plan provided the basis for the procedure adopted by the IAC on 20 October[a] and for the initial organization of the National Estimates Staff[b]—but not for the Board of National Estimates. His conditions were met during the next few months, except the first, which was only half met. The departmental agencies became willing to render research support, but the doubtful reliability of their contributions remained a continuing problem.

On 13 October 1950 William Donovan urged upon Bedell Smith, apparently not for the first time, the importance of establishing in the CIA an "Evaluation Group" composed of men of "experience and imagination and constructive intellect." Donovan suggested that the group might consist of a mature scholar (for example, William Langer), a strategist familiar with the uses and capabilities of all of the various military services, a scientist with current knowledge of new inventions, and two or three broad-gauged men of affairs. (No professional intelligence officers need apply.) A "working committee" familiar with "the skills of research and analysis" would "collate the information" for submission to the group, but "final evaluation" would be the group's responsibility. To impose that duty on the analysts would be "like a cashier being his own auditor."[51c]

Donovan conceived of this "Evaluation Group" as being at the apex of a CIA "R&A Branch" obviously analogous to the R&A Branch in the OSS—or to a properly manned and competent ORE! It should be remembered that William Donovan never had any use whatever for the interde-

---

[a]See Part Two, page 68.

[b]See pages 136–37.

[c]In August 1941, when Donovan established the Research and Analysis Branch, COI (later OSS), he put it under the direction of a collegial body of eminent scholars called the Board of Analysts. He probably intended this board to review and approve the intelligence production of R&A, but it never functioned in that way.[52] Donovan's proposal of 13 October 1950 may have been a modified revival of his original idea of such a board.

partmental coordination of estimates—in contrast to William Jackson, for whom such coordination was the primary consideration.

In arguing for the "collective responsibility" of the IAC, Jackson contended that no one man could bear sole responsibility for a national intelligence estimate. Bedell Smith could and did accept such personal responsibility—but he may have seen in Donovan's proposal a way to obtain for himself the reassurance of the collective judgment of a highly qualified group independent of the IAC, free of departmental bias or other institutional predilections[a] and dedicated solely to the service of the DCI in his role as the deciding voice in national estimates.[b] Bedell Smith never imposed his personal view on any estimate, but on one notable occasion he did adopt, as his personal position, the position recommended to him by his board, in preference to the majority view of the IAC.[53c]

THE BOARD OF NATIONAL ESTIMATES

At his first formal meeting with the IAC, held on 20 October 1950, General Smith announced that, at the earliest practicable date, he would establish in the CIA an Office of National Estimates. In his judgment (and intention) that office would become "the heart of the Central Intelligence Agency and of the national intelligence machinery."[54] It would include a "panel" of five or six outstanding men. Smith was trying to get Admiral Leslie Stevens[d] to head the panel and General Clarence Huebner[e] to be a member of it, possibly the head if Stevens were not available.[55f]

---

[a]Such as, for example, a predilection in favor of information collected by OSO or of the findings of OSI's research.

[b]Smith can have had no other reason to create the Board of National Estimates. The interdepartmental coordination of opinion contemplated by Jackson could have been accomplished without it. The creation of the board implied the exercise of independent judgment by the DCI.

[c]See page 145.

[d]Stevens was then Deputy Director of the Joint Staff for Subsidiary Plans, a position that he proved to be unwilling to leave. Smith had known him as Naval Attaché in Moscow.

[e]At the time of his retirement in 1950, Huebner was the commanding general of all U.S. forces in Europe. Smith had known him as the forceful combat commander of the 1st Division and V Corps.

[f]Jackson omitted any reference to this "panel" in his official minutes of that meeting—which suggests that he did not want to emphasize the idea to the members of the IAC. Smith's statement was recorded, however, in Colonel Howze's notes for General Bolling. Howze seems to have been more impressed by the names of Stevens and Huebner than by the significance of the creation of such a "panel."

The "panel" was, of course, the Board of National Estimates. Smith's announcement regarding it on 20 October evidently reflected his adoption of the recommendation in Donovan's letter of 13 October.[a] But when Jackson explained the idea to Montague a few days later, he used the language of Bross's report to the Eberstadt Committee in 1948.[b] Montague was struck by that because it was also the language of his own description of an ideal Global Survey Group, written in 1947. Thus, the idea of the Board of National Estimates was derived from both Donovan and Bross.

It was this idea that made the Office of National Estimates significantly different from, and superior to, any organization that had yet been devised for the production of intelligence estimates for use at the highest level of government. Indeed, more than twenty years later, the Board of National Estimates, as a group of experienced senior officers freed from all administrative responsibilities, distractions, and biases, in order to concentrate on the substance of intelligence, is still (1971) unique in all the world.

On 20 October 1950 General Smith had Leslie Stevens or else Clarence Huebner in mind to head this board, but in the event it was William Langer who was appointed to be Assistant Director for National Estimates and Chairman of the Board of National Estimates.[c] Before 20 October, Smith had been interested in obtaining Langer's services in some unspecified capacity, presumably in ONE; Donovan's letter of 13 October had been prompted by a telephonic inquiry from Smith regarding Langer.[56] Who, then, had proposed Langer to Smith? Donovan evidently had not, although he heartily seconded the nomination. Neither had William Jackson, who had a different idea.[d] It might have been Allen Dulles or Park Armstrong.

Langer, fifty-four in 1950, was a native of Boston with a Ph.D. from Harvard University (1923). Since 1936 he had been Coolidge Professor of History at Harvard. He was a member of the Board of Analysts, COI, from 1941 to 1942, and Director of the Research and Analysis Branch, OSS, from 1942 to 1946.[e] For two months in 1946 he was Special Assistant to the Secretary of State and the State Department member of the Intelligence Advisory Board.

---

[a]The number of members specified (five or six) was identical with the number suggested by Donovan.

[b]See page 124.

[c]Stevens was unwilling to accept the position. Huebner would come only as a consultant. That status was then deemed necessary in order to protect his military retired pay and perquisites.

[d]See page 131.

[e]Including seven months after R&A's transfer to State.

Langer was embarrassed by Smith's invitation to come to the CIA. He had just returned to Harvard after a nine-year absence;[a] he was unwilling to ask for further leave. Smith, however, appealed directly to the President of the University, stressing, no doubt, the state of national emergency and the possible imminence of World War III.[b] Grudgingly, Langer was granted leave for one more year.[57] He took office on 8 November. The establishment of ONE was formally announced on 13 November. Until 22 November, however, Montague remained in charge of the production of national intelligence estimates.[58]

Bedell Smith took a great personal interest in the Board of National Estimates, selecting its members himself with care. (They were to be the counsellors on whom he would rely in his lonely responsibility for the substance of national estimates.) He frequently consulted their judgment, apart from their formal submission of estimates, and he probed to discover whether any significant divergence of opinion existed among them, concealed by their consensus.[59]

In addition to Huebner and Langer, three other men were designated from the beginning to be members of the Board of National Estimates. They were Sherman Kent, Ludwell Montague, and DeForest Van Slyck. Montague and Van Slyck were already on deck. Kent was in Washington as a consultant as early as 20 November,[60] but his obligations to Yale University prevented him from accepting a full-time appointment until 12 January 1951.

Kent, forty-seven in 1950, was a native of Chicago, had a Ph.D. from Yale University, and was Professor of History at Yale. He had been a section and division chief under Langer in the R&A Branch of the OSS and Langer's deputy and successor as director of intelligence research in State. During the fall of 1946 he was a member of the faculty at the National War College. During the first nine months of 1947 he wrote *Strategic Intelligence* as a Guggenheim Fellow.[61]

There is reason to believe that Kent had been Jackson's choice to be Assistant Director for National Estimates but that Jackson's intention had been temporarily frustrated by Smith's appointment of Langer. Jackson never approved of Langer.[62] He esteemed Kent as an outstanding authority on intelligence.[63c] When Kent reported for full-time duty in

---

[a]Since 1946 he had been working on *The Challenge of Isolation* and *The Undeclared War* for the Council on Foreign Relations.

[b]This appeal had been used by President Truman to persuade Smith himself to become DCI. Smith used it to persuade several reluctant men to come to his aid at the CIA. (See Part Two, pages 56 and 57.)

[c]They became acquainted in 1949, when Jackson reviewed *Strategic Intelligence* for the *New York Times.* Jackson opened that book with prejudice, expecting nothing much from a

January, he was made Deputy Assistant Director with Jackson's promise of the eventual succession.[64] Kent did succeed Langer as Assistant Director, on 3 January 1952.[a]

Ludwell Montague, forty-three in 1950, was a native of Richmond, a graduate of the Virginia Military Institute, and had a Ph.D. from Duke University. He had been Assistant Professor of History at V.M.I. when called to active duty in Army G-2 in 1940. He was the first Secretary of the U.S. JIC from 1941 to 1943 and senior Army member of the JIS from 1943 to 1945; Assistant Director, CIG, in 1946; and Chief of the Intelligence Staff, ORE, from 1946 to 1947, and of the Global Survey Group, ORE, from 1947 to 1950. He had also been the CIA member of the NSC Staff from 1947 to 1950.[65]

Concurrently with his appointment to the Board, Montague was continued as the CIA member of the NSC Staff. That had the advantage of keeping the Board directly informed of the intelligence requirements of the NSC. Montague's particular concern was to ensure that national intelligence estimates were responsive to such requirements. Having just distinguished himself before General Smith by producing ORE 58-50 overnight and six fully coordinated NIEs in four weeks,[b] he became very impatient about the tendency of his academic colleagues to indulge in self-gratifying talk when decision and action were required. They considered their discussions of the profound issues of war and peace to be more important than the immediate needs of the NSC, which they regarded with disdain as merely bureaucratic.[66c]

Van Slyck, fifty-two in 1950, was a native of New York City and had a Ph.D. from Yale University. After nine years as a member of the Yale history faculty, he quit the academic world in 1929 to seek his fortune in investment banking. Eventually he became a partner in Fahnestock and Company, in charge of economic research. From May 1942 to July 1945 he served in A-2, at one time as chief of current intelligence and ultimately as a Far East specialist and estimator. During the last three months of his military service, July–September 1945, he was an execu-

professor and less from one who had served in the OSS. He was agreeably surprised and greatly impressed. Thereafter Jackson excepted Kent from his generally poor opinion of professors.

[a]Kent held that office for sixteen years, until his retirement on 1 January 1968. Langer became one of the "Princeton Consultants" (see pages 135–36). He resigned that position in 1963, when he perceived that there might be a conflict of interest between it and his position as a member of the President's Foreign Intelligence Advisory Board.

[b]See Part Two, pages 65–66 and 69–70.

[c]See pages 140 and 145–46. Montague remained a member of the Board for twenty years, until his retirement on 31 July 1970.

tive assistant to the Commanding General, AAF, concerned with demobilization plans.

After these wartime experiences Van Slyck found it hard to settle down to humdrum investment banking. In March 1946 Kingman Douglass, then DDCI, persuaded him to come to the CIG. Thereafter he served as Montague's deputy, generally minding the store in the CIG/CIA while Montague went off to the NSC Staff and elsewhere. Jackson is likely to have selected Van Slyck for the Board, not as an experienced intelligence officer but as one whom he had known in New York as a "man of affairs."[a] He made an outstanding contribution as a remarkably perceptive critic of other men's drafts. He was particularly concerned to distinguish between what was reasonably well supported by evidence and what was mere surmise.[67b]

Lieutenant General Clarence Huebner, sixty-two in 1950, reported for duty on 19 December as a consultant.[c] He was a native of Kansas who had enlisted as a private soldier in 1910, had been commissioned in 1916, and had proved himself to be a forceful combat commander on D-day in Normandy. Personally esteemed by his colleagues, he had little to contribute to their discussions, but was useful in other ways. As a distinguished soldier, he enjoyed the confidence of the JCS as well as the DCI; he had privileged access to U.S. military information that would otherwise have been inaccessible to the Board.[d] And if any IAC representatives from the Pentagon ever got out of hand, a growl from General Huebner was sufficient to restore good order and military discipline.[68e]

Calvin Hoover, fifty-three in 1950, was the sixth member of the Board to report in, on 20 December. A native of Illinois with a Ph.D. from the University of Wisconsin, he had been Professor of Economics at Duke University since 1927. He had served with Langer in the R&A Branch, OSS, from 1941 to 1944 and after that with the U.S. Group, Control Council, Germany, in 1945. During 1948 he was Chief of Economic Intelligence for the Economic Cooperation Administration in Europe. As a distinguished student of Soviet as well as German affairs, Hoover had a substantial contribution to make, but he remained a member of the Board for only eight months.[f]

---

[a]See page 135.

[b]Van Slyck remained a member of the Board for ten years, until his retirement on 29 October 1960.

[c]During General Smith's time, all of the military members of the Board were in this status, as was then deemed to be necessary in order to protect their retired pay and perquisites.

[d]See Part Five, page 246.

[e]Huebner remained a member of the Board until 30 June 1954, when he was sixty-six.

[f]Hoover resigned on 31 August 1951 but then became one of the "Princeton Consultants" (see page 135). He resigned that position in December 1969, when he was seventy-two.

The seventh member to arrive, on 8 January 1951, was Maxwell Foster, a Boston lawyer esteemed by Jackson as a skillful drafter and also, no doubt, as a practical "man of affairs." He soon came to resent what he regarded as Langer's tendency to override his colleagues, himself in particular,[69] and resigned on 30 June 1951, after less than six months.

Raymond Sontag, fifty-three in 1950, was the eighth member of the Board to report for duty, on 16 January 1951. He was a native of Chicago, with a Ph.D. from the University of Pennsylvania, and Professor of History at the University of California at Berkeley.[a] He was a specialist in German foreign relations, particularly Nazi–Soviet relations. From 1946 to 1949 he had been Chief of the German War Documents Project in the Department of State.

Sontag was magisterial in his coordination of national intelligence estimates. He conducted the meeting with the IAC representatives as though it were a seminar and the representatives his students. Any of them who attempted to stick to his departmental brief was made to look like an idiot. Having thus led all to concur in his own conclusions, Sontag then went before the IAC as *their* spokesman—and let no ignorant major general dare to quibble with the agreed conclusions of the substantive experts! General Smith must have inwardly enjoyed watching Sontag overawe his IAC colleagues. He never lifted a finger to protect them from the professor.[b]

When Sherman Kent became Assistant Director, in January 1952, Sontag was made his deputy.[c]

Sontag's appointment completed the original Board of National Estimates. In contrast to Donovan's prescription (one scholar, one strategist, one scientist, two or three "men of affairs"), Smith's original Board consisted of four eminent professors, one distinguished combat commander, one lawyer, and two men experienced in the interdepartmental coordination of intelligence estimates. It should also be noted that five of the eight held doctorates in history—excellent training for the exercise of critical judgment on the basis of incomplete evidence.

The six other men whom Smith subsequently appointed to the Board were Lieutenant General William Morris (April 1952 to August 1952), Vice Admiral Bernard Bieri (June 1951 to May 1953), Ambassador Nelson Johnson (December 1951 to June 1953), Dr. Edgar Hoover (January 1952

---

[a]He had been a member of the history faculty at Princeton from 1924 to 1941.

[b]The author imitated Sontag's IAC technique with some success until Allen Dulles became DCI and put him down.[70]

[c]Sontag resigned from the Board on 20 June 1953 but then became one of the "Princeton Consultants," a position that he still holds (1971).

to June 1954), James Cooley (August 1952 to May 1970), and Lieutenant General Harold Bull (October 1952 to December 1957).

Because some of these fourteen men replaced others, the total number of Board members present at any one time during the Smith period never exceeded eleven. The number was ten at the time of General Smith's departure in February 1953.

THE "PRINCETON CONSULTANTS"

Smith and Jackson had no confidence in the judgment of intelligence analysts, whether in the CIA or in the departmental agencies. Jackson regarded them all as bureaucrats out of touch with reality. He shared Donovan's conception that a board composed of "men of affairs" was needed to subject the findings of the analysts to the test of credibility in the light of practical experience. When he realized that the Board of National Estimates was being filled up with *professors* (the sort of people Langer knew), he was disgusted. In his estimation professors were even more out of touch with reality than were intelligence analysts![71]

When Smith and Jackson found it impossible to recruit for the Board "men of great prestige with practical experience,"[a] they conceived of creating another body of such men who, while not available for full-time service, might be willing to meet occasionally to give counsel on the most important and difficult estimative problems. This "Consulting Board" would meet in Princeton.[72][b] It came to be known as the "Princeton Consultants."

What Jackson meant by "men of great prestige with practical experience" is indicated by the names of the first three men chosen for this group: Vannevar Bush, George Kennan, and Hamilton Fish Armstrong.[73][c]

---

[a]These are Jackson's words for what Donovan meant by "men of affairs."

[b]The basic idea was to get away from the bureaucratic atmosphere of Washington. Since "men of affairs" would, of course, come from the Northeast, Princeton would be a convenient midpoint. Besides, Princeton is a pleasant place and Jackson had a home there.

[c]Bush, sixty, had been a professor, at M.I.T., but was also a practical scientist, an inventor. He had been Chairman of the Research and Development Board in the Department of Defense and in 1950 was President of the Carnegie Institution in Washington. Kennan, forty-six, was an outstanding Foreign Service officer and a specialist in Soviet and German affairs; he had been Minister-Counselor in Moscow while General Smith was Ambassador. In 1950 he was at the Institute for Advanced Study at Princeton. Armstrong, sixty-three, had long been a close collaborator with Allen Dulles in the Council on Foreign Relations and was Editor of *Foreign Affairs*.

The other original members of the Princeton group were Alexander Standish, a partner in J. H. Whitney and Company, Barklie Henry, a director of various corporations, and Burton Fahs, director of humanities for the Rockefeller Foundation.[47] The first two were evidently Jackson's friends, the third was Langer's.[a]

Jackson intended these consultants to exercise, in relation to the Board of National Estimates, the corrective authority that the Board had been intended to exercise in relation to the intelligence analysts. Their knowledgeable comments would set the professors straight; their concurrence would give prestige and authority to national intelligence estimates. Langer had a different view of the relationship. He saw these consultants as eminent men whose views were certainly worthy of respectful consideration, but they were not responsible to anyone for the substance of national intelligence estimates. The Board of National Estimates was responsible and should therefore exercise final judgment, subject only to the responsibility and consequent authority of the DCI.[75]

Ironically, the consultants came to value the information that they obtained from ONE more highly than ONE valued the advice that it obtained from them. The ultimate irony, in view of Jackson's preconceptions, is that the Board of National Estimates is now (1971) composed predominantly of professional intelligence officers, former analysts, while the consultants are for the most part professors.[b]

THE NATIONAL ESTIMATES STAFF

All of the Office of National Estimates below the level of the Board came eventually to be known as the National Estimates Staff.

Langer was authorized to draft from ORE anyone he wanted for ONE. He began on 15 November by taking a complete unit, the Global Survey Division, which was then composed of Ludwell Montague, DeForest Van Slyck, Ray Cline, Paul Borel, Willard Matthias, and George Jackson.[76] Montague and Van Slyck became members of the Board; Borel became Langer's Executive Officer.[c] Soon afterward Langer drafted [number

---

[a]Fahs had been Chief of the Far East Division, R&A Branch, OSS, under Langer.

[b]The intelligence professionalism of CIA today (1971) is far superior to anything known in 1950.

[c]Borel subsequently became DADNE for administration (1952), a member of the Board (1956), Assistant Director, Central Reference (1957), Assistant DDI (1963), Director, Intelligence Support Services (1966), Special Advisor to the DDI (1967), and Director, Foreign Broadcast Information Service (1969).

deleted] additional men and women from ORE. They had been recommended to him individually by Montague, Van Slyck, Cline, and Jack Smith[a] as the persons in ORE who were best suited to ONE's requirements. In the circumstances of that time a call to ONE was regarded in ORE as an invitation to enter Noah's Ark.[77]

By 29 November 1950 there were [number deleted] people in ONE [words deleted] including four Board members.[b] An eventual strength of [number deleted] was then contemplated.[78]

Montague's plan for an "Office of Estimates"[c] provided for a current intelligence division, five regional divisions, and a general division. The first would edit and publish the *CIA Daily Summary*, maintain secure custody of specially sensitive materials, and operate a CIA situation room and after-hours watch.[d] The regional divisions would be composed of area specialists who would follow the high-level cable traffic, produce copy for the *CIA Daily*, and contribute area expertise to the drafting of national intelligence estimates. The general division would be composed of more broadly experienced men. They would concern themselves with the more far-reaching implications of area developments, and would head the ad hoc task groups to be formed to draft estimates involving more than one regional division (for example, Soviet intentions in Germany).[79e]

Langer was determined to keep ONE small and flexible. He feared that the appointment of seven division chiefs would introduce bureaucratic evils into the purely intellectual republic that he desired ONE to be. He therefore decided that ONE should have no internal organization whatever. Langer did recognize that there were within his republic of intellects four general categories (not to say classes) of citizens: the members of the Board; senior members of the staff, whom he called generalists[f]; junior staff officers, called specialists; and clerical personnel. Langer himself would form ad hoc "task teams" composed of particular generalists and specialists to perform particular tasks as they arose.[80]

---

[a]Smith had been Chief of the Publications Division, ORE. He subsequently became a member of the Board (1957), Assistant Director, Current Intelligence (1962), and Deputy Director, Intelligence (1966).

[b]Langer, Kent (as a consultant), Montague, and Van Slyck.

[c]See page 127.

[d]These had been functions of the Publications Division in ORE. The current intelligence function was included in ONE in order to assure the estimators of access to sensitive current information, particularly the highest-level State Department cables, and also to ensure that current reporting would be guided by estimative judgment.

[e]This had been the function of the Global Survey Division in ORE.

[f]This term, reflecting Montague's conception of a general division, was a misnomer. Six of the nine original "generalists" were area specialists. The real criterion was grade (GS-15 or -14), which was indicative of age and experience.

There was, however, one task that required stable organization, procedure, and control. That was the daily publication of the *CIA Daily Summary*. Without any title, Jack Smith continued to publish the *Daily* as a matter of course with the support of the Publications Division personnel and the selected area specialists that he had brought with him from ORE.[81]

The CIA management's requirement for an ONE table of organization forced Langer to adopt some measure of internal organization. In that initial table Smith's de facto organization was recognized as the ONE Support Staff. It had a chief (Smith, of course) and included not only the three functional elements of the former Publications Division[a] but also the area specialists. The "generalists" were designated the Estimates Staff (they would draft *all* of the estimates), but they remained an unorganized pool of individuals without any chief.[82b]

The members of the Estimates Staff were dissatisfied by their lack of organization and direction. Led by Ray Cline, then thirty-two, they organized themselves and petitioned for leave to send a representative to the morning meeting of the Board in order to find out what estimative work there was to be done.[84c]

This initiative from below was strongly supported by Montague and Van Slyck. Langer was reluctantly persuaded to invite Cline to propose a more effective organization of the staff.[86] Cline proposed that all substantive personnel, specialist as well as "generalist," be assigned to the Estimates Staff and that Cline be designated as Chief of the Estimates Staff. That would have left Smith the chief of a strictly housekeeping Support Staff.[87]

Smith objected strenuously, on the ground that he had to have the specialists under his own control in order to produce the *Daily,* but that argument collapsed when the current intelligence function was transferred from ONE to a newly created Office of Current Intelligence.[d] Langer thereupon adopted Cline's plan, with the difference that he made Smith a generalist under Cline, with only part-time responsibility for continuing supervision of the residual Support Staff.[88e]

---

[a]That is, information control, reproduction, and the reading room, units that still exist in ONE.

[b]They were Derwood Lockard, John Maury, and Hiram Stout (GS-15s), and Ray Cline, George Jackson, Robert Komer, Willard Matthias, John Pendleton, and Abbot Smith (GS-14s).[83]

[c]There was plenty of estimative work to be done for the NSC, but the Board, absorbed in its own discussions, was paying no attention to it. (See page 132.)[85]

[d]See page 161.

[e]The personal relationship between Ray Cline and Jack Smith deserves passing notice.

As Chief of the Estimates Staff, Cline introduced system and order into the scheduling and preparation of estimates, but the capacity of ONE was limited by Cline's personal capacity to rewrite the drafts produced by his staff. Cline was a skillful and quick draftsman—the drafts that he presented to the Board were no doubt superior to those that he had received—but he was a bottleneck. Moreover, once Cline had perfected a draft, let no Board member dare to touch it! He had some warrant for this attitude. His drafts were derived from the consideration of evidence, or at least of responsible departmental contributions, while the novice Board members were merely expressing their uninformed preconceptions. Thus, Cline was practicing against the Board the tactic that Sontag later employed against the IAC—he represented the substantive experts.[a] The Board was not thereby ingratiated.[89]

[two lines, with[b] note, deleted] When Cline departed, in October 1951, Jack Smith had already gone off to the National War College and Abbot Smith to the Naval War College. By that time Abbot Smith, forty-five, was the staff member most highly esteemed by the Board. In absentia, he was appointed Chief of the Estimates Staff. William Bundy substituted for him until his return from Newport in June 1952.[90c]

In 1953 the distinction continued, within the Estimates Staff, between the "generalists," who drafted the estimates, and the specialists, who rendered expert assistance to them. In the fall of 1951, however, Chester Cooper, a Far East specialist, made an issue of the fact that there was no "generalist" who knew and understood the Far East. Specifically, he was complaining of what some "generalist" had done to "improve" (that is, ruin) his draft for a Far East estimate. The immediate consequence of Cooper's protest was that Cooper was made a "generalist"—because he was an outstanding specialist![91d] In time other "generalists" came to have

---

In 1945 Cline hired Smith to be a member of his current intelligence unit in the OSS. In 1949 Smith recommended Cline to be a member of the Global Survey Group in ORE. After this clash in ONE, their paths diverged, but in 1962, when Cline became DDI, he made Smith ADCI. Smith succeeded Cline as DDI in 1966.

[a]See page 136.

[b][note deleted]

[c]Bundy, a thirty-four-year-old Washington lawyer, had been recruited for the Estimates Staff by Langer in June 1951. He was afterwards Deputy ADNE for administration from 1957 to 1960, Deputy Assistant Secretary and Assistant Secretary of Defense, from 1961 to 1964, and Assistant Secretary of State from 1964 to 1969. Abbot Smith was made a member of the Board in 1953 and its Vice Chairman (DADNE) in 1958. In January 1968 he became Director of the Office of National Estimates. He retired in April 1971.

[d]Subsequently Cooper was made DADNE for administration (1958) and Assistant DDI for Policy Support (1962). He was detailed to the White House staff in 1965 and resigned from the CIA in 1968.

specific area assignments. On 9 February 1953 the "General Group" had [number deleted] members, of whom [number deleted] were in charge of particular areas.[92a] Those [deleted] and their associated specialists were in effect regional divisions of the staff. Finally, in June 1953 the existence of [number deleted] such regional divisions was recognized in the table of organization.[93b]

In February 1953 (at the time of General Smith's departure) the total strength of ONE was [number deleted], including [number deleted] members of the Board, [number deleted] members of the Estimates Staff, and [number deleted] members of the Support Staff, which included all clerical personnel.[94]

SOME EARLY PROBLEMS

In November 1950, when Montague was still functioning as a one-man Board of National Estimates,[c] he met with the IAC representatives on draft terms of reference for a scheduled estimate on Communist China. Montague's draft was problem-oriented: "to estimate the stability of the Chinese Communist regime, its relations with the USSR, and its probable courses of action toward the non-Communist world."[95] It reflected a specific request by the Senior NSC Staff.[96]

The four service representatives flatly rejected Montague's draft and insisted upon the adoption of an outline applicable to any country in the world. Montague recognized it as the outline for the Army's *Strategic Intelligence Digest*, a series of general-purpose descriptive handbooks with very little estimative content. He was unable to persuade his colleagues that a national intelligence estimate should be something else: intelligence required by the President and the NSC in relation to a specific policy problem. He refused to yield to the majority and referred the issue to the DCI and IAC.

Montague put the general issue to the IAC in these terms:

---

a[note deleted]

bThus, the [number deleted] regional divisions proposed by Montague in October 1950 came into being two and a half years later. Langer's antipathy toward bureaucratic hierarchy still prevails, however, in that they are not called divisions. At first they were called "groups." Now they are called "staffs."

cSee Part Two, pages 69–70.

The adoption of a set format requiring the inclusion of much basic descriptive matter and formal consideration of all conceivable contingencies would tend to destroy the utility of national estimates as contributions to the understanding and solution of specific national policy problems. The resultant compartmentation and volume of descriptive data would tend to obscure any analytical consideration of the critical issues.

Policy-formulating bodies such as the NSC require intelligence bearing directly on specific policy problems rather than generalized and descriptive country studies. The estimation of specific situations and contingencies must, of course, rest on basic intelligence data and thorough analysis. The policymaker, however, requires only the conclusions derived from such basic data, with reasonable indication of the supporting argument, but without recitation of the basic data itself or step-by-step exposition of the analytical process.[a]

Montague called upon the IAC to agree, in general, that national intelligence estimates "should endeavor to answer specific questions related to policy determination (rather than be generalized country studies)."[97]

When this matter came before the IAC on 30 November, General Smith entertained no discussion of the subject, but instead laid down the law himself. NIEs must address directly the problems before the policymakers. They must be brief; the argumentation must summarize the findings drawn from the supporting data. All readers must understand that for a more detailed examination of the data they must go to the experts (that is, to the departmental agencies). The IAC accepted that dictum without demur and adopted the recommended concept.[98]

On that basis, the early NIEs normally contained only one page of conclusions and a very few (one to five) pages of supporting discussion. Even the landmark NIE-25 ("Probable Soviet Courses of Action to Mid-1952," 2 August 1951) contained only five pages. That estimate was a landmark in that it recorded agreement, for the first time, that the USSR would not deliberately initiate nuclear general war if it could avoid doing so.[99b]

Another early problem was the character of IAC representation in coordination with the Board of National Estimates. At first these repre-

---

[a]This passage is quoted at length because a different view prevails today (1971).

[b]Subsequently, a good many largely descriptive "country studies" were published as NIEs. They related, however, to strange lands in South Asia, Africa, and Latin America, lands presumably unfamiliar to the policymakers.

sentatives tended to be front-office "policy" men. They came briefed by the departmental analysts, but they knew nothing of the substance of the matter, beyond their briefs, and were quite incapable of entering into a searching substantive discussion with the members of the Board.[100]

In January 1951 Langer conveyed his concern about this matter to General Smith. Smith had Langer speak to the IAC about it, which he did with diffidence. Smith thereupon took over in his own emphatic style.[101] Thereafter more substantively competent representatives were sent to meet with the Board, but that meant that they were men of lesser rank, more remote from their IAC principals in the departmental hierarchy. This had two disadvantages. The "representatives" did not represent their principals; they represented only themselves, or else some authority in the intervening hierarchy. And, no matter what the "representatives" had agreed to, the principals would be advised by men who had never participated in joint discussion of the subject.[102]

No satisfactory resolution of this dilemma has ever been devised.[103] Montague's plan of 1950, copying that of 1946, sought to avoid it by providing for the assignment of permanent representatives of the IAC principals as advisers to ADNE. The idea was that these men would serve not only as departmental representatives in ONE but also as ONE representatives in direct contact with the IAC principals, as the Senior Team of the wartime JIS had done.[104] That idea, however, was apparently beyond the comprehension of anyone who had not observed its operation in practice. In January 1951 provision was made for the assignment of four military officers to ONE, but only as technically expert staff officers, not as representatives of the service members of the IAC.[105a]

In the concept of 1950, ONE was to be entirely dependent on departmental contributions for research support, except for such in-house aid as it might obtain from ORR and OSI as "service of common concern." Obviously, the validity of national intelligence estimates could not rise much above the validity of these departmental contributions. The independent, knowledgeable, and experienced Board of National Estimates might suspect that some departmental contributions were slanted and self-serving, it might exert pressure on IAC representatives for further explanation and justification, but it had no independent sources of information except the *New York Times*, its own direct access to the State Department cables, and the narrowly limited research of ORR and OSI.

In June 1951 Langer declared that the contributions received by ONE were inadequate. He proposed that ONE be authorized to give "guidance"

---

[a]The last vestige of this arrangement is the Army position in the National Estimates Staff.

(direction?) to the research programs of ORR, OSI, and the IAC agencies. He suggested also that the ONE staff might be enlarged so that ONE itself could produce "national intelligence studies" (as distinguished from estimates) through its own research.[106]

Langer can hardly have realized it, but he was addressing the question first raised by Vandenberg in 1946—How can the DCI accept personal responsibility for the validity of national intelligence estimates while dependent upon the research support of agencies not under his own control?—and was proposing the solution that Vandenberg had adopted, the creation of a new ORE.[a] (It would certainly have been a better ORE under Langer's direction.)

It was not to be expected that Smith and Jackson would take kindly to the idea of enlarging ONE so that it could accomplish its own independent research. Nothing more was heard of that idea.

Langer was permitted to propose a "national intelligence study" to be made by G-2. That was intended to be the first of a series of such studies to provide "more detailed and rigorous analysis of certain key problems . . . than now exists" in order to provide a firmer base for estimative conclusions.[107] That was one way in which ONE could give guidance to departmental research. The IAC approved the idea,[108] but no other "national intelligence study" was ever proposed.

In July 1951 Langer made another approach to the problem by submitting to the IAC a paper on "Intelligence Gaps as Revealed by NIE-32."[109] The IAC referred that paper to OIC with instructions to develop "essential elements of information" related to the "gaps" specified,[110] and that is the last that was ever heard of it. That paper was, however, the prototype of the "Post-Mortem" series. General Smith later declared that "the identification of intelligence deficiencies in our production, including the conduct of post-mortems on estimates, was an essential part of the intelligence process."[111] The defect of the system was that the post-mortem findings regarding intelligence deficiencies were simply referred to the members of the IAC for such remedial action as they might deem appropriate, which might be much or nothing. Some post-mortems, however, were indeed effective in bringing about a significant redirection of intelligence collection and research.[112]

In general, however, nothing was accomplished during General Smith's time to relieve ONE of the vulnerability of complete dependence on self-serving departmental contributions. As Smith himself put it to the NSC[113]:

---

[a]See Part One, page 28.

> The Central Intelligence Agency is basically an assembly plant for information produced by collaborating organizations of the Government, and its final product is necessarily dependent upon the quality of the contributions of these collaborating organizations.[a]

General Smith's fine flow of rhetoric on the importance of interdepartmental collaboration and agreement left the Board of National Estimates uncertain of its authority to take a stand and invite a dissent. The largely professional Board spent a good deal of time and patience in an effort to educate, enlighten, and persuade the IAC representatives. Inasmuch as the professors were indeed persuasive and were also regarded with considerable awe by most representatives, this educational effort had a generally beneficial effect over time. Occasionally, however, it had no effect upon a particularly stubborn or strongly instructed representative. In such cases the Board tended to evade the issue rather than to force it.[114]

Thus, the early NIEs tended to be joint estimates and there was little occasion for IAC dissent. Such dissents as were registered were hardly substantial. A member of the IAC would exercise his privilege to rephrase a passage in the text in such a way as to give it a special slant or emphasis not acceptable to his colleagues. The departmental interest involved was readily apparent in such cases.[115]

In January 1951 IAC consideration of the Board's coordinated draft for NIE-10 ("Communist China") produced an interesting case. General Charles P. Cabell[b] objected, not to the substance of the draft but to its policy implications. He produced a revised text slanted to support his preferred policy. William Jackson, the DDCI, then in the chair, ruled that proposal out of order. Did Cabell dissent from the intelligence presented in the text as written? No, he did not, but might he then attach to it a statement expressing his own view of the policy that should be adopted with regard to China? Jackson would not allow that either, since it was not a dissent from the substance of the intelligence estimate.[116c]

---

[a]As a result of the gradual development of research capabilities in the DDI and DDS&T areas over a period of twenty years, the CIA is no longer dependent on departmental contributions. This present self-sufficiency, which is a realization of Vandenberg's purpose in 1946, has led some people to forget the primary value of interdepartmental coordination for the user of the NIE: the assurance that all pertinent authorities have been consulted and that all substantially divergent judgments have been recorded in one document.

[b]Then Lieutenant General and Director of Intelligence, USAF. Later Cabell was DDCI (1953–62).

[c]In later years many dissenting footnotes contained stump speeches of policy advocacy, which were allowed on the ground that one should be free to say anything he pleased in a statement for which he was solely responsible—a false doctrine.

The first really substantial difference to develop in the IAC had to do with the estimate in SE-11, "Probability of a Communist Assault on Japan in 1951," dated 17 August 1951,[a] and then it was the DCI himself who dissented, to the horror of all who knew of and valued the Lovett doctrine.[b] General Smith knew what he was doing; he stipulated that it was not to be taken as a precedent. Apparently he took the occasion to make the point that he gave more weight to the advice of his Board of National Estimates than he did to that of the IAC.[117]

The issue was a rather subtle one. The majority of the IAC (State, Army, Air Force, and the Joint Staff) held that a Soviet invasion of Japan would be unlikely *except* in the event of a general war. On the advice of the Board of National Estimates and with the support of the Director of Naval Intelligence, the Director of Central Intelligence held that to be unlikely *even* in the event of general war. The DCI did not put himself into a footnote. The majority view was expressed in one paragraph of the text, the view of the DCI and the DNI in the following paragraph.[118]

The underlying issue was the denial of U.S. military information to Intelligence.[c] The majority expressly excluded U.S. military capabilities from consideration. The DCI and the DNI held that to be unrealistic. They held that the Soviets would take into account U.S. capabilities to defeat an invasion of Japan and would be deterred thereby.[119]

In January 1952 the subordination of ONE to the newly created DCI, Loftus Becker, produced a tense situation. With reason, Sherman Kent, the newly appointed ADNE, regarded as essential the direct relationship between the Board of National Estimates and the DCI. Kent had no intention of submitting coordinated national estimates, or even Board memoranda for the DCI, to the judgment of some intervening bureaucrat. Kent and his deputy, Sontag, regarded Becker, personally, with contempt. That feeling was reciprocated.[120]

In February 1952 Becker declared to Smith that any adolescent who had been reading the newspaper could have produced a better estimate of the Iranian situation than NIE-56. Smith acknowledged that estimates were being watered down in the process of interdepartmental coordination but condoned that practice in the circumstances of that time.[d]

---

[a]The SE (Special Estimate) series consisted of NIEs closely limited in distribution because their contents would reveal specially sensitive matters under policy consideration: e.g., SE-1, "International Implications of Maintaining a Beachhead in South Korea," 11 January 1951. At that time the 8th Army was in pell-mell retreat and the policy question was whether to attempt to hold a beachhead at Pusan or to abandon Korea altogether.

[b]See Part One, page 24.

[c]See Part Five, pages 245–48.

[d]See Part Two, page 72.

Becker's principal complaint against ONE was that its estimates were not relevant or timely in relation to the intelligence requirements of the Senior NSC Staff, of which he was the CIA member. There was irony in that complaint, for it was Becker's responsibility to keep the Board informed of NSC requirements and he had neglected to do so.[a] But the other side of this matter was that the Board of National Estimates did indeed take a rather cavalier attitude toward the "bureaucratic" requirements of the NSC Staff.[b]

In February 1952 Bundy informed Becker that the Board was proceeding at a leisurely pace with an estimate required by the Senior NSC Staff in conjunction with a scheduled policy paper and would not meet the NSC schedule.[121c] Becker laid on a "crash" and demanded of Kent an account of the responsiveness of ONE estimates to NSC requirements. A review of the record revealed that:

(1) One or more NIEs had been produced on almost every problem that had been before the NSC.

(2) In some problem areas (for example, the Far East) the coverage had been extensive.

(3) There was, however, little correlation between the publication dates of estimates and NSC consideration of the subject.

(4) There was also a lack of comparability in scope between some estimates and some policy papers.

(5) Although there were no major gaps in coverage, some old estimates were "expiring."[d]

(6) The NSC had called for very few estimates on likely reactions to the adoption of a given U.S. course of action.[e]

(7) A closer "integration" of the estimates program and the NSC program would be feasible (with closer liaison).[123]

---

[a] During the summer of 1951 Montague was relieved of his assignment to the NSC Staff so that he might spend full time with the Board. By February 1952 Becker was the CIA member of the Senior NSC Staff and Bundy the NSC Staff Assistant.

[b] See pages 132 and 138.

[c] Another case in point occurred in April 1952, when Becker was outraged to discover that the Board had cancelled an estimate required by the Senior NSC Staff because a State contribution had not been forthcoming.[122]

[d] The "expiration" of estimates resulted from the early practice of giving them short-term terminal dates. For example, NIE-25, 17 August 1951, committed itself only to mid-1952. [one-and-a-half lines deleted] In the early 1950s the estimators dared not commit themselves for a longer term.

[e] The first such "contingency estimate" was SE-20, "The Effect on the Communists of Certain U.S. Courses of Action," 15 December 1951.

With reference to this report, Becker laid down the law that there must be more systematic planning, not only with regard to the estimates schedule but also with regard to the research required for estimates.[124]

On Kent's initiative, the Board of National Estimates met with the Steering Committee of the Senior NSC Staff on 10 April 1952 to discuss how NIEs could be made more useful in the preparation of NSC policy papers. One result was the preparation of a long-term (twelve-month) estimates program, which the Steering Committee considered and approved on 25 April.[125] Since then it has been the practice to review and extend this program quarterly, in consultation with the NSC (later, the White House) Staff and of course in coordination with the IAC (later, USIB).

On 1 July 1952 the Steering Committee of the Senior NSC Staff agreed with Becker that it would be desirable for NIEs to show more of the "factual" basis for the discussion and conclusions and also to give some clearer indication of the reliability of these basic "facts."[126] ONE sought to meet this requirement by adding appendices, called "Tabs," to the standard NIE format.

The service representatives rebelled against this innovation—a reaction quite inconsistent with their demand a year earlier that NIEs should consist predominantly of basic data.[a] Specifically, they demanded the deletion of the eight-page appendix of background information that State and ONE had prepared to go with the nine-page NIE-69, "Probable Developments in North Africa," then a relatively unfamiliar area. The service representatives had no objection to "Tabs" that presented, in tabular form, military order of battle or weapons characteristics. What they were balking at was the commitment of their IAC principals to concur in an additional eight pages of discussion of the political, economic, and social factors involved in the North African situation—matters with regard to which they had little interest and less competence.[127]

The Board of National Estimates urged the Director to retain the appendix to NIE-69 in view of the Senior NSC Staff's request for more information. At the IAC General Smith decided to disseminate the appendix with the estimate, but separately bound as a supplement. The members of the IAC were required only to note the supplement, not to concur in it (or dissent). In the future the DDI would decide, in consultation with the IAC agencies, what similar supplements should be similarly disseminated with NIEs. They would consist of background information only and would be prepared by the IAC agencies, not by ONE.[128]

---

[a]See page 140.

The Board of National Estimates did not regard this Judgment of Solomon as a good solution of the problem. It had no confidence in what the IAC agencies might produce in the way of supplements. It circumvented General Smith's decision by introducing more and more background material into the discussion part of estimates. And so it was that the once-slender NIEs began to grow stout.[129a]

---

[a][note deleted]

X

THE OFFICE OF RESEARCH AND REPORTS

The NSC Survey Group recommended in January 1949 that out of ORE there should be created not only a "small Estimates Division" but also a "Research and Reports Division" to perform such research services in fields of common interest as the NSC might determine could best be performed centrally.[a] [one-and-a-half lines deleted] in this connection but doubted that the U.S. central research agency should have so broad a mission.[b] It suggested that science, technology, and economics would be appropriate fields for centralized research. It emphatically excluded political intelligence research. That should be exclusively the business of the State Department's Office of Intelligence Research (OIR).[130]

The same order that announced on 13 November 1950 the creation of ONE also changed the name of ORE to Office of Research and Reports (ORR). All concerned knew that the change in name was but the beginning of the end of ORE. Some ORE personnel would be selected out for ONE. Some might be retained for the residual ORR dimly outlined in the Dulles Report. Some, particularly among the political analysts, might be taken up by OIR to meet its increased responsibilities for political research[c]—but, from the ORE point of view, that would be the same as going over to the enemy. The rest would be fired. Some escaped that fate by finding refuge in OSO and OPC, which were expanding. Others resigned.[131]

From the first it was evident that two divisions of ORE would survive in ORR: [one-and-a-half lines, with [d]note, deleted][e] The Dulles Report

---

[a]For a more extensive account, see the history of this Office now in preparation (1971).

[b][note deleted]

[c]See page 164.

[d][note deleted]

[e]This division had no research function; rather it was a coordinating and editing staff in

had recommended their inclusion. But what else? Science and technology, as the Dulles Report had suggested? At the end of 1948 the Scientific Branch of ORE had been made a separate Office of Scientific Intelligence (OSI)[a]; it was soon evident that OSI would not be resubordinated to ORR. Economics? ORE had some economic assets: an Economics Division, a Transportation Division, [remainder of list, covering a little over a line, with [b]note, deleted].

William Jackson discussed the question of what functions should be assigned to ORR at length with members of the IAC, especially with Park Armstrong, the State Department member. State claimed primary jurisdiction in economic as well as political intelligence[c] but, getting so much that it wanted from the demolition of ORE, was willing to permit ORR to engage in some subsidiary tasks of economic research, mainly related to Soviet war potential: [three lines deleted] But State did not insist that ORR confine itself to the Soviet Bloc; it was willing for ORR to study commodities production and trade on a global basis.[133] It was William Jackson who decided that ORR's economic research should be addressed primarily to the Soviet Bloc.[134d]

There was reason in that. The Soviet Bloc was later defined to include Communist China and North Korea, but not Yugoslavia and Finland.[135] [two and a half lines deleted] Economic information with regard to the rest of the world was abundant and easily obtainable.

As eventually defined in NSCID 15, dated 13 June 1951, the economic research responsibilities of the CIA (ORR) were perhaps deliberately left vague. The CIA would merely *supplement* the economic research done by the several departments, an echo of Vandenberg's evasion in 1946.[136e]

---

charge of the production of National Intelligence Surveys, compendia of descriptive information of interest primarily to war planning agencies such as the Joint Staff. The CIA (ORE) had assumed that function in 1948, in succession to the JIC's Joint Intelligence Studies Publication Board. The division chief, Kenneth Knowles, had been in ORE since 1946. In August 1955 Basic Intelligence was made a separate DDI office and Knowles became ADBI.

[a]See pages 173–75.

[b][note deleted]

[c]The pertinent NSCID said that each department should produce its own economic intelligence according to its own needs.

[d]This voluntary restriction later came to be regarded as a contract. ORR eventually escaped from it by observing that it could not measure the menace of Soviet trade and aid penetrations without studying the economies of the target countries.

[e]See Part One, page 28.

THE CREATION OF ORR

Theodore Babbitt, the former ADRE, was temporarily retained as ADRR, but it was evident to all, except perhaps to him, that his days were numbered.[a] It was also evident that his replacement should be a first-rate economist and administrator: [two and a half lines deleted] a coherent and capable Soviet Bloc economic research organization would have to be created from generally mediocre material and then be strengthened by recruitment. Seeking a man to perform this Herculean task, William Jackson consulted Sherman Kent, who recommended Max Millikan.[139]

Millikan, thirty-seven in 1950, was a native of Chicago and the son of a Nobel Laureate in physics. He received his Ph.D. in economics from Yale in 1941 and afterward served in the Office of Price Administration and in the War Shipping Administration. In 1946 Kent recruited him for the intelligence research organization in State. He left State in 1947 to be assistant secretary of the President's Committee on Foreign Aid. In 1949 he became Associate Professor of Economics at the Massachusetts Institute of Technology.

Millikan reported for duty on 15 January 1951. His arrival had an electric effect in raising from the depths the morale of ORR.[140] He gave the leftover personnel of ORE a sense of commitment to a well-defined and important mission pursuant to a well-conceived plan and under an able and forceful but considerate leader. They had known nothing like that in ORE, much less during the three-month interregnum.

The new ADRR intended to stay for only one year. He did not bring his family to Washington, but lodged in the home of Richard Bissell, with whom he had worked in the War Shipping Administration.[b] Having no family life, he did most of his paper work at night and spent much of the day visiting the economic units of ORR, becoming acquainted with his people, showing a personal interest in them and their work, consulting and encouraging them.[141]

---

[a]On the evening of 10 October 1950 (see Part Two, page 65), when General Smith learned that the CIA had no current coordinated estimate of the situation in Korea, he ordered that Babbitt be summarily fired, but Jackson persuaded him that it should not be done that abruptly.[137] Babbitt, or rather the chief of his Planning Staff, spent considerable effort developing unrealistic plans for the organization of ORR,[138] which suggests that they hoped to survive the cataclysm. When superseded in ORR, Babbitt became the Director of Intelligence in the Office of Civil Defense.

[b]Bissell was afterward Special Assistant to the DCI from 1954 to 1958 and Deputy Director, Plans, from 1959 to 1962.

Millikan left [one line deleted] to run themselves and devoted his personal attention to organizing and directing the new economic intelligence effort. [twelve lines, with ᵃnote, deleted] Millikan abolished Babbitt's overweening Planning Staff on the ground that planning should be done by the men responsible for substantive results—that is, by the ADRR and his division chiefs.[142]

Millikan reanimated the economic elements of ORR by putting long-idle hands hard to work compiling what he called an "Inventory of Ignorance"—that is, a systematic inventory of what was reasonably well-known about the Soviet Bloc economies and what more needed to be learned in order to complete the picture. That provided a useful guide to collection and research. Since perfect information was unlikely to be obtained, he proposed to proceed by the "method of successive approximations"—that is, to estimate what Soviet production might be, at least and at most, and then to work to narrow the difference between those extremes.[143]

Millikan had been authorized to dismiss anyone in ORR who, in his judgment, would be unable to make a positive contribution to the new Soviet Bloc economic research program, but he conducted no purge. Instead, he decided to keep the personnel he had, training them on the job if need be, while he pursued a vigorous recruitment program designed to raise the general competence of the Office as well as to enlarge it. He hoped to recruit experienced economists, especially among those who had worked with him at State in 1946, but he was hindered in that by delays in obtaining security clearances and by the subsidence of apprehension regarding the imminence of general war. He then turned instead to the recruitment of well-recommended graduate students. He devoted most of his own time to that effort, with good results.[144]

[eight-line paragraph deleted]

THE ECONOMIC INTELLIGENCE COMMITTEE

A week after Millikan's arrival, William Jackson declared that the IAC should be briefed on the reorganization of the CIA, with particular emphasis on the point that henceforth the CIA (ORR) research would be limited to Soviet economics.[147] On 15 February Dr. Millikan delivered a briefing on ORR. His Office would concentrate on Soviet economics as a

---

ᵃ[note deleted]

"service of common concern." It could also fill gaps in the economic research undertaken by State and Defense and serve as a useful *coordinator* of the entire economic intelligence effort.[148] At the staff meeting the next morning particular note was taken of the fact that no member of the IAC had objected to the idea of ORR as coordinator of economic intelligence.[149]

This gingerly approach to the IAC suggests that in February 1951 Smith, Jackson, Reber, and Millikan, all newcomers on the scene, were not aware that eleven months earlier the NSC had directed the DCI (Hillenkoetter) to study the adequacy of existing arrangements for coordinating the production of economic intelligence and to submit a "comprehensive" plan. However, when Smith proposed such a plan to the IAC, on 9 May 1951, it was as a response to an NSC directive dated 3 March 1950![150]

It would be interesting to know who discovered (or revealed) the existence of this year-old and unfulfilled NSC directive.[a] In any case, Millikan seized the opportunity that it presented. He made a quick survey and found that twenty-four Government departments and agencies were producing economic intelligence according to their various needs without any coordination whatever.[151] He proposed the establishment of an Economic Intelligence Committee (EIC) to effect the coordination that was obviously needed. Its basic membership would correspond to that of the IAC, but the other departments and agencies interested in economic intelligence would be invited to participate on an ad hoc basis. The seven functions that Millikan proposed for the EIC all related to various aspects of coordination.[152]

Millikan also proposed a new NSCID on economic intelligence. It assigned to the CIA three broadly stated coordinating functions and a supplemental research function, as a "service of common concern."[153]

Smith submitted these proposals to the IAC, which concurred in them, as amended, on 17 May 1951.[154] The principal amendment was the assignment of an eighth function to the EIC, that of preparing "coordinated reports that present the best available foreign economic intelligence."[155] It was agreed that the EIC should publish such reports without submitting them to the IAC except in cases of serious disagreement.[156]

The NSC adopted NSCID 15, "Coordination and Production of Foreign Economic Intelligence," on 13 June, and the Economic Intelligence Committee was formally established soon thereafter. The ADRR was its

---

[a]Presumably this NSC directive had been lost from sight during CIA's preoccupation with the "Webb proposals," the outbreak of the Korean War, the advent of General Smith, and the ensuing reorganization.

Chairman, ex officio; the EIC Secretariat was an element of his personal staff. The EIC established thirteen permanent subcommittees and various ad hoc working groups. During the next two years the Committee produced seventeen "surveys" related to coordination and thirteen substantive intelligence reports. In addition to the six IAC agencies, twenty non-IAC agencies participated in some part of this work, as appropriate.[157]

In practice, EIC papers were drafted in ORR and were then put through the EIC machinery in much the same way that ONE produced NIEs. Through the EIC, however, ORR was able to exercise a much stronger influence on the direction and coordination of departmental intelligence research than could ONE.

THE REORGANIZATION OF ORR

After a year as ADRR, Max Millikan was satisfied that both ORR and the EIC were well launched and well able to develop further without him. Meanwhile, he had developed the idea of a Center for International Studies (CENIS) at M.I.T. He was impatient to return to M.I.T. to organize and direct CENIS.[158a] He was impervious to Bedell Smith's appeals to him to stay on, even to Smith's suggestion that he was just the man to succeed eventually as DCI.[159]

Robert Amory, Millikan's successor as ADRR, was thirty-seven in 1952. He was a native of Boston and a graduate of Harvard (1936) and of Harvard Law School (1938). After practicing law in New York, he enlisted as a private soldier in 1941 and rose to the rank of colonel in 1946; he commanded a battalion of combat engineers in New Guinea and a regiment in the Philippines. After the war he was Professor of Law at Harvard until called to the CIA. Loftus Becker, the new DDI, proposed him to General Smith;[160] Becker and Amory had worked together in the same New York law firm before the war. Becker recruited Amory by holding out to him the prospect of becoming DDI after about a year as ADRR.[161] Amory became a consultant on 11 February 1952 and ADRR on 17 March.

Inasmuch as Amory was a lawyer and accountant rather than an economist, he felt a need to put a professional economist in charge of the five economic research divisions that Millikan had personally directed.

---

[a]On leaving ORR, Millikan became a CIA consultant and, somewhat later, one of ONE's "Princeton Consultants."

The consequence was a reorganization of ORR announced on 24 August 1952. This reorganization was, however, a consolidation rather than a radical innovation.

Amory reduced his span of control by having three subordinate chiefs reporting directly to him. [fifteen lines deleted]

During the spring of 1952, ORR was devoting an increasing proportion of its time and effort to direct intelligence support for the working groups of the Economic Defense Advisory Committee (EDAC), [two lines deleted]. In that forum, however, ORR's intelligence findings were condemned as unreliable by the representatives of OIR, although they had nothing better to offer. Conceding the uncertainties in all Bloc economic intelligence in 1952, this criticism was plainly a matter of jealous spite.[a] Contention regarding it hindered the work of the EDAC working groups.[163]

On 23 April 1952 the EDAC delivered to the NSC a report, over the signatures of Dean Acheson and Averell Harriman, that condemned "the general inadequacy of intelligence pertaining to East–West economic relations" and blamed "the absence of intelligence support" for the U.S. failure to obtain West European cooperation in restricting the use of Western ships in Bloc trade. These strictures in an NSC paper of limited distribution were widely disseminated by publication in the State Department's *Current Economic Developments*.[164]

This incident aroused the ire of Robert Amory and of Bedell Smith as well. On 3 June, Smith addressed a strong and scornful rebuttal to the NSC. He showed that substantial intelligence support had in fact been rendered to the EDAC, particularly with regard to the use of Western shipping in Bloc trade, and recommended that future EDAC program reports "reflect a more accurate appraisal of the information and intelligence support that is available in the economic field."[165]

One of Bedell Smith's specific complaints was that the EDAC report had failed to note that a special "intelligence working group" was being set up to coordinate intelligence support for the EDAC. This Intelligence Working Group (IWG) was formally chartered by the IAC on 14 August 1952. Because the content and sources of the required intelligence were highly sensitive, it was established outside of the EIC system.[166] [several words deleted] ORR's Coordination Staff was to it as the EIC Secretariat was to the EIC.

[five-line paragraph deleted]

Robert Amory exercised command and control by assigning tasks and deadlines. Having done that, he kept in touch but did not interfere. He

---

[a]See page 161.

expected the work to be well done and to be completed on time, and if he was disappointed in those respects, he could be explosive.[169]

During Amory's tenure as Assistant Director, ORR continued to grow. [one-and-a-half lines deleted]

On 23 February 1953 Amory was made Assistant DDI and Otto Guthe, Chief of the Geographic Research Area, became ADRR.[a] On 1 May, Amory succeeded Becker as DDI.

---

[a]Although economic intelligence was ORR's long suit and Guthe was a geographer, Amory had decided that Guthe was best qualified to head the Office as a whole.

XI

THE OFFICE OF CURRENT INTELLIGENCE

OCI was a third office derived from ORE, but one that had not been originally contemplated. The report of the NSC Survey Group had questioned the propriety of ORE's production of current intelligence and had strongly condemned its political research in duplication of that of the State Department's Office of Intelligence Research. William Jackson had intended that OIR should have its pick of ORE's political analysts, after ONE had taken its choice, and that any not chosen by ONE or OIR should be declared surplus and dismissed. As it turned out, however, OCI was the haven in which the surplus analysts of ORE found refuge, to Jackson's great chagrin!

The nucleus of OCI was the short-lived Office of Special Services (OSS). [two lines deleted] OCI was formed through the piecemeal accretion of former ORE functions and personnel to OSS.

CURRENT INTELLIGENCE IN THE CIA

Neither the President's letter of 22 January 1946 nor the National Security Act of 1947 said anything about a current intelligence function in the CIG or the CIA. Every intelligence organization, however, produces current intelligence for the information and the authority that it serves. The day the CIG came into existence (on 8 February 1946, with the adoption of NIA Directives 1 and 2), President Truman impatiently demanded of it the immediate production of a daily summary of current intelligence. He wanted a single, all-sufficient daily summary to replace, at least insofar as he was concerned, the multiplicity of departmental summaries that he was required to read.[a] He received the first number of the *CIG Daily Summary* on 15 February and was well pleased with it.[171]

The Secretary of State (Mr. Byrnes) protested the publication of the *CIG Daily Summary*. In the circumstances of 1946 it was derived almost entirely from State cables, duplicating the State Department's daily summary. The President rejected that protest, saying that the CIG was his own personal intelligence staff. The Secretary forbade the CIG to comment on the significance of State cables, reserving that function to State. Not long afterward, however, President Truman demanded, and of course got, CIG comments on items in the *CIA Daily Summary*.[172]

The CIA's publication of current intelligence was more formally sanctioned by NSCID 3, dated 13 January 1948. It provided that all intelligence agencies should produce and disseminate current intelligence as might be necessary to meet "their own internal requirements or external responsibilities."[173] DCID 3/1, dated 8 July 1948, provided that current intelligence was not subject to coordination.[174]

The NSC Survey Group noted that the CIA *Daily Summary, Weekly Summary*, and monthly *Review of the World Magazine*[b] were almost entirely political in content. Probably at the instigation of OIR, it questioned the propriety of those publications and recommended their discontinuance.[176] In response, Admiral Hillenkoetter pointed out that they were the only current intelligence publications prepared expressly for the President and the NSC, as distinguished from specialized departmental audiences.[177] He knew, as the NSC Survey Group apparently did not, that the *Daily* was prepared at the express direction of the President and the monthly *Review* at that of the NSC.

---

[a]President Truman was a remarkably dutiful reader of intelligence. He desired the *CIG Daily* to summarize operational as well as intelligence information for his convenience but was disappointed in that—the War and Navy Departments refused to release operational information to the CIG. State, on the other hand, furnished its most sensitive ("S/S") cables, under some restrictions with regard to their use.

[b]This *Review* deserves passing notice. The first number was prepared by the Global Survey Group (GSG), ORE, as a briefing for Admiral Hillenkoetter to present to the newly constituted NSC, at its request. It was fully coordinated with the IAC agencies. Hillenkoetter was pleased with it and ordered it to be published as an estimate. The NSC was also pleased and requested that it be repeated on a monthly basis. When Montague attempted to coordinate subsequent numbers with the IAC agencies, they begged off, insisting that a monthly estimate was current intelligence. The true reason was that no IAC agency had anyone cognizant of the global situation. To coordinate with the GSG, each agency had to send a squad of regional specialists, and these regional specialists fell to quarreling among themselves as each sought preferment for his particular region.[175]

To General Smith it was as axiomatic as it had been to Admiral Hillenkoetter that the CIA had a responsibility to keep the President currently informed. In October–November 1950 there was no question of discontinuing the *CIA Daily Summary*, but the current intelligence function was then transferred from ORR (later ORE) to ONE in accordance with Montague's plan.[a] Langer then discontinued the *Weekly* and the monthly *Review*.

[four-and-a-half page section deleted][b]

THE OFFICE OF SPECIAL SERVICES

Such was the situation [several words deleted] when Bedell Smith became DCI. His first concern was to pull together under one clear command authority the several elements in the CIA [several words deleted]. He did that by combining the functions and personnel of the Advisory Council and the Special Research Center[c] into one Office of Special Services (OSS). The creation of that Office was announced on 1 December 1950.[185]

[five-line paragraph deleted]

The first Assistant Director for Special Services was Horace Craig, who had been Chief of the Advisory Council since August 1950, but after only a month as Assistant Director, Craig was transferred to the Office of Training and Kingman Douglass was designated ADSS in his stead on 4 January 1951.[187]

Kingman Douglass, fifty-four in 1950, was a financial consultant to Dillon, Reed and Company. A native of Chicago and graduate of Yale University, he had earned a Distinguished Service Cross as an Army aviator in 1918. During World War II he had been the senior U.S. Army Air Force intelligence liaison officer in the British Air Ministry. In 1946 he had been Acting Deputy Director of Central Intelligence under Souers.

William Jackson had known Kingman Douglass in New York and in London. It was Jackson who induced Douglass to return to the CIA. Douglass would hardly have consented to come just to be ADSS; some-

---

[a]See page 137.

[b][note deleted]

[c]The Special Research Center was not a command but a place, the secure area that housed [word deleted] the General Division of ORE. [one line deleted]

thing grander than that must have been held out to him in prospect. In his discussion of the subject with Jackson, they must have agreed upon the conception of OCI as an "all-source" current intelligence service for the President and the DCI.

THE CREATION OF OCI

On 18 December 1950 William Jackson announced that he was now ready to take up the problem of current intelligence.[188] Three days later he met with Langer, Craig, and Babbitt to consider the proper location of that function in the CIA.[189] Babbitt contended that current intelligence could not properly be produced without immediately available research support. That was ORE doctrine. Jackson angrily accused Babbitt of trying to perpetuate ORE in ORR, and Babbitt acknowledged that to be true. Jackson could not be expected to agree to that conception.[a] Langer, for his part, did not want to be responsible for current intelligence if ONE could otherwise be assured of prompt access to the "S/S" cables. Saying that, he resigned the current intelligence function to OSS.[190]

As soon as Kingman Douglass took office, he put his staff to work on trial runs for a new all-source *Daily*.[191] When Jack Smith learned of this, he protested vigorously,[192] but in vain. On 12 January it was announced that "OCI" would produce the *Daily Summary*.[193] Three days later the name of OSS was publicly changed to Office of Current Intelligence.[194]

In this case OCI got the function without the personnel; the experienced staff that Jack Smith had selected out of ORE (ORR) remained in ONE. Jack Smith continued to publish the *CIA Daily Summary* until 28 February when OCI, after two months of practice, finally put out the first number of its new *Current Intelligence Bulletin (CIB)*.[195] It was not until two months later that Bedell Smith finally declared himself to be entirely satisfied with the *CIB*.[196b]

Bedell Smith sent a copy of the first number of the *CIB* to the Secretary of State with a note emphasizing that it was an *all-source* publication, not just a summary of State Department cables, as the former *Daily Summary* had been.[197] He sought thus to answer State's repeated com-

---

[a]Nevertheless, Babbitt's conception ultimately prevailed in the actual development of OCI. (See pages 164–65.)

[b]In August 1951 OCI supplemented the daily *CIB* with an all-source weekly *Current Intelligence Review*.

plaints about the publication of "political summaries" by the CIA. The difference was attributable as much to the Korean War as to the reorganization of the CIA. [two and a half lines deleted]

OCI and the *CIB* were a good, albeit belated, response to the new current intelligence requirements generated by the war. Current intelligence was necessarily a very incidental function in ONE. [four lines deleted] OCI was not limited in that way, but it still had to find the integral research support that Babbitt, with reason, had declared to be indispensable to the proper performance of the current intelligence function.

POLITICAL RESEARCH IN THE CIA

ORE had felt free to engage in any research that it deemed to be useful in the service of the President, the NSC, any defense-related Government agency that had no intelligence capabilities of its own (for example, the NSRB) or, of course, the other components of the CIA (such as the OSO). It was disposed to rely on the military intelligence agencies for technical military data but, with reason, had only scorn for their strongly held but extremely naive political views. ORE's regard for the political interpretations of the State Department's OIR was not much higher. It knew that OIR was a pariah within the Department. Relations between ORE and OIR were poisoned by OIR's resentment of ORE's intrusion into the field of political intelligence and by ORE's resentment of OIR's consequently captious criticisms intended to demonstrate the incompetence of ORE.[198]

The NSC Survey Group was strongly sympathetic with OIR in this matter. It held most emphatically that the CIA should engage in no political intelligence research whatever[199]—and political intelligence could be construed to cover everything except the most narrowly and technically defined scientific, economic, and military matters.

At his first formal meeting with the IAC Bedell Smith was as emphatic in stating that the CIA (ORR) would not thereafter engage in political intelligence research.[200]

During the next three months William Jackson and Park Armstrong discussed the practical consequences of that determination. Then, on 1 February 1951, Bedell Smith dispatched a letter to the Secretary of State reminding him that NSCID 3 made the Department of State primarily responsible for political, cultural, and sociological intelligence research, informing him that the CIA, relying on State, was no longer engaged in such research, and suggesting to him that the State Department might have to increase its intelligence research staff in order to meet the requirements of the CIA and the other IAC agencies for political research support.[201]

Jackson's letter of the same date to Armstrong was more explicit. State (OIR) was now responsible for the political, cultural, and sociological work formerly done by ORE, including (a) the initiation of appropriate collection requirements, (b) the evaluation of OSO reports, (c) research to meet the requirements of the NSC, the JCS, and other departments, (d) intelligence support for psychological warfare, (e) research on international organizations—such as the UN, (f) research on International Communism, and (g) research support for the CIA. [four lines deleted].[202a]

At the same time, Jackson forwarded to Armstrong a request from the Joint Staff to the CIA for material for a JIC psychological warfare intelligence estimate, requesting that OIR respond to it.[204] Two months having passed without response, the Joint Staff again addressed the DCI. Smith passed that inquiry on to Armstrong for direct response.[205]

Thus, Smith and Jackson were firmly determined to take literally State's claim to a monopoly of political intelligence research, to permit nothing of that sort to be done in the CIA under any pretext, to require all requests for political research support to be addressed to State, and to require State to respond directly to the requestors.

The denouement came in June 1951 when Armstrong addressed an appeal to Smith. State had included in its 1952 supplemental budget 250 positions required to meet the additional responsibilities set forth in Jackson's letter of 1 February. The Bureau of the Budget had allowed only 40 percent of the positions and 31 percent of the funds requested for this purpose. The reason was that the surplus personnel of ORE had been absorbed in the CIA instead of being transferred to State, so that the proposed increase in OIR's personnel strength was an addition to the Federal payroll. Would the DCI please intervene with the Bureau of the Budget on State's behalf?[206]

[three lines deleted] Jackson was deeply chagrined to learn that, but Kingman Douglass knew what he was doing. He was acquiring the integral research support that Babbitt had declared to be indispensable to the proper production of current intelligence.

But more than research support for current intelligence was involved. The fact is that no sooner had ORE disappeared than it was sorely

---

a[note deleted]

missed, especially by OSO. As early as 13 February OSO expressed its concern at being made dependent on OIR for political research support, especially as regards the integrated study of the ramifications of the international Communist conspiracy.[208] ORE had performed that service for OSO; in his letter of 1 February Jackson had listed it specifically as one of the ORE functions to be assumed by State. OIR, however, was extremely reluctant to take up that task; by May it was apparent that it would not do so.[209] (OIR regarded the product as domestic propaganda rather than intelligence.) There ensued, in the Deputy Director's daily staff meeting, earnest discussion of the proper location in the CIA of a unit to render operational research support to OSO and OPC and significantly, in that connection, of the amount of research that could appropriately be done in OCI.[210]

This trend of thought alarmed William Jackson. He expressed to the Director his concern about the development of research tendencies in OCI and proposed to inspect that Office, with the apparent intention of arresting that development. Bedell Smith authorized that inspection but stressed the point that assistant directors should be permitted to organize and run their offices as they thought best, so long as they produced the desired results.[211] In the end it was Stuart Hedden who made the inspection of OCI, as a practice run before his formal appointment as Inspector General.[a] His report, dated 7 December 1951, suggested some few administrative improvements. Hedden did not concern himself with the doctrinal principle that had concerned Jackson.

In late November Allen Dulles spoke up to question the propriety of OCI's unilateral reporting on purely political matters in the *CIB*. He suggested prior coordination with OIR in such cases.[b] Bedell Smith answered curtly that the purpose of the *CIB* was to report on *every* matter that the *CIA* thought should be brought to the President's attention and that the President had so directed.[212]

Thus it was that the development of "research tendencies" in OCI went unchecked and OCI became an independent political research organization comparable to ORE. Although ORR was administratively the continuation of ORE, OIR (and ONE) came to realize that ORE had actually survived in OCI.[213]

[nine-and-a-half lines, with [c]note, deleted] regional divisions followed the developing situation in their respective areas on an all-source basis

---

[a]See Part Two, page 106.

[b]Almost certainly this intervention was prompted by Park Armstrong. Dulles and Armstrong had been in close rapport at least since 1948. (See Part One, page 44.)

[c][note deleted]

and prepared copy for the daily *Current Intelligence Bulletin* and the weekly *Current Intelligence Review*. The material that they submitted was reviewed and accepted, modified, or rejected by a Publications Board composed of the Chief of the Intelligence Staff and the [number deleted] division chiefs. A subordinate editorial staff then perfected the English and attended to reproduction and dissemination.[215]

BAD BLOOD BETWEEN OCI AND ONE

The spirit of ORE still dwelt in OCI. The prevailing doctrine in ORE was that the ultimate authority on any subject was the desk man who studied it daily—even though he might be in rank and experience the most junior person concerned. Pure truth resided only in his independent, well-informed, and expert judgment. Any higher-level review must necessarily introduce adulteration; the higher the rank of the reviewer, the less well informed he would be. And any deference to the views of other agencies in interdepartmental coordination was shameless prostitution. This ORE view became the prevailing view in OCI, at least among the analysts.[216]

This unofficial but nevertheless prevailing view was of course diametrically opposite to the doctrine of William Jackson and to the conception of ONE, which included review by a distinguished Board of National Estimates as well as interdepartmental coordination.

This philosophical difference between OCI and ONE was sharpened by personal animus. The personnel of the National Estimates Staff were the elect of ORE. The personnel of OCI were the rejected, those not wanted in ONE, or ORR, or OSO and OPC. They could assuage their feelings, however, by thinking of themselves as the purveyors of pure truth in the service of the President, in contrast to those *coordinators* in ONE, hopelessly entangled in their time-consuming and humiliating procedures.

The conflict that ensued between ONE and OCI was perhaps inherent in the difference between their respective functions in dealing with the same subject matter, but its intensity can be fully understood only with reference to this psychological background.

On 13 February 1951, two weeks before the publication of the first number of the *CIB*, General Smith declared that it was to be a "joint production" prepared by OCI in collaboration with ONE, ORR, and

OSI.[218a] Subsequently the OCI Publications Board considered occasional contributions from ORR or OSI on economic and scientific subjects on the same basis as contributions from the regional divisions of OCI. ONE never submitted such contributions, and OCI never voluntarily consulted ONE.

From the outset the *CIB* contained "CIA" (that is, OCI) comments on the significance of the items reported. Bedell Smith tried to explain the standing of those comments in his letter to the Secretary of State transmitting the first number of the *CIB*:[b]

> It should be emphasized [he wrote] that the comments do not necessarily represent the mature appreciation of the Central Intelligence Agency and have not been coordinated with the other intelligence agencies represented on the Intelligence Advisory Committee. They are actually the first impressions of CIA on "spot" information and are subject to later revision.

In the opinion of ONE, OCI's "CIA comments" were often ill-considered and misleading. More particularly, ONE observed that many of them contained far-reaching estimates and that some of these estimates, published by OCI in the name of the CIA, flagrantly contradicted national intelligence estimates recently published in the name of the DCI.

In May 1951 Langer complained to Douglass about this "casual estimating" in a current intelligence publication,[219] but his remonstrance had no apparent effect. In June, Langer complained to Jackson, who brought the matter to Smith's attention. Smith's response was that Langer, who knew that OCI would be commenting in the name of the CIA, "should take the necessary steps for coordination"[220]—that is, any lack of internal coordination was Langer's fault.

That remark was not understood at the time; certainly nothing was done in response to it. Smith seemed to have inverted the standard rule of coordination, that he who would publish a statement must himself seek and obtain the concurrence of other interested parties. What Smith meant can be understood only with reference to the special circumstances of this case. He meant that it would be unreasonable to expect

---

[a]He said also that he wanted the *CIB* to be on his desk "first thing in the morning," which meant that it would have to be produced before the beginning of the normal working day. Since 1946 the *CIA Daily* had been published at noon, on the principle that a morning paper can publish only *yesterday's* news, while a midday paper can publish *today's* news from the Eastern Hemisphere.[217] Either no one present understood that point, or no one dared to point it out to General Smith.

[b]See page 162.

OCI, working to a before-office-hours deadline, to withhold comment because it could not coordinate with ONE, no one in ONE having yet come to work. If Langer objected to what OCI was saying, he should arrange to have an ONE representative available to be consulted by OCI's "dawn patrol."

Jackson brought the subject up again in July, and this time Smith made himself clear: someone from ONE should monitor OCI's production. Jack Maury was immediately appointed to sit with the OCI Publications Board.[221a]

Apparently Maury was not able to control OCI's estimative tendencies. In September, Langer again complained about OCI estimates, this time to Dulles, the new DDCI. Dulles had evidently been receiving similar complaints from Armstrong (State).[b] It appears that Dulles proposed that OCI be forbidden to comment on current intelligence. Smith and Jackson[c] both jumped on him for that, declaring that the President wanted CIA comments. Maury was supposed to control their estimative content. Smith added that he was not excited about any minor inconsistencies between OCI's "flash" comments and ONE's deliberately considered estimates. The difference in standing between those two forms of expression should be obvious to all concerned.[222]

This dismissal of the subject did not quiet ONE's complaints. A month later Larocque and Becker thought that Jackson ought to investigate the embattled relations between ONE and OCI.[223] In March 1952 the new ADNE, Sherman Kent, reported to the new DDI, Loftus Becker, that whereas ONE's relations with ORR and OSI were excellent, its relations with OCI left much to be desired. ONE's last words on the subject of "CIA" comment in current intelligence publications were as follows:

> Evaluation and comment on raw intelligence currently reported is essential. It is undesirable on the other hand to pass on to high officials of the government estimates hastily produced by a single CIA office which does not represent and may actually conflict with considered and coordinated judgments. In practice, the distinction between evaluation of intelligence and the drawing of estimates is difficult to maintain and O/CI comments in the CIA Daily and Weekly publications frequently ignore the distinction.

---

[a]Maury had been Deputy Chief of the [name deleted] Division in ORE and was in 1951 a "generalist" in ONE. He served also as ONE's watchdog with the Watch Committee (see page 171). He is now (1971) the DCI's Legislative Counsel.

[b]See pages 163–64.

[c]Present as the DCI's Senior Consultant.

. . . Up to now CIA current publications often seem to have ignored the agreed views of the IAC agencies as expressed in national intelligence estimates.[224]

Another aspect of this problem was OCI's complaint, first made in December 1951, that it was allowed no voice in the preparation of national intelligence estimates.[225a]

ONE understood that its drafts for national intelligence estimates were to be based on its evaluation of contributions received from the IAC agencies and from ORR and OSI as accepted "services of common concern." It knew that OCI's political research was a bootleg operation without acceptance and standing in the IAC community. It considered itself sufficiently informed by OCI's current intelligence publications and had no regard for OCI's estimative judgment.[226]

The issue being raised, however, Sherman Kent was accommodating. He invited OCI comment on the contributions received by ONE and the drafts prepared by ONE, and OCI representation at all meetings of the Board of National Estimates to review both terms of reference and draft estimates. He told the ADCI, "I wish to assure you of the Board's interest in having your people participate as much and as directly as possible, and always as members of the family."[227]

In taking this conciliatory line, Kent sought to develop a better spirit of collaboration between ONE and OCI—or else to create a sharp contrast between ONE's willingness to consider the views of OCI and OCI's disregard of the views of ONE. OCI took some advantage of the opportunity to make disparaging comments on departmental contributions and ONE drafts but would not attend meetings with the Board. In short, OCI was ever ready to criticize, but not to enter into joint discussion of the subject.[228] Why not? Did it fear to compromise its independence, or to be worsted in argument, or to be arbitrarily overruled by the Board?

A third aspect of this problem was the estimative content of OCI special memoranda prepared for the information of the DCI or the President. Requests for such memoranda on particular subjects were usually referred to ONE when it was perceived that major estimative judgments were involved, but OCI got the bulk of that trade for the simple reason that OCI, with its integral research facilities, could produce "factual" information faster than ONE could.

On 1 February 1952 Kent sought to get this matter under some control

---

[a]The specific occasion was OCI's criticism of a draft for NIE-46 (Iran). Becker's subsequent criticism of that estimate as finally adopted by the DCI and IAC (see page 145) was evidently inspired by OCI.

by proposing to Douglass that each office should supply the other with copies of all of the intelligence memoranda that it produced for the DCI, the DDCI, or the DDI.[229] At the same time, he proposed to Becker that, if a current situation threatened to develop into a crisis requiring estimative judgment, the DDI should form a joint OCI-ONE "Task Team" to deal with it. OCI would be responsible for the initial reporting, keeping ONE fully informed, but when a "spot estimate" was judged to be needed, the action would pass to ONE, with the "factual" support of OCI and with OCI's participation in the Board's consideration of the subject.[230]

It appears that nothing came of this initiative, for in July Sontag (then Acting ADNE) returned to the subject with a simpler proposal. He urged Becker to establish the principle that *every* intelligence memorandum destined for the White House or the NSC should be reviewed by the Board of National Estimates. He suggested that *all* requests for such memoranda should be referred to OCI for the preparation of a first draft, but that *all* OCI drafts should be reviewed by the Board with the ADCI sitting as an ad hoc member.[231]

Becker's decision on Sontag's proposal was that intelligence memoranda for the White House might be prepared by either office, according to the nature of the request, but that *all* such memoranda should be reviewed by the Board of National Estimates and the ADCI, acting jointly. The ADCI would be supported by the appropriate members of the OCI Publications Board.[232]

By this time there was a new ADCI, Huntington D. Sheldon. A native of Greenwich, Connecticut, and a graduate of Eton College and Yale College, he was forty-nine in 1952. After a career as an investment banker and corporation executive, he entered Air Intelligence in 1942 and eventually became the Deputy A-2 of the U.S. Strategic Air Force in Europe. After the war he operated a chicken hatchery in New Jersey. Kingman Douglass recruited him to be his successor as ADCI.[a] Sheldon entered on duty in OCI on 27 June 1952 and succeeded Douglass on 12 July.[b]

Sheldon's subordinates in OCI regarded him as an aloof but strong and forceful character, unquestionably in complete command of OCI, as

---

[a]Douglass retired from the Agency on 11 July 1952 to return to his personal business in New York City. He died on 8 October 1971.

[b]Sheldon subsequently pursued a distinguished career in the CIA. He normally served as Acting DDI during Amory's absences but did not succeed Amory in that office. He was appointed Assistant DDI under Cline (April 1962) and afterward Special Assistant to the DDS&T (November 1963). In that position he was actually a special assistant to the DCI for various important and sensitive tasks. He retired in January 1970, when he was sixty-seven.

Douglass had not been.[233] On the other hand, Sherman Kent later said that dealing with Sheldon was like pressing upon a pillow: there was no resistance, but also no lasting effect.[234] In short, Sheldon would agreeably appear to acquiesce in whatever was proposed to him, but then do as he pleased as though nothing had been said.

In August 1952 the CIA was committed to briefing the two principal candidates for the Presidency on foreign situations related to the national security.[a] Kent understood that these briefings would be prepared in accordance with Becker's decision on 25 July—that is, that OCI would prepare briefings on the current situation in the countries under consideration on each occasion, that ONE would prepare estimative paragraphs to be attached to OCI's country briefings, and that the Board and the ADCI would meet to review and combine these drafts. Sheldon apparently acquiesced in this idea, for he asked that the meeting be kept small, that the whole Board not attend. Apparently he was concerned lest the OCI delegation be heavily outnumbered.[235]

It did not work out that way. In casual conversation with Sheldon at lunch Kent was astonished to learn that OCI had already briefed one of the candidates without consulting ONE. Naturally, Sheldon was reluctant to give a different briefing to the other. Kent, however, insisted in going through with the agreed procedure and understood that Sheldon finally acquiesced. Nevertheless, when Sheldon was later notified of the time of the Board meeting, he flatly refused to attend. His position was that he had no interest in what ONE might choose to say on the subject and that what OCI had said or might say was none of ONE's business.[236]

On Sunday, 10 August, the Board of National Estimates met to review the OCI and ONE drafts. Becker, the DDI, was present. Becker certainly was not partial toward ONE.[b] He was impressed, however, by the cooperative attitude of the Board and by the refusal of OCI to participate.[237]

In September, Sheldon told Amory (then the Acting DDI) that Becker had authorized OCI to make short-term (up to six months) estimates.[238] If so, that was no solution of the problem, which concerned the distinction between evaluating the credibility of a report and estimating the likely consequences of the reported fact.[c]

On 25 October, Sontag obtained from Becker, in Sheldon's presence, a reaffirmation of Becker's decision of 25 July.[239] That made no difference. Sheldon simply ignored it.

This issue was never officially resolved, in General Smith's time or

---

[a]See Part Five, page 262.
[b]See pages 94 and 145–46.
[c]See page 167.

later. It did, however, fade away with the passage of time—perhaps as the proportion of ORE alumni gradually diminished in both OCI and ONE.

THE WATCH COMMITTEE OF THE IAC

One of OCI's important functions was to provide CIA support for the Watch Committee of the IAC.

The failure of Intelligence to give clear warning of the impending attack on South Korea in June 1950 stimulated the development of mechanisms intended to give timely warning of any military attack likely to affect the security interest of the United States. The Joint Intelligence Committee established a Joint Intelligence Indications Committee, of which Brigadier General John Weckerling, the Chief of the Intelligence Division, Army G-2, was chairman. At the same time, the CIA developed an interdepartmental "Check List Group" with an identical function: to compile a check list of specific actions indicative of the imminence of military operations, and to give warning if any significant combination of these listed indications was seen to be occurring.

On 24 November 1950 James Reber (Acting Secretary, IAC) proposed, with the concurrence of the Standing Committee of the IAC, that the "Check List Group" be formally established as the Watch Committee of the IAC, under the chairmanship of the CIA.[240]

Soon afterward Reber learned that the military members of the IAC would resist this proposal, presumably out of jealous concern for the JIIC and on the ground that warning of impending attack was a military function not to be entrusted to civilians. It should also be noted that COMINT was then the most likely source of warning and that the Army was then extremely jealous of its control of that source. In accordance with the maxim "if you can't beat 'em, join 'em," Reber recommended to General Smith that the "Check List Group" be scrapped and that the JIIC be made the Watch Committee of the IAC.[241]

When the IAC met to consider this matter, on the ninth anniversary of Pearl Harbor, General Smith declared that he was responsible for seeing to it that the Government had an effective Watch Committee but that it need not be headed by the CIA. He withdrew the proposal before the house, announced the dissolution of the "Check List Group," and proposed that the JIIC be established as the Watch Committee of the IAC, with its membership expanded to include all members of the IAC.[242]

The military were delighted, of course. General Bolling, the G-2, hastened to have the JIC charter of the JIIC rescinded and to propose to the IAC a suitably modified charter for the Watch Committee.[243] It was adopted on 28 December 1950.[244]

It was agreed that Watch Committee reports should be strictly factual, with evaluative comments, of course, but no estimating.[245] This was a delicate matter, similar to that at issue between OCI and ONE.[a] Inevitably, estimates sometimes crept into Watch Committee reports. The members of the IAC, however, were as jealous as ONE of their prerogative to do any estimating that was done. Consequently any objection to the appearance of an estimate in a Watch Report was generally sufficient to obtain its immediate deletion by the IAC.[246]

General Weckerling served as Chairman of the Watch Committee until August 1952 and was succeeded by Brigadier General John Willems, his successor in Army G-2.[b]

General Smith listed the establishment of the Watch Committee among his major achievements but retained a realistic view of what it could be expected to accomplish. As he put it to the NSC:

> Despite the utmost vigilance, despite watch committees, and all of the other mechanisms for the prompt evaluation and transmission of intelligence, there is no real assurance that, in the event of sudden undeclared hostilities, certain advance warning can be given.[247]

---

[a]OCI represented the CIA in the Watch Committee, but Jack Maury went along as watchdog for ONE.

[b]Eventually, in 1954, the DDCI (then General Cabell) became Chairman of the Watch Committee. In 1965, when General Carter retired as DDCI, Huntington D. Sheldon became the first civilian chairman.

XII

THE OFFICE OF SCIENTIFIC INTELLIGENCE

Smith and Jackson found an Office of Scientific Intelligence already established in the CIA, and a Scientific Intelligence Committee already formed to coordinate scientific intelligence activities.[a] Although the NSC Survey Group had contemplated the inclusion of scientific intelligence research in ORR, they decided to leave well enough alone. In 1952, however, Smith and Becker, under pressure from the military intelligence agencies, did act to curb the scope of OSI's independent research and to reduce its role in interdepartmental coordination. Remarkably, this development was the reverse of that which had occurred with regard to economic intelligence through the creation of ORR and the EIC. The difference was that the military intelligence agencies wanted the services rendered by ORR and the EIC, while they resented the intrusion of OSI and the SIC into areas that they regarded as exclusively military.

THE CREATION OF OSI AND THE SIC

Under prodding by the Joint Research and Development Board,[b] a Scientific Branch was established in ORE late in 1946. It was conceived to

---

[a]For more extensive treatment of OSI, see Karl Weber, "History of the Office of Scientific Intelligence," DDS&T Historical Paper No. OSI-1.

[b]A joint board of the War and Navy Departments headed by Dr. Vannevar Bush and concerned with the development of U.S. weapon systems.

be a panel of in-house consultants who would provide expert advice to the regional branches of ORE with regard to scientific matters. The Scientific Branch itself had no considerable scientific intelligence research capabilities.[248]

[ten-line paragraph deleted]

In 1948 both the Eberstadt Committee and the NSC Survey Group were shocked to discover the inadequacy of the U.S. scientific intelligence effort.[a] The Survey Group recommended that centralized scientific intelligence research and the coordination of all such research be made the principal business of its proposed "Research and Reports Division."[250] Instead, Admiral Hillenkoetter chose to reunite the Scientific Branch and the [one-half line deleted] in a new Office of Scientific Intelligence [one line deleted]. OSI came into being on 1 January 1949—two weeks before the report of the Survey Group was submitted to the NSC.[251]

The first Assistant Director for Scientific Intelligence was Dr. Willard Machle, a forceful character with a strong sense of mission. Unencumbered by responsibility for the situation that the Survey Group had condemned, he was determined to carry out its prescription.[b] His efforts to develop the internal research capabilities of OSI were hindered by the difficulty of recruiting suitably qualified personnel, who were in great demand elsewhere. His principal achievement was the creation of the Scientific Intelligence Committee as a means of coordinating the entire scientific intelligence effort. The SIC was, plainly, the model for the later (and more successful) EIC.

The SIC was established by DCID-3/3, which was drafted by Karl Weber,[c] coordinated through ICAPS, and accepted by the IAC on 28 October 1949. The coordination was stormy. The military intelligence agencies were outraged by the prospective intrusion of the CIA into the area of weapon-systems development. Machle and Weber adhered to the British conception that scientific and technical intelligence included all research and development up to the initiation of series production. The military sought to distinguish between basic scientific capabilities and weapon-systems applications, reserving the latter to themselves exclusively. It happened, however, that the Research and Development Board in the Department of Defense was extremely dissatisfied with the intelligence support obtainable from the military intelligence agencies and was correspondingly in favor of Machle's plan, which in effect commis-

---

[a]One of their principal informants was Ralph Clark, then of the staff of the Research and Development Board. In October 1949 Clark became the DADSI.

[b]Compare the resistance of ORE, pages 125–26.

[c]As Acting ADSI. Machle, who had directed that it be done, was absent in Europe.[252]

sioned the SIC (Machle) to be the primary source of intelligence support for the RDB.[253] The prestige of the RDB within the Department of Defense outweighed the resistance of the military intelligence agencies. DCID-3/3, as finally adopted, conformed to Machle's conception.[254]

DCID-3/3 authorized the SIC to "plan, support, and coordinate the production of scientific intelligence as it affects the national security." The SIC and its subcommittees would formulate national scientific intelligence requirements, prepare interdepartmental intelligence production plans, assign production tasks to the various constituent agencies, and evaluate scientific intelligence collection activities. The chairman would be from the CIA (Machle), the members from the Army, Navy, Air Force, State, and the AEC.[255]

Willard Machle was outraged that scientific intelligence should be dependent on clandestine collection by ignorant "spooks." He insisted that the collection of such information should be controlled and conducted by scientifically qualified personnel. [three lines deleted] Moreover, when Machle suspected OSO of withholding information from OSI,[a] he encouraged the members of his [one-half line deleted] to exploit their former OSO contacts to get it—that is, OSI effected a clandestine penetration of OSO! When that was discovered, the earth trembled with the shock and Machle was asked to resign.[257]

Machle's successor as ADSI, announced on 6 March 1950, was Dr. Marshall Chadwell from the New York office of the Atomic Energy Commission. In contrast to Machle, Chadwell was a notably mild-mannered and conciliatory man.[258b]

General Smith not only maintained OSI but also authorized a gradual increase in its personnel strength. [two lines deleted] Smith yielded, however, to a military counterattack on the jurisdiction that Machle had established for OSI and the SIC.

Late in 1950 a number of noted scientists in the Boston area, men involved in U.S. weapon-systems development and deeply concerned about the poverty of U.S. intelligence on corresponding Soviet developments, approached Chadwell with an offer of assistance. Out of this offer developed the Boston Scientific Advisory Panel, a body analogous to

---

[a]At about this time an OPC officer characterized OSO as a great repository of unused information—gathered at great expense but unused because OSO would let no one see it for security reasons.

[b]Chadwell, fifty-two in 1950, was a native of Amesbury, Massachusetts, with a Ph.D. from Harvard University in physical chemistry. He had served during the war in the Office of Scientific Research and Development and since then with the Rockefeller Foundation in New York. He had been Deputy Manager of the New York office of the AEC for eighteen months when called to the CIA.

ONE's "Princeton Consultants." The group included, for example, the men who later became the first three Presidential scientific advisers: James Killian, George Kistiakowsky, Jerome Wiesner. Whatever the value of their scientific advice, the active interest and moral support of such men were of inestimable value to OSI during its time of trouble.[260]

THE MILITARY COUNTEROFFENSIVE

With recognition of the special competence of OSI [two lines deleted] the military accepted the Joint Atomic Energy Intelligence Committee (JAEIC), the subcommittee of the SIC concerned with that subject. With reluctance, they accepted also the subcommittee on biological warfare, chemical warfare, electronics, and guided missiles that Machle established in November 1949, and the subcommittees on aircraft and antiaircraft weapon systems that Chadwell established in June 1950. They were outraged, however, when they learned that Chadwell was considering the establishment of SIC subcommittees on undersea warfare and army ordnance. These were subjects plainly within the jurisdiction of single military services and therefore, it was contended, not subject to coordination.[261]

In February 1951 the Army member of the SIC opened the military counteroffensive by questioning the justification for any SIC subcommittees on weapon-systems applications. There ensued a prolonged wrangle within the SIC, which was evenly divided between its military and civilian members: Army–Navy–Air Force versus CIA–State–AEC. In April, after a formal three to three vote, Chadwell undertook to consult the DCI. In July, presumably pursuant to instructions, he finally consented to dissolve the aircraft and antiaircraft subcommittees of the SIC.[262] That sacrifice did not appease the military, who continued their attack on the chemical warfare, electronics, and guided missiles subcommittees.[263]

The persistence of the military evidently irritated General Smith. Jackson told Larocque that Smith would take up the matter with the IAC and, if he got no satisfaction there, would take it to the NSC. Smith was considering the idea of asking Dr. Compton to investigate the entire field of scientific intelligence.[264] Dr. Karl Compton was the former Chairman of the Research and Development Board who had insisted on the adoption of DCID-3/3. At this point Smith was evidently disposed to uphold the SIC and to put down the military.

Smith did take up the matter with the IAC, on 2 August, but not with the force that Jackson had expected him to use. His position was that the SIC had no authority to abolish a subcommittee, that only the IAC could do that.[265] That seems to have been a misconception: the IAC had established the SIC, but the SIC had established the subcommittees and presumably could disestablish them. The effect, however, was to change the venue from the SIC to the IAC, where Smith (rather than Chadwell) would be in the chair, and that plainly was General Smith's purpose.

Smith went on to say that, before the IAC acted on this matter, he wished to obtain the advice of President Conant of Harvard.[266] His reference to Conant must have been a slip for an intended reference to Compton. If so, it was unfortunate; the name of Compton would have struck more terror in the ranks of the military than the name of Conant did. Smith may have expected the military to fall back before this threat of an independent (and hardly impartial) investigation. If so, he was disappointed.[a] General Bolling, the G-2, replied that four of the SIC subcommittees were a waste of time for their military members. Smith had to agree that any subcommittee that was not useful should be abolished.[267]

In any case, action had to be suspended while General Smith took counsel. In September Dr. Compton agreed to make the desired survey of the entire field of scientific intelligence,[268] but later he excused himself. Smith then directed Stuart Hedden to survey OSI.

In January 1952 Marshall Chadwell and Ralph Clark[b] were alarmed to learn that the exclusively military Joint Intelligence Committee was setting up a Joint Technical Intelligence Subcommittee. They spoke to Loftus Becker, the new DDI, about that, and Becker spoke to Bedell Smith. Becker's thought was that the military should be encouraged to improve their coverage of scientific and technical matters, that the SIC should confine itself to subjects that the military could not handle as well. Apparently Becker was not aware that the SIC existed only because of the intense dissatisfaction of the Research and Development Board with military scientific and technical intelligence. Smith was probably aware of that. His thought was that, even where the CIA's jurisdiction had been established, as in the case of the SIC, he was prepared to reconsider if the military did take effective action to improve their performance.[269]

At the February meeting of the SIC, the Army member announced that the JTIS had established subcommittees on guided missiles, biological

---

[a]This tactic worked, however, when General Smith employed it for a second time, one month later. (See Part Two, pages 72–73.)

[b]See page 174. Clark had been DADSI since 21 October 1949.

warfare, chemical warfare, and military electronics. He perceived unnecessary duplication and moved for the abolition of the SIC subcommittees on those subjects.[270] (That was, of course, Vandenberg's 1946 strategy in reverse.[a]) At about the same time, the military refused to participate in a conference that the SIC had arranged with the British on guided missiles and electronics.[271] And at this point the CIA Inspector General made the unkindest cut of all by reporting his conclusion that OSI should cease duplicating the scientific intelligence research of the military intelligence agencies.[272]

General Smith was not stampeded. He declared that the situation was more complicated than anyone realized. But he ordered that Hedden's report be distributed to the members of the IAC and that the subject be put on the agenda of the next meeting of the IAC.[273]

At that meeting (6 March 1952) General Smith forcefully reiterated his position that no SIC subcommittee could be dissolved by a majority vote of its members.[b] Only the IAC could do that. However, that forceful pronouncement was only an artillery barrage to cover his retreat. He announced the establishment of an "Ad Hoc Committee to Survey Existing Arrangements Relating to the Production of Scientific and Technical Intelligence," the mission of which would be to prepare a revision of DCID-3/3. Loftus Becker, the DDI, would be chairman. The IAC members should name their representatives.[274]

DCID-3/4 AND THE SCIENTIFIC ESTIMATES COMMITTEE

It must be noted that the survey conducted by Becker's Ad Hoc Committee was not an independent survey such as Dr. Compton might have made. Instead, it was in fact an interagency negotiation accomplished through an IAC subcommittee. And with Loftus Becker in the chair the result was a foregone conclusion, in view of his previously stated attitude.

At the same time, it must be noted that Bedell Smith had little option in the matter. With the military members of the SIC in effect on strike, the SIC could no longer function. Smith must have concluded that it would prove counterproductive to carry the issue to the NSC and that instead he should do whatever he could to salvage something from the

---

[a]See Part One, page 28.

[b]Apparently the military majorities in the four SIC subcommittees under attack had voted to dissolve them.

wreck. Moreover, there was some hope that the military, having set up the JTIS, might now do better than they had hitherto in the field of scientific and technical intelligence.

On 15 July 1952 Becker discussed his draft report with Ralph Clark, the DADSI. Clark, who remembered well the circumstances in which the SIC had been set up,[a] observed with distress that the CIA was abandoning its role of leadership in the field of science and technology. He must have expressed his long-held view that the military intelligence agencies were simply incompetent in that field. Becker refused to accept either point. He could not, he said, prejudge that the JTIS would prove to be incompetent.[275]

On 14 August 1952 the DCI and IAC approved the report of the Ad Hoc Committee, rescinded DCID-3/3, and adopted DCID-3/4.[276]

DCID-3/4 assigned to the intelligence agencies of the Department of Defense primary intelligence production responsibility with regard to weapons, weapon systems, and military equipment and techniques, including intelligence on related scientific research and development. It assigned to the CIA (OSI) primary responsibility with regard to scientific resources in general, fundamental research in the basic sciences, and medicine (other than military medicine). Atomic energy intelligence was made free for all.[277]

DCID-3/4 stipulated, however, that no single agency was to be regarded as the final authority on any subject. The interest of each agency in the work of the others was recognized; provision was made for the exchange of papers and for working-level conferences "as appropriate." Nothing was said about how any disagreements discovered at these conferences were to be resolved.[278]

The SIC and all of its subcommittees were dissolved, except that JAEIC was retained as a subcommittee of the IAC itself. JAEIC actually antedated the SIC. It had been established in November 1946 as the Joint Nuclear Energy Intelligence Committee (JNEIC) and since 1947 had been producing a semi-annual estimate of the Soviet atomic energy program that went directly to the IAC for approval without passing through the processes of ORE or, later, ONE. This function and this relationship were simply continued.[279]

DCID-3/4 created a new IAC subcommittee called the Scientific Estimates Committee. This SEC differed from the SIC in that it had no authority to coordinate scientific intelligence activities, although it was charged with stimulating and guiding interagency liaison and working-level conferences. Its primary function was to prepare "integrated" sci-

---

[a]See page 174.

entific and technical intelligence as required for "national intelligence."[280] That passage was understood to mean that the SEC could produce only integrated contributions to national intelligence estimates and surveys (the NIE and NIS series), that it could publish nothing in its own name (as did the EIC),[281] although the passage could have been more broadly construed.

It was left up to the SEC to elect its own chairman. It elected John Routh, the OSI member. He was chief of [name deleted] Division of OSI. Chadwell and Clark, in their chagrin, would have nothing to do with the SEC; they had appointed Routh to it in their stead.[282]

The adoption of DCID-3/4 had a devastating effect upon the morale of OSI. Becker resented OSI's resistance; it was an implicit criticism of him. He was particularly sensitive to the charge that he had cravenly abandoned the CIA's established position of leadership in the field of scientific intelligence.

On 21 August, Becker met with the senior officers of OSI for the purpose of jacking them up. He freely acknowledged that there was serious doubt whether the military intelligence agencies and the JTIS were competent to meet the responsibilities assigned to them by the DCID, but he demanded that OSI quit its petty quibbling and make a loyal effort to make the Director's directive work effectively. If OSI wanted to exercise leadership, it must earn that position by superior performance. If its performance was really superior, it could exert leadership in the working-level conferences, whether or not it was in the chair. Becker flatly refused to produce a detailed explanation in writing of how he expected the new system to function. It was up to OSI to work that out.[283]

This performance did not convince OSI that Becker had known what he was doing when he produced DCID-3/4. OSI never reconciled itself to that document. But Becker's speech did have an effect. Thenceforward OSI devoted less of its attention and energy to asserting the CIA's authority to coordinate scientific intelligence activities and more to developing OSI's internal capabilities for intelligence research in all fields of scientific intelligence, including weapon-systems development, in anticipation of a day when a new DCI and a new DDI would value such independent capabilities.[284] And that day did come.

XIII

THE OFFICE OF COLLECTION AND DISSEMINATION

The NSC Survey Group recommended the dismemberment of OCD.[a] Two years later William Jackson, the DDCI, moved to carry out that recommendation, which was his own idea. Bedell Smith, however, decided not to do this. Smith's reversal of Jackson must be attributed to the persuasive powers of James M. Andrews, the Assistant Director for Collection and Dissemination.[b] Thus, OCD survived untouched the general reorganization of the CIA pursuant to NSC 50.

The cabal of colonels who came to the CIG with General Vandenberg[c] had read in an Army regulation that the intelligence process consisted of collection, evaluation, and dissemination. On their advice, Vandenberg established an Office of Collection, an Office of Evaluation (ORE), and an Office of Dissemination.[285] The Office of Collection had nothing to do with the collection of information in foreign parts. Its function was to gather from State and the Pentagon the intelligence materials that ORE would "correlate and evaluate." The Office of Dissemination would then distribute to the White House, State, and the Pentagon the "strategic and national policy intelligence" that ORE had produced. Two months passed before it occurred to some bright mind that the same set of liaison officers and couriers who collected information for ORE could also disseminate the ORE product, that two separate offices for collection and dissemination were not required. The two offices were then combined to form one Office of Collection and Dissemination.[286]

---

[a]For a more extended treatment of OCD, see George Jackson and Martin Claussen, *Organizational History of the Central Intelligence Agency, 1950–1953*, DCI Historical Series, HS-2, Chapter 5.

[b]James M. Andrews, the ADCD, is not to be confused with James D. Andrews, the contemporary Advisor for Management.

[c]See Part One, page 28.

This episode is indicative of the level of sophistication that General Vandenberg and his preferred advisers brought to the direction of intelligence.

The plan for ORE included a "Library," which was to contain not only standard reference works but also a central file of all the intelligence documents that would come into ORE's possession. Ted Shannon, then the CIA Executive for Administration and Management, and Kenneth Addicott, then in ORE, took particular interest in this "Library" and from it developed the idea of a Reference Center in which all of the intelligence materials in the possession of the Government would be deposited, indexed, and made available to all intelligence agencies. As might have been expected, the departmental agencies flatly refused to surrender their files to the CIG; the Reference Center could be no more than the CIG's central reference facility.[287]

The management of ORE, engrossed in more urgent internal and external problems, paid no attention to the development of the Reference Center. For that reason Shannon transferred it from ORE to his own office in September 1947.[288] In January 1948 he engaged James M. Andrews to be its chief.[289] Andrews was an enthusiastic advocate of the use of business machines for the indexing, retrieval, and analysis of information.[a] In May 1948 the Reference Center was merged into the original OCD and Andrews was made the Assistant Director for Collection and Dissemination.[290]

[six lines deleted] Thus, it was the Reference Center that had taken over OCD, rather than vice versa.

Andrews sought to instill in OCD personnel the idea that OCD existed only to serve the other components of the CIA, and the departmental agencies as well, insofar as practicable. They must forget about pretensions to superior coordinating authority and do their utmost to service every demand or request that came to them, no matter what the source.[292] That was indeed a remarkable doctrine in the CIA of 1948.

The NSC Survey Group examined OCD just after this reorganization had gone into effect. It had no cognizance of the previous period of trial and error. It could not know how the new arrangement would work out.

On theoretical rather than empirical grounds, the Survey Group concluded that the Liaison Branch of OCD had a coordinating function that

---

[a]Andrews, forty-three in 1948, was a native of Schenectady with a Ph.D. from Harvard University. He was, before the war, a research associate in anthropology and Assistant Curator of Somatology at Harvard. During the war he was a specialist in statistical analysis in ONI. It appears that he was recommended to Shannon by Captain A. H. McCullom, who had served in ONI and in 1947 was DADRE. Andrews came to the CIG from Harvard.

should be assigned to its proposed "Coordination Division."[a] The rest of OCD (the former Reference Center) was plainly related to research and should therefore be assigned to the proposed "Research and Reports Division."[293] Andrews's comment on this proposal was that it was, in effect, a return to the situation that had existed before September 1947, which had been unsatisfactory.[294] Hillenkoetter rejected the proposal, but the NSC approved it in NSC 50.[295]

In accordance with the Dulles Report and NSC 50, Jackson included in his plan for ORR a Reference Division composed of the former Reference Center elements of OCD. The Liaison Branch would go to OIC, and OCD would cease to exist.[296]

Andrews was resigned to the demise of OCD but determined that the Reference Center he had created should not be subordinated to ORR, as the "Library" had been in ORE. No doubt with the support of Shannon, Andrews appealed to General Smith. His line was that OCD was a service organization, in the service of all of the components of the CIA and of the IAC agencies as well. It should not be subordinated to just one of its many customers. The result would be the neglect from which the Library had suffered in ORE, or at least a reduction in its functions to suit the limited interests of ORR. If OCD must be abolished, let all of its elements be assigned to OIC, where they could continue to serve the whole intelligence community.[297]

General Smith was no doubt impressed by this argument—and even more by Jamie Andrews's spirit and his grasp of his business. Smith readily agreed that the Reference Center elements of OCD should not be subordinated to ORR. At the same time, he perceived that the day-to-day service operations of OCD would be incongruous in OIC. Most important, he saw that James Reber was not the man to take the place of James Andrews in charge of that business.[298] His decision was to leave Andrews and OCD exactly as he had found them.[299]

[one-and-a-half pages deleted]

---

[a]By this time the Liaison Branch had undertaken the coordination of specific collection requirements, as distinguished from the general coordination of collection operations, which remained a function of ICAPS.

XIV

THE OFFICE OF
OPERATIONS

The advent of Bedell Smith had little effect on the operations of the three constituent elements of the Office of Operations. The Office as a whole was subordinated to the Deputy Director, Plans, during 1951, but was transferred to the Deputy Director, Intelligence, on 1 March 1952.[a]

[seventeen-line paragraph, with [b]note deleted]

The FBID had its origins in a unit formed by the Federal Communications Commission in 1940 to monitor foreign propaganda broadcasts. It was transferred to the CIG as a "service of common concern" by NIA Directive No. 5, dated 29 June 1946, and was at first assigned to the Office of Collection.[301]

The FDD originated in the Army and Navy units organized in 1944 to exploit the rapidly growing volume of captured documents. These units were merged as the Washington Document Center in April 1946. It was transferred to the CIG in December 1946 and was briefly assigned to ORE.[302]

The OSS had engaged in the exploitation of domestic contacts for foreign intelligence purposes. When the Office of Special Operations was established in the CIG on 11 July 1946, the ADSO was given a "B" Deputy in charge of domestic contacts. He was Kingman Douglass, who had been Admiral Souers's Acting DDCI and was later to be General Smith's ADCI. Douglass developed a plan for a domestic contacts organization but favored its separation from OSO.[303]

In July 1946 General Vandenberg sent Kingman Douglass and William

---

[a]For a more extended treatment of OO, see Louise Dickey Davison, *Office of Operations: Overt Collection, 1946–65,* DDI Historical Series, in preparation (1971).

[b][note deleted]

Jackson to London [one line deleted] and to Frankfurt to see whether Brigadier General Edwin Sibert could be recruited for the CIG. Later Vandenberg himself, accompanied by Wright and Galloway,[a] visited Sibert in Frankfurt. Sibert readily agreed to come to the CIG.[b]

All accounts indicate that Sibert was offered something grand as an inducement to come. Jackson's recollection was that Sibert was to be DDCI, or else to be chief of all CIG collection activities. As Douglass remembered it, Sibert was to be both DDCI and chief of all field collection, with the prospect of the succession as DCI. Sibert himself was reticent on the subject. He later said that his primary motive in consenting to come to the CIG had been to get home after three years overseas. Vandenberg had offered to make him Assistant Director in charge of *all* collection activities; Wright and Galloway had demurred; and Vandenberg had then deferred the precise definition of what Sibert's function would be.[304]

General Sibert reported for duty on 13 September 1946. He was kept in the DCI's office until 17 October, when the Office of Operations was created and Sibert was made ADO. On the same date Colonel Galloway was made ADSO, a position in which he had been acting since July.

[six lines deleted]

Thus, the Office of Operations was a makeshift combination of three elements, each valuable in itself but none essentially related to another or to any other CIG Office. It appears to have been put together primarily for the expedient purpose of providing an Assistant Directorship for General Sibert in lieu of whatever it was that General Vandenberg had in mind when he first sent Douglass and Jackson to recruit him.

Certainly Sibert himself was bitterly disappointed by the position that he actually got in the CIG.[307] No matter what had or had not been promised him, he had a right to expect something better as a senior brigadier general with four years of intelligence experience, three of them in positions of great responsibility. He was a more broadly experienced intelligence officer than any other then in the CIG, including the DCI himself and his Executive, Colonel Wright.

Kingman Douglass was mortified to think that he had induced Sibert to come to the CIG with promises that had proved false.[c] He attributed the disappointment of Sibert's expectations to a personal attack on him

---

[a]Two of the colonels Vandenberg had brought from Army G-2. (See Part One, page 28.)

[b]Sibert, forty-nine in 1946, was a graduate of West Point (1918) and a professional Army officer. His first intelligence experience was as military attaché in Brazil, 1940–41. He was G-2, ETO, 1943–44; G-2, 12th Army Group, 1944–45; and G-2, U.S. Forces, European Theater, 1945–46.

[c]Douglass's departure from the CIG coincided approximately with Sibert's arrival.

by Drew Pearson. Pearson had charged that Sibert, as G-2, 12th Army Group, was responsible for the heavy American casualties in the "Battle of the Bulge" and that he was unfit to hold any high position in the CIG.[308]

Richard Helms[a] had a different explanation: the intimate relationship between Vandenberg and Galloway. When Galloway heard that Sibert was to have charge of *all* CIG collection, he protested vigorously that Vandenberg could not do that to him. Galloway had been Vandenberg's classmate at West Point; the two families were very close socially.[309]

Both of those considerations no doubt had bearing on the outcome. So did the determination of Colonel Wright, Vandenberg's *éminence grise*, that Wright should be DDCI and Galloway ADSO. Wright had driven away all of Souers's assistant directors that could possibly have contested his preeminence: Kingman Douglass, Louis Fortier, and William Goggins.[b] He can hardly have welcomed the arrival of a brigadier general of Sibert's stature as an intelligence officer. He may have thought to provoke Sibert's resignation by disappointing his expectations.[c] Sibert, however, knew that he had no commitment from Vandenberg beyond an undefined Assistant Directorship, and, having committed himself, he probably thought it unsoldierly to quit before serving out a minimal two-year tour.[311] Actually, he returned to the Army on 14 June 1948.[d]

Sibert's Deputy Assistant Director was George Carey, a remarkably engaging individual. A native of Ilchester, Maryland, he left Johns Hopkins University in 1918, at the age of eighteen, to become a lieutenant in the Royal Canadian Air Force. What he did with himself from 1919 to 1921 is not recorded. From 1921 to 1931 he was employed in alternate years as a collector of big game for the Field Museum and as an investment banker. From 1932 to 1941 he was engaged in organizing and conducting big game hunting expeditions to East Africa and South Asia, at first for Thomas Cook and Son and later in the same business for himself. During the war he was in the Operations Division of the Headquarters, Army Air Forces, but was generally in the field negotiating for the establishment of airbases in the areas in which he had hunted big game. He left the service, a colonel, in 1946, to become a farmer in Maryland.

---

[a][note deleted]

[b]See Part Two, page 76.

[c]Wright's point of view on this deserves mention. Wright knew that he was an abler man than Sibert (he was), yet Sibert had got a star and Wright had not, presumably because Sibert was a West Pointer while Wright was a "mustang." Despite that handicap, Wright eventually became a major general.[310]

[d][note deleted]

Carey was recruited late in 1946 to succeed Kingman Douglass. [one line deleted] As soon as Sibert met him, he made him his Deputy.[313] When Sibert departed on 14 June 1948, Carey succeeded him as ADO. He was then forty-eight.[a]

The NSC Survey Group praised the constituent branches of the Office of Operations but perceived no rationale for their combination in OO. [nine lines deleted]

When the time came to respond to this recommendation, George Carey was at home with a broken leg. Lyman Kirkpatrick [several words deleted] secretly favored the integration of that branch with the clandestine services[b]; his defense of the integrity of OO was feeble.[316] Carey, however, entered a vigorous defense.[c] His general argument was similar to Andrews's with regard to OCD: OO was in the service of the entire intelligence community; its components should not be subordinated to particular customers. [two lines deleted] Hillenkoetter adopted Carey's position, [nine lines deleted]

SUBORDINATION TO THE DDP

[three pages deleted]

SUBORDINATION TO THE DDI

Having successfully averted the dissolution of OO, through its subordination to the DDP, Carey began to importune the DCI, the DDCI

---

[a]As further evidence of the universal esteem in which Carey was held, it may be noted that, when General Wright departed in March 1949, Hillenkoetter asked Carey to be DDCI. Carey declined on the advice of Stuart Symington (then Secretary of the Air Force), who told him that Hillenkoetter's ship was sinking and that he had better remain ADO. Carey's personal friendships with important people in Washington were of great value to the CIA, quite apart from his services as ADO.

[b]Kirkpatrick's ambition to pursue a career in the clandestine services was forwarded when Bedell Smith made him DADSO on 1 July 1951 and ADSO in December, but was frustrated when he was stricken with polio in July 1952. He later became Inspector General (April 1953) and Executive Director (April 1962).

[c][note deleted]

(Dulles), and the DDP (Wisner) for its separation from the clandestine services. Bedell Smith once declared in exasperation that he would have to subordinate OO to himself directly since it was neither overt nor covert.[323]

During 1951 William Jackson was "surveying" the offices subordinate to the DDP, first as DDCI, then as the DCI's Special Assistant and Senior Consultant (in effect, as Inspector General[a]). In August he got around to OO, and in November, persuaded by Carey, he recommended that OO be separated from the DDP and subordinated to the prospective DDI.[324] That was a reversal of the position taken in the Dulles Report, to which Jackson was a party, but that part of the Dulles Report reflected the conceptions of Allen Dulles rather than those of William Jackson.

Frank Wisner (the DDP) was strongly opposed to this recommendation and argued strenuously against it, repeating the considerations marshalled by Dulles in 1948 to show an essential relationship between the [deleted] and the clandestine services. Dulles himself, as DDCI, was less strongly opposed; he suggested that the decision be deferred until the new DDI had been chosen and consulted. Carey heartily endorsed Jackson's recommendation (which was his own). [three lines deleted]

Loftus Becker, the new DDI, had no interest in acquiring OO, but he was persuaded by George Carey's strong feelings on the subject. He spent considerable time reviewing the matter with Dulles, Wisner, Jackson, Hedden, Carey, and Larocque. It was finally settled on 12 February 1952, when Dulles and Wisner agreed to what Becker proposed.[326] Bedell Smith was not personally involved, although he must have approved the agreed solution. On 1 March the Office of Operations was transferred from the DDP to the DDI. [two lines deleted] Thus, the final solution was just what George Carey had wanted it to be.

---

[a]See Part Two, page 105.

XV

PROGRESS REPORT TO
THE NSC

On 11 June 1951 Bedell Smith evidently considered that his reorganization of the CIA pursuant to NSC 50 had been completed. He then directed the preparation of a final report to the NSC on the implementation of NSC 50.[327a]

Because of the pressure of more urgent business, this report was not ready for the Director's signature until 22 April 1952.[328] It covered the reorganization of the CIA through 31 December 1951.

In this document Bedell Smith reported and commented on the "reactivation" of the IAC and the creation of ONE, ORR, the EIC, the Watch Committee, and the CIA Career Service, in that order. He also mentioned four instances of special operational services rendered pursuant to specific NSC direction—a matter that was hardly germane to NSC 50 but that did show the new CIA to be alert, capable, and responsive. Finally, Smith discussed four unsolved problems.[329] They were as follows:

(1) The relation between Intelligence and Operational Planning (see Part Five, page 241).
(2) The security problem resulting from the dispersal of the CIA among twenty-eight buildings in the Washington area and the consequent need to construct a secure new building large enough to house the entire Agency (see Part Four, pages 200–202).
(3) The confusion of responsibility for COMINT. The matter was currently under study by a committee appointed by the President (see Part Five, pages 253–54).

---

[a]Hillenkoetter had rendered previous reports on the subject. This "final" report by Smith with reference to NSC 50 is not to be confused with other similar reports rendered by him with reference to the implementation of NSC 68/4, for which see Part Four.

(4) The coordination of scientific and technical intelligence, concerning which there had been less progress than in any other field. The matter was currently under study by an interagency committee, the Becker Committee (see Part Three, page 178).

Thus, the reorganization of the CIA directed by the NSC in July 1949 was finally accomplished by Bedell Smith during 1951. In accordance with their agreement at the 21 Club,[a] it was chiefly the work of William Jackson, with only occasional personal interventions by Smith. Everything that was done, however, was done by Smith's authority. It could not have been done without his mastery of the situation.[330]

The reorganization of 1950–51 was an essential part of Bedell Smith's performance as Director of Central Intelligence. It was one of his three principal achievements.[b]

---

[a]See Part Two, page 57.

[b]The other two were his mastery of the IAC (Part Two, Chapter V) and his organization of the Clandestine Services (Part Four, Chapter XIX).

PART FOUR

THE WAR
EMERGENCY AND
THE CLANDESTINE
SERVICES

XVI

THE INTENSIFICATION OF INTELLIGENCE ACTIVITIES

It is axiomatic that the situation appreciated in NSC 68 and the policy proposed to meet it require the improvement and intensification of U.S. foreign intelligence and related activities, as a safeguard against political and military surprise, and as essential to the conduct of the affirmative program envisaged.

—NSC 68/1,
21 September 1950

By adopting NSC 50, dated 1 July 1949, the NSC directed the reformation of the CIA as its agency for the coordination of intelligence activities, the production of national intelligence estimates, the performance of intelligence services of common concern, and the conduct of other "activities related to intelligence." How Bedell Smith carried out that direction is recounted in Part Three of this history.

Coincident with Smith's arrival on the scene, the NSC adopted another directive, NSC 68/1, calling for a general intensification of intelligence and related activities to meet the requirements of a national emergency. The sense of emergency that prevailed at that time is hard to imagine nowadays; the war in Indochina has never elicited such a response. It was then thought that the Communist attack in Korea might be the opening gambit of World War III.

Under the terms of NSC 50, the leader of the directed intensification of intelligence activities must be the Director of Central Intelligence. Bedell Smith was called to Washington to perform that service, not just to reform the CIA.

On 31 January 1950 President Truman directed the Secretaries of State and Defense (Dean Acheson and Louis Johnson) to reexamine "our objectives in peace and war and the effect of these objectives on our strategic plans, in the light of the probable fission bomb capability and possible thermonuclear bomb capability of the Soviet Union." The Secretaries submitted their report on 7 April. Its main conclusion was that the development of a Soviet nuclear capability had greatly increased the danger to the United States inherent in the implacable hostility of the Kremlin. This situation required deterrent countermeasures, including an intensification of the U.S. intelligence effort. In general, the report advocated a substantial mobilization of U.S. economic and military resources in the interest of national security. For example, the ceiling on military expenditures, then set at $13.2 billion, should be raised to about $50 billion.[a]

Before making a decision, the President transmitted the Secretaries' report to the National Security Council as NSC 68, requesting a clearer delineation of the specific programs required to carry out the recommended policy.[1] It may be noted in passing that the consequent development of specific programs fortuitously enabled the United States to react quickly to the Communist invasion of South Korea late in June.

NSC 68/1, dated 21 September 1950, was the formal response prepared by an NSC Ad Hoc Committee in which the CIA was represented by Ludwell Montague. The theme of Annex No. 6, "Intelligence and Related Activities," prepared by Montague and adopted without change, was that no considerable improvement of such activities could be accomplished until the NSC itself resolved the still unresolved issues regarding the implementation of NSC 50. As Montague then put it:

> The basic requirement for the improvement of the U.S. intelligence effort is a positive and definitive determination as to the role of the Central Intelligence Agency in relation thereto. The Agency was created to coordinate the intelligence activities of the several departments and agencies of the Government in the interest of national security. In consequence it is responsible for the quality and efficiency, not only of its own operations, but of the total intelligence effort. Its capability to accomplish its mission, however, has been impaired by continuing rivalries among the intelligence agencies and consequent differences as to the true intent and meaning of the pertinent statute and directives. These differ-

---

[a]For the genesis, rationale, and tenor of this report, see Dean Acheson, *Present at the Creation*, pages 344–49 and 373–77.

ences as to the manner in which coordination was to be effected have impeded coordination by any means. In the circumstances the attitude of all concerned has tended to become negative and defensive, inhibiting positive and constructive action in the national interest. The existence of this situation has long been realized. Previous efforts to resolve it by superior direction have resulted only in further differences of interpretation as to intent. Until a clear and positive doctrine is established and maintained, effective coordination of the total U.S. intelligence effort cannot be achieved.[2a]

The foregoing excerpt is a fair description of the situation that Bedell Smith was summoned to master. How he did so is set forth in Part Two, chapter V.

NSC 68/1 provided for its own periodical updating as the specific programs that it recommended were more fully developed and put into execution. Bedell Smith had his first say on the subject in the Annex No. 6 prepared for NSC 68/3, dated 8 December 1950. At his direction, that Annex contained only two sentences. The first was a verbatim quotation of the opening sentence of Annex No. 6 in NSC 68/1 (the text at the head of this chapter). The second was a simple assertion that the DCI and IAC had the matter in hand. It was formally noted that this Annex had been prepared by the CIA with the concurrence of the IAC.[3]

On the next go around, the DCI and IAC had more to say concerning NSC 114.[b] Their contribution consisted of three parts: (1) the text of Appendix A, which was in fact a national intelligence estimate on "Changes in the World Situation Since NSC 68," coordinated by ONE and the IAC in the manner by then established; (2) a revision of Annex No. 6 containing extended comment on coordination, intensification, and difficulties encountered; and (3) a five-paragraph summary of Annex No. 6, which was included in the main text as paragraphs 45–49.[4]

Montague produced the revised Annex No. 6 on the basis of contributions received from the component offices of the CIA and the IAC agencies, and James Q. Reber, the Assistant Director for Intelligence

---

[a]This was the occasion on which Hillenkoetter told Montague, "I will support anything that you say." (See Part One, page 47.) Montague has no recollection of consulting others in the CIA. Interdepartmental coordination was accomplished, not through the IAC, but through the NSC Ad Hoc Committee.

[b]NSC 114, adopted by the NSC Senior Staff on 31 July 1951, was an updating of NSC 68/4, dated 14 December 1950, which was the main text of NSC 68/3 as amended and adopted by the NSC and the President.

Coordination (ADIC), cleared it informally with the members of the IAC on 23 July.[5]

The revised Annex opened with the two one-sentence paragraphs from the previous Annex. It went on to praise the substantial progress made in the development of cooperation and coordination through the active participation of the IAC. Under the heading of *Coordination* it mentioned also the thorough reorganization of the CIA to eliminate duplication of departmental activities and to develop agencies for interdepartmental coordination and for the provision of services of common concern. Specifically mentioned in this connection were ONE and the Board of National Estimates, ORR and the Economic Intelligence Committee, and the Interdepartmental Watch Committee.[6]

Under the heading of *Intensification* the revised Annex declared that as much had been accomplished as could be with the means presently available. Further progress would depend on the augmentation of personnel and facilities. Under *Difficulties* it was noted that all of the intelligence agencies were having difficulty in recruiting qualified personnel. The chief problem was to find them, although the time lag in clearing them was a hindrance. Only State (OIR) was impeded by the lack of an adequate budget. Another problem was lack of space, especially as regards the CIA. This lack imposed intolerable security hazards and operating inefficiencies.[7]

The revised Annex concluded with an estimate that the expansion of the national intelligence effort was now (July 1951) about halfway toward the goal set for mid-1952 and that that goal would be attained.[8]

A new report, NSC 114/2, was almost immediately scheduled for completion on 10 September, primarily because State and the CIA were dissatisfied with the main text of NSC 114.[9] The entire process was repeated, but this time there was less attention paid to what had happened since NSC 68 (April 1950) and more to future prospects and problems. For instance, the Board of National Estimates produced a new estimate for Appendix A, SE-13, with a new title, "Probable Developments in the World Situation."[10]

James Reber, ADIC, undertook to produce as well as coordinate the new text for Annex No. 6. The military representatives rejected his paragraph in praise of the IAC, but their IAC principals overruled them on that.[a]

Reber's draft Annex covered the same ground as the preceding one but added some further specifications of problems requiring solution. The increasing difficulty of clandestine collection in denied areas made

---

[a]See Part Two, pages 72–73.

necessary the development of "scientific" means of collection. There was a general need for increased emphasis on specific collection requirements, for the coordination of collection requirements and priorities, and for periodic reassessment of collection resources. This need was particularly acute with regard to clandestine collection.[a] There was also a need to fix responsibility for the safekeeping and welfare of defectors.[12b]

Reber concluded that the need for more and better intelligence was obvious but that the policymakers and planners could never be fully satisfied. It was imperative that intelligence agencies be granted the personnel and facilities required to do a better job.[13]

The DCI and IAC adopted the 13 September version of this Annex (IAC-D-29/4), and it was incorporated in NSC 114/2, dated 12 October 1951.

In March 1952 the President requested that NSC 68 and NSC 114/2 be reappraised in the light of the revised estimate of Soviet atomic capabilities and the net evaluation of Soviet capabilities to deliver a nuclear attack on the continental United States. The NSC Senior Staff had more than usual difficulty in responding to this request, presumably because of strong internal policy differences. Its draft response went through innumerable revisions before it was finally adopted by the NSC in September as NSC 135/3.[14]

Meanwhile, the intelligence community[c] had developed a new Annex No. 6. It was a new text, by a new and unidentified hand, offered on 9 April in substitution for the text that Reber had coordinated with the IAC representatives.[d] The new version was adopted by the DCI and IAC on 14 April.[16] It provides an interesting review of the state of U.S. intelligence two years after NSC 68 called for the "improvement and intensification" of intelligence activities and eighteen months after General Smith took office as DCI.

With implicit reference to a passage in the "Dulles Report," the new Annex boldly asserted that, under the arrangements made since October

---

[a]The Interagency Clandestine Collection Priorities Committee (IPC) had already been created to meet this problem, on 26 July 1951.[11]

[b]The responsibility of the CIA had already been established by NSCID No. 12 [word deleted]. This problem was therefore internal to the CIA, as between OO and OPC-OSO, with some FBI involvement.

[c]This term first appeared, as "Federal intelligence community," in IAC-D-29/8, dated 9 April 1952, para. 1.

[d]William Bundy was probably the author of this new version. He was then the NSC Staff Assistant. Reber's coordinated draft was overloaded with detail of interest only at the working level. The new draft showed a better sense of what would be of interest at the NSC level.[15]

1950, *national intelligence estimates* were now the authoritative intelligence opinion of the Government. With regard to intelligence research, however, it emphasized that the resources available were insufficient. *Political research* was the responsibility of the Department of State, the intelligence resources of which were inadequate. *Military research* must meet the requirements of the war in Korea and of NATO as well as the requirements for NIEs; the resources available were insufficient. *Economic research* was progressing well under EIC coordination, but the demands for intelligence support to be expected from the newly created economic warfare agencies would probably be beyond the present capacity of the Community. The coordination of effort now planned in the field of *scientific and technical research* should result in some improvement.[17a]

With regard to *intelligence collection,* the new Annex stressed the limitations imposed by Soviet security measures and the consequent need to eliminate marginal targets and to concentrate on truly significant ones. Success would depend on a cooperative concentration of effort and on the development of technological and scientific means. The best effort could not guarantee warning of a surprise attack.[18]

Related programs (covert action operations) would require increasing money and manpower. The chief difficulty was in the recruitment and training of personnel. Greater use of military personnel would be necessary.[19]

This was the last such report rendered by Bedell Smith as DCI.

A crude measure of the intensification of the CIA's activity is the growth of the Agency's personnel strength [three lines deleted].[b]

[two pages deleted]

The indicated increase in personnel presented an acute problem of finding space to house them all.

In October 1950 the CIA was housed chiefly in the former OSS complex at 2430 E Street—four old masonry buildings on the hill and four "temporaries" at its foot. OSO and OPC were isolated in two other temporary structures, K and L, beyond the Reflecting Pool. Other elements were scattered about in makeshift quarters.

This dispersion of the CIA in old buildings constructed for other purposes offended Bedell Smith. It militated against close supervision and control. It also imposed costly operational inefficiencies and security

---

[a]Ironically, at this time the SIC was being destroyed and a weaker SEC was being planned to replace it. (See Part Three, page 178.)

[b]It should also be noted that on 18 December 1950 the CIA went on a "war footing"—that is, a six-day working week.[20]

hazards. Smith soon concluded that the only satisfactory long-term solution of the problem would be to build a new, secure building large enough to house the entire Agency under one roof and designed expressly to meet its needs. Before that could be accomplished, however, it would be urgently necessary to obtain more space for the rapidly increasing Agency population. In April 1951 he obtained Tempos I and J, contiguous to K and L, and in June the Recreation Building in that area as well.[22] That would temporarily accommodate the rapid growth of OPC.

Smith had his eye also on the Munitions Building on Constitution Avenue, where he had once flourished as Secretary of the War Department General Staff.[a] In May 1951 there was thought to be a "strong chance" that it could be obtained within sixty days, but a month later it was said to be "not available."[23] It must have been kept under consideration, however. In July 1952 it was declared to be inadequate, but the adjacent Navy Building would do. "Red" White, the Assistant DDA, was instructed to keep after the Navy Building.[24]

Meanwhile, the plans for a newly constructed building were being developed. In June 1951 it had been expected that it would be authorized by Congress within the next three months and would be completed a year later (by September 1952).[25] In October, however, Smith announced that the new building had been lost for the time being. He would resume with Congress in January. Meanwhile, the plan should be revised. The building planned had been too big. It must be simple and austere.[26]

One problem with regard to a new building was to find a site for it. Smith preferred the "Nevius Tract,"[b] although the Soldiers' Home, Arlington Hall, and Langley were also under consideration. The Agency had requested $38 million for its new building but expected to get only $25 million. It was estimated that a building on the Nevius Tract would cost at least $38 million; one at the Soldiers' Home would cost more. Smith proposed to cut the cost by erecting a simple steel and concrete, windowless, "warehouse-type" building on the Nevius Tract, but Wolf, the DDA, told him that the "Planning Commission" would never allow such a structure to be built on that site.[c] Langley was the only place where a $25 million, "warehouse-type" structure could be built, but Langley was too remote.[28]

In March 1952 Smith decided to ask for $42 million in the hope of

---

[a]The Munitions Building, a 1917 "temporary," was the seat of the War Department until the Pentagon was completed in 1943.

[b]Now the site of the Iwo Jima monument.

[c]The approval of both the National Capital Planning Commission and the Fine Arts Commission would be needed. They would require a "monumental" structure on such a prominent site.[27]

getting $38 million, estimated to be enough for a proper building on the Nevius Tract.[29] In April he reported that the CIA was scattered among twenty-eight buildings in the Washington area and listed the construction of an adequate and secure new building as one among his four most urgent unsolved problems.[30] In June, however, when Wolf told him that a draft bill on the subject was ready for presentation to Congress, Smith told him abruptly and without explanation to withdraw the CIA's request for funds for that purpose.[31]

Why did Smith do that? He had not lost interest in obtaining a new building. He had concluded that it would be inexpedient to press for extra funds in an election year.[32] It appears that he had concluded also that the authorization of a new building would militate against obtaining additional space urgently needed before a new building could be completed. In August he told White that a new building could not be ready before 1955 or 1956.[33] They must therefore try again to get the Navy Building on Constitution Avenue. But if that building proved not available (it was not), then they must again go all out for a new building.[34]

Allen Dulles built the new CIA Headquarters Building at Langley, completed in 1962. A plaque in the entrance declares it to be his monument. But the original impetus for the construction of such a building was Bedell Smith's.

XVII

PSYCHOLOGICAL WARFARE

*We have accepted these responsibilities as agents for the major depart-
ments concerned and for projects approved by the Psychological Strategy Board. . . . The presently projected scope of these activities has . . .
produced a threefold increase in the clandestine operations of this
Agency and will require next year a budget three times larger than that
required for our intelligence activities.*

—Bedell Smith, 23 April 1952

NSC 68 (April 1950)[a] held that the Free World in general and the United
States in particular were already under political, psychological, and
clandestine subversive attack by the Soviet Union and that it behooved
the United States to fight back with the same weapons. The Communist
military attack in Korea (June 1950) intensified the feeling that the U.S.
and the USSR were actually at war. For the time being at least, the
military operations of that war were limited to Korea by mutual choice,
but its other aspects were not thus limited.

The United States already had an agency for the conduct of covert
political action on a rather small scale: the Office of Policy Coordination
in the Central Intelligence Agency.[b] Manifestly, however, its operations
would have to be radically expanded in both variety and scale in order to
carry out the policy adopted by the President when he approved the
conclusions of NSC 68. The general term employed to describe this

---

[a]See page 196.
[b][note deleted]

variety of covert action operations was "psychological warfare." The body established in April 1951 to coordinate this effort was called the Psychological Strategy Board.[a]

Bedell Smith was dismayed by the variety and magnitude of the covert action operations that he was called upon to conduct. [nine lines deleted][36]

Smith feared that preoccupation with such operations on such a scale would divert the CIA from its primary intelligence mission.[37] The Government, he said, must make up its mind whether the CIA was to remain an intelligence agency or whether it was to become a "Cold War Department."[38] He strove to limit his covert operational commitments—with only marginal effect. In particular, he strove to distinguish between covert action operations and guerrilla warfare, which could hardly remain covert. The latter, he contended, should be the responsibility of the Department of Defense and its military theater commanders.[39] Only reluctantly did he come to accept the idea that the CIA must do such things because no one else could or would do them. He then insisted that in such cases the CIA would be acting only as the executive agent for State and Defense, contrary to its own interest as an intelligence organization, and that State and Defense must therefore bear the political responsibility and provide the necessary support.[40]

At the same time, Bedell Smith engaged in a resounding quarrel with the Joints Chiefs of Staff over the control of truly clandestine operations in time of war, an issue on which he was not disposed to yield. At issue was a JCS attempt to take control of both covert action operations[b] and clandestine intelligence collection.[c]

It is convenient to trace the development of the situation with regard to "psychological warfare" along two separate lines: (1) Smith's effort to revise NSC 10/2 and to distinguish between covert action and guerilla warfare, and (2) [six lines deleted].

THE CREATION OF THE PSYCHOLOGICAL STRATEGY BOARD

The initiative for the creation of the Psychological Strategy Board (PSB) came not from Bedell Smith or the CIA, but rather from the NSC Senior

---

[a]There had been an earlier Psychological Strategy Board established within the Department of State (August 1950) with JCS and CIA liaison.[35] It was concerned with overt propaganda and with the coordination of covert action therewith.

[b]See pages 207 and 210.

[c]See Part Five, pages 241–42.

Staff. That body was unable to agree on where in the Government the responsibility for policy formation, coordination, and evaluation with regard to the multifarious "psychological warfare" operations envisaged in NSC 68 should be located. It presented three alternatives to the NSC. They were: (1) closer interdepartmental coordination, without the creation of a new agency; (2) the creation of a planning authority with no operational functions; or (3) the creation of a new executive agency to take over all "psychological warfare" operations, including those of the CIA.[41]

At this time Bedell Smith was not much interested in Allen Dulles's views on the subject. [two lines deleted] He instructed Dulles and Wisner to distinguish between covert action and guerrilla warfare and to limit the CIA's commitment with regard to the latter.[42]

The President chose the second of the three alternatives, mentioned above. With the aid of the Bureau of the Budget, Sidney Souers drafted a directive providing for the establishment of a Psychological Strategy Board under an independent chairman. William Jackson thought that the creation of such an authority would be advantageous to the CIA, and Frank Wisner agreed. Allen Dulles doubted that an adequate chairman could be found outside of the Government.[43]

On 4 April 1951 the President signed a slightly modified directive to the Secretaries of State and Defense and the Director of Central Intelligence. It provided that the PSB would be composed of three members: the Under Secretary of State (then James Webb), the Deputy Secretary of Defense (then Robert Lovett), and the Director of Central Intelligence (Bedell Smith).[a] Those three would decide which of them would be chairman. A representative of the Joint Chiefs of Staff would sit with them as military adviser. Under the Board there would be a staff headed by a director to be appointed by the President.[44]

The PSB would be responsible to the NSC. Its functions would be to provide guidance to the departments and agencies engaged in psychological warfare and to coordinate and evaluate their operations. Responsibility for the planning and execution of such operations would remain as assigned in NSC 10/2 and NSC 59/1.[45]

Webb and Lovett made Bedell Smith the chairman of the PSB.[46] The military adviser was Admiral Leslie Stevens.[47][b] Gordon Gray was chosen to be director of the staff.[48][c]

---

[a]William Foster succeeded Lovett in September 1951; David Bruce succeeded Webb in January 1952.

[b]See Part Two, pages 79 and 93.

[c]Gray, forty-two in 1951, was a graduate of the University of North Carolina and the Yale

The PSB had no voice in Bedell Smith's struggle with the Joint Chiefs of Staff, but it assured him of the sympathetic consideration of the Secretaries of State and Defense, and ultimately it became the means whereby he obtained departmental support for the CIA's covert action operations.

THE REVISION OF NSC 10/2

The basic directive for OPC was NSC 10/2, dated 18 June 1948. Bedell Smith's initial concern with regard to that directive was to counter its implication that OPC was subject to direction by State and Defense rather than by the DCI and to assert his own command and control over that office. He rejected a proposal for the formal revision of NSC 10/2, declaring that his authority as DCI was sufficient, and instead had Frank Wisner, the ADPC, obtain the concurrence of his State, Defense, and JCS advisers in the DCI's interpretation of that document.[a]

That satisfied Smith but not Wisner, who remained concerned regarding the ambiguities of NSC 10/2 respecting control of OPC's operations in time of war. The question was not academic. There was a war already in progress in Korea, no matter what other name might be given to it, and there was acute apprehension that war in Europe might break out at any time. The Joint Chiefs of Staff were pressing urgently for effective planning for that contingency.[49]

Wisner's particular concern was with the conflicting interpretations of paragraph 4 of NSC 10/2, which had been inserted at the insistence of the Joint Chiefs of Staff in 1948. It reads as follows:

In time of war or national emergency, or when the President directs, all plans for covert operations shall be coordinated with

---

Law School. He had worked with William Jackson in the law firm of Carter, Ledyard & Millburn, but was afterwards a publisher and politician in North Carolina. He was Assistant Secretary of the Army, 1947–49, and Secretary, 1949–50. He became President of the University of North Carolina in February 1950 but remained in Washington as Secretary of the Army until April of that year and as Special Assistant to the President until November. Now, only six months after taking office full-time at Chapel Hill, he returned to Washington as Director, PSB. He held that office for only six months, July–December 1951.

[a]See Part Two, page 79. As in other instances, Smith preferred to assert his authority in practice rather than attempt to define it in writing, lest the formulation of a text provoke controversy and result in some undesirable limitation through compromise.

the Joint Chiefs of Staff, and the execution of covert operations in military theaters shall be under the control of the Joint Chiefs of Staff.

By repeated memoranda and direct discussions of the subject, Wisner persuaded Smith to share his concern. On 14 December 1950, just before President Truman proclaimed a state of national emergency, Bedell Smith persuaded the NSC to suspend the operation of paragraph 4 of NSC 10/2 pending its clarification. So doing, he contracted to submit to the NSC as soon as possible a complete revision of NSC 10/2.[50]

This proposed revision of NSC 10/2 was prepared by Wisner in consultation with Admiral Stevens (the designated representative of the JCS), General Magruder (OSD), and Robert Joyce (State), and was submitted by Smith to the NSC on 8 January 1951.[51] [four-and-half pages deleted][a]

The next day Bedell Smith received from James Lay, the Executive Secretary, NSC, President Truman's own copy of the JCS paper. It was sent by direction of the President himself. Its margins were full of scathing comments in the President's own hand.[58]

Meanwhile, General John Magruder, OSD, was advising the Deputy Secretary of Defense (Robert Lovett). The DCI, Magruder said, was trying to work out a reasonable solution, one that would protect the legitimate interests of all concerned, not only the DCI but also the Secretary of State, the JCS, and the theater commander. In contrast, the JCS version was "an example of the extreme positions which can emerge from an insulated atmosphere in which strictly unilateral consideration is given to national issues." The other departments and agencies would not stand for it; both the tone and the content of the JCS position would evoke in them "further prejudice against the JCS, which is now of unwholesome proportions." The Secretary of Defense was faced with a choice between rejecting the JCS position or creating a deadlock in the NSC that could be broken only by the President. To avoid that dilemma, Magruder urged that the Deputy Secretary of Defense (Lovett) meet informally with the Under Secretary of State (Webb), the Director of Central Intelligence (Smith), and the Chairman of the Joint Chiefs of Staff (Bradley) to settle the matter out of court.[59]

The meeting recommended by Magruder was held on 5 April.[b] Bedell Smith then noted that the Department of State and the National Security Resources Board (two of the three statutory members of the NSC) had

---

[a][note deleted]

[b]It may be noted that this was, in effect, the first meeting of the PSB (created the day before—see page 205), with Bradley as the JCS representative.

already approved [fifteen lines deleted]. The others present seized upon the way out of the dilemma that Smith offered them, and so it was done exactly as Smith proposed.[61a]

NSC 10/2, as amended on 16 April 1951, lacked the clarity of [word deleted], but the effect of Smith's revision of paragraph 4 was substantially what [word deleted] had been intended to accomplish. The important difference between the original language of paragraph 4 and the revised version was that the orders to be *transmitted through* the JCS (for their information) would be those of the *DCI*.

[WORDS DELETED] "MAGNITUDE"

The other approach to a definition of the DCI's responsibilities with regard to "psychological warfare" sprang from Bedell Smith's concern regarding the magnitude of OPC's commitments and his desire to reduce them, particularly to foist off upon the JCS the responsibility for supporting guerrilla operations in active theaters of war [word deleted]. In this Smith was discreetly opposed and eventually frustrated by Allen Dulles and Frank Wisner. For sound doctrinal reasons, they wanted to retain control of any guerrilla movements that the CIA had generated, even in time of war and even after such operations had grown to such a scale as would require military direction and logistical support. [one-and-a-half lines deleted][b] That is why he was readily disposed to suspend NSC consideration of it until he could make another attempt to transfer to the JCS the responsibility for guerrilla warfare.[c]

In February 1951 Bedell Smith observed that the OPC budget for Fiscal 1952 provided for operations that were beyond the CIA's present authority and administrative capacity. That budget was useful for planning purposes, but the CIA could undertake such planning only pending a determination with regard to the executive responsibility for such operations. The business of the CIA was to gather intelligence. If other tasks kept being piled on, the CIA would have to turn them over to other

---

[a]In submitting this agreement to the NSC, Smith proposed to submit further recommendations with regard to when it had been determined whether responsibility [one-half line deleted] could be transferred to another agency (for example, to the JCS).

[b][note deleted]

[c]The JCS, for their part, desired to control the CIA's operations in the sense of directing what the CIA should undertake, but still wanted the CIA to do the dirty work of implementation for them.

agencies.[62] A week later, when the JCS was briefed on the CIA's covert operations, Smith emphasized that the CIA was doing the advanced planning indicated only because no one else was doing it, and without commitment to carry out such plans.[63]

In order to obtain a decision regarding the extent of the CIA's responsibilities in this field, Smith submitted to the NSC a memorandum on the "Scope and Pace of Covert Operations." It was in the form of a JCS staff study. The stated problem was

> to obtain more specific guidance from the National Security Council in order to define the projected scope and pace of covert operations in aid of the current covert cold war and of military preparations to meet overt global war, and to insure timely and effective support for such operations.[64]

In this memorandum, dated 8 May 1951, Bedell Smith argued that the scope of the CIA's covert operations already far exceeded what had been contemplated in NSC 10/2 (1948) and that still greater increases would be required to discharge the missions now proposed by State, Defense, and the JCS, and implicit in NSC 68. Operations on this scale were beyond the CIA's present administrative capabilities. Some policy decisions were required. For instance, to what extent would the United States support counterrevolution in the "slave states" (the Soviet satellite states)? NSC 10/2 required that covert operations be conducted in such a way that U.S. involvement could be plausibly denied. U.S. involvement in a counterrevolution in Eastern Europe would be as obvious as Soviet involvement in Greece had been.[a] Moreover, the Joint Chiefs of Staff were demanding first priority for "retardation" in the event of war.[b] Priority was a political question.[65c]

Smith recommended that, in view of the magnitude of the issue and the policy guidance needed, the NSC should initiate a comprehensive review of the subject, including a restatement or redetermination of the responsibilities and authorities involved in such operations. If the CIA were to be made responsible, then provision should be made for (1) joint planning with the military authorities; (2) specific guidance with regard

---

[a] It is now thought that the Greek civil war was a Yugoslav operation of which Stalin disapproved and that Stalin's objection to Tito's adventurism in Greece was the beginning of the breach between Yugoslavia and the USSR.

[b] [note deleted]

[c] To foment counterrevolution would expose whatever assets the CIA might have for retardation. To conserve those assets would preclude counterrevolution. Thus, counterrevolution and retardation were mutually exclusive policy choices.

to dual cold war and military missions; (3) bringing political considerations to bear; and (4) the provision of personnel and of administrative and logistical support. Finally, Smith suggested that, when the interests of both State and Defense were involved, the recently established PSB should provide the required guidance.[66]

Smith's "Magnitude Paper" was referred to a special committee of the NSC Senior Staff composed of Paul Nitze (State), Frank Nash (Defense), Admiral Wooldridge (JCS), and William Jackson (CIA). Seven weeks later (27 June) this special committee recommended that the NSC (1) approve in principle the immediate expansion of OPC and the intensification of its activities; (2) reaffirm the responsibility and authority of the DCI for the conduct of covert operations, subject to the policy guidance provided for in NSC 10/2 and the approval of the PSB; and (3) charge the PSB with responsibility for determining the desirability and feasibility of particular operations, and their scope, pace, timing, and priorities, and for ensuring the provision of adequate personnel, funds, and logistic support for them by the Departments of State and Defense. [four lines deleted]

This response was not exactly the one that Smith had sought. It committed him to the conduct of covert operations on a very large scale, [two lines deleted]. At the same time, it did "reaffirm" his authority to conduct such operations, and it did make the PSB responsible for determining what covert operations should be undertaken and for obtaining adequate support for them from State and Defense.

The recommendations of the special committee were sent to the Joint Chiefs of Staff for comment prior to NSC consideration of them.[a] Another seven weeks passed before the Chiefs vouchsafed to present their views (15 August). They recommended the development of a program of covert action against the USSR of "great magnitude." To that end, the PSB should develop a strategic concept and a national program consistent with current military planning and should present them to the NSC for approval. That approval having been obtained, the appropriate executive agencies should submit their detailed operational plans to the PSB for approval. Any case of interdepartmental conflict with regard to these plans should be referred to the NSC for decision. All this having been done, the Department of Defense should support the covert operations approved by the NSC to the extent that the Joint Chiefs of Staff found it convenient to do so without hindrance to any military program. Only the President could override the judgment of the Joint Chiefs of Staff on such a matter.[68]

---

[a]This was the standard practice. See page [deleted].

The obvious purpose of this elaborate procedure proposed by the Joint Chiefs of Staff, requiring NSC, even Presidential, decisions on the details of operational plans, was to gain for the Joint Chiefs of Staff [two lines deleted]. The JCS had no voice in the PSB, except insofar as they were represented by a "military adviser," but custom at least required the Secretary of Defense to obtain their advice (and consent?) before participating in an NSC action.

Frank Wisner was most dismayed to observe that he could expect no military support for his planned operations until this elaborate bureaucratic rigmarole had been accomplished, if then.[69]

On 28 August, William Jackson reported that the NSC Senior Staff had summarily rejected as irrelevant the procedure recommended by the Joint Chiefs of Staff. With the JCS representative participating and concurring, they had reviewed their 27 June recommendations to the NSC and had readopted them with only three insignificant verbal changes. Jackson was confident that the NSC itself would adopt that paper. Whether the CIA would be able to obtain adequate military support thereafter was another question.[70]

The Joint Chiefs of Staff were not to be dismissed as easily as that. Admiral Wooldridge was forced to reopen the subject; the matter remained in contention for another two months. Not until 23 October did the NSC itself finally adopt a text substantially identical with that submitted to it on 27 June.[a] [one line deleted]

In conjunction with the amendment of paragraph 4 of NSC 10/2, [three lines deleted]. At the same time, the PSB was made responsible for determining what covert operations should be undertaken and for obtaining adequate support for them from the Departments of State and Defense.

[nine-line paragraph deleted]

Smith's position on this subject, [several words deleted], was set forth in his report to the NSC dated 23 April 1952.[74] [fourteen lines deleted]

Given the necessary support from State and Defense, the CIA could perform the task, Smith said, but in view of the large increase in the Agency's budget and personnel strength there were three points that should be noted. They were: [twelve lines deleted].

Thus, Bedell Smith yielded, regretfully, to the doctrine of Allen Dulles that clandestine intelligence collection and covert "psychological warfare" were inseparable,[b] [two lines deleted]. He remained determined to force State and Defense to accept responsibility for each covert undertaking and to support it adequately, through the mechanism of the PSB.

---

[a]See page 210.
[b]See Part Two, page 72.

THE FUNCTIONING OF THE PSB

On 27 June 1951 the special committee of the NSC Senior Staff had noted that the Psychological Strategy Board, created on 4 April, was not yet functioning.[a] That statement was repeated in [word deleted] 23 October 1951. The reasons for this delay were the difficulty of finding a director for the PSB staff and then Gordon Gray's personal difficulty in leaving the University of North Carolina to make himself available full time in Washington.[b] Bedell Smith was exasperated by Gray's slowness in getting the PSB staff organized and functioning.[75]

Smith became even more dissatisfied when the PSB staff did begin to function. In September he objected that Gray was intruding into operational matters. According to the President's directive of 4 April, the PSB was to coordinate psychological warfare strategy but was expressly prohibited from engaging in operations.[76c] In October, Smith and Webb agreed that the PSB (that is, the PSB staff) was headed in the wrong direction. The PSB (the staff) should be a small steering committee but instead had become a large papermill.[77d]

At the end of the year Gordon Gray returned to the University of North Carolina and was succeeded by Admiral Alan Kirk.[e] That change relieved some of the tension, because of Smith's personal liking for Kirk, but it did not relieve Smith's dissatisfaction with the staff that Gray had created. That staff was composed of psychological warfare theorists without operational experience. It was pestering the DDI and others with demands for "intelligence support" far beyond its need to know.[f] Smith held that the regular briefings that it received from OCI were sufficient for its general information; it must justify any further intelligence requirements in relation to specific projects.[79] He agreed with Dulles that the formal papers that the staff was submitting to the PSB were at a level

---

[a]See page 210.

[b]See page 206.

[c]See page 205. The PSB was, however, charged with evaluating the operations of the CIA and others.

[d]Defense and the JCS, however, wanted the PSB to engage in elaborate paper exercises. (See pages 210–11.)

[e]Kirk, sixty-four in 1952, was well known to Bedell Smith. He had crowned a distinguished career in the Navy by commanding the U.S. naval forces engaged in the invasions of Sicily and Normandy and had succeeded Smith as Ambassador to Moscow, 1949–52.

[f]ORE had planned a major effort to provide specialized intelligence support for psychological warfare. Jackson had included that among the functions transferred from ORE to State (OTR) (see Part Three, pages 161–62), but State had done nothing about it. Finally, in June 1952, State undertook to establish a Psychological Warfare Support Staff in OIR.[78]

of generality more appropriate to the NSC or the JCS than to the practical concerns of the PSB.[80] At the same time, he insisted that the PSB must act to control the intrusions of its staff into operational matters.[81]

One gathers that Bedell Smith considered the PSB staff incompetent and its work irrelevant. He created another body to attend to what he regarded as the real business of the PSB.[a]

From the first, Smith had been concerned about the magnitude and growth rate of the OPC budget. He directed that in that budget a distinction should be made between those covert operations that produced some intelligence information and those that did not.[82] He felt that as DCI he should be responsible to justify only those CIA operations that produced intelligence. If with respect to other covert operations he was merely the executive agent for State and Defense, then the expense of those operations should be chargeable to those departments and be justified by them. In November 1951 he actually persuaded the sympathetic representatives of State, Defense, and the JCS[b] to agree to that proposition.[83] In February 1952 it turned out, however, that the CIA would have to defend the entire OPC budget.[84]

Bedell Smith was convinced that OPC had undertaken numerous projects of doubtful value, at the casual suggestion of its departmental consultants or through its own enthusiasm for covert operations. He appointed a special board to review in detail every OPC project and to eliminate every one that could not be justified as necessary to carry out a formal commitment to State, Defense, or the NSC. This group soon came to be known as the "Murder Board."[85] It recommended the elimination of about one-third of OPC's projects.[86c]

In October 1952 Smith announced a new procedure to govern the initiation of new covert action projects. Any proposal would first be reviewed by a committee within the CIA, which would submit its recommendation to the DDP (Wisner). If he approved, he would submit it to the DCI, who, if he approved, would pass it to a high-level review board under the PSB, which would submit its recommendation to the PSB. No project would be undertaken unless and until it had been approved by the PSB. The function of the PSB, however, was not to pass on operational details, but only to consider projects in relation to the overall programs and policies of State and Defense.[87]

When on 30 October 1952 Bedell Smith formally proposed to the PSB

---

[a]See below and next page.

[b]That is, Robert Joyce, John Magruder, and Leslie Stevens.

[c]These were by definition a multitude of minor projects of doubtful or marginal value. They did not amount to one-third of the actual work in progress.

the creation of this "high-level review board," he already had oral agreement with regard to it[88] and was writing only for the record. He declared that the CIA, as an operating agency, required more than policy guidance. The programs and projects proposed must be scrutinized for PSB *approval*, and their net value must be periodically assessed. The existing arrangements forced the CIA to assume too much responsibility and authority. On the other hand, the distinguished members of the PSB (the Under Secretary of State and the Deputy Secretary of Defense) could not be expected to review operational plans in detail. What they needed was the recommendations of qualified subordinates, one for each, chaired by the director of the PSB staff (Admiral Kirk). This reviewing group should not only recommend the approval or disapproval of projects but also check periodically as to whether they should be continued or discounted, speeded or slowed, increased or decreased.[89]

Bedell Smith's evident motives in presenting this proposal were (1) to cut out the worthless PSB staff, (2) to obtain the endorsement of acceptable projects by technically competent (and friendly) departmental representatives, and (3) through their recommendations to obtain the personal approval of the distinguished members of the PSB as a means of committing their departments to responsibility for and adequate support of the projects approved by them. Besides Admiral Kirk, the members of the "high-level" reviewing group were Robert Joyce and John Magruder, who had long been associated with OPC as representatives of State and Defense, and Wayne Jackson representing the CIA.[90a]

This arrangement had hardly been made when the PSB itself was abolished. Probably at the instigation of C. D. Jackson,[b] President-elect Eisenhower decided that the entire system for the direction and conduct of "cold war activities" should be reappraised.

---

[a]Wayne Jackson, forty-seven in 1952, was a graduate of the Yale Law School who had shared an office with William Jackson in Carter, Ledyard & Millburn. He had served in the War Production Board and the Department of State from 1941 to 1951. In January 1951 William Jackson brought him into the CIA to be Allen Dulles's only personal assistant as DDP. From September 1952 until January 1957 Wayne Jackson was special assistant to the DCI. He was a member of the Board of National Estimates from January 1957 until his retirement in January 1969.

[b]C. D. Jackson, an important figure in the Time–Life–Fortune complex, had been active in Eisenhower's campaign for the presidency. Before that he had been Eisenhower's principal psychological warrior in Europe. Bedell Smith once praised Jackson as the most successful psychological warrior he had ever known. While Jackson preened himself, Smith went on to explain that C.D. had planned a leaflet drop on Polish and Russian "slave labor" camps in Germany. The bundle of leaflets had failed to open. It struck and sank a barge in the Rhine—and that, said Smith, was the greatest achievement of psychological warfare in Europe! [four lines deleted]

Bedell Smith rejected C. D. Jackson's plan for accomplishing this purpose. He rejected also the idea of a DCI-appointed committee: "We cannot adequately appraise ourselves." He preferred to have the new Secretaries of State and Defense appoint and instruct a committee. That would have to be deferred until the new Administration took office. "We will not win or lose the Cold War within the next two months."[92]

In the event, the Jackson Committee was appointed by President Eisenhower just as Bedell Smith was leaving office as DCI. William Jackson was its Chairman, C. D. Jackson was a member, and Wayne Jackson was its chief of staff. This multiplicity of CIA-related Jacksons occasioned some merriment.

The Jackson Committee held that the Psychological Strategy Board was based on a false premise. There could be no such thing as a psychological strategy distinguishable from the general policy of the Government as determined by the President with the advice of the NSC. Consequently the Psychological Strategy Board was abolished and the Operations Coordinating Board (OCB) was substituted for it. The function of this Board was to coordinate the program undertaken by the various departments and agencies in implementation of particular NSC policy papers.[93] This was similar to the work of the PSB, but no longer was there any premise of devising a distinct psychological strategy. That was quite in accord with the views of Bedell Smith.[a]

The members of the PSB (the Under Secretary of State, the Deputy Secretary of Defense, and the Director of Central Intelligence) continued to be the principal members of the OCB. When Bedell Smith ceased to be DCI and became Under Secretary of State, some question arose about the chairmanship, but not in the mind of Bedell Smith. Who could imagine Bedell Smith being a member of a board without being its chairman? Without a break in stride, Bedell Smith, the Under Secretary of State, continued to preside over the PSB in its last days and over the OCB.

---

[a]Compare the contrasting position taken by the Joint Chiefs of Staff in August 1951, pages 210–11.

XVIII

THE ORGANIZATION OF THE CLANDESTINE SERVICES

This paper . . . is designed to create a single overseas clandestine service, while at the same time preserving the integrity of the long-range espionage and counterespionage mission of CIA from amalgamation into those clandestine activities which are subject to short term variations in the prosecution of the cold war. . . . There is no reason why the establishment of a single chain of command and of uniform administrative procedures would have any effect of submerging specialized OSO or OPC missions and techniques if intelligently applied.

—Bedell Smith, 15 July 1952

Bedell Smith's third major achievement as Director of Central Intelligence was his organization of the Clandestine Services.[a] The idea of integrating OSO and OPC had been advocated by Allen Dulles since 1948, but was initially opposed by Smith. [one line deleted] Smith sought to make a clear distinction between the intelligence activities of the CIA, including clandestine collection by OSO, and the covert operations of OPC.[b] Thereafter this idea became less important to him and the advantages of a simpler chain of command and control over all overseas operations more attractive. In the end, it was Smith who dictated the

---

[a]The other two were his development of a cooperative relationship with the IAC (see Part Two, Chapter V) and his reorganization of the DDI offices pursuant to NSC 50 (see Part Three). In general, Smith preferred to say that he had *organized* the CIA (which he had found *un*organized). That was substantially true. (See Part Two, pages 76–77.)

[b]See Chapter XVII.

terms of the merger, in July 1952. Only a man of his force of character could have imposed it on OSO.

THE DULLES CONCEPTION

In May 1948 Allen Dulles moved to counter a State Department proposal by advising the NSC that clandestine intelligence collection and covert operations should be under the control of a single director. That intervention resulted in the establishment of OPC in the CIA, though not under the clear control of the DCI.[a]

In the division of labor within the NSC Survey Group, Allen Dulles took as his province not only all CIA clandestine operations, for both intelligence collection and political action, but also all of the CIA's overt collection activities as well.[b] Not surprisingly, the NSC Survey Group found that all such activities should be brought under a single direction below the level of the DCI. Specifically, its recommendation was that OSO, OPC, [words deleted] and perhaps also the Foreign Broadcast Information Branch (FBIB) of OO should be "integrated" in a new self-sufficient and semi-autonomous "Operations Division."[94]

In adopting the recommendations of NSC 50, the NSC adopted this recommendation, excluding the FBIB, and directed the DCI to carry it out.[95] Admiral Hillenkoetter promptly submitted a plan for this purpose, but inasmuch as it required the amendment of NSC 10/2 in a way that would transfer the effective control of OPC from State to the DCI, it was not adopted.[c] (Apparently that consequence of the Survey Group's recommendation had not been foreseen!) Thus, when Bedell Smith became DCI in October 1950, the situation with regard to OSO, OPC, and OO remained exactly as it had been in January 1949, when the NSC Survey Group submitted the recommendations of Allen Dulles to the NSC.

BEDELL SMITH'S INITIAL CONCEPTION

On 12 October 1950 General Smith told the NSC that he would promptly comply with the direction contained in NSC 50, with one exception: he

---

[a]See Part Two, pages 77–79.
[b]See Part One, page 43.
[c]See Part Three, page 111.

would not merge OSO, OPC, and [words deleted] OO. The NSC accepted that exception without inquiring why the DCI was opposed to the merger or what alternative arrangement he had in mind.[a]

There is no record of Smith's reasons for making this exception. From his subsequent actions, however, two considerations can be inferred: (1) he wished to maintain a clear distinction between clandestine intelligence collection and covert action operations by preserving an organizational distinction between OSO and OPC, and (2) he hoped to effect the necessary coordination between them by appointing a Deputy Director to have supervision of both. That Deputy Director was, of course, Allen Dulles.[b]

Although it thus appears that Bedell Smith intended from the first to have a deputy particularly charged with the supervision and coordination of OSO and OPC, he realized also from the first that two CIA units operating independently in the same overseas area would require some local supervision and coordination. For this purpose he devised a system of Senior Representatives (of the DCI) abroad.

Smith's intention to appoint such Senior Representatives was known in OSO as early as 12 October 1950—one week after Smith had taken office as DCI, one month before Dulles came to Washington as a consultant, two and a half months before Dulles took office as DDP. In short, this was Smith's idea, not Dulles's, and it, like the appointment of a DDP, was intended to be a substitute for the integration of OSO and OPC, not a step in that direction.[96c]

[fifteen-line paragraph, with note(s), deleted]

These Senior Representatives were not in the chain of command. That still ran from the ADSO or the ADPC to their respective station chiefs in the field. The Senior Representatives were, essentially, local observers for the DCI, reporting directly to him and not subject to let or hindrance by the ADSO, the ADPC, or the DDP. They were to be kept fully informed by the field stations under their supervision and could intervene with advice, though not with orders.[97] Their leverage was that, if their advice was disregarded, they would submit their recommendations to the DCI, who would then issue his own orders to the ADSO or ADPC.

---

[a]See Part Two, page 62.

[b]For the considerations that entered into the selection of Dulles, see Part Two, page 91.

[c]To quiet apprehensions in OSO that the appointment of Senior Representatives would be a first step toward integration, the ADSO (Colonel Schow) gave out assurances that General Smith had no such intention.

[d][note deleted]

[e][notes deleted]

This was not a good system of command and control. It was perhaps the best that could be contrived at the time, given a basic decision that the operations of OSO and OPC must be kept separate and distinct.

CREEPING INTEGRATION

Allen Dulles was of the same opinion still. The steps that he took as DDP to coordinate the activities of OSO and OPC were plainly designed to lead eventually to integration.

That coordination was sorely needed is evidenced by a memorandum dated 7 February 1951 from the DCI's Executive Assistant (Lyman Kirkpatrick) for the DDP (Allen Dulles). Both OSO and OPC had made independent approaches to the same individuals and groups with a view to recruitment. There was similar confusing duplication in the two offices' operational liaison with other U.S. agencies [words deleted] and further duplication in such matters as communications and procurement. OSO was concerned lest the security of its long-term clandestine penetrations be jeopardized by OPC's widespread contacts.[98a]

This memorandum prompted Dulles to call a meeting on the subject of OSO-OPC coordination. The outcome of that meeting was merely the appointment of a committee to study the subject and submit recommendations. It is significant, however, that Kirkpatrick recorded the proceedings under the title of "Meeting on Integration of OSO and OPC."[100] Thus, it appears that the thrust of the discussion was toward integration, although integration was contrary to the policy of the DCI at the time.

The committee appointed on 14 February [one-and-a-half lines deleted]. They rendered their report a month later. In essence, it recommended that certain administrative and support functions common to OSO and OPC be integrated but that the operational elements of the two offices be kept distinctly separate.[101]

Meanwhile, by direction of the DDP, a process had already been begun that plainly pointed toward the eventual integration of the operating elements of the two offices. As a first step, the ADPC, Frank Wisner, met on 3 March with the new ADSO, Major General Willard Wyman,[b] and

---

[a]Kirkpatrick was a highly ambitious young man (thirty-five in 1951). As Executive Assistant and later as ADSO, he was always "playing his own game" (not OSO's). His constant object was to outflank Frank Wisner as ADPC and later as DDP.[99] (See Part Three, page 188, and page 223, below.)

[b]General Wyman relieved Colonel Schow as ADSO on 15 February 1951. Wyman had had no intelligence experience, but considerable command experience overseas.

they agreed upon a redefinition of the territories to be covered by their respective area divisions so that they would correspond exactly to one another.[102] The next step was to rearrange the office space allotted to these divisions so that the corresponding divisions would be adjacent to each other. That was not easily done in the cramped quarters available.[a] By the end of June, however, it had been accomplished.[103] And it could be anticipated that, when this rearrangement had been made, the next step would be the appointment of a common chief for each pair of divisions.

So it happened. On 9 June 1951 the ADSO and the ADPC agreed to combine their small Latin American divisions into one common Western Hemisphere Division. Its chief, from OSO, reported to both Assistant Directors. Below him the OSO and OPC elements of the combined division remained distinct.[104] This was not yet true integration, but it was coming close.

Meanwhile, in March, Wyman proposed to Wisner that their overseas operating bases targeted against the USSR should be combined, [words deleted].[105] The DCI himself approved that proposal on 18 April.[106]

Thus, it will be seen that by the summer of 1951 Allen Dulles, Frank Wisner, and Willard Wyman had gone a long way toward integrating OSO and OPC—despite the fact that during the same period Bedell Smith was constantly directing them to keep the operations of OSO and OPC separate and distinct.[b] Dulles, Wisner, and Wyman complied, technically, with Smith's direction, but it is evident that they were working toward integration as an ultimate objective, an objective that General Smith was not yet prepared to approve.

It is also evident that General Wyman's attitude in this respect was quite different from that of the old hands in OSO as represented by Richard Helms.[c]

THE OSO ATTITUDE TOWARD INTEGRATION

OSO was derived from the clandestine services of the OSS.[d] By 1951 it had been a going concern for ten years, and its old hands regarded

---

[a]It was necessary to find enough additional space to hold one complete division while another moved into the space that it had vacated, and so on.

[b]See Chapter XVII, above. At this time Smith hoped to rid himself of most of OPC's operational commitments, which was his reason for seeking to preserve the distinction between OSO and OPC.

[c]See pages 219 and 220.

[d]When the OSS was dismembered on 1 October 1945, these elements became the War

themselves as professional clandestine operators. From their point of view, OPC was a parvenu, its ranks composed of enthusiastic but inexperienced amateurs. To be sure, some members of OPC were OSS veterans, notably Frank Wisner, the ADPC, but they had left the service at the end of the war and so had not had the continuous experience of the OSO professionals. Moreover, they had not shared in OSO's struggle to survive in the postwar world and so could not really be members of the clan.

Another factor in OSO's antipathy toward OPC was that OPC was born rich, while OSO remained relatively poor. That was true not only of office budgets but of personal pay as well. Since the establishment of the OSO grade and pay structure, there had been a general inflation in such matters. In order to recruit, OPC had to offer higher grades than were available in OSO for similar work. Thus, the "amateurs" in OPC were generally better paid than the professionals in OSO. That must have rankled. A related factor was that OPC was expanding rapidly while OSO remained generally static. Consequently not only the pay but also the prospects for promotion were better in OPC.

Another source of institutional jealousy was that OSO was committed to a long-term and, by definition, unspectacular task, while much of OPC's work was designed to produce an immediate or early impact, from which a sense of current achievement could be derived.[a] The urgency with which OPC undertook these tasks made it easy for the OSO professionals to regard the OPC "amateurs" as reckless adventurists. And, given OPC's dependence on OSO's clandestine contacts, there was some substance to OSO's concern lest OPC's operations expose OSO's assets. OSO's operations were not by nature self-revealing, but the effect of any successful OPC operation would necessarily be noticeable and therefore might provoke investigation and counteraction by the enemy.[107]

On 24 May 1951 William Jackson, the DDCI, brought the subject of integration into the open. In reporting on his survey of OPC, he recommended "that ultimately covert intelligence and covert operations be administered through a single command chain down to the station level."[108] That recommendation evidently reflected OPC's then current view. It was made subject to confirmation after Jackson had completed his survey of OSO.

Department's Strategic Services Unit (SSU). OSO was derived from SSU and activated on 11 July 1946, although organizational continuity was then technically broken. (See Part Two, page 87.)

[a]It should be noticed, however, that a large part of OPC's work consisted of planning and preparations for contingencies that might never arise.

[nine-line paragraph deleted]

It appears that William Jackson never rendered a written report on his survey of OSO, which was made during July and August.[a] There is in the record, however, a lengthy memorandum from Lyman Kirkpatrick, the new DADSO,[b] to Jackson, dated 31 August 1951, which states itself to be based on Kirkpatrick's participation in Jackson's survey of OSO.[110] This memorandum may have been intended to serve as a contribution to Jackson's eventual report, but it was decidedly at variance with the view that Jackson had acquired in OPC.

Kirkpatrick certainly did not contemplate an integrated chain of command down to station level. Rather, he recommended a redefinition of functions so that OSO would hold a monopoly of all contacts with clandestine agents and underground organizations, whether for intelligence collection or for covert action operations, and OPC would be left with only such political and psychological activities as did not involve such contacts.[111c] This proposal became the key to OSO's attitude toward integration from that time forward: that any merger of OSO and OPC functions should occur within OSO, under OSO control.

Kirkpatrick recommended also "that the staff of the DDP be held to an absolute minimum so that the present operating offices will not be echeloned down to a lower level, and that the operating support units being currently gathered around DDP not become the tail wagging the operating dog, just as the CIA administrative staff once did."[112] Whatever the merits of that matter, this reference to the findings of the NSC Survey Group was a plain appeal to Jackson's prejudice against Hillenkoetter's administrative staff.

[nineteen lines, with [d]note, deleted]

On 24 October, General Wyman, on his return from a visit to the Far East, strongly urged upon General Smith the necessity of integrating the field operations of OSO and OPC, but his idea of how that should be done was similar to Kirkpatrick's recommendation to Jackson in August.[115e]

---

[a]Jackson ceased to be DDCI on 3 August, when he signed a personal services contract (WAE). He returned to private business but remained active in CIA affairs as the DCI's Special Assistant and Senior Consultant. In 1956 President Eisenhower named Jackson Special Assistant for National Security Affairs. Jackson later retired to Arizona, where he died on 28 September 1971. Allen Dulles succeeded Jackson as DDCI on 23 August 1951, at which time Frank Wisner became DDP and Kilbourne Johnson ADPC.

[b]Kirkpatrick, the DCI's first Executive Assistant, became DADSO on 1 July and ADSO on 17 December.

[c][note deleted]

[d][note deleted]

[e]See above.

Wyman supplemented his memorandum for Smith with another for Jackson that supplies the following quotation: "I strongly believe that those functions now regarded as belonging to OPC, but which are of a purely clandestine intelligence nature, should be controlled by those individuals engaged in intelligence work."[116] On 13 November Allen Dulles (DDCI) reported to the Director's morning meeting that General Wyman felt strongly "that operations should be subordinated to intelligence."[117] That generalized statement was not a precise reflection of the Wyman–Kirkpatrick position, but shows how it was understood (and reacted to) by Dulles, and also by Wisner and Johnston.

General Wyman departed on 13 December 1951 to accept a command in Korea. Lyman Kirkpatrick succeeded him as ADSO on 17 December and Richard Helms became DADSO.

THE DCI ACCEPTS INTEGRATION AS A GOAL

It appears that the turning point in Bedell Smith's attitude toward integration was the NSC's adoption of [eight lines deleted]. He promptly withdrew [word deleted] from further consideration.[a]

From that point onward the question was not whether OSO and OPC would be integrated, but only how that should be done.

On 8 January 1952 Smith signed an order prepared by Wisner directing that the remaining area divisions of OSO and OPC be merged.[b] The merged divisions would be responsible directly to the DDP as a single operating service.[118] Thus, the chain of command would run from the DCI through the DDP to the division chiefs, and the ADSO and ADPC would become merely staff officers to the DDP.

At the same time, Wisner mentioned the low state of morale in OSO and OPC. Both Kirkpatrick (the ADSO) and Johnston (the ADPC) wished to see Smith about that. Smith evaded Kirkpatrick's request to brief him on the merger but consented to visit OPC for morale-building purposes.[119] There Smith confessed to the principal officers of OPC that he "screamed like a wounded buffalo" when disappointed but said that they must not take that too hard. He really appreciated their operational skill and devoted service; he depended on them.[120] That apparently took care of the moral problem in OPC.

---

[a]See pages 208 and 211.

[b][note deleted]

Meanwhile, OSO was fighting a rearguard action. On 31 January [name deleted] then Acting ADSO, saw Frank Wisner and [name deleted] (DADPC) and persuaded them, he believed, to slow down the merger process. He said that he was not opposing the merger as such but that he was concerned regarding the security of OSO's clandestine assets if the ADSO were to lose control of his own operations and personnel to the chiefs of the merged divisions.[121] In short, the ADSO must be kept in the chain of command, at least for the time being.

By March 1952 it was felt in the ADPC's staff that any further progress toward integration, particularly in the field, would be resisted by the ADSO and his immediate staff, though not by the OSO personnel in the merged divisions.[122]

[three pages, including one whole section, deleted]

INTEGRATION ACCOMPLISHED

On 17 April 1952 Wisner, Johnston, and Kirkpatrick met at Johnston's home in Fairfax. Wisner and Johnston understood that Kirkpatrick then agreed to proceed toward the more complete integration of OSO and OPC, and in particular to clarify the *command* position of the DDP and the *staff* positions of the ADSO and the ADPC.[131] The next morning Wisner reported this happy development at the Director's morning meeting. Smith then remarked that it was not necessary to go too far toward integration, that the merger was really a matter of coordination.[132]

The substance of this so-called Fairfax Agreement was already clearly implicit in General Smith's order of 8 January.[a] Thus, the agreement, if there was one, was nothing more than an agreement to proceed further toward the implementation of that order. Two weeks later, on 2 May 1952, however, Kirkpatrick submitted a plan for "integration" that was radically at variance with Smith's order as well as with the supposed "Fairfax Agreement" but entirely consistent with Kirkpatrick's recommendations to Jackson in August 1951[b] and with the principle advocated by Helms in March 1951 and January 1952.[c] The essence of it was that the ADSO would retain *command* of OSO.

Kirkpatrick proposed that OPC should be divided into two offices,

---

[a]See page 224.
[b]See page 223.
[c]See page 220 and above.

Psychological Warfare and Paramilitary Activities. Those two offices and OSO "should retain their integrity as offices with separate, independent staffs and with full command control under DDP of their personnel, budget and missions." There should, however, be a strong Vice DDP to give operational and management direction to them and to control compartmentalization between them.[133a]

Kirkpatrick's proposal of 2 May 1952 was the last stand of OSO against integration.

Kilbourne Johnston, the ADPC, forwarded Kirkpatrick's proposal to Frank Wisner, the DDP, with a furious but cogent memorandum of dissent.[134] It is not apparent what Wisner did then, but it is evident that Kirkpatrick's paper did reach Bedell Smith in one way or another. Smith rejected Kirkpatrick's conception of a trifurcated command structure, but he adapted some of Kirkpatrick's ideas to his own conception of a single chain of command down to the chiefs of merged overseas stations.[b]

The next development was a meeting in late May arranged by Wisner and attended by Smith, Wisner, Johnston, and Helms (as Acting ADSO in Kirkpatrick's absence).[135] The result of that meeting was that Helms prepared at Smith's direction a draft dated 4 June 1952 and entitled "A Proposed Organization of the CIA Clandestine Services."[136] The military analogies contained in that paper strongly suggest that its organizational conception had been dictated by Bedell Smith himself. Certainly that conception differed radically from Helms's previous ideas on the subject,[c] while conforming to the concept of Smith's order of 8 January.[d] One may infer that Helms perceived that the time for argument was over and that he loyally wrote as Smith directed. One may infer also that he was made the drafter in order to silence OSO opposition. Nevertheless, it is notable that much of the language of Smith's final version, dated 15 July, was taken verbatim from Helms's 4 June draft. Thus, ironically, it was Richard Helms who drafted the final order for the integration of OSO and OPC.

Bedell Smith, however, personally prepared his own text for that final order. On 30 June 1952 he desired to have Wisner, Kirkpatrick, Johnston, Hedden (the Inspector General), and White (the Assistant DDA) review a revised draft of his own paper entitled "CIA Clandestine Services— Description of Proposed Organization" and suggest any final changes they might wish to make in it.[137] The next day [name deleted], the Acting

---

[a]Kirkpatrick would have been the logical candidate for appointment as Vice DDP. It is not clear what there would have been left for the DDP to do.

[b]See page 227.

[c]See pages 220 and 225.

[d]See page 224.

ADPC, advised Wisner that he should accept Smith's draft "with enthusiasm" and press to have it issued as a directive.[138a]

In early July, Bedell Smith personally cleared his draft with David Bruce, the Under Secretary of State, Robert Lovett, the Secretary of Defense, and Sidney Souers, the Special Assistant to the President for National Security Affairs.[139]

The final version of Smith's paper was issued as a directive on 15 July 1952 under the title "Organization of CIA Clandestine Services."[140] Its stated purpose was to create a single overseas clandestine service while at the same time protecting the long-term espionage mission of the CIA from becoming lost in multifarious opportunistic and urgent covert operations.[b]

Smith reaffirmed his decision of 8 January to establish a single chain of command from himself as DCI through the DDP and the chiefs of the merged area divisions to the chiefs of merged stations overseas. To this end, the DDP would assume the residual command functions of the ADSO and the ADPC.

The DDP would be assisted by a Chief of Operations who would serve as both his deputy and his chief of staff. This position may have been suggested by Kirkpatrick's proposed "Vice DDP," but it reflected also Smith's military experience. Kirkpatrick was appointed to the office but was unable to serve because of his severe illness (polio), which began on 20 July. Richard Helms substituted for Kirkpatrick as Acting Chief of Operations until he was appointed to that position in his own right on 26 February 1953.

[fourteen-line paragraph, with note(s), deleted][c]

The DCI's Senior Representatives abroad were assigned *command* authority over all CIA activities in their respective areas of responsibility.

General Smith emphasized that in this structure there were only two echelons of command authority: the DCI in Washington and the Senior Representatives abroad. The DDP and his division chiefs had only delegated authority, as the executive agents of the DCI.

This order went into effect on 1 August 1952. OSO and OPC then ceased to exist as separate entities. In their stead there was a single organization with a plural name, The Clandestine Services.

---

[a]Given the textual correspondence between Helms's 4 June draft and Smith's 15 July text, it is virtually certain that Smith's 30 June text was derived from Helms's draft and substantially identical with the 15 July version.

[b]See the epigraph to this chapter, page 217.

[c][note(s) deleted]

PART V

EXTERNAL RELATIONS

XIX

RELATIONS OUTSIDE OF THE IAC COMMUNITY

The Director noted . . . that he would not go along with any committee that would interpose itself between the President and him.

—Minutes, Director's Meeting
16 April 1952[a]

The minutes of the Director's morning meeting indicate, in general, that Bedell Smith devoted far more of his time and attention to his relations with the President, the Secretaries of State and Defense, and the Joint Chiefs of Staff than he did to his relations with his colleagues on the Intelligence Advisory Committee.[b] Smith regularly attended the meetings of the National Security Council and also had a private weekly meeting with the President.[c] Through the favor of the Secretary of Defense, his former patron, General George Marshall, he was invited to attend the weekly meetings of the Joint Chiefs of Staff.[2] He also had periodic luncheons with his colleagues on the Psychological Strategy

---

[a]This statement expressed Bedell Smith's reaction to a suggestion that the CIA might protect itself against public criticism by having a Congressional or else a Presidential committee to "front" for it. It is cited to show the importance that Smith attached to his direct relationship with the President.

[b]These minutes do not cover Smith's first five months in office, when he was working hard to establish a cooperative relationship with the IAC. (See Part Two, Chapter V.)

[c]He saw the President on special occasions as well. Typically, when a paper before him moved him to wish to speak to the President, he would call for an appointment, call for his car, and dash off to the White House unaccompanied. He had easy access to the President whenever he asked for it.[1]

Board (the Under Secretary of State and the Deputy Secretary of Defense), with the Secretaries of the Army, Navy, and Air Force, and with selected Congressmen in rotation. Smith enjoyed high favor in all these quarters, except for his running battle with the Joint Chiefs of Staff.

THE PRESIDENT

President Truman had held Bedell Smith in high regard at least since Smith's selection in 1946 to be Ambassador to Moscow. Truman had personally selected Smith to be DCI, had personally overcome Smith's reluctance to accept that office, and probably felt a corresponding personal obligation to Smith for having done so.[a]

Truman's personal regard for Smith is further illustrated by the story of Smith's promotion to four-star rank. When General Eisenhower was appointed to be the NATO Supreme Commander in Europe, Smith begged to go with him again as Chief of Staff.[3] Eisenhower was willing, but President Truman declared that to be Director of Central Intelligence was a more important service than to be Chief of Staff at SHAPE, and that was that. Eisenhower therefore took Lieutenant General Alfred Gruenther to be his Chief of Staff. Subsequently Eisenhower recommended Gruenther's promotion to four-star rank. Reminded by Souers of his dictum regarding the relative importance of the two positions, Truman directed that Smith be promoted also. Nevertheless, Smith's name was somehow omitted from the promotion list.[b] President Truman thereupon refused to promote anybody until General Smith had been promoted.[4] Smith was made a four-star general effective 1 August 1951.

Every Friday morning General Smith went to the White House to brief the President. He took this duty very seriously; he was always tense while he prepared himself for it and on his way to the White House. There he conferred briefly with Sidney Souers, the President's special consultant for national security affairs,[c] before they went in together to see the President. No one else was present, except that James Lay, the Executive Secretary of the NSC, attended on occasion. Smith's presentation was

---

[a]See Part Two, pages 55–56.

[b]Souers attributed this omission to the coolness toward Smith of the West Pointers in general and General Bradley in particular. (See Part One, pages 5 and 10.)

[c]Souers had previously been the first DCI, of course, and also Executive Secretary of the NSC.

brisk and soldierly, the President was closely attentive, but the attitude of both was completely informal. After the briefing, Smith and Souers relaxed over coffee, noted whatever had particularly interested the President, and discussed other matters of mutual interest. On his way back to his own office, General Smith was almost always in a jovial mood.[5a]

The briefing materials that Smith took to the White House always included an annotated world map, a detailed order-of-battle map of Korea, and the President's "black book," a black loose-leaf binder inscribed "The President" in gold lettering. The "black book" always contained the *Watch Report*, the CIA weekly *Current Intelligence Review*, [line deleted]. It might contain other printed materials, such as a national intelligence estimate to which Smith wished to draw the President's particular attention. The "black book" was left with the President until the following Friday, when a new one was exchanged for it.[6b]

Smith's private briefing of the President followed only twenty-four hours after his briefing of the NSC on Thursday mornings. What, then, had he to tell the President that the President had not already heard at the NSC? Almost certainly the chief difference was that Bedell Smith gave President Truman his personal judgment regarding the military situation in Korea. Smith never touched upon that subject at the NSC, in the presence of General Bradley, whose responsibility it was.[7] President Truman, however, did not greatly trust the judgment of the Joint Chiefs of Staff, while he regarded Bedell Smith as an outstandingly intelligent general and his own man as well. In preparing himself to brief the President, Smith's chief concern was to make himself letter-perfect on the situation in Korea and to make his Korean situation map more precise than General Bradley's.[8] Smith must have known that the President would question him most closely regarding the military situation in Korea as a check on General Bradley's briefing on the same subject the day before.

One reason for Smith's tension as he prepared to brief the President was Harry Truman's phenomenal memory for detail. On one occasion the numbered symbols for a group of divisions had been affixed to the Korean map in a different order from that of the week before. Truman noticed and inquired regarding that difference, after the passage of a week. Smith was amazed.[9c]

---

[a]On these occasions Smith was accompanied by Meredith Davidson, his own briefing officer, who was thirty-one in 1951. Davidson prepared Smith's briefing materials and shared in the postbriefing coffee, but did not enter the President's office.

[b]President Truman was a dutiful and diligent reader of all the intelligence publications presented to him by the CIA.

[c]Smith himself had a phenomenal memory, though it was aural rather than visual. More than once Davidson was amazed to hear his own oral briefing being repeated verbatim by Smith hours later.

In the mutual esteem that Harry Truman and Bedell Smith felt for each other there was a psychological bond: they were both "mustangs." Truman had been an artillery captain when Smith was an infantry lieutenant—but in a larger sense Truman also had risen from the ranks to high station against all odds. When Harry Truman sent to Bedell Smith his scathing comments on a JCS paper,[a] he had references to the substance, but it was also one "mustang" deriding the West Pointers to another.[10]

THE NATIONAL SECURITY COUNCIL

The National Security Act of 1947 made the Central Intelligence Agency subject to the supervision and direction of the National Security Council and made the Director of Central Intelligence the Council's intelligence adviser. By direction of the President, the DCI attended all meetings of the Council in that capacity. Bedell Smith took this duty very seriously. In return, he enjoyed the complete confidence of the members of the Council.

In the meetings of the Council, Smith was associated with the President, the Vice President (Alben Barkley), the Secretary of State (Dean Acheson), the Secretary of the Treasury (John Snyder), the Secretary of Defense (George Marshall, 1950–51, and Robert Lovett, 1951–53), and the Chairman of the National Security Resources Board (Stuart Symington, 1950, and afterward Jack Gorrie). Also regularly present were Omar Bradley (Chairman, Joint Chiefs of Staff), Averell Harriman (Special Assistant to the President), Sidney Souers (Special Consultant to the President), and James Lay (the Executive Secretary, NSC).[11]

The meetings of the Council were always opened with a briefing by General Bradley on the military situation in Korea and another by General Smith on new intelligence in general and on intelligence pertaining to the day's agenda. Thereafter Smith generally remained silent unless his comments were requested, but he did not hesitate to intervene in the discussion if he felt that the intelligence bearing on the problem was being mistakenly interpreted or ignored.[12]

On one remembered occasion Smith waxed enthusiastic in his analysis of a political situation and was called to order by the President, who reminded him that the Secretary of State was present and that the

[a]See Part Four, page 207.

subject was his business. Smith was greatly abashed by that incident. In general, however, his occasional interventions were received with attention and respect.[13]

THE SENIOR NSC STAFF

In July 1950 President Truman established a Senior NSC Staff composed of men holding positions of authority in their respective departments and agencies. NSC papers, prepared by full-time Staff Assistants (in effect, the former NSC Staff), would be reviewed and perfected by this Senior Staff before presentation to the NSC.[14]

Admiral Hillenkoetter nominated himself to be the CIA member of the Senior Staff, with Ludwell Montague as his alternate,[15] and also named Montague to be the CIA Staff Assistant.[a] Inasmuch as Hillenkoetter rarely attended the meetings of the Senior Staff, Montague normally covered both positions.

In October 1950 Bedell Smith nominated his Deputy, William Jackson, to be the CIA member of the Senior Staff.[16] Montague was continued as Staff Assistant (supposedly a full-time job) while serving also as a member of the Board of National Estimates. Hiram Stout, a member of the Estimates Staff, was designated to substitute for him on occasion.[17]

Jackson came to feel that the meetings of the Senior Staff were a waste of his valuable time. Much of the interdepartmental debate on policy questions was of no concern to the CIA, even as guidance to the intelligence effort. Moreover, much of the time of that high-level Staff was taken up with just plain nitpicking. Jackson's attendance became increasingly infrequent, with Montague again substituting in that position. In July 1951, while Montague was on leave, the CIA was represented by Hiram Stout.[18]

At that point James Lay, the Executive Secretary, complained to Bedell Smith regarding the low level of CIA representation at the meetings of the Senior Staff, over which he presided. Smith thereupon declared that he would himself attend the Tuesday afternoon meetings of the Senior Staff, accompanied by Dr. Langer, the ADNE, and that Jackson and Langer would attend on Thursday afternoons.[19b] Langer thereupon ar-

---

[a]Montague had represented the CIA in the NSC Staff since the fall of 1947.

[b]Smith met with the NSC on Thursday mornings and with the IAC on Thursday afternoons.

ranged to have Stout replace Montague as Staff Assistant, so that Montague could devote full time to the business of the Board of National Estimates.[20]

This arrangement did not last long. After only two weeks of it Smith declared that too much of the time of the Senior Staff was taken up with matters that should have been settled at the drafting stage.[21] He never went again. Langer also dropped out.

When Allen Dulles succeeded Jackson as DDCI in August 1951, he inherited Jackson's position on the Senior Staff. Dulles declared that the meetings of the Senior Staff were important, that he would try to attend every one of them himself.[22] By December, however, Loftus Becker, the Executive Assistant, was regularly substituting for him.[23] When Becker was made DDI in January 1952, he was also made the regular CIA member of the Senior Staff.[a] In May 1952 William Bundy, of the Estimates Staff, replaced Stout as Staff Assistant. That arrangement was continued through the remainder of Bedell Smith's term as DCI.

In short, Bedell Smith, William Jackson, and Allen Dulles, all came to have a poor opinion of the Senior NSC Staff and to avoid attendance at its meetings. In addition to their impatience with its tedious proceedings, they were offended by the blandness of its policy recommendations to the NSC.

The latter point is illustrated by an indignant exchange between Dulles and Smith in July 1952. Dulles reported that a draft policy paper before the Senior Staff simply ignored the most striking development in the Soviet-American worldwide confrontation: the fact that the United States was now the target of a Soviet propaganda campaign of greater intensity than had ever been seen in the world before. Smith responded by denouncing the "inadaptability" of U.S. policy to changes in the situation. "We are sitting on our hands until the situation has deteriorated to a point where open conflict or a complete failure of our policy is the consequence.[24][b] Both Smith and Dulles felt that the United States was under heavy attack by the USSR, throughout the world, and that the United States should respond with wartime vigor and tactical flexibility.

THE DEPARTMENT OF STATE

It appears that Bedell Smith had no close personal relationship with Dean Acheson, the Secretary of State, although they met regularly at the

---

[a]See Part Two, pages 93–94.
[b]Presumably Smith meant to say "are the only remaining alternatives."

NSC. Smith's inability to establish such a relationship may have rankled. On one occasion James Webb (the Under Secretary) called Smith by telephone to say that Acheson had taken exception to something that Smith had said at the NSC that morning. Plainly Webb meant to be helpful, but Bedell Smith responded, in his most emphatic style, that if the Secretary of State had anything to say to him, he could make his own phone call—and with that the Director of Central Intelligence hung up on the Under Secretary of State![25]

Smith's sensitivity on this score is further illustrated by his instruction to Frank Wisner, the DDP, not to accept any summons to the State Department.[a] Smith did not want any of his deputies to go hat-in-hand to any department. If State had anything to say to Wisner, let it come to him.[26]

As matters settled out, Smith's principal personal point of contact within the State Department was with the Under Secretary, James Webb, who was also the State Department member of the Psychological Strategy Board.[b] Correspondingly, Dulles's principal contact at this time was with Freeman Matthews, Webb's Deputy,[c] and Wisner's was with Robert Joyce, Matthews's emissary.[27]

Of course, Smith had contact also with Park Armstrong, the Special Assistant for Intelligence Research and State Department member of the IAC, but Smith rebuffed Armstrong's repeated efforts to interpose between the CIA and the Under Secretary's office in matters relating to clandestine operations.[28]

THE DEPARTMENT OF DEFENSE

In contrast, Bedell Smith enjoyed a close personal relationship with the Secretary of Defense, George Marshall, his former patron.[d] Smith venerated Marshall,[29] but Marshall, for his part, was always cool, correct, and impersonal in his official relations. The correspondence between the DCI and "the Honorable, the Secretary of Defense" was evidently written by staff officers for signature—as was the DCI's correspondence with "the

---

[a]Before Smith's arrival, Wisner had been the State Department's man, not Hillenkoetter's. (See Part Two, page 78.)

[b]In January 1952 David Bruce succeeded Webb in both positions.

[c]Ambassador Matthews later became a member of the Board of National Estimates (1962–69).

[d]See Part One, pages 5–6.

Honorable, the Secretary of State." In the Defense file, however, there are also notes addressed to "Dear General Marshall" and "Dear Smith." They too are correct and businesslike, but they have a distinctly different tone and were evidently composed by the signers themselves.[30]

These more personal notes show that Smith always knew that he could obtain fair consideration from the Secretary of Defense, no matter what the position of the Joint Chiefs of Staff or the Service Secretaries might be. That knowledge was invaluable to Smith in view of the state of his relations with the Joint Chiefs of Staff.[a] In one such note Marshall told Smith that, if he could not obtain satisfaction from the Secretary of the Army (Frank Pace), he should let Marshall know about it and Marshall would then see what he could do.[31] In another, a handwritten note attached to a more formal letter, Marshall assured Smith that he had spoken personally to the Chiefs of Staff and that they would cooperate.[32] In yet another note, Smith offered his "sincere thanks" for Marshall's personal good offices in obtaining an "eminently satisfactory" solution for an urgent problem.[33]

Bedell Smith was also aware, however, that he could invoke the personal intervention of the Secretary of Defense only as a last resort and only if he had a very strong case. Insofar as the record shows, he did so only three times: to obtain an adequate field training area for the clandestine services, to obtain military training for CIA recruits,[b] and with regard to an attempt by the Joint Chiefs of Staff to revise NSCID 5.[c] It is notable that he did not do so with regard to so serious a matter as the JCS attempt to revise NSC 10/2. He reckoned that he could handle that matter himself, with the aid of John Magruder and Robert Lovett.[d]

In September 1951 Robert Lovett succeeded George Marshall as Secretary of Defense. Lovett had been an early advocate of the establishment of a Central Intelligence Agency.[e] He had been personally associated with Smith in the Psychological Strategy Board.[f] As Deputy Secretary of Defense, Lovett signed himself to Smith as "Bob".[34] As Secretary of Defense, he became "Robert Lovett,"[35] but that made no difference in their relationship of mutual appreciation and respect.

The correspondence between the DCI and the Secretary of the Army, Frank Pace, was signed simply "Bedell" and "Frank." So was that between

---

[a]See Part Four, page 207.
[b]See pages 243–44.
[c]See pages 241–42.
[d]See Part Four, pages 207–8.
[e]See Part One, pages 11 and 24.
[f]See Part Four, pages 205 and 207.

the DCI and the Assistant to the Secretary of Defense for International Security Affairs, Frank Nash.[36a]

In his struggle to obtain proper military consideration for the CIA's personnel requirements in a time of war and manpower stringency, the DCI was greatly aided by the personal friendship of Anna Rosenberg, the Assistant Secretary of Defense for Manpower. Indeed, the personal relationship of Bedell Smith and Anna Rosenberg was warm enough to excite gossip. That apparently pleased and amused Bedell Smith. He laughingly dismissed the subject by declaring that his reputation greatly exceeded his capabilities.[37] Be that as it may, it did the CIA no harm that the Assistant Secretary of Defense admired Bedell Smith and was personally concerned to protect his interest.[b]

THE JOINT CHIEFS OF STAFF

It would be too simple to attribute Bedell Smith's conflict with the Joint Chiefs of Staff to the coolness toward him of West Pointers in general and General Bradley in particular.[c] Whatever Bradley may personally have thought of Smith, he was perfectly correct in his official relations with him, insofar as the record shows. The conflict was really institutional and therefore perhaps inevitable in the circumstances of the time.

During World War II the Joint Chiefs of Staff had directly advised a President who had little regard for his Department of State and was pleased to think of himself as the Commander-in-Chief, enjoying an intimacy with his generals and admirals that no other civilian could share. The Chiefs of that time (Leahy, Marshall, King, and Arnold) had all been taught in service schools that it was potentially disastrous to permit politicians to interfere in matters requiring professional military judgment. That lesson was driven home by heavy stress on a historical example, the patent presumption and stupidity of President Lincoln's interference in the military operations of General McClellan. That war had been won only after General Grant was given a free hand. Thus, the Chiefs of Staff were politely deferential toward the President, but firm with him. They had him pretty well in hand, except for the ever-present

---

[a]Nash was the Defense Department member of the Senior NSC Staff.

[b]It was Anna Rosenberg who alerted Sidney Souers to the fact that Smith's name had been omitted from the Army's promotion list. (See page 232.)

[c]See Part One, pages 5 and 10.

danger of Mr. Churchill's influence. They treated with scorn British military proposals that were evidently inspired by Churchill for ulterior political purposes. They were accustomed to dispose of an unwelcome civilian idea by unexplained references to "overriding military necessity," the existence of which only they could judge. In time of war the sole national objective had to be to win the war in the shortest possible time. After that the politicians could take over again.[38]

The Chiefs of Staff had not maintained so brave a figure during the years before 1950, when the military budget was being arbitrarily cut, but the unpreparedness of the United States for war in 1950 seemed to vindicate the proposition that military affairs were too serious a matter to be left to politicians. After June 1950 there was a real war in progress in Korea, no matter what the President might call it. More important, there was acute apprehension that war might break out in Europe at any time.[39]

To a considerable degree, the Joint Chiefs of Staff and their joint and single-service staffs were indeed isolated in the Pentagon. Nevertheless, much of what others regarded as their overweening arrogance was nothing more than a natural presumption on their part that the precedents of 1941–45 applied in the circumstances of 1950–53. When the Joint Chiefs of Staff were confronted with the Central Intelligence Agency, the precedent they had in mind was the wartime subordination of the OSS to the JCS from 1942 to 1945.[40]

General Bedell Smith, for his part, regarded the incumbent Chiefs of Staff (Bradley, Vandenberg, Collins, and Sherman) with no awe. Bradley outranked Smith, but Smith had dealt with him on even terms or better as Chief of Staff at SHAEF. Moreover, he was well aware that he was by statute subordinate only to the NSC, that he was actually working in the service of the President, the Secretary of State, and the Secretary of Defense, and that he could rely on their sympathetic understanding and support. Nevertheless, Smith himself understood the legitimate interests of the Joint Chiefs of Staff and their theater commanders. He always sought a reasonable accommodation of all of the interests involved. It was the Chiefs who were demanding and intransigent.[41]

Bedell Smith's confrontations with the Chiefs of Staff over the revision of NSC 10/2 [one-half line deleted] have been recounted above. Those were typical experiences. By giving way on nonessentials, Smith accomplished his essential purpose in both cases.[a]

Recounted below are Smith's encounters with the Joint Chiefs of Staff

---

[a]See Part Four, pages 207–11.

on five other matters: (1) the revision of NSCID 5; (2) the recruitment and training of CIA career personnel from among young men subject to military service; (3) the intelligence exploitation of captured sources; (4) intelligence access to U.S. military information; and (5) the preparation of estimates of Soviet net military capabilities, taking into account opposing U.S. capabilities.

The Revision of NSCID 5

NSCID 5, dated 12 December 1947, provided that the DCI should conduct all Federal espionage and counterespionage operations outside of the United States, except for certain "agreed activities" to be conducted by others and except for military counterintelligence operations necessary for the security of U.S. forces and military installations. The DCI was, moreover, made responsible for coordinating covert and overt intelligence collection activities.[42]

"Agreed activities" meant espionage operations to be conducted by others with the knowledge and expressed consent of the DCI. No agreement, however, had ever been reached on that subject. Without consulting the DCI, the military simply extended their licensed counterintelligence operations to include a considerable amount of amateurish espionage and covert action. That was done on the ground of an inherent right to ensure the security of U.S. forces.[43]

As early as May 1950 the Joint Intelligence Committee of the JCS was considering a revision of NSCID 5 designed to bring all U.S. espionage and counterespionage operations under the control of the JCS in time of war.[44] The underlying thought was the same as that underlying the later JCS attempt to assert a similar control over covert action operations.[a] The precedent for it was the subordination of the OSS to the JCS from 1942 to 1945.

During the discussion of the revision of NSC 10/2 in February 1951, Bedell Smith himself proposed to the JCS a new NSC directive that would have consolidated NSCID 5, NSC 10/2, [deleted] in accordance with Smith's conception.[45] That draft, however, was discarded in the circumstances of the actual revision of NSC 10/2.[b]

---

[a]See Part Four, page [deleted].
[b]See Part Four, pages 207–8.

In June 1951 the Joint Chiefs of Staff submitted to the Secretary of Defense, for transmission to the NSC, a proposed revision of NSCID 5 that incorporated the JIC's May 1950 draft but went beyond it to authorize the military services to engage in espionage operations without the knowledge and consent of the DCI. Secretary Marshall invited the DCI's comments. General Wyman, the ADSO, denounced the JCS draft as completely unacceptable on both legal and doctrinal grounds.[46] After studying the matter for four weeks, Bedell Smith dispatched a personal letter to Secretary Marshall.[47]

In this letter dated 2 July, Smith showed dispassionately that the Joint Chiefs of Staff had simply ignored the National Security Act of 1947. He cited the President's own handwritten comments on the JCS proposal to revise NSC 10/2 (April 1951)[a] as a recent reaffirmation of the principle that the DCI was subject to the direction of only the NSC and the President. He demonstrated that in practical terms the idea of mounting independent and uncoordinated clandestine operations in the same area was "a thoroughly bad business."

Having established these points, Bedell Smith turned conciliatory. He was ever ready to consider on its merits any proposal made to him regarding "agreed activities." He recognized explicitly the necessary authority of a military theater commander within his theater. That could be accommodated by using the language recently approved in the revision of paragraph 4 of NSC 10/2 (April 1951).[b]

Bedell Smith concluded by advising the Secretary of Defense that the JCS proposal was unworthy of being submitted to the consideration of the NSC.

Secretary Marshall evidently accepted Bedell Smith's advice. The JCS proposal was not forwarded to the NSC. Instead, Smith prepared his own revision of NSCID 5, in accordance with his own prescription. He kept the 1947 text but added to it four short paragraphs that defined the CIA's relationship with the "Senior U.S. Representatives" (the Ambassador or the equivalent), the "Senior U.S. Military Commander" (the theater commander where applicable), and the Joint Chiefs of Staff, with regard to the clandestine collection of intelligence. The key added paragraph was the same as paragraph 4 of NSC 10/2 as revised in April 1951.[c] The NSC adopted this revision of NSCID 5 on 28 August 1951.[48]

[two pages deleted]

---

[a]See Part Four, page 207.
[b]See Part Four, pages 207–8.
[c]See Part Four, page 208.

Recruitment and Training

[ten-line paragraph deleted]

General Smith desired to develop a CIA career service. He considered that military training, experience, and discipline would be highly beneficial for the young men to be recruited into that service.[a] What he had in mind was not only basic military training but also specialized training, including language school and two or three years of actual military service in the field or at sea. Smith requested the Secretary of Defense to arrange for the services to provide such training for 150 college graduates (per year) to be selected by the CIA.[55]

The Joint Chiefs of Staff were willing to do that, on a reimbursable basis (although they were to get two or three years of service from the trainees), but they stipulated that none of Smith's recruits could be from "service-controlled sources," particularly from the ROTC or the Reserve.[56]

Bedell Smith asked Anna Rosenberg what the Chiefs of Staff meant by that. Every able-bodied young man in the country was under service control, through the draft if not otherwise. He argued that even if his recruits were ROTC graduates, the services would be getting all of the active service out of them that they could expect, short of all-out war. He provided a way out by volunteering to count his recruit-trainees against his present allotment of [number deleted] officers.[57]

In the end the Secretary of Defense informed Smith that the services would train, as Smith proposed, up to two hundred men recruited by the CIA from sources other than the ROTC, the service academies, and the active military establishment. If the CIA wanted to recruit ROTC graduates, let it first obtain (from Congress) an expansion of the ROTC program to meet its needs.[58b]

Bedell Smith was thus disappointed with respect to the recruitment of ROTC graduates, but he was pleased to get this military training program established. He thanked Secretary Marshall for his support[59]—although the Secretary had actually obtained for him no more than the Joint Chiefs had been willing to grant at the beginning.[c] The training program was put into effect. The Army, Navy, Marine Corps, and Air Force accepted

---

[a]See Part Two, pages 97–98. Initially at least, Smith was thinking primarily of recruits for the clandestine services.

[b]It was to this disappointing letter that Secretary Marshall attached his handwritten personal assurance that the Chiefs of Staff would cooperate. (See page 238.)

[c]At about the same time, Secretary Marshall did obtain for Smith a good field training area that otherwise would not have been available to him.[60]

non-ROTC college graduates recruited by the CIA, put them through basic training and officer candidate school, and gave them a year of experience in active service at sea or overseas. They were then assigned to the CIA in active duty status until the expiration of their military obligation.[61a]

The Exploitation of Captured Sources

The war in Korea was producing quantities of captured sources of intelligence: North Korean and Chinese documents and prisoners of war, Soviet weapons, and other military equipment. It was an obvious function of the DCI to coordinate the intelligence exploitation of these sources, but they were under the actual control of the military—that is, of the Joint Chiefs of Staff.

The JCS proposed to the Secretary of Defense the establishment of three JCS agencies to conduct this exploitation: an Armed Services Document Intelligence Center (ASDIC), an Armed Services Personnel Interrogation Center (ASPIC), and a Joint Material Intelligence Agency (JMIA). The Secretary requested the DCI to ascertain the views of the non-Defense intelligence agencies. The FBI opted out; it preferred to do its business (such as it was in this case) by direct liaison, free of CIA coordination.[b] State and the AEC agreed to permit the CIA to represent their interests, apparently to hold down the number of civilians intruding upon the military. Smith proposed the amendment of the JCS paper to provide for the appointment by the CIA of assistant directors for ASDIC and ASPIC, and a special adviser for the JMIA, to ensure that the interests of the CIA, State, and the AEC received adequate attention.[62]

On 5 March 1951, in the absence of General Smith, General Wyman (ADSO) reported to William Jackson (DDCI) that General Megee (Deputy Director of the Joint Staff for Intelligence) had said that the Joint Staff was strongly opposed to the idea of CIA participation in the direction of the JCS agencies to be established for the exploitation of captured sources. Jackson emphatically declared that, if the IAC did not concur in General Smith's proposals, the issue would be taken to the NSC.[63] The IAC (including General Megee) concurred.[64]

For whatever reason, none of the three agencies proposed by the JCS

---

[a]This program continued in effect until 1966.

[b]See pages 254–56.

in December 1950 was actually set up until December 1951, when the JMIA was finally established.[a] Lyman Kirkpatrick (the Executive Assistant) then noted hotly that the JCS had established the JMIA without consulting the CIA. General Smith, however, was quite relaxed about that. He said that the CIA's real objective was only to make sure that the CIA received the product of such military intelligence agencies and that proper attention was paid by them to CIA requirements. He directed James Reber (the ADIC) to make sure of this, if possible without direct CIA participation.[65]

Bedell Smith understood, better than did his civilian associates, the prerogatives of a theater commander and the sensitivities of the military in general. During 1951 Smith had fought two big battles with the JCS, over NSC 10/2 [deleted].[b] In December he was seeking to induce the Department of Defense to assume the cost of the OPC's paramilitary operations.[c] He did not choose to expend his credit in Defense over what was to him a peripheral issue. His own proposals in March had provided for nothing more than a CIA adviser with the JMIA.[d]

The arrangements that Reber made with the JMIA were evidently satisfactory. [two lines, with [e]note, deleted] The research units of ORR and OSI were able to obtain the data that they required.

Access to U.S. Military Information

On 1 February 1951 General Smith briefed the JCS regarding his proposed revision of NSC 10/2 and the CIA's requirements for military support for covert operations. He took advantage of the opportunity to say:

> In addition to the above, we need to be kept informed by receiving the papers of the Joint Chiefs of Staff and the military cable traffic. These papers are essential to keep our operational planning cur-

---

[a]One may suppose that the Joint Staff, of the same opinion still, had arranged to have the work done by the Far East Command, [several words deleted] to keep it beyond the reach of the CIA.

[b]See Part Four, pages 207–11.

[c]See Part Four, page 213.

[d]It may be noted also that this was the period of the military onslaught on the SIC, before which Bedell Smith retreated. (See Part Three, pages 177–78.)

[e][note deleted]

rent and up-to-date, and to keep our Office of National Estimates informed. These papers will naturally be handled with maximum security and minimum circulation.[67]

The Joint Chiefs of Staff were not responsive to this plea.[68] Rather, they evidently gave instruction that no JCS paper and no military operational cables should be released to the CIA. Even the Joint Intelligence Committee refused to permit the Director of Central Intelligence to see its estimates.[a] Prior to JIC approval they were merely drafts that it would be improper to send outside of the Pentagon. After JIC approval they were JCS papers, no longer under JIC control.[69]

The only concession that the JCS would make on this point was to permit ONE Board member General Clarence Huebner to see some JCS papers in the Pentagon.[b] Huebner could not quote such papers to the Board of National Estimates, but he could advise the Board with cognizance of their contents.[70] No doubt he kept General Smith more explicitly informed.

In January 1951 President Truman requested of General Smith an estimate of "the prospects for the creation of an adequate Western European defense."[c] Such an estimate would of course require the collaboration of the Joint Strategic Planning Group of the Joint Staff. General Smith told the IAC that he would arrange that with General Bradley.[71]

Two weeks later General Smith told the IAC that he had discussed the subject with the Joint Chiefs of Staff, with negative results. NIE 13 (the number assigned to the project in ordinary sequence) would have to be completed strictly as an intelligence paper. He would then send it to the JCS requesting their comments on particular aspects of an operational nature.[72]

Even on this basis, NIE 13 was not viable. The military members of the IAC objected strenuously that the draft conveyed an implicit judgment on the adequacy of JCS-approved plans.[73] In the end the project was cancelled.[74] Thus, it was demonstrated that not even the President of the United States could obtain a combined assessment of intelligence and operational information.[d]

It happened that in February 1951 Senator Brien McMahon, Chairman of the Congressional Joint Committee on Atomic Energy, requested of

---

[a]The JIC was composed of the military members of the IAC.

[b]See Part Three, page 133.

[c]President Truman never recognized any distinction between intelligence and operational information and judgments. (See Part Three, pages 157–58.)

[d]But see pages 248–51.

General Smith an estimate of the Soviet capability to prevent the delivery of U.S. atomic weapons on targets in the Soviet Union. This time the subject was an enemy capability, rather than the capabilities of the U.S. side, but again the estimate would require cognizance of the capabilities and vulnerabilities of U.S. forces. Noting that such an estimate would serve to ensure Congressional support for related U.S. military programs, General Smith requested the Secretary of Defense to authorize the participation of the Defense Department's Weapons Systems Evaluation Group, which had recently completed certain relevant operational analyses.[75]

General Smith may have hoped thereby to bypass the JCS and their Joint Staff, but Secretary Marshall referred his request to the JCS for their advice and the JCS pronounced a veto. Senator McMahon was not authorized to request such an estimate, and in any case he had not addressed his request to the proper agency (themselves). Secretary Marshall adopted the JCS position.[76] The project (NIE 30) was cancelled.[77]

A third case of this kind arose in May 1951. General Bolling, the Assistant Chief of Staff, G-2, requested a national estimate on "the probability of a Communist attack on Japan during 1951."[78a] An estimate, NIE 37, was laid on, but in July it was cancelled[79]—because the intelligence community had been unable to obtain information on the strength and dispositions of U.S. forces in and near Japan, information that the Soviets would certainly have and would take into account in deciding whether or not to attack Japan.[80]

In August, however, the same subject was up again, this time as SE-11.[b] [sixteen lines, with [c]note, deleted]

In proceeding as he did in this case, Bedell Smith had two purposes. He took the occasion to demonstrate that he gave more weight to the advice of his own Board of National Estimates than he did to that of the Intelligence Advisory Committee.[d] He sought also to demonstrate, to the President, the National Security Council, and the Chiefs of Staff themselves, the absurdity of the JCS position. Enemy intentions could not be estimated without regard to the capabilities of U.S. forces that the enemy knew to be present. Bedell Smith would never make an estimate without

---

[a]Soviet activities on Shakhalin had raised an alarm. Bolling wanted others to share responsibility for his estimate that no attack was impending.

[b]SEs (Special Estimates) were national intelligence estimates prepared for a special purpose and for specially limited dissemination.

[c][note deleted]

[d]See Part Three, page 162.

taking the presence of U.S. forces into account. The only question was whether he would be well or ill informed about them.

In April 1952 Bedell Smith was still pleading. He then told the NSC that it was not necessary for intelligence officers to know very much about U.S. plans, but if they were to make a timely intelligence contribution to U.S. planning, they must have in advance at least a general idea of what was up for consideration and what future U.S. actions foreign powers would be reacting to. Liaison with State in this respect was reasonably satisfactory, but that with the armed services was less than satisfactory.[82]

This problem was never resolved during General Smith's time. In January 1953 it was again presented, as follows:

> As Western strength increases, estimates of Soviet military capabilities are increasingly meaningless without cognizance of Western capabilities to resist. Thus, the 1952 NIE on Soviet air defense capabilities is nothing but an inventory of Soviet hardware applicable to the subject. The Council's recent directive for an evaluation of the Soviet net capability to inflict injury on CONUS[a] is an example of what is required in major cases.[83]

This passage is from a draft report to the NSC prepared at General Smith's direction. That report was never submitted. In February the new DCI, Allen Dulles, cancelled the project.[b]

Net Evaluations

In July 1951 the Senior NSC Staff requested an estimate of Soviet capabilities for direct attack on the continental United States. Again Bedell Smith observed that such an estimate could not be made without cognizance of U.S. capabilities to repel the attack—that is, without the

---

[a]That is, the continental United States.

[b]The issue of intelligence access to U.S. military information was still sensitive in 1955, when the author was assigned to the permanent staff of the Net Evaluation Subcommittee of the NSC. The participation of a CIA representative was indispensable, but such a representative would necessarily have access to sensitive U.S. military information. It was hoped that the Chairman of the JCS (Admiral Radford) would not notice the author's presence in the NESC Staff. Whether he did or not, he made no issue of it, and that was regarded as an important breakthrough.

collaboration of the Joint Staff.[84] Since it was by then evident that it would be futile to propose direct Joint Staff collaboration in an NIE, Smith worked out with the Executive Secretary of the NSC a five-part procedure, as follows:[85]

1. An NIE on the maximum scale of the direct military attack that the Soviets were capable of launching against the continental United States. (In 1951 such an attack would have had to be delivered primarily by propeller-driven medium bombers carrying atomic bombs, the Soviet version of the U.S. B-29.)
2. A JCS evaluation of the U.S. capability to repel an attack of that scale and nature.
3. An IIC[a] estimate of Soviet capabilities for clandestine attack (that is, for the delivery of atomic bombs on targets in the United States by clandestine means).
4. An ICIS[b] evaluation of U.S. capabilities to counter such an attack.
5. On the basis of these four contributions, a final evaluation of the net result by the DCI in collaboration with the Chairmen of the JCS, IIC, and ICIS.

The NSC did not adopt this plan until September,[88] but meanwhile action was proceeding in accordance with it. The IIC refused to estimate,[c] but ONE produced an estimate on the basis of data furnished by the IIC, and the IAC adopted it on 30 August. [six lines deleted]

It remained to obtain the judgment of the JCS and the ICIS on the ability of the United States to defend itself against attacks of the scale and nature indicated by these intelligence estimates. That took longer—a full year in fact. For one thing, the Joint Chiefs of Staff were determined not to expose their judgment on such a subject to profane eyes. For another, they were caught in a dilemma. The honor of the services required that U.S. defensive forces be shown to be wonderfully efficient, but budgetary considerations required that they be shown to be dangerously deficient. The Joint Chiefs of Staff avoided ever pronouncing on.

---

[a]The Interdepartmental Intelligence Conference (IIC) was established in 1939 to coordinate the investigation of foreign clandestine activities in the Western Hemisphere. J. Edgar Hoover, Director of the FBI, was chairman; State, Army, Navy, and Air Force participated.[86]

[b]The Interdepartmental Committee on Internal Security (ICIS), composed of representatives of State, the Treasury, Defense, and Justice, was established in 1949.[87]

[c]One of J. Edgar Hoover's cardinal principles was that the FBI, an investigative agency, should not evaluate or interpret the information that it collected. [two lines deleted]

that subject themselves. As for the ICIS, it shamelessly thumped the tub for greatly increased appropriations to defend against the dire threat of clandestine attack with weapons of mass destruction.[92]

On 26 June 1952 General Smith announced to the IAC that at last all of the preliminary returns, from the IAC, IIC, ICIS, and Joint Staff, were in. The fifth step, the preparation of a Summary Evaluation, remained to be accomplished. Smith asked for the designation of an Air Force officer to represent the interest of the IAC in that work, in company with representatives of the DCI, JCS, IIC, and ICIS.[93a]

The actual work of preparing the Summary Evaluation was accomplished by a group in the CIA specially constituted by Smith for the purpose. Robert Amory, the ADRR, was in charge.[b] He was assisted by Vice Admiral Bieri, Lieutenant General Bull, and Dr. Edgar Hoover[c]—members of the Board of National Estimates—and by William Bundy, the NSC Staff Assistant.[94] In short, Bundy drafted the report, subject to the direction and approval of the others.

On 10 December the Summary Evaluation had been through all the lower levels of review and acceptance and was ready for presentation to the Joint Chiefs of Staff on the 15th. Smith announced that he would attend, with Amory and Bull. Amory would do the talking, as instructed by Smith.[95]

Two weeks later Smith was baffled by his inability to get the Joint Chiefs of Staff to act on the Summary Evaluation either one way or the other. He went to see General Bradley about that. Bradley proposed that the entire problem be transferred to an NSC subcommittee with General Edwards in the chair.[96] No doubt Smith perceived that this was a multipurpose device to get Smith out of the chair, to put a JCS man in it, to absolve the members of the JCS of any personal responsibility for the findings of the Summary Evaluation, and to make an ad hoc committee (the "Edwards Committee") responsible for it.[97] Nevertheless, Smith acquiesced, in order to get the task done. The NSC established the "Edwards Committee,"[98] and Smith appointed General Bull to it.[d]

The real work had already been done. The Edwards Committee had only to go through the motions of taking testimony and reviewing extant studies in order to show that it had done something. Its report was

---

[a]The DCI would be representing the NSC interest, not that of the IAC.

[b]Amory may have already been identified as the future DDI. (See Part Three, page 154.) He was Acting DDI when the draft report was presented.

[c]Hoover was an economist. The Summary Evaluation was largely concerned with industrial damage in the United States and the consequences for the U.S. war economy.

[d]As the former G-3 at SHAEF, "Pinky" Bull knew how to serve General Smith and also how to cope with the Joint Staff.

drafted by Willard Matthias, a member of the National Estimates Staff, who had accompanied General Bull as amanuensis.[99]

The last difficulty was that of obtaining the concurrence of the Director of the Federal Bureau of Investigation. Mr. Hoover was outraged by a conclusion of the Summary Evaluation that the Soviets would not risk forfeiting at least tactical surprise in their bomber attack by smuggling atomic weapons into the United States before D-day, as would be necessary in the case of a clandestine attack. Even though the FBI could not guarantee the detection of such an operation, its accidental detection would alert the United States and risk provoking a decisive preemptive attack on the USSR.[100] Robert Amory finally succeeded in bringing J. Edgar Hoover into camp, but only at the last minute before the presentation of the Summary Evaluation to the NSC.[101]

The procedure that Bedell Smith succeeded in establishing in this case was continued after he had ceased to be DCI. In 1954 a second Summary Evaluation was made by a second ad hoc committee. In 1955, on the initiative of Allen Dulles as DCI, the NSC established a permanent Net Evaluation Subcommittee. The procedure was applied, however, only to the case of a Soviet attack on the continental United States. It was never used to estimate the net capabilities of Soviet forces in other cases.[102]

SERVICE TO OTHER COMPONENTS OF THE DEFENSE DEPARTMENT

The nonmilitary components of the Department of Defense were highly dissatisfied with the quality of the intelligence support available to them within that Department from the service intelligence agencies and the Joint Intelligence Committee. Consequently they turned to the CIA for such support.[a] General Vandenberg and Admiral Hillenkoetter were always glad to oblige, but General Smith tried to put a stop to that practice.

General Smith had been DCI for only two months when he observed that the policymakers were turning more and more to the CIA for advice and assistance. (Evidently he was not aware that they had long been

---

[a]See Part Three, pages 173–74, with regard to the interest of the Research and Development Board in obtaining intelligence support from the CIA. The Assistant to the Secretary of Defense for International Security Affairs (ISA) also preferred intelligence obtained from CIA to that obtainable from the military intelligence agencies.[103]

doing so; he had been given a false impression by the "Dulles Report.") He said that the problem now was to get the departments to make full use of their own intelligence agencies.[104]

In April 1952 Loftus Becker, the DDI, and Sherman Kent, the ADNE, met with the Joint Intelligence Committee to seek a better allocation of requests for estimates between the JIC and the IAC.[105] The CIA (ONE) was not trying to take business away from the JIC. On the contrary, it was trying to get the JIC to relieve it of the burden of responding to requests that were properly the business of the JIC. The root of that problem was of course the requesters' judgment that estimates prepared by ONE were greatly superior to those produced by the JIC.

In June the Research and Development Board (RDB) requested of the DCI an estimate of the capabilities of Soviet science and technology. Bedell Smith told the members of the JIC, present as members of the IAC, that his business was to attend to the requirements of the NSC. The RDB, a component of the Department of Defense, should have gone to the JIC with its request. The CIA would be glad to help the JIC on a spare-time basis, but the CIA did not participate in JIC estimates and would accept no responsibility for them. The DCI would not act on the RDB request unless the JIC told him that it was incapable of satisfying it.[106]

The RDB must have continued to beat on the DCI's door, for Smith returned to the subject seven weeks later. The RDB request, he said in exasperation, could readily be answered (by the JIC) out of OSI publications. The CIA did not propose to do the JIC's work for it, but would of course honor a request from the Secretary of Defense through the NSC.[107a]

Bedell Smith was not always so strict about this matter. In October 1952, in response to a request from Lieutenant General Geoffry Keyes, Director of the Weapons Systems Evaluation Group (WSEG), Smith undertook to propose to the IAC the initiation of the desired estimate. As before, he stressed that his prior responsibility was to satisfy the requirements of the NSC, but he shifted his ground from a none-of-our-business to a time-available basis, as follows: "While we are glad to assist agencies of the Department of Defense by furnishing intelligence which transcends the capabilities of any single department or agency, our acceptance of such requirements must be understood to be subject to priority tasks which may be set by the National Security Council."[108]

Having said that for the record, Bedell Smith added in longhand: "Jeff—I think we have a lot of data on this already, so it won't take as long as if we started from scratch. WBS."

---

a[note deleted]

One may speculate on the difference between Smith's treatment of the RDB and the WSEG. Both were components of the Department of Defense independent of the JCS and the three services. The RDB was civilian; WSEG was military. But the chief difference seems to have been that "Jeff" Keyes was an old friend in need of help.

It should be noted that the Secretary of Defense did not really have to go through the NSC to get service from the DCI. In November 1952 the Acting DDI, Robert Amory, responded to an urgent request from the Secretary of Defense, Robert Lovett, by providing the Secretary with an uncoordinated memorandum from the Board of National Estimates. Amory was careful to point out that this memorandum was supplementary to NIE 21 and that it would be coordinated as soon as possible as NIE 21/1.[109]

THE UNITED STATES COMMUNICATIONS INTELLIGENCE BOARD

Communications intelligence (COMINT) was a critically important source of information during the period from 1950 to 1953, but under the terms of NSCID 9, dated 1 July 1948, it was excepted from the coordinating jurisdiction of the DCI and IAC. The function of coordinating COMINT activities was assigned instead to a special body, the United States Communications Intelligence Board (USCIB), in which the DCI was just one among the several members. Inasmuch as the leaderless USCIB could act only with unanimous consent, it could accomplish no effective coordination.[a] One can readily imagine what Bedell Smith thought of such a fatuous arrangement.

On 20 October 1951 Kingman Douglass, the ADCI, urged upon Smith the need for "a fresh look at the entire communications intelligence picture."[110] On 10 December Smith expressed to the NSC his grave concern regarding the security and effectiveness of U.S. COMINT activities and proposed a high-level survey of the situation.[111]

The ground must have been well prepared in advance. Within three days the NSC proposed and the President approved the assignment of the task of making such a survey to the Secretaries of State and Defense. By 18 December it was known that they would appoint a select committee to make the survey and that it would be composed of George Brownell

---

[a]See Part Three, pages [deleted].

(Chairman), Charles Bohlen for State, John Magruder for Defense, and William Jackson for CIA.[a] General Ralph J. Canine, representing the JCS, would serve as a consultant, not as a member of the committee.[112] The committee was formally appointed and instructed on 28 December and went to work on 5 January.[113]

The Brownell Committee submitted its report to the Secretaries of State and Defense on 13 June 1952. This was fast work for a committee dealing with such a complex and controversial matter. It was possible because all concerned knew that Dean Acheson, Robert Lovett, and Bedell Smith were determined to obtain a prompt and effective solution to the problem—and also because the responsible military authorities were themselves disgusted by the infighting of the past three years and by the inefficiencies inherent in the existing setup.[114]

The recommendations of the Brownell Committee were subsequently embodied in the revision of NSCID 9 adopted by the NSC on 29 December 1952. [twenty-four lines, with note(s), deleted][b]

This revised NSCID still maintained communications intelligence as an activity separate and distinct from the IAC community but brought it under the effective control of the DCI. Not until 15 September 1958 were the IAC and USCIB combined to form the all-inclusive United States Intelligence Board.

THE FEDERAL BUREAU OF INVESTIGATION AND THE IIC

Bedell Smith was unsuccessful in his efforts to obtain CIA participation in the Interdepartmental Intelligence Conference (IIC), which was the personal preserve of J. Edgar Hoover.[c] In this case, his usually irresistible force came up against an immovable object.

In October 1945 the FBI had aspired to be assigned the task of conducting U.S. secret intelligence operations worldwide.[d] That aspiration was frustrated by the postwar creation of the CIG and OSO. The FBI remained resentful of the existence of the CIG/CIA and determined to

---

[a]Brownell was a New York lawyer and reserve brigadier general who had served as special assistant to the Secretary of the Air Force. Bohlen was Counsellor of the Department of State; Magruder, deputy for "psychological" affairs in ISA. Jackson was of course the DCI's senior consultant.

[b][note(s) deleted]

[c]See page 251.

[d]See Part One, page 21.

prevent any CIA encroachment upon its internal security functions. The National Security Act of 1947 contained two provisos to protect the Bureau's prerogatives.[a] Relations between [one-half line deleted] OO and the FBI were difficult.

In 1948 the NSC Survey Group took cognizance of the strained relationship between the CIA and the FBI. It sought to ease the tension and facilitate coordination by recommending that the FBI be made a member of the IAC.[116] That was done, but J. Edgar Hoover refused to attend the IAC, where he would have had to sit below the DCI. His representative almost always abstained from the proceedings of the IAC, "the subject being outside of his jurisdiction," as indeed it almost always was. His responsibility was clear—to see that the IAC took no action prejudicial to the interest of the FBI.[117]

[eight lines deleted] a seat at the Interdepartmental Intelligence Conference analogous to the FBI seat in the IAC. These requests were rebuffed.

[four lines deleted] A new effort must be made to obtain [one-and-a-half lines deleted] for [name illegible] a seat on the IIC. He mentioned darkly that the FBI's seat on the IAC was subject to review.[118b]

The task of persuading J. Edgar Hoover was assigned to Allen Dulles, but Bedell Smith laid down the line that Dulles should take. The matter was too important for those involved to quibble about media of exchange or details of protocol. [two lines deleted] The CIA was willing to give to the FBI whatever information it obtained overseas, but it would make no special collection effort for the FBI unless it got something in return.[119]

Evidently Dulles accomplished nothing, for in November Smith took up the task himself. He had Hoover and two of his henchmen come to lunch with Dulles, Wyman, Kirkpatrick, and himself. When his guests had been properly regaled, Smith said that his purpose was to work out closer cooperation between the CIA and the FBI. Past misunderstandings had resulted from a clash of personalities, not of policies. [eight lines, with [c]note, deleted] Smith handed Hoover a staff study on the subject.[120]

J. Edgar Hoover was genial. He welcomed the idea of a monthly luncheon with Bedell Smith. His staff would take up with Kirkpatrick the details regarding a reciprocal exchange of information. But Hoover was adamant in refusing the CIA a permanent seat in the IIC. The CIA would be specially invited to attend whenever (in Hoover's judgment) the

---

[a]Sections 102(d)(3) and 102(e).

[b]Colonel Sheffield Edwards, USA (Ret.), was the CIA's Director of Security (under various titles) from 1947 to 1963.

[c][note deleted]

CIA had a legitimate interest in the subject under discussion.[121] That was the best Bedell Smith could get out of J. Edgar Hoover.

CONGRESSIONAL RELATIONS

Members of Congress in general regarded the Director of Central Intelligence as personally responsible for all U.S. intelligence activities, under the terms of the National Security Act of 1947. In the event of an "intelligence failure" it would be the DCI whom they would hold accountable, not the chief of any departmental intelligence agency nor the IAC collectively.[122a]

Bedell Smith's relations with Congressional leaders were characterized by a strong mutual respect rather than by personal warmth. Like others of his generation in the military, Smith had been brought up to regard Congressmen with respect. His bearing toward them was generally deferential, responsive, and soldierly—although he did practice a bit of showmanship on them on occasion. One of his favorite devices, when being questioned too closely, was to divert attention from the subject by saying, "Now, as I recall, Marshal Stalin once told me. . . ."[b] That always made a big impression.[123] There were not many men in Washington who could recall what Marshal Stalin, the archenemy, had once told them.

The record of the Senate subcommittee hearing on Smith's nomination to the DCI reveals clearly the immense respect in which he was held by those senators even before he took office,[124] and afterward Congressmen naturally responded in kind to such a distinguished man's evident respect for them.

There was one senator who disliked Smith—before he had met him. He was Senator Brien McMahon, Chairman of the Joint Committee on Atomic Energy. McMahon had been offended by a speech that Smith had made before becoming DCI in which Smith had criticized the AEC's control of the development of atomic weapons. When the time came for the periodic briefing of the Joint Committee on the Soviet atomic energy program, Walter Pforzheimer, the Legislative Counsel, ventured to tell

---

[a]For a fuller treatment of the subject, see the history of the CIA's Congressional relations to be prepared by Walter Pforzheimer, who was the CIA's Legislative Counsel from 1946 to 1956.

[b]Actually, Smith had had only seven conversations with Stalin during his three years as Ambassador.

General Smith of Senator McMahon's dislike of him.[a] Forewarned, Bedell Smith turned on his charm, with the result that Brien McMahon became one of Smith's strongest admirers.[125]

At a later briefing, Senator McMahon wanted to know how Smith knew what he was saying about the Soviet program. The source of Smith's information was too sensitive to be revealed to a Congressional committee. Smith invited McMahon to come to his office for a personal briefing, on McMahon's solemn promise not to reveal what he would hear to his committee. McMahon came and a battery of CIA staff officers gave him a formal briefing. Then Smith cleared the room and remained closeted with the Senator. During that time he could have said nothing that he had not himself been told by the staff officers he had dramatically dismissed, but he gave McMahon the impression that he was sharing with him secrets that even his own staff could not be permitted to overhear.[126b]

In September 1952 Bedell Smith got himself into some trouble by his incautious testimony in Senator Joseph McCarthy's libel suit against Senator William Benton. Smith had been subpoenaed by Benton to refute McCarthy's slanderous attack on the patriotic loyalty of George Marshall, which Smith was of course glad to do. In cross-examination he was asked whether he did not know it to be a fact that the State Department had been infiltrated with Communists in 1947 (when Marshall was Secretary of State and Smith was Ambassador in Moscow). Smith replied that he did not know that to be a fact. He was then asked whether he agreed with Senator Benton's testimony that Benton had known that there were Communists in the Department in 1947 (when Benton was Assistant Secretary of State). To that Smith replied that he did believe it—and then added gratuitously that he believed that there were Communists in his own organization![127]

Smith went on to explain that this was only a prudent assumption. He knew of no Communist in the CIA; if he had found one, he would already have disposed of him.[128] His explanation was lost in a crescendo of bold black headlines such as "Gen. Smith Believes Reds Are in U.S. Intelligence!"[129]

A quotation to the effect that the DCI believed that there were unidentified Communists in the CIA would be sensational at any time. To appreciate the impact of Smith's incidental remark one must recall the atmosphere of the Cold War, the McCarthy phenomenon, and the Repub-

---

[a]Smith's response to Pforzheimer's apology for mentioning this unpleasant fact was "That's your job."

[b]Smith used this technique on others on other occasions.

lican presidential campaign of 1952, which sought to make a major issue of Communist infiltration of the Government under the lax administration of the Democrats. Harry Truman's initial reaction was to suppose that Bedell Smith, Eisenhower's man, had deliberately betrayed him to the Republicans![130]

Bedell Smith made his embarrassed explanations to Harry Truman, Dwight Eisenhower, Adlai Stevenson, the Press, and the House Un-American Activities Committee, and got Eisenhower's promise not to exploit the incident, but the echoes continued to reverberate. No less an authority than General Smith believed that the Government was infiltrated with Communists!

At this same time, Bedell Smith was even more seriously involved in the case regarding the loyalty of John Paton Davies.[a]

Davies was born in China, of missionary parentage, in 1908. He entered the Foreign Service in 1931, and served in China from 1942 to 1945 and in Moscow from 1945 to 1947. In Moscow he impressed the Ambassador, General Smith, as "a very loyal and very capable officer of sound judgment."[131]

From 1947 to 1952 Davies was a member of the State Department's Policy Planning Staff under George Kennan, with whom he had served in Moscow. By training and experience he was particularly well qualified to appreciate the developing situation in China. His comment on the decline and fall of the Nationalist regime was that, in Chinese eyes, it had "lost the Mandate of Heaven."[b] This line of thought, however, brought Davies (and his entire generation of Foreign Service China specialists) under increasing attack as having been treasonously responsible for the "loss of China."[132c]

George Kennan was charged with providing policy guidance to OPC. His man Davies acted for him with regard to China. [fifteen lines, with [d]note, deleted]

Bedell Smith was bedeviled by this problem throughout his tenure as DCI. Smith's personal position was that he still thought Davies a very

---

[a][note deleted]

[b]The author, who was associated with Davies in the NSC Staff, remembers well his exposition of this theme, which seemed particularly apt in the light of Chinese history and ideas.

[c]Nelson Johnson, Ambassador to China (1929–41), sympathized with these young men, although he did not share their view. He considered them victims of having been sent to language school in Peking, where their mandarin tutors had poisoned their minds against the Nationalist regime, which had moved the capital from Peking to Nanking. Johnson had no doubt of their sincerity and loyalty.

[d][note deleted]

loyal and very capable officer. He said that he believed he would know a Communist when he saw one and that he did not believe Davies to be one. He had not been DCI at the time of the incident in question, but if he had been he would have been disposed to act on Davies's suggestion, which he considered good. [four lines deleted][a]

The matter came to a showdown when Bedell Smith was nominated to be Under Secretary of State in January 1953. Senator McCarran then got the Senate Committee on Foreign Relations to hold up the confirmation of Smith's appointment until McCarran could conduct a full-dress hearing on the Davies case with Smith as DCI.

At the eventual hearing on his nomination Bedell Smith was asked the direct question, should Davies continue to be a Foreign Service officer? He answered as follows:

> I will give you a categorical answer, no. Moreover, I do not think that John Davies, even if he is the most loyal man in the world—and I do not answer for his loyalty except from observation—that he is of any use now to the Foreign Service or to the United States, if it were for no other reason than for the fact that Davies does not have the confidence and, indeed, has the complete suspicion of very important members of this body, and the State Department cannot afford to have people like that.

Bedell Smith was confirmed as Under Secretary of State. John Davies remained a member of the Foreign Service until November 1954, when he was dismissed by the Secretary of State, John Foster Dulles, on the basis of a finding by the President's Security Hearing Board that he lacked judgment, discretion, and reliability, without prejudice with regard to his loyalty.[133] The evident motivation of that finding was that mentioned by Bedell Smith: the State Department could not afford to keep an officer so thoroughly condemned by important senators.

---

[a][note(s) deleted]

[thirty-six-page chapter deleted]

XXI

THE DEPARTURE OF GENERAL SMITH

As Director of Central Intelligence, he made an outstanding contribution to the national security of the United States. Through his firmness and tact, perceptiveness and judgment, and withal, through his brilliant leadership in a position of highest responsibility, he assured the realization of that ideal of a coordinated intelligence effort which was set forth by the Congress in 1947, and brought to a new height of effectiveness the intelligence machinery of the United States Government. Through his well-grounded and clearly defined concept of intelligence, reinforced by his recognized integrity and high personal prestige, he won acceptance of the principle that policy decisions must be based upon sound intelligence.

—*Dwight D. Eisenhower*
21 February 1953[a]

As we take leave of Bedell Smith as DCI, it is well to consider again President Eisenhower's excellent summation of his accomplishment during his twenty-eight months in that role. As this history has shown, he had indeed (1) realized for the first time the conception of a coordinated intelligence effort set forth by the Congress in 1947, (2) brought to a new height of effectiveness the intelligence machinery of the United States Government, and (3) won acceptance of the principle that policy decisions must be based upon sound intelligence. The history of U.S. intelligence is indeed divisible into two distinct eras, before Smith and after Smith.

---

[a]Reprise. See Part One, page 3.

The Director of Central Intelligence expressed no view, of course, with regard to the presidential election of 1952. At the direction of President Truman, he arranged to provide intelligence briefings for both of the major candidates. His intention was that both should be briefed by Meredith Davidson, who prepared the DCI's own briefings for the President. It happened, however, that both asked to have their initial briefings on the same day, Stevenson in Springfield and Eisenhower in New York. Davidson, the DCI's Assistant, was then sent to Springfield, and Melvin Hendrickson, Davidson's assistant and later successor in OCI, was sent to New York. This arrangement was maintained during the rest of the campaign. Stevenson was always briefed in Springfield, to which he returned every weekend to function as governor, but Hendrickson traveled all over the United States. Davidson and Hendrickson took care to make their briefings substantially identical. The only difference was that items derived from COMINT were identified as such to Eisenhower, who had a COMINT clearance.[212]

One must suppose that, personally, Bedell Smith favored the election of his former commander, "Ike" Eisenhower. Certainly he had more to expect from that outcome in the way of influence and favor. But Bedell Smith was a great admirer of Harry Truman—and, when Adlai Stevenson's questions and comments on his briefings were reported to him, Smith remarked admiringly on the acuteness of Stevenson's perception. When Bedell Smith noted that, it was remembered that he had once said Ike was not so bright.[213] Not so bright as Bedell Smith, that is. Few men were. But there should be no doubt about the sincerity—indeed, the sentimental extravagance—of Bedell Smith's admiration of Dwight Eisenhower.[214]

Smith lost no time in paying court to the President-elect. After the election Eisenhower disappeared for a time. On 21 November he traveled clandestinely to Washington in a private railroad car for the purpose of conferring privately with old Army friends there, particularly with regard to his undertaking to go to Korea. But Eisenhower's train made an unscheduled stop in Baltimore, where Bedell Smith and Meredith Davidson got on board.[215] Bedell Smith had stolen a march on the Pentagon establishment!

Smith briefed Eisenhower on the situation in Korea, but the occasion was primarily a sociable reunion of two old comrades. At Washington the Eisenhower car was shunted off into the railroad yard. Smith and Davidson made their surreptitious departure from it at 12:45 A.M., and the Eisenhowers, after that.

On 28 November Smith and Davidson went up to the President-elect's headquarters in the Commodore Hotel in New York. Smith was alone with Eisenhower for about an hour. During that time the President-elect asked him to initiate action on several matters. One of them was a reappraisal of "cold war activities."[a] Smith went directly from Eisenhower's office to an apartment that was at his disposal in New York and summoned William Jackson and C. D. Jackson to join him there. After their discussion of how to conduct the reappraisal, as William Jackson was leaving, Smith remarked to him, "You know what I want—to be Chairman of the Joint Chiefs of Staff."[216]

One can readily imagine what satisfaction Bedell Smith, the former private soldier in the Indiana National Guard, would have derived from becoming the ranking U.S. military officer in active service. Remembering all the trouble the Joint Chiefs of Staff had given him as DCI, what personal satisfaction there would have been in stalking in and taking the chair vacated by Omar Bradley! And it was not unreasonable for Bedell Smith to suppose that Eisenhower, who had esteemed him as his Chief of Staff, would appreciate what he could do to improve the performance of the Joint Chiefs of Staff and the Joint Staff.

But that could not be. Even if Eisenhower would have liked to have had Bedell Smith as his Chairman of the Joint Chiefs, there was an established custom that precluded it. Omar Bradley was an Army general. His successor must be a Navy admiral. The only question was which admiral.[b]

On another occasion Robert Amory, the Acting DDI, accompanied Bedell Smith to Eisenhower's headquarters in New York. Smith entered Eisenhower's office in high spirits. He came out crushed. He never explained what had happened, but sat in morose silence all the way back to Washington, finally muttering, "And I thought that it was going to be great."[217]

One can only conjecture that it was at this meeting that Bedell Smith learned not only that he could not be Chairman of the Joint Chiefs of Staff but also that the President-elect wanted him to be Under Secretary of State.

Bedell Smith loathed the thought of becoming Under Secretary of State. For one thing, he did not like John Foster Dulles, the Secretary-designate.[c] For another, he considered the State Department a hopeless

---

[a]See Part Four, pages 214–15.

[b]Forrest Sherman would have been the obvious choice had he lived. Eisenhower chose Arthur Radford, Commander-in-Chief, Pacific, who impressed him when he was en route to Korea.

[c]Meredith Davidson tells how Smith coldly rebuked J. F. Dulles for rudeness in failing to acknowledge Smith's introduction of Davidson.[218] Dulles, of course, was totally preoccupied with his own concerns.

case. Even the great General Marshall, although he had introduced procedural innovations derived from his experience as Chief of Staff of the Army, had never been able to make the Department function with good military discipline and efficiency. Finally, Smith foresaw that his successor as DCI would be Allen Dulles,[a] and he had misgivings about that.

Bedell Smith had reservations about Allen Dulles.[220] Apart from issues of substance,[b] Dulles often "rubbed him the wrong way."[221c] Nevertheless, Smith did respect Dulles's general ability and his particular mastery of the tradecraft of clandestine operations. After two years of close personal observation, however, Smith lacked confidence in Dulles's self-restraint. It was all right for Dulles to be an enthusiastic advocate of covert operations as long as the decision rested with Bedell Smith, but if Dulles himself were DCI, who then would control and restrain him? Smith feared that Dulles's enthusiasm for covert operations would eventually lead him into some ill-conceived and disastrous adventure.[222] In short, Bedell Smith anticipated a fiasco like the Bay of Pigs, although that did not happen until eight years later.

It was widely known that Bedell Smith did not want to be Under Secretary of State. Consequently it has been widely supposed that Smith's transfer to State was forced upon him by John Foster Dulles pursuant to a devious scheme to make Allen Dulles Director of Central Intelligence.[d] It was well known that Allen Dulles had wanted to be DCI ever since that office was created.[e] Foster Dulles was regarded by Smith as a crafty and calculating man.[227]

It was not Foster Dulles's idea, however, to make Bedell Smith Under Secretary of State. That idea was conceived by Dwight Eisenhower for his own purposes. Dulles could of course perceive the advantage in it for his brother. That consideration may have reconciled him to an appointment that he might otherwise have opposed.

As Bedell Smith understood it, there were two parts to Dwight Eisenhower's consideration of this matter. He first concluded that Bedell Smith

---

[a]It appears that the only other person who wanted to succeed Smith as DCI was William Donovan, but his appointment was not seriously considered.[219]

[b]See Part Two, pages 91–92, and Part Four, page 221.

[c]It seemed that almost every name that came up in discussion was that of some old acquaintance of Allen Dulles. This was so—Dulles had a remarkably wide acquaintance in American and European "ruling circles"—but Smith felt that he was being constantly upstaged by Dulles.

[d]This opinion is held, for example, by Sidney Souers,[223] William Jackson,[224] Lyman Kirkpatrick,[225] and Robert Amory.[226]

[e]See Part One, page 13.

should not remain DCI. He then perceived that Smith could be useful to him in State.

Bedell Smith attributed the first idea, not to Foster Dulles, but to Lucius Clay.[a] Smith told Souers that Clay had told Eisenhower it would be improper for both the President and the DCI to be military men. (Souers's comment was that it was more obviously improper for the Secretary of State and the DCI to be brothers.)[228]

The idea attributed to Clay seems far-fetched. Smith regarded it bitterly as an example of the length to which the West Pointers would go in order to get rid of him. Whether Eisenhower took it seriously or not, he apparently used it as an argument in his efforts to persuade Smith to agree to go to State.

There is another man who may well have exerted his considerable influence to persuade the President-elect to relieve Smith as DCI. He was Sherman Adams, the prospective White House "Chief of Staff." When Smith proposed to open an office in the Commodore Hotel, next door to Eisenhower's, Adams assigned a distant broom closet to the CIA.[229] Evidently Eisenhower's new Chief of Staff did not want the old one to have such access to him as Smith had had to Truman.

Bedell Smith later explained to Sidney Souers the positive side of Eisenhower's desire for him to accept appointment as Under Secretary. For political reasons antedating his nomination, Eisenhower was obliged to make John Foster Dulles his Secretary of State, but Dulles was essentially a stranger to him. For that reason he desired to have a man whom he knew well and in whom he had confidence as No. 2 in the State Department.[230]

There was an interval between the time when Bedell Smith realized that he could not remain as DCI and the time when he reluctantly consented to be Under Secretary of State. During that interval he was heard to mutter that it was time for him to "get out and make some money" (as Lucius Clay had done).[231] But in the end Bedell Smith simply could not refuse any service that Dwight Eisenhower demanded of him.

Bedell Smith had one clearance to obtain, however, before he finally submitted. He asked the President if it would embarrass him in any way if his DCI were to accept a political appointment in the Eisenhower Administration. Harry Truman was deeply moved by Smith's loyal consideration; he had tears in his eyes when he told Congressman John McCormack about it.[232]

---

[a]General Clay, USMA '18, had been Commander-in-Chief, U.S. Forces, Europe, and Military Governor, U.S. Zone, Germany, and since his retirement in 1949 Chairman of the Board and Chief Executive Officer of the Continental Can Company.

Bedell Smith attended his last IAC meeting on 8 January 1953 but did not then mention his impending departure.[233] He never took formal leave of the IAC.

The President-elect's intention to nominate Bedell Smith to be Under Secretary of State was announced to the press on 11 January 1953. The next morning Allen Dulles proposed to send a message informing the CIA's overseas stations.[234] That was the first mention of the subject at the Director's morning meeting. Smith attended these meetings for the last time on 23 January. Thereafter Allen Dulles presided.

The Senate confirmed Smith's appointment to be Under Secretary on 6 February.[a] Three days later he formally resigned as DCI. Allen Dulles continued as Acting Director until 26 February, when he formally took office as the fifth Director of Central Intelligence.[235b]

---

[a]His confirmation was delayed by Senator McCarran. (See page 259.)

[b]Bedell Smith served as Under Secretary of State for only a year and a half and then resigned, in August 1954. Apparently he had intended from the first to stay no longer than military honor required. Then he went to "making money," principally as Vice Chairman of the American Machine and Foundry Company. He died seven years later, in August 1961.

Chronology

1950

May: President Truman personally selects Lieutenant General Walter Bedell Smith to be DCI, replacing Admiral Hillenkoetter. Smith begs off on grounds of ill health. (He was facing a serious operation for a stomach ulcer. If he recovered well from that, he intended to retire from the Army and to seek a remunerative position in industry or the presidency of a university.)

June: Admiral Hillenkoetter asks to be reassigned to duty at sea.

25 June: North Korean forces invade South Korea.

27 June: President Truman commits U.S. naval and air forces in defense of South Korea.

30 June: President Truman commits U.S. ground forces in South Korea.

August: Smith recovers well from operation. President Truman induces him to accept appointment as DCI in a time of national peril.

August: Smith persuades William Harding Jackson to accept appointment as DDCI.

18 August: The White House announces Smith's appointment to be DCI. Smith announces that Jackson will be DDCI.

28 August: The Senate confirms Smith's appointment to be DCI.

29 August: At Smith's request (23 August), Lawrence Houston, CIA General Counsel, provides him with a comprehensive review of the problems confronting the CIA.

September: Smith confers with William Donovan and Allen Dulles in New York.

2 October: William Jackson enters on duty as a consultant. (Hillenkoetter refused to make him DDCI.)

7 October: Smith and Jackson take office as DCI and DDCI.

10 October: Ludwell Montague submits to Jackson, at his request, a plan for an "Office of Estimates."

10 October: Smith summons the IAC to an emergency meeting in his office.

12 October: Smith attends his first NSC meeting and undertakes to carry out NSC 50, except with regard to the integration of OSO and OPC. The NSC agrees to that exception.

12 October: Frank Wisner (the ADPC) explains Smith's interpretation of NSC 10/2 to the representatives of State, Defense, and the JCS, who accept it.

16 October: Murray McConnel enters on duty as the CIA Executive.

20 October: Smith holds his first formal meeting with the IAC, calls for "rapid cooperative work," and announces his intention to establish an Office of National Estimates including a Board of National Estimates.

[six lines deleted]

8 November: William Langer enters on duty as prospective Assistant Director for National Estimates.

11 November: Smith asserts before the IAC his personal responsibility as DCI (in contrast to the "board of directors" concept).

13 November: The establishment of the Office of National Estimates is announced, with Langer as ADNE. The residue of ORE is redesignated Office of Research and Reports, with Theodore Babbitt, former ADRE, as ADRR.

16 November: Allen Dulles enters on duty as a consultant.

1 December: McConnel is redesignated Deputy Director for Administration; provision is made for a Deputy Director for Operations; the Office of Special Services is established, with Horace Craig as ADSS; Colonel Matthew Baird is named Director of Training, DDA.

13 December: Lyman Kirkpatrick is made Executive Assistant to the DCI. James Reber is designated Assistant Director for Intelligence Coordination.

18 December: Smith holds first weekly Staff Conference (of Assistant Directors).

18 December: The "Princeton Consultants" established.

18 December: On or about this date Allen Dulles agrees to become Deputy Director for Operations (redesignated Deputy Director for Plans by 21 December, when announcement of the appointment is discussed at the Deputy Director's Staff Meeting).

22 December: Allen Dulles drafts memorandum of understanding under which he is to start full-time work as DDP on 2 January 1951 (announced 4 January).

[eight lines deleted]

28 December: The Watch Committee of the IAC is established.

1951

[two lines deleted]

2 January: Allen Dulles officially assumes duties as DDP.

4 January: Kingman Douglass designated ADSS, replacing Craig.

4 January: Max Millikan designated ADRR, replacing Babbitt; enters on duty 15 January.

8 January: Smith submits to the NSC a proposed revision of NSC 10/2. [two lines deleted]

15 January: The Office of Special Services is redesignated Office of Current Intelligence.

16 January: William Jackson, Acting DCI, submits NSC 10/4, [one line deleted].

[three lines deleted]

1 February: Smith requests access to JCS papers and cables for the information and guidance of DDP and ONE.

8 February: JCS refuses to release U.S. military information to the DCI.

9 February: Executive Registry established.

14 February: Allen Dulles (DDP) holds meeting on "the integration of OSO and OPC" (which was at this time contrary to Smith's policy).

15 February: Major General W. G. Wyman enters on duty as ADSO, replacing Colonel Schow.

16 February: Walter Reid Wolf made Special Assistant to the DCI.

[four lines deleted]

28 February: OCI publishes the first number of the CIA *Current Intelligence Bulletin* (replacing the CIA *Daily Summary* published since 1946).

3 March: Wisner (ADPC) and Wyman (ADSO) agree to a redefinition of OPC and OSO area divisions to make them correspond to each other.

23 March: The minutes of the Director's morning meeting with his Deputies begin.

27 March: The Joint Chiefs of Staff recommend that NSC 10/3 and 10/4 be rejected, and that the NSC adopt a directive that would have subordinated the DCI to the JCS in time of war.

1 April: Wolf made DDA, replacing McConnel.

4 April: President Truman establishes the Psychological Strategy Board composed of the Under Secretary of State, the Deputy Secretary of Defense, and the DCI. (Smith was later elected Chairman.)

5 April: Webb, Lovett, Smith, and Bradley meet and agree on Smith's proposed revision of para. 4 of NSC 10/2. [two lines deleted]

16 April: The NSC adopts Smith's revision of para. 4 of NSC 10/2.

18 April: Smith subordinates the Office of Training directly to the DCI.

May: Lieutenant Colonel Chester Hansen made Assistant to the DCI and first Chief of the Historical Staff.

8 May: Smith submits to the NSC a memorandum on the "Scope and Pace of Covert Operations" calling for a reappraisal and redefinition of CIA functions and responsibilities.

17 May: The IAC establishes the Economic Intelligence Committee.

24 May: William Jackson (DDCI) recommends the eventual integration of OSO and OPC.

June: The Joint Chiefs of Staff propose a revision of NSCID 5.

[two lines deleted]

11 June: Smith considers that the reorganization of the CIA pursuant to NSC 50 has been completed and orders the preparation of a final report to the NSC.

13 June: The NSC adopts NSCID 15 on the coordination of economic intelligence.

[four lines deleted]

25 June: Smith wants a full-time Inspector.

[four lines deleted]

1 July: Lyman Kirkpatrick is made DADSO. Joseph Larocque succeeds him as the DCI's Executive Assistant.

2 July: Smith advises the Secretary of Defense (Marshall) that the JCS proposal to revise NSCID 5 is unworthy of being submitted to NSC consideration.

3 July: Baird, DTR, submits a staff study proposing the creation of an "elite corps" within the CIA.

[three lines deleted]

30 July: In response to an attack by the military intelligence agencies on the weapons applications subcommittees of the Scientific Intelligence Committee, Smith proposes to call on Dr. Karl Compton to investigate the entire field of scientific and technical intelligence.

[two lines deleted]

1 August: Smith is made a four-star general.

2 August: Smith proposes a complex procedure for evaluating the net capabilities of the USSR to inflict damage on the continental United States.

3 August: William Jackson resigns as DDCI and is made the DCI's "Special Assistant and Senior Consultant."

15 August: The Joint Chiefs of Staff submit their views on "Scope and Pace."

23 August: Allen Dulles is made DDCI, replacing Jackson; Frank Wisner is made DDP, replacing Dulles; Kilbourne Johnson is made ADPC, replacing Wisner.

28 August: The NSC Senior Staff rejects the views of the JCS on "Scope and Pace."

28 August: The NSC adopts Smith's revision of NSCID 5.

31 August: Kirkpatrick (DADSO) recommends a redefinition of functions that would give OSO a monopoly of clandestine contacts, whether for intelligence collection or covert action operations.

[three lines deleted]

10 September: Major General Harold McClelland enters on duty as Assistant Director for Communications, subordinate to the DDP.

10 September: The NSC adopts Smith's proposed procedure for net evaluations.

17 September: Smith rejects the concept of a "small elite corps" within the CIA and appoints a committee to develop a career service program covering all employees.

27 September: Allen Dulles, presiding at the IAC, insists that the U.S. position in an international intelligence estimate is perforce a national intelligence estimate and therefore the responsibility of the DCI and IAC, rather than the JIC. The Joint Staff accepted this ruling and requested of the DCI a U.S. position paper for use in preparing a NATO intelligence estimate (SG 161).

[two lines deleted]

October: Arthur Darling enters on duty as a historical consultant.

20 October: Kingman Douglass (ADCI) urges "a fresh look at the entire communications intelligence picture."

[five lines deleted]

24 October: Wyman urges the integration of the field operations of OSO and OPC.

30 October: Stuart Hedden enters on duty as Special Assistant to the DCI.

31 October: Smith withdraws NSC 10/4 from further consideration.

29 November: Loftus Becker replaces Larocque as the DCI's Executive Assistant.

10 December: Smith lays down the law regarding administrative support for the clandestine services. Colonel Lawrence White is appointed Assistant DDA, replacing Shannon, on 28 December. (White does not take office until 1 January 1952.)

11 December: Larocque made DADO, replacing White.

17 December: Kirkpatrick made ADSO, replacing Wyman.

17 December: Last meeting of the weekly Staff Conference.

[four lines deleted]

28 December: The Brownell Committee is appointed to investigate communications intelligence.

1952

1 January: Loftus Becker made Deputy Director for Intelligence and Stuart Hedden made Inspector General.

3 January: Sherman Kent made ADNE, replacing Langer.

4 January: John Earman listed as Executive Assistant, replacing Becker.

8 January: Smith directs the integration of the OSO and OPC area divisions. The integrated divisions are to be directly responsible to the DDP, rather than to the ADSO and ADPC.

[two lines deleted]

11 February: Robert Amory enters on duty as a consultant.

[nine lines deleted]

1 March: The Office of Operations is transferred from the DDP to the DDI.

3 March: General Lucian Truscott [line deleted] brief Smith on plans for the integration of the OSO and OPC stations [word(s) deleted]. At Smith's request, [name deleted] outlines a plan for the general integration of OSO and OPC substantially the same as that adopted by Smith in July.

6 March: Smith establishes an ad hoc committee to review DCID 3/3 (scientific intelligence).

[five lines deleted]

17 March: Robert Amory made ADRR, replacing Millikan.

28 March: NSCID 1 is amended to authorize the DCI, with the concurrence of the IAC, to release U.S. national intelligence to foreign governments and international bodies (NATO).

[three lines deleted]

17 April: Wisner (DDP), Johnson (ADPC), and Kirkpatrick (ADSO) agree to proceed with the further integration of OSO and OPC pursuant to Smith's 8 January order.

23 April: Smith submits to the NSC his final report on the reorganization of the CIA pursuant to NSC 50.

2 May: Kirkpatrick (ADSO) proposes a plan of integration that would divide OPC into two offices and leave the three ADs in command of their respective operations subject to coordination by a Vice DDP (Kirkpatrick).

3 June: Smith emphatically rebuts an EDAC report critical of ORR.

4 June: At Smith's direction, Richard Helms submits a plan of organization for the integrated Clandestine Services.

5 June: Smith refuses to produce estimates for components of the Department of Defense. That is the JIC's business.

13 June: The Brownell Committee submits its recommendations regarding communications intelligence.

19 June: Smith adopts a Career Service plan.

26 June: Work begun on the "Summary Evaluation" of Soviet net capabilities to inflict damage on the continental United States.

27 June: Huntington D. Sheldon enters on duty in OCI.

30 June: Smith invites comment on his own draft of a plan for the integration of the Clandestine Services derived from the submissions of [name deleted] Kirkpatrick, and Helms.

[four lines deleted]

12 July: Sheldon replaces Douglass as ADCI.

15 July: Smith orders the integration of OSO and OPC under the direct command of the DDP in accordance with his own plan, effective 1 August. The offices of the ADSO and the ADPC will become staff units.

20 July: Kirkpatrick stricken by polio.

22 July: Major Gordon Butler reports for duty as Chief of the DCI's Cable Secretariat.

1 August: Smith's order integrating the Clandestine Services goes into effect. Kirkpatrick (ADSO) made Chief of Operations (deputy and chief of staff to the DDP); [one-and-a-half lines deleted] (Johnson, ADPC, resigned. [name deleted] served as Acting Chief of Operations during Kirkpatrick's illness.)

1 August: The Office of Communications is subordinated directly to the DCI.

14 August: The IAC adopts DCID 3/4 abolishing the Scientific Intelligence Committee and establishing the Scientific Estimates Committee (a victory of the military over OSI).

14 August: The IAC establishes the Intelligence Working Group to coordinate intelligence support for the EDAC.

24 August: Amory (ADRR) reorganizes ORR.

[two lines deleted]

7 October: Colonel Stanley J. Grogan made Assistant to the DCI and Chief of the Historical Staff, replacing Hansen.

30 October: Smith formally proposes to the PSB a revised procedure for reviewing and approving psychological warfare projects.

4 November: Dwight Eisenhower elected President.

21 November: Smith meets Eisenhower's train in Baltimore and travels with him to Washington.

28 November: Smith consults William Jackson and C. D. Jackson regarding the establishment of the "Jackson Committee" to reappraise procedures for the direction and conduct of "cold war activities." Smith confides to William Jackson that he wants to be Chairman of the Joint Chiefs of Staff.

[five lines deleted]

15 December: The "Summary Evaluation" is presented to the JCS.

29 December: The NSC adopts a revision of NSCID 9 embodying the recommendations of the Brownell Committee. [three-and-a-half lines deleted]

31 December: The "Edwards Committee" is established to produce the "Summary Evaluation."

1953

January: The "Jackson Committee" is appointed to reappraise procedures for the direction of "cold war activities."

8 January: Smith attends IAC for the last time.

11 January: Smith's nomination to be Under Secretary of State is announced.

16 January: The "Summary Evaluation" produced by the "Edwards Committee" is presented to the NSC.

19 January: Hedden resigns as Inspector General.

20 January: Eisenhower inaugurated as President.

23 January: Smith attends the Director's morning meeting for the last time and decides that Darling should be replaced as the CIA Historian.

24 January: Dulles's appointment to be DCI is announced.

6 February: The Senate confirms Smith's appointment to be Under Secretary of State.

9 February: Smith resigns as DCI.

Notes

PART ONE: THE ESSENTIAL BACKGROUND

1. Letter, Forrest C. Pogue to Ludwell L. Montague, 27 Feb. 1970, Historical Staff/ Historical Collection (HS/HC)-400, item 1. (Dr. Pogue is Director of the George C. Marshall Research Library, Lexington, Virginia, and the biographer of General Marshall. His information on this point is derived from interviews with General Smith regarding Marshall.)

2. Ibid.

3. *New York Times*, 8 Jan. 1953; *U.S. News & World Report*, 31 July 1953.

4. Memo for record, Ludwell L. Montague, "Interview with William Harding Jackson, 8–9 Dec. 1969," HS/HC-400, item 2, p. 1.

5. Walter Bedell Smith, *Eisenhower's Six Great Decisions* (New York, 1956).

6. Walter Bedell Smith, *My Three Years in Moscow* (Philadelphia, 1950), pp. 13–15.

7. Ibid.; transcript of Ludwell L. Montague's recorded interview with Averell Harriman, 11 March 1970 HS/HC-400, item 3, pp. 4, 5–6.

8. Smith, *My Three Years in Moscow*, p. 334.

9. *U.S. News & World Report*, 31 July 1953.

10. Memo, William Jackson to Montague (see n. 4), p. 6.

11. Memo for record, Ludwell L. Montague, "Interview with Lawrence Houston, 30 July 1969," HS/HC-400, item 4.

12. Memo for record, Ludwell L. Montague, "Personal Recollections of General W. B. Smith," 3 April 1970, HS/HC-400, item 5.

13. Meredith Davidson to Ludwell Montague, 12 May 1971; Robert Amory to Ludwell Montague, 9 Aug. 1971.

14. U.S. Senate, Committee on Foreign Relations, *Hearing on the Nomination of Walter Bedell Smith to Be Under Secretary of State* (Washington, 1953), p. 1.

15. Memo for record, Ludwell Montague, "Interview with Jack Earman, 27 August 1969," HS/HC-400, item 6.

16. Ibid.

17. Memo, Jackson to Montague (see n. 4), p. 8.

18. Memo, Earman to Montague (see n. 15).

19. Memo, Jackson to Montague (see n. 4), p. 8.

20. Walter Pforzheimer to Ludwell Montague, 24 July 1970.

21. Ibid.

22. Winston S. Churchill, *The Hinge of Fate* (Boston, 1950), p. 526.

23. Letter, William Jackson to Ludwell Montague, 1 April 1970, HS/HC-400, item 7.

24. William H. Jackson, "Memories of a Hero" (Thomas Hitchcock, Jr.), HS/HC-466, pp. 9, 11–13, 17–23, 30–33.

25. Memo, Jackson to Montague (see n. 4), p. 1.

26. Ibid., p. 2.

27. Ibid., pp. 1–2.

28. [two lines deleted]

29. Memo, Jackson to Montague (see n. 4), p. 2.

30. Letter, Gen. Hoyt Vandenberg, DCI, to Allen Dulles, 28 Aug. 1946, Personal Papers of Allen W. Dulles. [line deleted]

31. Allen W. Dulles, *Germany's Underground* (New York, 1947), and *The Secret Surrender* (New York, 1966). (See also Edward P. Morgan, "The Spy the Nazis Missed," in Allen W. Dulles, *Great True Spy Stories* [New York, 1968], and scattered references in Allen W. Dulles, *The Craft of Intelligence* [New York, 1963].)

32. Minutes of a meeting of the Secretaries of State, War, and Navy, 14 Nov. 1945, Miscellaneous Papers on Origins of CIA, from DCI Souers's Personal File, HS/HC-135.

33. Memo for record, Ludwell L. Montague, "The State Department's Intention to Nominate Allen Dulles to be DCI in Succession to Vandenberg, February 1947," 7 April 1970, HS/HC-400, item 8.

34. Allen W. Dulles, "Memorandum respecting Section 202 (Central Intelligence Agency) of the bill to provide for a National Defense Establishment," 25 April 1947, HS/HC-400, item 9.

35. Memo for record, Ludwell L. Montague, "Interview with Sidney Souers, 4 December 1969," HS/HC-400, item 10, pp. 3–4.

36. Dulles, "Memorandum" (see n. 34).

37. Memo, Souers to Montague (see n. 35), p. 6.

38. Ludwell Montague, "Intelligence Service 1940–1950," HS/HC-401, (see n. 28), pp. 16–17, 19–20.

39. Revised Draft, Departmental Order, "Creation of an Office of Foreign Intelligence," 30 Sept. 1944, HS/HC-31, item 7.

40. Draft Executive Order, "Transferring the Office of Strategic Services to the Executive Office of the President," n.d., HS/HC-31, item 5.

41. Memo, Mr. Lubin to the President, "A Permanent United States Foreign Intelligence Service," 25 Oct. 1944, HS/HC-31, item 8.

42. Memo for the President, William J. Donovan, 18 Nov. 1944, HS/HC-400, item 12.

43. JIC 239/1, reproduced as Appendix A to Memo (DDIM-52-52), Brig. Gen. R. C. Partridge, Deputy Director for Intelligence, The Joint Staff, for Mr. Darling, CIA, 15 July 1952, HS/HC-67. (The author drafted JIC 239/1 as instructed by the Army G-2 Policy Staff. See HS/HC-401 [at n. 28], pp. 22–24.)

44. Ibid.

45. JIC 239/5, reproduced as Appendix D, HS/HC-67 (see n. 43). (The author drafted JIC 239/5. See HS/HC-401 [at n. 28], pp. 24–26.)

46. Ibid.

47. Author's recollection. The text of JCS 1181/1 as published in the *Times Herald* is in HS/HC-450, item 1. [two lines deleted]

48. Correspondence in HS/HC-31, items 13–16 (see n. 39).

49. Memo, John Magruder to General Donovan, 2 May 1945, HS/HC-31, item 16 (see n. 39).

50. Executive Order 9621, 20 Sept. 1945, HS/HC-31, item 20 (see n. 39).

51. Memo, the President to the Secretary of State, 20 Sept. 1945, HS/HC-31, item 23 (see n. 39).

52. Dean Acheson, *Present at the Creation* (New York, 1969), pp. 157–63.

53. Staff Study, "Development of a National Intelligence Program" (n.d.), and Annex A thereto, "Establishment of an Interdepartmental Intelligence Coordinating Authority and an Interdepartmental Security Coordinating Authority," now filed separately, HS/HC-135.

(The date on which this Staff Study and Annex were presented to the War and Navy Departments is indicated in a draft letter from the Secretary of War and Secretary of the Navy to the Secretary of State, n.d., HS/HC-135.)

54. Ibid.

55. Ibid.

56. Memo, Souers to Montague (see n. 35), para. 5.

57. Policy Documents Copied by A. B. Darling, HS/HC-31, items 19 and 21 (see n. 39).

58. Report to the Honorable James Forrestal, Secretary of the Navy, *Unification of the War and Navy Departments and Postwar Organization for National Security*, 22 Oct. 1945, chapter 2, "Intelligence," HS/HC-135 (see n. 53).

59. Summary of Report by a Committee Headed by Mr. Robert A. Lovett, Assistant Secretary of War for Air, 3 Nov. 1945, HS/HC-135 (see n. 53).

60. Minutes of a meeting of the Secretaries of State, War, and Navy, 14 Nov. 1945, HS/HC-135 (see n. 53). (This report of the meeting appears to have been prepared by H. Freeman Matthews, Department of State.)

61. Memo, Rear Adm. Thomas B. Inglis (DNI) to Fleet Admiral King, 20 Nov. 1945, HS/HC-135 (see n. 53).

62. Memo, Alfred McCormack to Admiral Inglis, 12 Dec. 1945, HS/HC-135 (see n. 53).

63. Memo, Admiral Souers to Commander Clifford, 27 Dec. 1945, HS/HC-135 (see n. 53).

64. Harry S. Truman, *Years of Trial and Hope* (New York, 1956), p. 57.

65. Memo, Souers to Montague (see n. 35), paras. 2, 3, and 6.

66. Letter, President Truman to Secretaries of State, War, and Navy, Enclosure, NIA Directive No. 1, HS/HC-244.

67. Statement of Admiral Souers to the author, 1946, borne out by a comparison of the two texts.

68. NIA Directive No. 1 (see n. 66), para. 1.

69. IAB minutes, 4 Feb.–10 June 1946, CIA Archives, and author's personal recollection. (The author was Souers's Assistant Director for current intelligence and national estimates.)

70. Ibid., 5th Meeting, 10 June 1946; Truman (see n. 64), p. 58; memo, Souers to Montague (see n. 35), para. 6.

71. Memo, Souers to Montague (see n. 35), para. 9.

72. Ibid.

73. The author's recollection of conversations with Gen. Vandenberg, partly reflected in HS/HC-401 (see n. 28), pp. 37–38. (The author was Vandenberg's Acting Assistant Director for Research and Evaluation.)

74. CIG 10, 20 June 1946, HS/HC-400, item 13.

75. IAB minutes (see n. 69) 28 June 1946; textual comparison of CIG 10 (see n. 74), Appendix "A," with NIA Directive No. 5, HS/HC-450 (see n. 66 [*sic*—47?]), item 6.

76. NIA Directive No. 2, Appendix "A," HS/HC-450 (see n. 66 [*sic*—47?]), item 4; ORE Administrative Order No. 1, 7 Aug. 1946, HS/HC-450, item 7; HS/HC-401 (see n. 28), p. 38.

77. HS/HC-401 (see n. 28), pp. 39–41; HS/HC-450 (see n. 66 [*sic*—47?]), item 12, Appendix.

78. CIG 16, "Intelligence Estimates Prepared by the Central Intelligence Group" (proposal by the Chief of Naval Intelligence), 14 Oct. 1946, HS/HC-400, item 14.

79. CIG 16/1, "Intelligence Estimates Prepared by the Central Intelligence Group" (proposal by the DCI), 26 Oct. 1946, HS/HC-400, item 15; IAB minutes (see n. 69), 9th Meeting, 31 Oct. 1946.

80. IAB minutes (see n. 69), 31 Oct. 1946.

81. Memo, Souers to Montague (see n. 35), para. 5.

82. IAB minutes (see n. 69), 8 April 1946.

83. Acheson (see n. 52), p. 161.

84. Ibid., p. 214.

85. HS/HC-401 (see n. 28), pp. 50–52; HS/HC-450 (see n. 66 [*sic*—47?]), items 14 and 17.

86. Letter, William H. Jackson to James Forrestal, 14 Nov. 1945 HS/HC-400, item 16.

87. HS/HC-450 (see n. 66 [*sic*—47?]), items 5, 10, and 11.

88. Personal file kept by the Curator of the Historical Intelligence Collection, Walter Pforzheimer, who was then Legislative Counsel, CIG.

89. National Security Act of 1947; recollections of Lawrence K. Houston, then General Counsel, CIG.

90. Memo, Montague (see n. 33).

91. Memo, Souers to Montague (see n. 35), para. 6.

92. A. B. Darling, "With Vandenberg as DCI: Part II, Coordination to Practice," *Studies in Intelligence* 12, no. 4, pp. 85–86.

93. A. B. Darling, "DCI Hillenkoetter," *Studies in Intelligence* 13, no. 1, p. 40.

94. Ibid., pp. 38–55; IAB minutes (see n. 69), 17 July 1947, 11 Sept. 1947: IAC minutes, 20 Nov. 1947, 8 Dec. 1947, CIA Archives.

95. IAC minutes (see n. 94), 8 Dec. 1947.

96. Ibid.; NSCID 1, 12 Dec. 1947 [several words deleted]; A. B. Darling, interview with R. H. Hillenkoetter, CIA Historical Staff Files.

97. U.S. Senate, Committee on Government Operations, Subcommittee on National Policy Machinery, *Organizational History of the National Security Council* (Washington, 1960), p. 5.

98. Memo, Souers to Montague (see n. 35), para. 12.

99. R. H. Hillenkoetter, written responses to A. B. Darling's questionnaire, 24 Oct. 1952, CIA Historical Staff Files, p. 22.

100. Hanson W. Baldwin, "Where the United States Is Weak," *Armed Force*, 18 Oct. 1947. A copy is available in "Baldwin Articles" [word deleted].

101. A. B. Darling, interview with Robert Blum, 10 March 1953, CIA Historical Staff Files.

102. Allen W. Dulles, William H. Jackson, and Matthias F. Correa, *Report to the National Security Council on the Central Intelligence Agency and National Organization for Intelligence*, hereafter *Report to the NSC*, 1 Jan. 1949, HS/HC-80, p. 166.

103. Ibid., p. 167.

104. Memo, Souers to Montague (see n. 35), paras. 13–15.

105. Memo, undated and unsigned, but evidently from a confidential informant in the OSO, Personal Papers of Allen W. Dulles. [one line deleted]

106. [one line deleted]

107. Allen W. Dulles, MS, statement for the Eberstadt Committee, Personal Papers (see n. 105).

108. A. B. Darling, MS, notes on the Survey Group papers in the NSC files (1953), HS/HC-350.

109. Dulles, Jackson, and Correa, *Report to the NSC* (see n. 102), pp. 2–5, 11, and passim.

110. Report of the Committee on National Security Organization ("the Eberstadt Committee") to the Commission on Organization of the Executive Branch of the Government ("the Hoover Commission"), 15 Nov. 1948, HS/HC-47, item 2, pp. 16, 76–77.

111. IAC minutes (see n. 94).

112. Dulles, Jackson, and Correa, *Report to the NSC* (see n. 102), pp. 4–5, 63.

113. Ibid., pp. 7, 69, 81.

114. Ibid., pp. 12, 137–38.

115. IAC minutes (see n. 94), 18 Feb. 1949.

116. Ibid.

117. Comments by the Central Intelligence Agency on "Conclusions and Recommendations" of a Report to the National Security Council . . . entitled "The Central Intelligence Agency and National Organization for Intelligence," 28 Feb. 1949, HS/HC-80.

118. Ibid.

119. Maj. Gen. S. Leroy Irwin, Director of Intelligence, GSA, memo for the DCI, 25 Feb. 1949. [one line deleted]

120. Rear Adm. Thomas B. Inglis, Director of Naval Intelligence, memo for the Executive Secretary, NSC, 4 March 1949.

121. Ibid.

122. A. B. Darling, interviews with R. H. Hillenkoetter and Robert Blum, CIA Historical Staff Files.

123. NSC 50, "A Report to the National Security Council by the Secretaries of State and Defense on the Central Intelligence Agency and National Organization for Intelligence," 1 July 1949, HS/HC-80.

124. Ibid.

125. Author's recollection, supported by Earman to Montague (see n. 15), para. 2.

126. IAC minutes (see n. 94).

127. Hillenkoetter, DCI, memo for the members of the IAC, "Implementation of NSC 50," 5 Aug. 1949, Report No. 13 [one-quarter line deleted].

128. Idem for idem, "State Department's Four Problems," 1 Nov. 1949, and "State's Four Papers re NSC 50," 30 Dec. 1949.

129. A. B. Darling, interview with John Magruder, 26 Feb. 1952, CIA Historical Staff Files.

130. Memo, Lawrence R. Houston, for Lt. Gen. W. B. Smith, 29 Aug. 1950, Office of the General Counsel, Tab E.

131. Magruder to Darling (see n. 129).

132. James E. Webb (Under Secretary of State) to Hillenkoetter, 7 July 1950. [one line deleted]

133. Hillenkoetter to Webb, 26 July 1950. [one line deleted]

134. Memo, Houston for Smith (see n. 130), Tab A.

135. Webb to Hillenkoetter, 3 Aug. 1950, 14 Aug. 1950. [one line deleted]

136. Houston to Chief, COAPS, 1 Sept. 1950.

PART TWO: BEDELL SMITH TAKES COMMAND

1. Memo, Souers to Montague (see Part One, n. 35), para. 16.

2. Hillenkoetter to Darling (see Part One, n. 122).

3. Memo, Souers to Montague (see Part One, n. 35), para. 17.

4. Ibid.

5. Ibid.

6. Ibid., para. 16.

7. Ibid., para. 17.

8. *Washington Post,* 3 July, 26 July, and 27 July 1950; *Washington Evening Star,* 18 Aug. 1950 [one-half line deleted].

9. Memo, Souers to Montague (see Part One, n. 35), para. 19. The date is derived from press reports that the appointment was first offered to Smith in May. *New York Times,* 19 Aug. 1950; *Washington Evening Star,* 21 Aug. 1950 [one-half line deleted].

10. Memo, Souers to Montague (see Part One, n. 35), para. 19.

11. *New York Times,* 19 Aug. 1950; *Washington Post,* 19 Aug. 1950 [one-half line deleted].

12. Memo, John R. Tietjen, Director of Medical Services, "Health of Gen. Walter Bedell Smith (1951–1953)," 6 April 1970, HS/HC-400, item 19.

13. *Washington Post,* 27 July 1950; *Washington Evening Star,* 18 Aug. and 21 Aug. 1950 [one-half line deleted].

14. *Congressional Record—Senate,* 28 Aug. 1950.

15. *Evening Star,* 18 Aug. 1950 [one-half line deleted].

16. Acheson (see Part One, n. 52), pp. 402–13.

17. Martin Claussen, "DCI Service Records," HS/HC-40.

18. *Washington Post,* 26 July 1950; *Washington Evening Star,* 21 Aug. 1950 [one-half line deleted].

19. Author's recollection of the oral testimony of several recruits to the Board of National Estimates.

20. U.S. Senate, Committee on Armed Services, "Nomination of General Walter Bedell Smith," 24 Aug. 1950 [word deleted].

21. Memo, Souers to Montague (see Part One, n. 35), para. 20.

22. Ibid., paras. 16 and 20.

23. Memo, Jackson to Montague (see Part One, n. 4), para. 9.

24. Ibid.

25. *New York Herald Tribune,* 18 Aug. 1950 [one-half line deleted].

26. Lawrence Houston to Ludwell Montague, 14 July 1970.

27. Magruder to Darling (see Part One, n. 129); author's recollections.

28. Letter, William Donovan to Maj. Gen. W. B. Smith, 17 Sept. 1943, HS/HC-497.

29. Ibid.

30. Sir Kenneth Strong, *Intelligence at the Top* (London, 1968), p. 85.

31. Ibid., p. 127.

32. Ibid., pp. 154–80; Senate Armed Services Committee (see n. 20); author's recollection of remarks by General Smith.

33. Memo, Jackson to Montague (see Part One, n. 4), paras. 10, 11, 13.

34. Senate Committee on Armed Services (see n. 20).

35. Memo, Houston to Montague (see Part One, n. 11).

36. Memo, Lawrence R. Houston, for Lt. Gen. W. B. Smith, 29 Aug. 1950, Office of the General Counsel.

37. Ibid.

38. Ibid.

39. Senate Armed Services Committee (see n. 20).

40. Letters, William Donovan to General Smith, various dates from 21 Sept. to 20 Oct. 1950. [line deleted]

41. Lawrence Houston to Ludwell Montague, 14 July 1970.

42. Dulles, *Craft of Intelligence* (see Part One, n. 31), p. 5.

43. Letter, Donovan to Smith, 21 Sept. 50 (see n. 40).

44. Walter Pforzheimer to Ludwell Montague, 29 July 1970.

45. Ibid.

46. [one-half line deleted] IAC minutes, USIB Secretariat.

47. Memo, Souers to Montague (see Part One, n. 35), para. 22.

48. William R. Harris, "March Crisis 1948, Act I," *Studies in Intelligence* 10, no. 4 (1966), pp. 1–22.

49. Dulles, Jackson, and Correa, *Report to the NSC* (see Part One, n. 102), pp. 74–75.

50. Memo, Earman to Montague (see Part One, n. 15).

51. Walter Pforzheimer to Ludwell Montague, 29 July 1970, quoting Gen. Charles F. Cabell, who was a member of the IAC in 1950 and was later DDCI.

52. Memo, Montague, "Personal Recollections" (see Part One, n. 12); HS/HC-401, pp. 64–67.

53. Memo, Jackson to Montague (see Part One, n. 4), para. 12.

54. Memo, Montague, "Personal Recollections" (see Part One, n. 12), para. 8.

55. ORE 58-50, "Critical Situations in the Far East," 12 Oct. 1950; CIA Historical Staff, "Study of CIA Reporting on Chinese Communist Intervention in the Korean War, September–December 1950," Tab H, HS/HC-55, item 1.

56. [several words deleted] (see n. 46), para. 2.

57. NSC 50 (see Part One, n. 123), pp. 2–3.

58. Col. Hamilton H. Howze, "Notes on IAC Meeting, 20 October 1950" (for Maj. Gen. A. R. Bolling, AC of S G-2), ICAPS File. [line deleted]

59. Dulles, Jackson, and Correa, *Report to the NSC* (see Part One, n. 102), pp. 65–70; [several words deleted] (see n. 46), para. 6.

60. W. H. Jackson to the DCI, 16 Oct. 1950, Office of the General Counsel [one-half line deleted].

61. Memo, Jackson to Montague (see Part One, n. 4), para. 11.

62. [several words deleted] (see n. 46), paras. 6–8.

63. Ibid., para. 7.

64. Ibid., paras. 9–10.

65. [several words deleted] IAC minutes, USIB Secretariat, paras. 2–3.

66. Ibid., paras. 7–8; author's recollection.

67. IAC minutes, 2, 9, 11, 16, and 21 Nov. 1950; IAC Progress Reports, 15 Nov. and 6 Dec. 1950. [line deleted]

68. Author's recollection.

69. James Q. Reber, memo for record, 14 Nov. 1950, IAC minutes (see n. 67).

70. Ibid.; author's recollection.

71. Minutes, Director's Staff Meeting, 18 April 1951. [line deleted]

72. DDI Diary, 1 Feb. 1952. [line deleted]

73. Memo, Houston to Montague (see Part One, n. 11).

74. Minutes, Director's Staff Meeting, 11 June 1951 (see n. 71).

75. NSC 68/4, Annex 6. [line deleted]

76. IAC-D-29/2, 7 Sept. 1951, USIB Secretariat.

77. IAC-M-44, 10 Sept. 1951, USIB Secretariat.

78. NIA Directive No. 2, 8 Feb. 1946 (see Part One, n. 76).

79. HS/HC-401, pp. 37–38.

80. Author's personal recollection and comment.

81. Dulles, Jackson, and Correa, Interim Report No. 2, "Relations Between Secret Operations and Secret Intelligence," 13 May 1948. [line deleted]

82. Memo, Hillenkoetter, DCI, to the Executive Secretary, NSC, 4 June 1948. [line deleted]

83. Frank Wisner, memorandum of conversation and understanding, "Implementation of NSC 10/2," 12 Aug. 1949. [line deleted]

84. Lawrence Houston to Ludwell Montague, 12 Nov. 1970.

85. Memo, Houston, Pforzheimer, and Wisner, for the DDCI [*sic*], "Proposed Revision of NSC 10/2," 5 Oct. 1950. [line deleted]

86. Memo, Houston to Montague (see Part One, n. 11).

87. Howze, "Notes" (see n. 58), para. 6.

88. Memo, Wisner for the DCI, "Interpretation of NSC 10/2 and Related Matters," 12 Oct. 1950. [line deleted]

89. Ibid.

90. Dulles, Jackson, and Correa, *Report to the NSC* (see Part One, n. 102), pp. 11, 136.

91. [several words deleted] to Ludwell Montague, 2 Dec. 1970.

92. Walter Pforzheimer to Ludwell Montague, 29 July 1970.

93. Lyman B. Kirkpatrick, Jr., *The Real CIA* (New York, 1969), p. 93.

94. Ibid., pp. 7–74.

95. Ibid., pp. 94–95.

96. Minutes, Staff Conference [word deleted], 12 Feb. 1951. [line deleted]

97. Minutes, Daily Staff Meeting, 9 Feb. 1951 (see n. 71).

98. Kirkpatrick (see n. 93), p. 93.

99. Minutes, Daily Staff Meeting, 13 Dec. 1950–7 Feb. 1951 (see n. 71).

100. Strong (see n. 30), pp. 182–84.

101. Minutes, Daily Staff Meeting (see n. 71) [several words deleted].

102. Minutes, Weekly Staff Meeting (see n. 71) [word deleted].

103. SC-M-1, 18 Dec. [1950?] (see n. 96).

104. SC-M-4, 8 Jan. 1951 (see n. 96).

105. Minutes, Director's Meeting, 24 Jan. 1952. [line deleted]

106. SC-M-19, 28 May 1951 (see n. 96) [word deleted].

107. SC-M-23, 9 July 1951 (see n. 96) [word deleted].

108. Walter Pforzheimer to Ludwell Montague, 16 Oct. 1970.

109. John Earman to Ludwell Montague, 10 Nov. 1970.

110. George Jackson and Martin Claussen, *Organization History of the Central Intelligence Agency, 1950–1953,* vol. 10, p. 41.

111. Lawrence Houston, [several names deleted], Walter Pforzheimer, and Lawrence White to Ludwell Montague during October 1970.

112. Walter Pforzheimer to Ludwell Montague, 13 Oct. 1970.

113. Lawrence White to Ludwell Montague, 15 Oct. 1970.

114. Jackson and Claussen, *Organizational History,* vol. 10, pp. 49–51.

115. Lawrence White to Ludwell Montague, 15 Oct. 1970.

116. Ibid.; also HS/HC-239. [line deleted]

117. Jackson and Claussen, *Organizational History,* vol. 10, p. 52.

118. Lawrence White to Ludwell Montague, 15 Oct. 1970.

119. General Order 38, 1 Dec. 1950 [word deleted].

120. Contract, A.W.D., 22 Dec. 1950, para. 2, HS/HC-231.

121. Dulles, Jackson, and Correa, *Report to the NSC* (see Part One, n. 102), pp. 10, 104–5, 129, 135.

122. Dulles, *Craft of Intelligence,* p. 5.

123. Minutes, Daily Staff Meeting, 21 Dec. 1950 (see n. 71).

124. Contract, A.W.D., 22 Dec. 1950 (see n. 120).

125. Memo, Jackson to Montague (see Part One, n. 4), para. 17.

126. John Earman to Ludwell Montague, 10 Nov. 1970.

127. Walter Pforzheimer to Ludwell Montague, 24 July 1970.

128. Memo, Jackson to Montague (see Part One, n. 4), paras. 5, 17, and 19.

129. Wayne Jackson to Ludwell Montague, quoting Gordon Gray.

130. Jackson and Claussen, *Organizational History*, vol. 2, pp. 47–48.

131. Howze, "Notes" (see n. 58).

132. Memo for record, George Jackson and Martin Claussen, "Interview with Loftus E. Becker," 18 April 1955, HS-2, Historical Staff.

133. Ibid.

134. Regulation 1-130, 20 March 1953 [several words deleted].

135. Author's recollection.

136. DDI Diary, 1 Feb. 1952 (see n. 72).

137. Jackson and Claussen, memo for record (see n. 132).

138. Minutes, Director's (Deputies') Meetings (see n. 71) [several words deleted].

139. Ibid.

140. Memo, Jackson to Montague (see Part One, n. 4); Meredith Davidson to Ludwell Montague, 12 May 1971, with regard to Smith's opinion of Wisner.

141. Personal recollections of the author, whose father was a military intelligence officer (1919–23) and who saw for himself the state of military intelligence in 1940.

142. Gen. W. B. Smith, DCI, *Report to the NSC on the Implementation of NSC 50*, 23 April 1952. [line deleted]

143. Letter, DCI to Secretary of Defense, 5 March 1951. [line deleted]

144. SC-M-7, 29 Jan. 1951 (see n. 96); minutes, Director's Meeting, 26 April 1951 (see n. 71).

145. Walter Pforzheimer to Ludwell Montague, 26 Oct. 1970.

146. Memo from the DCI to the DDA (McConnel), ADPC (Wisner), ADSO (Wyman), and DTR (Baird), 22 March 1951 [several words deleted].

147. CIA Regulation 70, 18 April 1951 [several words deleted].

148. Ibid., 1 July 1951.

149. SC-M-27, 17 Sept. 1951 (see n. 96) [several words deleted].

150. CIA Notice 78-52, 19 June 1952 [several words deleted].

151. CIA Notice P-11-52, 1 July 1952 [several words deleted].

152. Minutes, Director's Meeting, 7 Dec. 1951 (see n. 71) [several words deleted].

153. Ibid., 13 Dec. 1951.

154. SC-M-33, 17 Dec. 1951 (see n. 96) [several words deleted].

155. Minutes, Director's Meeting, 1 Aug. 1951 (see n. 71) [several words deleted].

156. Ibid., 11 Dec. 1952 [several words deleted].

157. Smith, *Report to the NSC* (see n. 142).

158. Frank R. Reynolds, draft, "The CIA Cable Secretariat-Message Center, 1952–69," pp. 4–24, Cable Secretariat.

159. Minutes, Director's Meeting, 16 Aug. 1951 (see n. 71) [several words deleted].

160. Ibid., 26 July 1951.

161. Frank Reynolds to Ludwell Montague, 13 Nov. 1970.

162. John Earman to Ludwell Montague, 10 Nov. 1970.

163. Reynolds (see n. 158), pp. 25–26.

164. Gordon Butler to Ludwell Montague, 12 Nov. 1970.

165. Reynolds (see n. 158), pp. 51–52.

166. Memo from the DCI (Smith) to the DDCI (Dulles), 15 July 1952, HS/CSG–17.

167. Minutes, Daily Staff Meeting, 19 Dec. 1950 (see n. 71) [several words deleted].

168. SC-M-7, 29 Jan. 1951 (see n. 96) [several words deleted].

169. Minutes, Daily Staff Meeting, 26 Dec. 1950 (see n. 71) [several words deleted].

170. SC-M-18, 14 May 1951 (see n. 96) [several words deleted].

171. Omar N. Bradley, *A Soldier's Story* (New York, 1951), pp. vii, xii, 17, 563.

172. The Executive Assistant's Official Diary, 24 Sept. 1951. [line deleted]

173. Martin Claussen, draft, "Status Report on the CIA History," 17 June 1958, pp. 3–4, Historical Staff.

174. Arthur Darling to Ludwell Montague, 1952.

175. Minutes, Director's Meeting, 15 May 1952 (see n. 71) [several words deleted].

176. Ibid., [sic—Deputies' Meeting?], 9 July 1952.

177. Ibid., 5 Sept. 1952 [several words deleted].

178. Author's comment on Darling history, The Central Intelligence Agency: An Instrument of Government, to 1950, CIA Historical Staff.

179. Memo, Earman to Montague (see Part One, n. 15).

180. Minutes, Director's [sic—Deputies'?] Meeting, 23 Jan. 1953 (see n. 71) [several words deleted].

181. Ibid., 25 June 1951 [several words deleted].

182. Jackson's "surveys" were frequently mentioned at the Director's meetings throughout 1951. Ibid. [several words deleted].

183. Ibid., 18 June 1951 [word deleted].

184. Ibid., 6 July 1951.

185. John Earman to Ludwell Montague, 10 Nov. 1970.

186. Walter Pforzheimer to Ludwell Montague, 26 Oct. 1970, quoting Stuart Hedden to Pforzheimer, 1952.

187. John Earman to Ludwell Montague, 10 Nov. 1970.

188. Minutes, Director's Meeting, 11 Sept. 1951 (see n. 71) [word deleted].

189. Ibid., 16 Oct. 1951.

190. Kenneth Greer, draft, "History of the Office of the Inspector General," pp. 5–6.

191. Minutes, Director's Meeting, 22 Aug. 1951 (see n. 71) [word deleted].

192. Greer (see n. 190), p. 7.

193. Ibid., pp. 21–23.

194. Ibid., pp. 23–25.

195. Ibid., pp. 8–15, 25–27.

196. Ibid., pp. 28–29.

197. Walter Pforzheimer to Ludwell Montague, 26 Oct. 1970.

198. Greer (see n. 190), p. 30.

199. Ibid., p. 29.

200. Walter Pforzheimer to Ludwell Montague, 26 Oct. 1970.

PART THREE: REORGANIZATION PURSUANT TO NSC 50

1. Letter from the DDI to the Secretary of State, 19 Aug. 1949 [several words deleted].

2. Memo from the DCI to the Executive Secretary, NSC, 27 Dec. 1949 [word deleted].

3. Letter from the President to the Secretaries of State, War, and Navy, 22 Jan. 1946, HS/HC-450, item 2, para. 3b.

4. NIA Directive No. 2, 8 Feb. 1946, HS/HC-450, item 4.

5. Author's recollection and comment.

6. Ibid.

7. Dulles, Jackson, and Correa, Report to the NSC (see Part One, n. 102), pp. 46–48, 63–64.

8. James Reber to Ludwell Montague, 20 Nov. 1970.

9. The Executive Assistant's Official Diary, 28 Nov. 1951. [line deleted]

10. SC-M-14, 4 April 1951. [line deleted]

11. IAC-M-24, 2 April 1951, IAC minutes [several words deleted].

12. SC-M-1, 18 Dec. 1950 (see n. 10) [several words deleted].

13. James Reber, ADIC, "Report on Coordination," 5 Oct. 1951 [line deleted]

14. The President's letter (see n. 3), para. 3a.

15. The National Security Act of 1947, Sec. 102(d)(3).

16. The President's letter (see n. 3), para. 3c.

17. Memo from Col. Montague to Col. McCormack, "Special Estimates Staff," 14 Jan. 1946, HS/HC-135 (see Part One, n. 53); NIA Directive No. 2 (see n. 4); CIG Administrative Order No. 3, 4 March 1946, HS/HC-333.

18. William Reitzel, "Analysis of ORE Production," 19 July 1949, HS/HC-502, p. 1.

19. Montague, "Intelligence Service" (see Part One, n. 38), pp. 43–46, 52–56.

20. Ibid., pp. 49–51.

21. Ibid., pp. 18, 31; CIG Administrative Order No. 3 (see n. 17).

22. Ibid., pp. 41–42; CIG 16/1 (see Part One, n. 49); IAB minutes, 31 Oct. 1946 [several words deleted].

23. Ibid., pp. 39–41.

24. Harris, "March Crisis 1948, Act I" (see Part Two, n. 48).

25. Author's recollection.

26. Dulles, Jackson, and Correa, *Report to the NSC* (see Part One, n. 102), pp. 6, 72.

27. Montague, "Intelligence Service" (see Part One, n. 38), pp. 59–61.

28. Dulles, Jackson, and Correa, *Report to the NSC* (see Part One, n. 102), pp. 5, 74–75.

29. Montague, "Intelligence Service" (see Part One, n. 38), pp. 53–55.

30. Author's recollection and comment; Reitzel, "Analysis of ORE Production" (see n. 18).

31. Dulles, Jackson, and Correa, *Report to the NSC* (see Part One, n. 102), pp. 5–6.

32. John A. Bross, "Chapter II, the Central Intelligence Agency, National and Service Intelligence," HS/HC-47, item 1, p. 49.

33. John Bross to Ludwell Montague, 27 Aug. 1969; memo from Ludwell Montague for the ADRE, "Functions of the Global Survey Group," 17 July 1947, HS/HC-450, item 22, para. 2; Montague, "Intelligence Service" (see Part One, n. 38), pp. 56–57.

34. Report of the Eberstadt Committee (see Part One, n. 110), p. 16.

35. Dulles, Jackson, and Correa, *Report to the NSC* (see Part One, n. 102), p. 83.

36. Ibid., p. 70.

37. Author's recollection.

38. CIG 16/1 (see Part One, n. 79); draft memo for the Director, 15 April 1947, HS/HC-450, item 18; memo from the ADRE to the DCI, 11 Aug. 1947, HS/HC-450, item 23.

39. Memo from the Chief, Global Survey Group (Montague) to the ADRE, "Comment on the Dulles–Jackson Report," 11 Feb. 1949, HS/HC-450, item 28.

40. NSC 50 (see Part One, n. 123), pp. 7–10.

41. Author's recollection and comment.

42. Memo from the DCI to the Executive Secretary, NSC, 27 Dec. 1949. [half line deleted]. "NSC 50–Dulles Report (1949)."

43. Memo from Chief, Global Survey Group (Montague) to the ADRE, 8 Sept. 1949, HS/HC-450, item 34.

44. Memo, Lawrence R. Houston to Lt. Gen. W. B. Smith, 29 Aug. 1950 [line deleted] (see Part Two, n. 36.)

45. CIG Administrative Order No. 3 (see n. 17).

46. Hillenkoetter to Webb, 26 July 1950. [line deleted]

47. Memo, Houston to Smith (see Part Two, n. 36).

48. Memo, W. H. Jackson to Gen. Smith, 3 Oct. 1950, HS/HC-400, item 23.

49. Memo, Theodore Babbitt, Ludwell Montague, and DeForest Van Slyck to the Deputy Director (Jackson), "Plan for a CIA Office of Estimates," 10 Oct. 1950, HS/HC-450, item 42.

50. Ibid.

51. Letter, William J. Donovan to Lt. Gen. W. Bedell Smith, 13 Oct. 1950. [line and a half deleted]

52. Letter, William Langer to Ludwell Montague, 19 Aug. 1969, HS/HC-400, item 21.

53. IAC-M-40, 13 Aug. 1951 [several words deleted].

54. IAC-M-1, 20 Oct. 1950 [several words deleted].

55. Howze, "Notes" (see Part Two, n. 58). [line deleted]

56. Letter, Donovan to Smith (see n. 51).

57. Letter, Langer to Montague (see n. 52).

58. Ludwell Montague, "Chronology, October–November, 1950," HS/HC-400, item 22.

59. Letter, Langer to Montague (see n. 52).

60. Memo, Sherman Kent to Dr. Langer, 20 Nov. 1950, HS/HC-296.

61. Sherman Kent, *Strategic Intelligence for American World Policy* (Princeton, 1949).

62. Memo, Jackson to Montague (see Part One, n. 4), para. 15.

63. Ibid., para. 16.

64. Sherman Kent to Ludwell Montague, 22 Dec. 1970.

65. Montague, "Intelligence Service" (see Part One, n. 38).

66. Author's recollection and comment.

67. Ibid.

68. Ibid.

69. Sherman Kent to Ludwell Montague, 22 Dec. 1970.

70. Author's recollection and comment.

71. Memo, Jackson to Montague (see Part One, n. 4), para. 14.

72. SC-M-1, 18 Dec. 1950 (see n. 10).

73. Ibid.

74. Memo, Langer, ADRE, for the DDCI, "Activities of the Office of National Estimates," 9 July 1951, Tab B, HS/HC-112, item 42.

75. Author's recollection and comment.

76. Montague, "Chronology" (see n. 58).

77. Author's recollection and comment.

78. ONE, Table of Organization, 29 Nov. 1950, HS/HC-296.

79. Memo, Jackson to Smith (see n. 48).

80. Author's recollection and comment.

81. Ibid.

82. Memo from William L. Langer, ADNE, for Advisor for Management, "Tentative Table of Organization for the Office of National Estimates," 29 Nov. 1950. [one-and-a-half lines deleted]

83. Ibid.

84. Memo for record, R. S. Cline, 18 Dec. 1950, HS/HC-296, item 9.

85. Montague, "Intelligence Service" (see Part One, n. 38), p. 68a.

86. Author's recollection.

87. Memo, R. S. Cline to Dr. Langer, 22 Dec. 1950, HS/HC-296, item 10.

88. Memo, Paul A. Borel for the Personnel Director, "Encumbrance of Position of the O/NE Revised T/O," 17 Jan. 1951. [line deleted]

89. Author's recollection and comment.

90. Ibid.; Sherman Kent, Abbot Smith, James Graham, and Willard Matthias to Ludwell Montague, 15 and 18 Jan. 1971.

91. James Graham to Ludwell Montague, 15 Jan. 1971.

92. ONE personnel data, 9 Feb. 1953. [line deleted]

93. ONE personnel data, 30 June 1953, ibid.

94. ONE personnel data, 9 Feb. 1953, ibid.

95. NIE 10, "Communist China," 17 Jan. 1951, ONE Reading Room.

96. IAC-D-7, 28 Nov. 1950 [several words deleted].

97. Ibid.

98. IAC-M-8, 30 Nov. 1950 [several words deleted].

99. NIE-25, ONE Reading Room.

100. Author's recollection and comment.

101. SC-M-3, 2 Jan. 1951 (see n. 10) [several words deleted]; Langer to Montague (see n. 52).

102. Author's recollection and comment.

103. Montague, "Intelligence Service" (see Part One, n. 38), pp. 18–19.

104. Ibid., p. 18.

105. Borel to the Personnel Director (see n. 88).

106. Minutes, Daily Staff Meeting, 28 June 1951. [line deleted]

107. IAC-D-24, 19 June 1951 [several words deleted].

108. IAC-M-34, 5 July 1951 [several words deleted].

109. IAC-D-25, 2 July 1951 [several words deleted].

110. IAC-M-34, 5 July 1951 [several words deleted].

111. IAC-M-71, 22 May 1952 [several words deleted].

112. Author's recollection and comment.

113. Smith, *Report to the NSC* (see Part Two, n. 142). [line deleted]

114. Author's recollection and comment.

115. The published versions of all NIEs adopted in Smith's time are available in the ONE Reading Room.

116. IAC-M-15, 15 Jan. 1951 [several words deleted].

117. IAC-M-40, 13 Aug. 1951 [several words deleted].

118. SE-11, 17 Aug. 1951, ONE Reading Room.

119. Ibid.

120. Author's recollection.

121. DDI Diary, 14 Feb. 1952 [line deleted] (see also Part Two, n. 12.)

122. Ibid., 7 April 1952.

123. ONE memo for the DDI, "Statement of Activities and Problems," 1 March 1952, HS/HC-112, item 19.

124. DDI Diary, 4 March 1952 (see n. 121).

125. Ibid., 10 and 29 April 1952.

126. Ibid., 1 July 1952.

127. Memo from Sherman Kent, ADNE, for the DCI, 2 Sept. 1952 HS/HC-112, item 7.

128. IAC-M-81, 4 Sept. 1952 [several words deleted].

129. Author's recollection and comment.

130. Dulles, Jackson, and Correa, *Report to the NSC* (see Part One, n. 102), pp. 8–9, 83–92.

131. Author's recollection and comment.

132. Otto Guthe to Ludwell Montague, 17 Feb. 1971.

133. Jackson and Claussen, *Organizational History,* vol. 7, p. 14. (See Part Two, n. 110.)

134. SC-M-1, 18 Dec. 1950 (see n. 10) [several words deleted].

135. Jackson and Claussen, *Organizational History* (see Part Two, n. 110), vol. 7, p. 30.

136. NSCID 15, "Coordination and Production of Foreign Economic Intelligence," 13 June 1951 [several words deleted].

137. Memo, Earman to Montague (see Part One, n. 15); Sherman Kent to Ludwell Montague, 27 Jan. 1971.

138. Jackson and Claussen, *Organizational History* (see Part Two, n. 110), vol. 7, pp. 22–24.

139. Sherman Kent to Ludwell Montague, 27 Jan. 1971.

140. Virginia Long to Ludwell Montague, 27 Jan. 1971.

141. Ibid. Mrs. Long was Millikan's secretary.

142. Jackson and Claussen, *Organizational History* (see Part Two, n. 110), vol. 7, pp. 24–28.

143. Ibid., vol. 7, p. 33.

144. Ibid., vol. 7, p. 35.

145. Ibid., vol. 7, p. 10n, p. 35.

146. Office of Personnel statistics [several words deleted].

147. SC-M-6, 22 Jan. 1951 (see n. 10) [several words deleted].

148. IAC-M-20, 15 Feb. 1951 [several words deleted].

149. Minutes, Daily Staff Meeting, 16 Feb. 1951 (see n. 106) [several words deleted].

150. IAC-D-22, "Action Proposed as a Result of a Survey of the Requirements, Facilities, and Arrangements of the United States Government for Foreign Economic Intelligence Relating to the National Security," 9 May 1951 [several words deleted]. In this document, Appendix A to Tab A is a memo from the Executive Secretary, NSC, to the DCI, 3 March 1950, informing him that the NSC had approved a proposal made by the Chairman, NSRB, 2 Feb. 1950.

151. Ibid., Tab A, Appendix C.

152. Ibid., Tab A.

153. Ibid., Tab B.

154. IAC-M-31, 17 May 1951. [several words deleted].

155. IAC-D-22/1 (revised), 29 May 1951 [several words deleted].

156. IAC-M-31, 17 May 1951 [several words deleted].

157. IAC-D-22/2, 17 Aug. 1953 [several words deleted].

158. [several words deleted] to Ludwell Montague, 26 Jan. 1971.

159. Robert Amory to Ludwell Montague, 9 Aug. 1971, quoting Millikan. The minutes of the Director's [*sic*—Deputies'?] Meeting (see n. 106) make it clear that Bedell Smith did indeed try hard to retain Millikan's services.

160. Minutes, Director's [*sic*—Deputies?] Meeting, 25, 30, and 31 Jan. 1952 (see n. 106) [several words deleted].

161. Robert Amory to Ludwell Montague, 9 Aug. 1971.

162. [two lines deleted]

163. Vladimir Grinioff, draft history of "CIA Participation in the Economic Defense Program, 1947–1971," vol. 1, chap. 3, pp. 19–20.

164. Ibid., pp. 21–22.

165. Ibid., pp. 23–23b, quoting in full memo from the DCI for the NSC, 3 June 1952.

166. IAC-D-53/1, 25 July 1952 [several words deleted]; memo from Robert Amory, ADRR, to the DDI, 6 Jan. 1953. [line deleted]

167. Jackson and Claussen, *Organizational History* (see Part Two, n. 110), vol. 7, p. 46.

168. [one line deleted]

169. Phyllis Beach to Ludwell Montague, 17 Feb. 1971.

170. [two lines deleted]

171. Author's recollection. The author was in charge of the production of the *CIG Daily Summary*.

172. Ibid.

173. NSCID 3, 13 Jan. 1948 [several words deleted].

174. DCID-3/1, 8 July 1948 [several words deleted].

175. Montague, "Intelligence Service" (see Part One, n. 38), pp. 57–59.

176. Dulles, Jackson, and Correa, *Report to the NSC* (see Part One, n. 102), pp. 84–86, 92.

177. "The Central Intelligence Agency and National Organization for Intelligence," HS/HC-80, p. 26.

178. [one line deleted]

179. [deleted]

180. [deleted]

181. [deleted]

182. [deleted]

183. [deleted]

184. [deleted]

185. General Order No. 38, 1 Dec. 1950 [several words deleted].

186. [two lines deleted]

187. General Order No. 40, 4 Jan. 1951 [several words deleted].

188. SC-M-1, 18 Dec. 1950 (see n. 10) [several words deleted].

189. Minutes, Daily Staff Meeting, 21 Dec. 1950 (see n. 106) [several words deleted].

190. Author's recollection and comment.

191. SC-M-4, 8 Jan. 1951 (see n. 10) [several words deleted].

192. Memo, R. J. Smith to W. L. Langer, "The CIA Daily Summary," 9 Jan. 1951, HS/HC-296.

193. Minutes, Daily Staff Meeting, 12 Jan. 1951 (see n. 106) [several words deleted].

194. General Order No. 41, 15 Jan. 1951 [several words deleted].

195. Jackson and Claussen, *Organizational History* (see Part Two, n. 110), vol. 8, p. 35.

196. SC-M-17, 30 April 1951 (see n. 10) [several words deleted].

197. Letter, W. B. Smith, DCI, to the Secretary of State, 28 Feb. 1951. [line deleted]

198. Author's recollection and comment.

199. Dulles, Jackson, and Correa, *Report to the NSC* (see Part One, n. 102), pp. 87, 92.

200. IAC-M-1, 20 Oct. 1950 [several words deleted].

201. Letter, W. B. Smith, DCI, to the Secretary of State, 1 Feb. 1951. [line deleted]

202. Letter, W. H. Jackson, DDCI, to Park Armstrong, 1 Feb. 1951 (see n. 201).

203. [one-and-a-half lines deleted]

204. Letter, Jackson to Armstrong, 29 Jan. 1951 (see n. 201).

205. Letter, Smith to Armstrong, 21 March 1951 (see n. 201).

206. Letter, Armstrong to Smith, 22 June 1951 (see n. 201).

207. [one-and-a-half lines deleted]

208. Minutes, Daily Staff Meeting, 13 Feb. 1951 (see n. 106) [several words deleted].

209. Ibid., 16 May 1951.

210. Ibid., 24 May 1951.

211. Minutes, Director's Meeting, 23 May 1951. [line deleted]

212. Ibid., 23 Nov. 1951 [several words deleted].

213. Author's recollection of OIR comment on the subject.

214. Office of Personnel statistics [several words deleted].

215. Jackson and Claussen, *Organizational History* (see Part Two, n. 110), vol. 8, pp. 31–34, and Annex B, Tab 6.

216. Author's recollection.

217. Montague, "Intelligence Service" (see Part One, n. 38), p. 35.

218. SC-M-8, 12 Feb. 1951 (see n. 10) [several words deleted].

219. Memo, Langer to Douglass, 22 May 1951, cited in Jackson and Claussen, *Organizational History* (see Part Two, n. 110), vol. 8, p. 41.

220. Minutes, Director's Meeting, 27 June 1951 (see n. 211) [several words deleted].

221. Ibid., 16 and 17 July 1951.

222. Ibid., 7 Sept. 1951 [several words deleted].

223. The Executive Assistant's Official Diary, 13 Oct. 1951 (see n. 9).

224. ONE memo for the DDI (see n. 123).

225. The Executive Assistant's Official Diary, 19 Dec. 1951 (see n. 9).

226. Author's recollection and comment. See also ONE memo for the DDI (n. 123).

227. Memo from Kent, ADNE, to the ADCI (Douglass), "Inter-Office Relationships in the Production of NIE's," 1 Feb. 1951, HS/HC-112, item 25.

228. Author's recollection and comment. Sherman Kent to Ludwell Montague, 12 Feb. 1971.

229. Memo from Kent, ADNE, to the ADCI (see n. 227).

230. Memo from Kent, ADNE, to the DDI (Becker), "Production for Making Spot Estimates," 31 Jan. 1952, HS/HC-112, item 26.

231. Memo from Sontag, ADNE, to the DDI, "Intra-CIA Coordination of Intelligence Memoranda Prepared for the White House and the NSC," 22 July 1952, HS/HC-112, item 9.

232. DDI Diary, 25 July 1952 (see n. 121).

233. Thomas Lawler to Ludwell Montague, 17 Feb. 1971.

234. Sherman Kent to Ludwell Montague, 12 Feb. 1971.

235. Sherman Kent, memo for record, 30 Sept. 1952, HS/HC-112, item 5.

236. Ibid.

237. DDI Diary, 10 Aug. 1952 (see n. 121).

238. Ibid., 19 Sept. 1952.

239. Paul Borel's note on a copy of Kent's memo for record (see n. 235).

240. IAC-D-6, 24 Nov. 1950 [several words deleted].

241. Jackson and Claussen, *Organizational History* (see Part Two, n. 110), vol. 8, pp. 48–49.

242. IAC-M-10, 7 Dec. 1950 [several words deleted].

243. IAC-D-61/2, 27 Dec. 1950 [several words deleted].

244. IAC-M-12, 28 Dec. 1950 [several words deleted].

245. IAC-M-11, 21 Dec. 1950 [several words deleted].

246. Author's recollection of such occasions.

247. Smith, *Report to the NSC* (see Part Two, n. 142).

248. Author's recollection and comment.

249. [two-and-a-half lines deleted]

250. Dulles, Jackson, and Correa, *Report to the NSC* (see Part One, n. 102), pp. 8–9, 83, 88, 90–91.

251. Weber (see n. 249), p. 8.

252. Karl Weber to Ludwell Montague, 11 March 1971.

253. Weber (see n. 249), p. 23.

254. Ibid., pp. 13–14, 18; Annex IV, pp. 2–3.

255. Ibid., Annex IV, pp. 1, 3.

256. [line deleted]

257. [several words deleted] to Ludwell Montague, 25 May 1971.

258. Weber (see n. 249), pp. 16–17, 19.

259. Ibid., p. 20. [line deleted]

260. Ibid., pp. 25–26.

261. Ibid., Annex IV, pp. 4–5.

262. Ibid., Annex IV, p. 6.

263. The Executive Assistant's Official Diary, 26 July 1951 (see n. 9).

264. Ibid., 30 July 1951.

265. IAC-M-30, 2 Aug. 51 [several words deleted].

266. Ibid.

267. Ibid.

268. The Executive Assistant's Official Diary, 13 Sept. 1951 (see n. 9).

269. DDI Diary, 6 Jan. 1952 (see n. 121).

270. Weber (see n. 249), p. 7.

271. DDI Diary, 18 Feb. 1952 (see n. 121).

272. Kenneth Greer, draft "History of the Office of the Inspector General," pp. 8–15.

273. Minutes, Director's Meeting, 3 March 1952 (see n. 211) [several words deleted].

274. The subject is not mentioned in IAC-M-63, 6 March 1952 (it must have been discussed in executive session), but the action in the IAC is covered in Becker's DDI Diary in the entry for 18 Feb. 1952, which must have been written up in final form after 6 March 1952.

275. DDI Diary, 15 July 1952 (see n. 121).

276. IAC-M-79, 14 Aug. 1952 [several words deleted].

277. DCID-3/4, 14 Aug. 1952 [several words deleted].

278. Ibid.

279. Weber (see n. 249), Annex II, pp. 14–16, 24. See also the IAC-D-10 series [several words deleted].

280. DCID-3/4, 14 Aug. 52 [several words deleted].

281. Weber (see n. 249), p. 21.

282. Karl Weber to Ludwell Montague, 26 Feb. 1971.

283. DDI Diary, 21 Aug. 1952 (see n. 121).

284. Karl Weber to Ludwell Montague, 22 Feb. 1971.

285. CIG Administrative Order No. 6, 11 July 1946, HS/HC-333.

286. CIG Personnel Order No. 13, 10 Sept. 1946 [several words deleted].

287. Jackson and Claussen, *Organizational History* (see Part Two, n. 110), vol. 5, p. 13.

288. Ibid.

289. Agency Notice No. 1-48, 13 Jan. 1948 [several words deleted].

290. Jackson and Claussen, *Organizational History* (see Part Two, n. 110), vol. 5, p. 15.

291. [one-half line deleted]

292. Ibid., vol. 5, pp. 23–25.

293. Dulles, Jackson, and Correa, *Report to the NSC* (see Part One, n. 102), pp. 48, 62, 64.

294. Jackson and Claussen, *Organizational History* (see Part Two, n. 110), vol. 5, p. 30.

295. NSC 50 (see Part One, n. 123), p. 10.

296. Jackson and Claussen, *Organizational History* (see Part Two, n. 110), vol. 5, p. 44.

297. Ibid.

298. Author's interpretation of the consideration that would have moved General Smith.

299. [line deleted]

300. [two-and-a-half lines deleted]

301. Ibid., vol. 4, pp. 3–4, as corrected by Louise Davison with regard to the number of the NIA Directive.

302. Ibid., pp. 4–5.

303. Ibid., pp. 6–7.

304. Louise Dickey Davison, draft history, "The Office of Operations: Overt Collection, 1946–1965," DDI Historical Series, DCS-Appendix A.

305. [one-and-a-half lines deleted]

306. [one-and-a-half lines deleted]

307. Lawrence White to Ludwell Montague, Nov. 1970.

308. A. B. Darling, interview with Kingman Douglass, 28 May 1951, HS/HC-800, vol. 1.

309. A. B. Darling, interview with Richard Helms, 10 Nov. 1952, HS/HC-800, vol. 2.

310. Walter Pforzheimer to Ludwell Montague, 1 July 1971.

311. Author's comment.

312. [line deleted]

313. Louise Davison to Ludwell Montague, 10 March 1971.

314. Ibid. Mrs. Davison's source was George Carey.

315. [one-and-a-half lines deleted]

316. Louise Davison to Ludwell Montague, 10 March 1971.

317. [deleted]

318. [deleted]

319. [deleted]

320. [deleted]

321. [deleted]

322. [deleted]

323. Ibid.

324. Ibid., vol. 4, pp. 62.

325. Ibid., vol. 4, pp. 64–65.

326. DDI Diary, 10–14 and 31 Jan. 1952 and 1, 8, and 10–12 Feb. 1952 (see n. 121).

327. Minutes, Director's Meeting, 11 June 1951 (see n. 211).

328. Ibid., 22 April 1952.

329. Smith, *Report to the NSC* (see Part Two, n. 142).

330. Memo, Jackson to Montague (see Part One, n. 4), para. 10.

PART FOUR: THE WAR EMERGENCY AND THE CLANDESTINE SERVICES

1. NSC 68, "United States Objectives and Programs for National Security," 14 April 1950. [one line deleted]

2. Ludwell Montague, memo for record, 17 March 1971, covering draft, "Intelligence and Related Activities," 10 Aug. 1950, HS/HC-400, item 24; NSC 68/1, 21 Sept. 1950. [one line deleted]

3. NSC 68/3, 8 Dec. 1950. [one line deleted]

4. IAC-D-29, 2 Aug. 1951 [several words deleted]. This IAC document was in fact the complete text of NSC 114 as adopted by the NSC Senior Staff, 31 July 1951, being distributed to the IAC for information.

5. SC-M-24, 16 July 1951 (see Part Three, n. 223) [several words deleted]. Official Diary (see Part Three, n. 9), 18, 21, and 23 July 51. [line deleted]

6. Draft Annex No. 6, 23 July 1951, NSC 68 File (see n. 1).

7. Ibid.

8. Ibid.

9. Minutes, Director's Meeting, 31 July and 1 Aug. 1951 [line deleted]

10. IAC-M-45, 20 Sept. 1951 [several words deleted].

11. IAC-M-36, 26 July 1951 [several words deleted].

12. IAC-D-29/1, 5 Sept. 1951; 29/2, 7 Sept.; 29/3, 11 Sept. [several words deleted]. (See Part Two, n. 76, and Part Four, n. 4.)

13. Ibid.

14. NSC 68 File (see n. 1).

15. IAC-D-29/7, 27 March 1952; 29/8, 9 April 1952 [several words deleted].

16. IAC-M-67, 14 April 1952 [several words deleted].

17. IAC-D-29/8, 9 April 1952 [several words deleted].

18. Ibid.

19. Ibid.

20. SC-M-1, 18 Dec. 1950. [line deleted]

21. [line deleted]

22. SC-M-14, 4 April 1951 (see n. 20); minutes, Director's Meeting, 13 June 1951 [several words deleted].

23. Minutes, Director's Meeting, 4 May and 13 June 1951 (see n. 9) [several words deleted].

24. Ibid., 11 July 1952 [several words deleted].

25. Ibid., 23 June 1951 [several words deleted].

26. Ibid., 22 Oct. 1951 [several words deleted].

27. Walter Pforzheimer to Ludwell Montague, 1 July 1971.

28. Minutes, Director's [sic—Deputies'?] Meeting, 9 and 15 Jan. 1952 and 13 Feb. 1952 (see n. 9) [several words deleted].

29. Ibid., 19 March 1952.

30. Smith, Report to the NSC (see Part Two, n. 142). [line deleted]

31. Minutes, Director's Meeting, 6 June 1952 (see n. 9) [several words deleted].

32. Walter Pforzheimer to Ludwell Montague, 1 July 1971.

33. Minutes, Director's Meeting, 1 Aug. 1952 (see n. 9) [several words deleted].

34. Ibid.

35. Jackson and Claussen, Organizational History (see Part Two, n. 110), vol. 2, p. 68.

36. Smith, Report to the NSC (see Part Two, n. 142).

37. SC-M-9, 21 Feb. 1951 (see n. 20) [several words deleted].

38. SC-M-29, 22 Oct. 1951 (see n. 20) [several words deleted].

39. SC-M-8, 12 Feb. 1951 (see n. 20) [several words deleted].

40. Smith, Report to the NSC (see Part Two, n. 142).

41. Record of Meeting of the Senior NSC Staff, 18 Dec. 1950. [line deleted]

42. SC-M-8, 12 Feb. 1951 (see n. 20) [several words deleted].

43. SC-M-11, 5 March 1951 (see n. 20) [several words deleted].

44. Harry Truman, Directive to the Secretary of State, Secretary of Defense, and Director of Central Intelligence, 4 April 1951, HS/CSG-587.

45. Ibid.

46. Minutes, Director's Meeting, 3 May 1951 (see n. 9) [several words deleted].

47. Ibid., 18 July 1951.

48. Ibid., 19 and 26 June, 27 July 1951.

49. Memo, Adm. Stevens to Wisner, "OPC Planning Personnel in Theaters (Europe)," 6 Dec. 1950; memo, Wisner to DCI, "War Planning—Covert Operations," 13 Dec. 1950. [line deleted]

50. Memo, Wisner to DCI, "Proposed Interpretation of NSC 10/2, paragraph 4," 23 Oct. 1950; Wisner to DCI, "War Planning—Covert Operations," 13 Dec. 50; Executive Secretary, NSC, to DCI, "NSC 10/2," 14 Dec. 1950 [several words deleted].

51. Memo, DCI to Executive Secretary, NSC. [line deleted]

52. [deleted]

53. [deleted]

54. [deleted]

55. [deleted]

56. [deleted]

57. [deleted]

58. Memo, James Lay for General Smith, 3 April 1951; Letter, W. B. Smith to George Marshall, 2 July 1951 [several words deleted].

59. Memo, John Magruder for the Deputy Secretary of Defense, "Joint Chiefs of Staff Comments and Recommendations Respecting [several words deleted], 30 March 1951 [several words deleted].

60. [deleted]

61. Memo, DCI for the NSC [several words deleted], 9 April 1951; James Lay, Executive Secretary, for the NSC, "NSC 10/2," 16 April 1951 [several words deleted].

62. SC-M-9, 21 Feb. 1951 (see n. 20) [several words deleted].

63. SC-M-10, 28 Feb. 1951 (see n. 20) [several words deleted].

64. Memo, DCI for the NSC, [line deleted] 8 May 1951 [several words deleted].

65. Ibid.

66. Ibid.

67. [three lines deleted]

68. Memo, Omar Bradley, Chairman, JCS, for the Secretary of Defense, [line deleted] 15 Aug. 1951 [several words deleted].

69. Memo, Frank Wisner, ADPC, for the DDCI, "CIA Position on JCS Recommendations re: Magnitude Paper," 24 Aug. 1951 [several words deleted].

70. Minutes, Director's Meeting, 28 Aug. 1951 [several words deleted].

71. [deleted]

72. [deleted]

73. [deleted]

74. Smith, *Report to the NSC* (see Part Three, n. 113).

75. Minutes, Director's Meeting, 27 July 1951 (see n. 9), envelope 5.

76. Ibid., 19 Sept. 1951 (see n. 9) [several words deleted].

77. Ibid., 25 Oct. 1951 (see n. 9) [several words deleted].

78. Ibid., 18 June 1952 (see n. 9) [several words deleted].

79. Ibid., 27 Feb. 1952 (see n. 9) [several words deleted].

80. Ibid., 27 March 1952 (see n. 9) [several words deleted].

81. Ibid., 14 May 1952 (see n. 9) [several words deleted].

82. Ibid., 14 Nov. 1951 (see n. 9) [several words deleted].

83. Ibid., 23 Nov. 1951 (see n. 9 [several words deleted].

84. Ibid., 11 and 13 Feb. 1952 (see n. 9) [several words deleted].

85. Ibid., 10 July 1952 (see n. 9) [several words deleted].

86. Ibid., 22 Aug. 1952 (see n. 9) [several words deleted].

87. Ibid., 17 Oct. 1952 (see n. 9) [several words deleted].

88. Ibid.

89. Memo, DCI to the PSB, [line deleted] 30 Oct. 1952, (see n. 9) [several words deleted].

90. Minutes, Director's Meeting, 29 Oct. 1952 (see n. 9) [several words deleted].

91. [two lines deleted]

92. Minutes, Director's Meeting, 25 Nov. 1952 (see n. 9) [several words deleted].

93. Wayne Jackson to Ludwell Montague, 7 April 1971.

94. Dulles, Jackson, and Correa, *Report to the NSC* (see Part One, n. 102), pp. 10, 104–5, 129, 134.

95. NSC 50 (Part One, n. 123), pp. 8–10.

96. Memo for the File, EXO/SO (William Tharp), 12 Oct. 1950, HS/HC-400, folder 71.

97. SC-M-4, 8 Jan. 1951 (see n. 20) [several words deleted].

98. Memo, EA/DCI (Kirkpatrick) for the DDP (Dulles), "Difficulties Between OSO and OPC," 7 Feb. 1951. [line deleted]

99. Richard Helms to Ludwell Montague, 13 May 1971.

100. Memo for record, Lyman Kirkpatrick, "Meeting on Integration of OSO and OPC," 14 Feb. 1951, HS/HC-200.

101. Memo to DDP, "Integration of OSO and OPC," 13 March 1951, HS/CSG-200.

102. Memo, ADSO and ADPC for DDP, 3 March 1951, HS/CSG-200.

103. Memo, ADSO for DDP, 28 March 1951; memo, ADSO for ADPC, 6 June 1951, HS/CSG-200.

104. Memo, ADSO and ADPC for DDP, 9 June 1951, HS/CSG-200.

105. Memo, ADSO to ADPC, 5 March 1951, Records Integration Division, Clandestine Services.

106. Minutes, Director's Meeting, 18 April 1951 (see n. 9) [several words deleted].

107. Author's comments, suggested in part by [several words deleted]. *The Office of Policy Coordination, 1 September 1948–1 August 1952*, draft chapter on "Circumstances Relating to the Merger of OSO and OPC," seen in April 1971, pp. 42–45.

108. Memo, DDCI for the DCI, "Survey of the Office of Policy Coordination," 24 May 1951. [line deleted]

109. [two lines deleted]

110. Memo, Kirkpatrick for Jackson, "Survey of OSO," 31 Aug. 1951, HS/CSG-36.

111. Ibid.

112. Ibid.

113. [deleted]

114. [deleted]

115. Memo, ADSO for DCI, "Closer Relationships Between OSO and OPC Activities," 25 Oct. 1951, HS/CSG-400, folder 71.

116. Memo, ADSO for W. H. Jackson, 9 Nov. 1951, HS/CSG-400, folder 71.

117. Minutes, Director's Meeting, 13 Nov. 1951 (see n. 9) [several words deleted].

118. Ibid., 8 Jan. 1952 (see n. 9) [line deleted]

119. Ibid., 7 Jan. 1952.

120. [several words deleted] to Ludwell Montague, Oct. 1970.

121. Memo, Acting ADSO [word deleted] to ADSO (Kirkpatrick), 4 Feb. 1952, HS/CSG-200.

122. [deleted]

123. [deleted]

124. [deleted]

125. [deleted]

126. [deleted]

127. [deleted]

128. [deleted]

129. [deleted]

130. [deleted]

131. Cover memo, ADPC for DDP, "Attached ADSO Secret Draft Labelled OSO/OPC Merger," 5 May 1952. [one line deleted]

132. Minutes, Director's Meeting, 18 April 1952 (see n. 9) [several words deleted].

133. Memo, ADSO to DCI, "OSO/OPC Merger," 2 May 1952, HS/CSG-200.

134. Cover memo, ADPC for DDP, 5 May 1952 (see n. 131).

135. Memo, DDP for ADSO, "Next Step on Merger," 20 May 1952. [line deleted]

136. Memo, Acting ADSO for DDP, "Merger Paper Requested by the Director," 4 June 1952. [line deleted]

137. Minutes, Director's Meeting, 30 June 1952 (see n. 9) [several words deleted].

138. Memo, Acting ADPC for DDP, "Draft Description of Proposed CIA Clandestine Organization," 1 July 1952. [line deleted]

139. Transcript of a meeting held on or about 15 July 1952, HS/CSG-348.

140. Memo, DCI for DDCI, DDP, DDA, DDI, Director of Training, Assistant Director for Communications, "Organization of CIA Clandestine Services," 15 July 1952, HS/CSG-17.

141. [several words deleted] to Ludwell Montague, May 1971.

PART FIVE: EXTERNAL RELATIONS

1. Meredith Davidson to Ludwell Montague, 12 May 1971.

2. Letter, Gen. Marshall Carter to Ludwell Montague, 13 Oct. 1970. In 1951 Gen. Carter (later DDCI) was Gen. Marshall's executive assistant as Secretary of Defense.

3. Walter Pforzheimer to Ludwell Montague, 1 July 1971.

4. Memo, Souers to Ludwell Montague (see Part One, n. 35).

5. Meredith Davidson, James Lay, and Sidney Souers to Ludwell Montague, various dates.

6. Meredith Davidson to Ludwell Montague, 12 May 1971.

7. James Lay to Ludwell Montague, 13 May 1971.

8. Meredith Davidson to Ludwell Montague, 12 May 1971.

9. Ibid.

10. Author's comment.

11. U.S. Senate, Committee on Government Operations, Subcommittee on National Policy Machinery, *Organizational History of the National Security Council* (Washington, 1960), p. 17.

12. James Lay to Ludwell Montague, 13 May 1971.

13. Ibid.

14. *Organizational History of the NSC* (see n. 11), pp. 17–19.

15. Letter, DCI (Hillenkoetter) to the President, 21 July 1950, HS/HC-450, item 38.

16. Record of Meeting of the Senior NSC Staff, 25 Oct. 1950 [several words deleted].

17. Author's recollection.

18. Ibid.

19. Minutes, Director's Meeting, 13 July 1951. [line deleted]

20. The Executive Assistant's Official Diary, 21 Aug. 1951 (see Part Three, n. 9). [one line deleted]

21. Minutes, Director's Meeting, 1 Aug. 1951 [several words deleted].

22. The Executive Assistant's Official Diary, 29 Aug. 1951 (see Part Three, n. 9) [several words deleted].

23. Ibid.

24. Minutes, Director's [*sic*—Deputies'?] Meeting, 31 July 1952 [several words deleted].

25. Walter Pforzheimer to Ludwell Montague, 29 July 1970. Pforzheimer was present on this occasion.

26. Minutes, Director's Meeting [several words deleted].

27. Correspondence with the Department of State, 1951–52. [line deleted]

28. Ibid.; minutes, Director's Meeting [several words deleted].

29. Letter, Pogue to Montague (see Part One, n. 1).

30. Correspondence with the Department of Defense, 1951 [several words deleted].

31. George Marshall to "Dear Smith," 25 May 1951 [word deleted].

32. GCM (George Catlett Marshall) to Smith, 25 June 1951 [several words deleted].

33. Bedell Smith to General Marshall, 5 July 1951 [several words deleted].

34. Bob Lovett to General Smith, 2 June 1951 [several words deleted].

35. Robert Lovett (Acting Secretary of Defense) to the DCI, 7 Aug. 1951 [several words deleted].

36. Correspondence with the Department of Defense (see n. 27).

37. Walter Pforzheimer to Ludwell Montague, 10 Nov. 1970.

38. Author's recollection.

39. Ibid.

40. Author's comment.

41. Ibid.

42. NSCID 5, 12 Dec. 1947, HS/HC-500.

43. Wayne Jackson to Ludwell Montague, 2 June 1971.

44. JIC draft, 19 May 1950, HS/HC-75, item 1.

45. Draft NSCID, 5 Feb. 1951, HS/HC-75, item 3.

46. Memo, W. G. Wyman, ADSO, to the DDP (Dulles), 6 June 1951. [line deleted]

47. Letter, W. B. Smith to Hon. George C. Marshall, 2 July 1951 [several words deleted].

48. NSCID 5, 28 Aug. 1951 [several words deleted].

49. IAC-M-35, 19 July 1951 [several words deleted].

50. [deleted]

51. [deleted]

52. [deleted]

53. [deleted]

54. [deleted]

55. Letter, DCI to Secretary of Defense, 5 March 1951 [several words deleted].

56. Memo, JCS to Secretary of Defense, 16 May 1951 [several words deleted].

57. Memo, DCI for Assistant Secretary of Defense, 23 May 1951 [several words deleted].

58. Letter, G. C. Marshall (Secretary of Defense) to General Smith, 23 June 1951 [several words deleted].

59. Letter, Smith (DCI) to General Marshall, 5 July 1951 [several words deleted].

60. Letter, G. C. Marshall to General Smith, 19 June 1951 [several words deleted].

61. Burney Bennett to Ludwell Montague, 26 May 1971. The subject will be more fully covered in Bennett's history of the Office of Training, now in preparation.

62. IAC-D-14, 6 Feb. 1951, and IAC-D-14/1, 3 March 1951 [several words deleted].

63. SC-M-11, 5 March 1951 [line deleted]

64. IAC-M-23, 15 March 1951 [several words deleted].

65. SC-M-33, 17 Dec. 1951 [several words deleted].

66. [one-and-a-half lines deleted]

67. Brief for discussion with the Joint Chiefs of Staff, 1 Feb. 1951 [several words deleted].

68. Minutes, Daily Staff Meeting, 5 Feb. 1951 [several words deleted].

69. Author's recollection.

70. Ibid.

71. IAC-M-17, 22 Jan. 1951 [several words deleted].

72. IAC-M-19, 8 Feb. 1951 [several words deleted].

73. IAC-M-21, 23 Feb. 1951 [several words deleted].

74. IAC-M-27, 23 April 1951 [several words deleted].

75. Memo, DCI for Secretary of Defense, 5 Feb. 1951 [several words deleted].

76. IAC-M-27, 23 April 1951 [several words deleted].

77. IAC-M-28, 26 April 1951 [several words deleted].

78. IAC-D-21, 9 May 1951 [several words deleted].

79. IAC-M-35, 19 July 1951 [several words deleted].

80. Author's recollection.

81. [one-half line deleted]

82. Smith, *Report to the NSC* (see Part Two, n. 142). [line deleted]

83. W. B. Bundy, draft report to the NSC, 15 Jan. 1953 (see n. 82).

84. IAC-M-35, 19 July 1951 [several words deleted].

85. IAC-M-38, 2 Aug. 1951 [several words deleted].

86. Thomas F. Troy, *The Coordinator of Information and British Intelligence* (Office of Training, 1970), pp. 147–51.

87. *Organizational History of the NSC* (see n. 11), p. 6.

88. IAC-M-44, 10 Sept. 1951 [several words deleted].

89. [line deleted]

90. [line deleted]

91. [line deleted]

92. Author's comment.

93. IAC-M-75, 26 June 1952 [several words deleted].

94. Minutes, Director's Meeting, 10 Dec. 1952 [several words deleted].

95. Ibid.

96. Ibid., 29 Dec. 1952.

97. Author's comment.

98. Minutes, Director's Meeting, 31 Dec. 1952 [several words deleted].

99. Willard Matthias to Ludwell Montague, 2 June 1971.

100. Author's recollection.

101. Minutes, Director's Meeting, 16 Jan. 1953 [several words deleted].

102. Author's recollection. The author was a member of the permanent NESC Staff from 1955 to 1958.

103. Author's recollection. The author was in contact with ISA in the NSC Staff.

104. SC-M-1, 18 Dec. 1950 (see n. 63) [several words deleted].

105. Minutes, Director's Meeting, 29 April 1952 [several words deleted].

106. IAC-M-73, 5 June 1952 [several words deleted].

107. Minutes, Director's Meeting, 24 July 1952 [several words deleted].

108. Letter, DCI to Director, WSEG, 22 Oct. 1952 [several words deleted].

109. Memo, Acting DDI for Secretary of Defense, 12 Nov. 1952 [several words deleted].

110. Memo, ADCI for the DCI, "Arrangements Governing Communications Intelligence Activities," 20 Oct. 1951 [several words deleted].

111. Memo, DCI for the Executive Secretary, NSC, "Proposed Survey of Communications Intelligence Activities," 10 Dec. 1951 [several words deleted].

112. Minutes, Director's Meeting, 18 Dec. 1951 [several words deleted].

113. The Executive Assistant's Official Diary, 28 Dec. 1951 (see Part Three, n. 9) [several words deleted].

114. [deleted]

115. [deleted]

116. Dulles, Jackson, and Correa, *Report to the NSC* (see Part One, n. 102), pp. 56–58, 63.

117. Author's observations.

118. Minutes, Director's Meeting, 7 May 1951 [several words deleted].

119. Ibid., 8 May 1951.

120. Memo for record, Lyman Kirkpatrick, DADSO, 7 Nov. 1951. [one line deleted]

121. Ibid.

122. Walter Pforzheimer to Ludwell Montague, 8 June 1971.

123. Ibid.

124. [U.S. Senate, Committee on Armed Services,] "Nomination of General Walter Bedell Smith," 24 Aug. 1950, HIC/CRS.

125. Walter Pforzheimer to Ludwell Montague, 8 June 1971.

126. Ibid.

127. *Hearings Before the Committee on Un-American Activities,* "Testimony of Gen. Walter Bedell Smith," 13 Oct. 1952 (Washington, 1952), pp. 4284–85. The published record of this Hearing quotes the transcript of Smith's deposition in the case of McCarthy vs. Benton, 29 Sept. 1952.

128. Ibid.

129. *New York Journal-American,* 29 Sept. 1952, HIC/CRS.

130. Walter Pforzheimer to Ludwell Montague, 9 June 1971.

131. Smith, *My Three Years in Moscow* (see Part One, n. 6), p. 88.

132. Author's recollection.

[four pages deleted]

212. Meredith Davidson to Ludwell Montague, 24 June 1971.

213. Meredith Davidson to Ludwell Montague, 12 May 1971.

214. Wayne Jackson to Ludwell Montague, 8 July 1971.

215. Meredith Davidson's personal diary, 21 Nov. 1952; Meredith Davidson to Ludwell Montague, 12 May 1971.

216. Meredith Davidson to Ludwell Montague, 28 Nov. 1952; ibid., 12 May, 27 July, and 11 Aug. 1971.

217. Robert Amory to Ludwell Montague, 9 Aug. 1971.

218. Meredith Davidson to Ludwell Montague, 12 May 1971.

219. Walter Pforzheimer to Ludwell Montague, 26 Oct. 1970.

220. Memo, Jackson to Montague (see Part One, n. 4) [several words illegible]. Memo, Souers to Montague (see Part One, n. 35), para. 24; Robert Amory to Ludwell Montague [date illegible] Aug. 1971.

221. Robert Amory to Ludwell Montague, 9 Aug. 1971.

222. John Earman to Ludwell Montague, 10 Nov. 1970.

223. Memo, Souers to Montague (see Part One, n. 35), paras. 24–25; letter, Souers to Montague, 19 July 1971.

224. Memo, Jackson to Montague (see Part One, n. 4), paras. 5 and 19.

225. Kirkpatrick, *The Real CIA* (see Part Two, n. 93), p. 120.

226. Robert Amory to Ludwell Montague, 9 Aug. 1971.

227. Memo, Jackson to Montague (see Part One, n. 4), para. 5.

228. Memo, Souers to Montague (see Part Two, n. 35), para. 24.

229. Robert Amory to Ludwell Montague, 9 Aug. 1971.

230. Letter, Sidney Souers to Montague, 19 July 1971.

231. Meredith Davidson to Ludwell Montague, 27 July 1971.

232. Memo, Walter Pforzheimer to Montague, 11 March 1970, HS/HC-400, item 25, quoting McCormack.

233. IAC-M-93, Jan. 1953 [several words deleted].

234. Minutes, Director's Meeting, 12 Jan. 1953 (see n. 9) [several words deleted].

235. Ibid., 23 Jan.–9 Feb. 1953.

Index